C000212743

FOOD WORDS

FOOD WORDS

Essays in Culinary Culture

Peter Jackson and the CONANX group

Foreword by Warren J. Belasco

Bloomsbury Academic
An imprint of Bloomsbury Publishing Plc

B L O O M S B U R Y
LONDON · OXFORD · NEW YORK · NEW DELHI · SYDNEY

Bloomsbury Academic
An imprint of Bloomsbury Publishing Plc

50 Bedford Square   1385 Broadway
London   New York
WC1B 3DP   NY 10018
UK   USA

www.bloomsbury.com

BLOOMSBURY and the Diana logo are trademarks of Bloomsbury Publishing Plc

First published 2013
Published in paperback 2015
Reprinted by Bloomsbury Academic 2015

© Peter Jackson and the CONANX group, 2013, 2015

Peter Jackson and the CONANX group have asserted their rights under the Copyright, Designs and
Patents Act, 1988, to be identified as Authors of this work.

All rights reserved. No part of this publication may be reproduced or transmitted in any form or by
any means, electronic or mechanical, including photocopying, recording, or any information storage or
retrieval system, without prior permission in writing from the publishers.

No responsibility for loss caused to any individual or organization acting on or refraining from action as
a result of the material in this publication can be accepted by Bloomsbury or the author.

British Library Cataloguing-in-Publication Data
A catalogue record for this book is available from the British Library.

ISBN: HB: 978-0-85785-195-6
PB: 978-0-85785-196-3
ePDF: 978-1-47252-103-3
ePUB: 978-0-85785-235-9

Library of Congress Cataloging-in-Publication Data
Jackson, Peter, 1955-
Food words: essays in culinary culture/Peter Jackson and the CONANX group; foreword by
Warren J. Belasco.
pages cm
Includes bibliographical references and index.
ISBN 978-0-85785-195-6 – ISBN 978-0-85785-196-3 – ISBN 978-0-85785-235-9
1.Food–Terminology. 2.Gastronomy–Terminology. 3.Culture–Semiotic models.
4.Figures of speech.I. Title.
TX349.J327 2013
641.5001'4–dc23
2013005626

Typeset by Deanta Global Publishing Services, Chennai, India
Printed and bound in Great Britain

Contents

Foreword

As this collection of essays attests, serious food scholarship is flourishing, indeed booming. For evidence, look at the growing number of reference books, monograph series, journals, conferences, workshops, documentaries, degree programs, museum exhibits, websites, and courses all devoted in some way to illuminating the many meanings of food. As a gauge of food's importance, one need look no further than this book's table of contents. Can all of these words be related to food? Yes, and more so, for as Peter Jackson notes, the list does not include quite a few other words, such as "natural," "organic," "dinner," "fat" or, for that matter, "food." The list's selectivity proves a larger point, however: food is so relevant to so many key categories of inquiry and experience that we can't even begin to cover the subject.

Even more amazing, such a list might not have existed as recently as the 1970s. Many senior food scholars can remember well the skepticism voiced by our colleagues and, more consequently, our deans when we first revealed that we were "doing food." For me, this perilous moment came during a job interview in 1979, when I was summarizing an article I'd written about the origins of one of the first fast food chains in the United States, and my prospective dean chortled, "Howard Johnson's, for God's sake?!" Suffice it to say this exclamation had more to do with disbelief than celebration. And even today, a declaration of interest in food studies may still be met by a bemused smirk. Today, however, we can feel reassured that we

have lots of company, for it is eminently OK to pay attention to food. As the CONANX group has proved, one can even get funded by highly respectable international agencies to pay attention to food, and not just in the well-established disciplines of agronomy, food science, and clinical nutrition but also in the murkier areas of the humanities and social sciences.

"Attention" is the operative word here. Humans can pay attention to only so many things before cognitive overload sets in. Surveying the growth of a scholarly field—in this case, food—the historian wonders, Why now? What's been going on over the past few decades that has encouraged us to notice food? Moreover, why wasn't it noticed before? People have been eating forever, but until thirty or so years ago, the academic literature on dining was rather spare. Yet, all of a sudden, we're all agreeing with Lord Byron that "much depends on dinner." That proposition now seems so obvious that one may be compelled to ask of our academic predecessors, "What were they *not* thinking?" (Conversely, one may wonder—but not here— what are we *not* paying attention to these days? Given the fact of attention deficit, what have we given up so we can think about food? Such a shadow list would make an interesting appendix to this book.)

Why now? Academia is more of a marketplace than many of us would like to admit. In an era of severe economic restraints on the growth of higher education, it has become quite clear that food "sells." Deans may still be privately skeptical, but they appreciate high enrollments, as well as the publicity accorded newsworthy food scholars. Students—undergraduates and postgraduates alike—love to study food, and their market demand encourages an increasing supply of instructors, books, courses, and concentrations, the last a synonym for the focusing of attention. Food scholars in turn have discovered that they are not as alone as they once thought, as kindred spirits emerge in their own schools, disciplines, and cyberspace. As for *why* food sells now but not before, we can sort the reasons into outside and inside perspectives. The outside category would include the current events, worries, policy priorities, and trends noted in Jackson's introduction, especially the crisis of authority, trust, and responsibility wrought by the growing distance between producers and consumers. Studying food thus becomes the logical extension of caveat emptor, as more and more consumers seek greater transparency in a system that feeds so many so abundantly yet also seems to concentrate too much power in too few hands. Similarly, in seeking to explain why the counterculture took on the food industry in the late 1960s (Belasco 1989), I suggested outside factors such as the Vietnam War, changes brought on by the civil rights movement, and the rise of environmentalism.

Unlike those of us who first discovered food issues through the counterculture and other vehicles of cultural radicalism, however, current students of food have a much stronger body of literature to consult, cite, and revise. Learning from past scholarship is the way a discipline grows. Our understanding of how the global food system works has improved markedly as today's generation of emerging scholars builds on the insights of those who pioneered the field in the 1970s and 1980s. My own introduction to the systematic study of food came after a chance encounter with Joan Dye Gussow's provocative reader, *The Feeding Web: Issues in Nutritional Ecology* (1978). While Gussow did an excellent job of directing me to the work of pioneering theorists such as Georg Borgstrom and Kenneth Boulding, the bibliographical resources supporting *Food Words* are far deeper and richer than anything imaginable twenty or thirty years ago. And as proof of current

maturity, we should note a marked decline in the usage of clichés such as "we are what we eat" and "food for thought"—overdone phrases now reserved for neophyte journalists cutting their teeth on the food beat.

In addressing the "why now?" question, I think it would be simplistic to attribute too much to current or recent events. Nor should the rise of food consciousness be reduced to a few well-worn conditions such as neoliberalism, status envy, or conspicuous consumption. Events and trends may provoke us to pay attention to the literature—much the way Hitler's invasion of the USSR in 1941 sparked an interest in Tolstoy's account of Napoleon's similar adventures in 1812—but if the literature is drab, unimaginative, and boring, attention diminishes fast. (Obviously that was not the case with *War and Peace*.) Context may be a necessary consideration, but it is not sufficient. That's where the inside explanation comes in: food may be inherently *interesting* to study. One should not underestimate the intrinsic fascination of investigating where our meals come from, marveling at the ingenuity and variety by which humans turn the raw into the cooked, or pondering how meals create social identities and obligations. We *all* have a stake in food. Matters of equity, health, heritage, and sustainability take on special resonance when they involve what we put in our mouths. There is no worry more pressing or tangible than hunger and famine, nor are there many experiences more pleasurable than a good meal shared with friends.

Moreover, thinking about food requires an interdisciplinary or multidisciplinary approach. It resists and subverts the academic overspecialization that may inhibit a quest for broader understanding. As this book's wide-angle essays prove, food becomes a way to integrate disparate issues because everything is connected. And thanks to the higher than average quality of food writing, exploring those connections can be innately pleasurable. For this we owe some gratitude to the large number of literary food writers, critics, collectors, and enthusiasts who have raised the bar for readability in this subject area. Knowing that we are entering a terrain also explored by the likes of Jean Anthelme Brillat-Savarin, M.F.K.

Fisher, A. J. Liebling, and Elizabeth David, we academics may feel the need to step up our prose, especially as we step out of the comfort zone of our native disciplines. That we may be addressing a wider public audience than normal for most academic scholarship may also be attributed to the remarkable growth of popular food media. We may privately regret the sensationalism and superficiality of celebrity chef spectacles, but we might also consider thanking TV stars like Jamie Oliver, Anthony Bourdain, and Nigella Lawson for priming audiences for more "serious" reflections about food. And few academic fields have such a largely supportive coterie of journalists competing to publicize our discoveries and translate our insights into understandable language. Some of these journalists—Michael Pollan and Eric Schlosser, for instance—have become major recruiters to the "good food" cause, and their bestselling books have found their way into many required reading lists, thereby setting a higher standard for accessibility and clarity. Instructors may experience a similar upgrade in the quality of writing assignments when students reflect on their food

memories, voice indignation about insufficient food safety regulation, investigate the hidden byways of the corporate food chain, or play ethnographer at the family dinner table. Hence, the decision of the CONANX team to organize the pieces herein as suggestive "essays"—an exalted and increasingly rare literary format—rather than as formulaic journal articles or "just the facts" encyclopedia entries.

Speaking of CONANX, I had the wonderful opportunity to visit, work, and, yes, dine with this team for several days. (Note that gatherings of food scholars are often provisioned at a gastronomic level significantly higher than the average academic chow.) During our meetings and meals, I was particularly struck by their collegiality and enthusiasm, as well as their remarkable collaborative style, which resembled the collective improvisation of a well-honed jazz band. Addressing a shared set of guidelines, questions, and cues, each still found ample room for self-expression in extended individual solos. The result is a book that really swings.

Warren J. Belasco

Contributors

Warren J. Belasco is a professor of American studies at the University of Maryland-Baltimore County

Helene Brembeck is a professor of ethnology and codirector of the Centre for Consumer Science (CFK) at the University of Gothenburg

Ben Coles is a lecturer in human geography at the University of Leicester

Maria Fuentes is a research associate at CFK Gothenburg

Qian Gong is a lecturer in Media and Communication at the University of Leicester

Peter Jackson is professor of human geography at the University of Sheffield

Richard Lee is a research associate in the Institute of Health and Society at Newcastle University

Angela Meah is a research fellow in the department of geography at the University of Sheffield

Richard Milne is a postdoctoral researcher in the Institute of Public Health at the University of Cambridge

Nick Piper is a postdoctoral researcher at the Leeds University Business School

Matt Watson is a senior lecturer in social and cultural geography at the University of Sheffield

Jakob Wenzer is a research associate at CFK Gothenburg

Introduction

Food Words is a bold, unique, and some might say brash, undertaking. It is bold in attempting to identify the keywords that define the emerging field of "food studies." It is unique in terms of how the book was written, by a group of scholars associated with the CONANX research program (investigating *Consumer culture in an "age of anxiety"*), and in the sense that (as far as we are aware) nothing similar has been undertaken previously.[1] It is brash (in the words of one of our critical friends, Warren Belasco) in the sense that the field we are attempting to describe is itself far from well defined, compared to many longer-established humanities and social science disciplines that contribute to this emergent field.

That the field is a contested and rapidly evolving one is revealed by looking back at an article by Jennifer Ruark in *The Chronicle of Higher Education* (1999), which defined food studies as a "hot commodity," a fashionable new field of intellectual endeavor, regarded with suspicion in some quarters where it was accused of being "scholarship lite" because of its supposed lack of disciplinary rigor and its associations with food enthusiasts and popular historians rather than more serious-minded academics.[2] Despite the many scholarly studies that have appeared in the intervening years, a recent piece in the *New York Times* by Jan Ellen Spiegel (April 13, 2012) repeated the idea that food studies is a "new" academic field and continued to express anxiety about whether certain aspects of food were worthy of serious study. Aware of these debates and reservations, we do not attempt to provide a definitive guide to this nascent field. That would be premature and contrary to the spirit of what we are attempting in *Food Words*. But nor do we wish to deny the intellectual depth of the field, aware that many of our current food words have a long history that previous generations of scholars have helped craft.

Food Words was inspired by Raymond Williams's *Keywords* (1976), which set out to provide a guide to the vocabulary of culture and society, mapping the language of cultural transformation that had occurred in Britain and the rest of the industrialized world during the eighteenth and nineteenth centuries.[3] Williams did not attempt to provide a singular or static definition of his selected keywords but sought to trace the dynamic "fields of meaning" associated with each term, tracking their changing use and reception in different social contexts. Starting with a small group of words (culture, class, art, industry, and democracy), he eventually provided detailed essays on over 100 words.[4] Opposing what he described as a "sacral" attitude toward the meaning of words, Williams sought to demonstrate the active and contested nature of our social vocabulary: a shared body of words and meanings in our most general discussions. Necessarily incomplete and selective, Williams's *Keywords* did not simply seek to provide more accurate (fixed and stable) definitions but to shed light on the social and historical context of their use ("not resolution but ... that extra edge of consciousness" [1976: 24]).

While "food" was not one of Williams's keywords, there were essays on "consumer" and "taste," tracing how the idea of consumption has had negative connotations since the fourteenth century (meaning to destroy, use up, waste, or exhaust), later developing a more neutral application in the eighteenth century in descriptions of bourgeois political economy, before taking on its current range of meanings through the influence of modern commercial culture. Likewise, his essay on "taste" traces the word's evolution from the physical sensation of tasting with the mouth to its metaphorical extension in references to "good taste" and socially approved manners or etiquette (cf. Mol 2009). In contrast to Williams, who specifically distinguished his book from a dictionary or glossary of a particular academic discipline, *Food Words* attempts to map out the shifting meanings of our core vocabulary as applied to the interdisciplinary field of food studies.

While we share Williams's concern to trace the "fields of meaning" of our culinary keywords, we are not linguists or philologists, interested primarily in the words' etymology. We are social scientists, interested in how meanings circulate within different sectors of society (from scientific and commercial applications to policy debates and popular culture) and how they are approached and appropriated within different disciplinary traditions. Our chronological scope stretches back to the nineteenth century (and occasionally earlier) but is mostly focused on the last fifty years or so. Our disciplinary range encompasses anthropology and sociology, human geography and social history, media and cultural studies, also touching on the environmental and life sciences as well as public health and social policy.[5]

Besides Williams's *Keywords*, the other inspiration for *Food Words* was Theodor Adorno's (1958) discussion of the essay form, which outlines a radical alternative to standard dictionary-style definitions or encyclopedia entries. In that work, Adorno argued that the essay form is characterized by a spirit of intellectual freedom that does not permit its domain to be prescribed. "Methodically unmethodical," it accentuates the fragmentary and emphasizes the partial. According to Adorno, the essay form

eschews certainty and abrogates the ideal. Its aspirations are critical and self-relativizing, playful and persuasive, seeking cross-connections and making visible the invisible. In the spirit of Williams and Adorno, *Food Words* does not aim to be comprehensive or to comprise an encyclopedia or dictionary of food research. Rather, we aim to provide a series of original essays addressing topics and issues that are central to current debates in the field. While each essay is research-based and fully referenced, our ambition is to reach a wider audience of nonspecialist readers (as Williams did so successfully with his *Keywords*).

THE SOCIAL SHAPING
OF *FOOD WORDS*

So what has shaped the selection of our particular culinary keywords? The historical context for this project includes the intensification of agricultural production and the globalization of food supply chains that has occurred over recent decades, making an unprecedented range of foods available to Western consumers (Goodman and Watts 1997; Morgan et al. 2006). Yet, we would argue, the growing distance between modern-day consumers and the conditions of agricultural production has increased our anxieties about the geographical provenance of food, decreasing our trust in food and making many consumers unsure about its safety and quality (Kjaernes et al. 2007). A recent survey of European consumers found that almost half (48%) were concerned that food may damage their health (up from 42% in 2005); that around two-thirds (68%) were worried about the quality and freshness of food; and that over half (51%) disagreed with the view that "food today is safer than ten years ago" (Eurobarometer 2010).

These pervasive anxieties about food have been exacerbated since the 1980s by a series of "food scares" and farming crises that have occurred across Europe and by significant fluctuations in the price of key agricultural commodities, giving rise to growing concerns about future global food security, which, in turn, has generated renewed debates about the future of genetically modified (GM) food and other socio-technical changes affecting the food supply (Atkins and Bowler 2001; Blay-Palmer 2008). As this book was in preparation, the world was witnessing what the UN Secretary General called the worst food crisis in a generation, coupled with an economic recession throughout much of the industrialized world.

During the same period, across Europe and North America, there has been a growth of "alternative food networks" (including the rise of farmers' markets, community-supported agriculture, and the much-publicized Slow Food movement). There has also been a "quality turn" toward free-range and organic production (Goodman 2003; Maye et al. 2007), with attempts to support more local and sustainable systems of production and more ethical forms of consumption, reinforcing the need for a greater sense of connection along food supply chains. Representing a new moral economy of agricultural production and a turn toward more ethical forms of consumption for some observers, others are suspicious about the elitist and socially exclusionary nature of these developments, which always seem to command premium prices and be readily appropriated by more conventional market forces (Guthman 2004a; Morgan et al. 2006; Maye et al. 2007).

This, then, was the immediate social and political context in which the *Food Words* project was conceived and written. We are deeply aware that the selection of our keywords derives from our particular perspective, reflecting how we are positioned and how we position ourselves in terms of our social, historical, and geographical location. All of the members of the writing team are social scientists based in academic institutions in the global North, and we are conscious of how different the book might have looked if it had been written from a different global or academic perspective. While, for us, food is abundant, relatively cheap, and readily available, we are all-too-aware that food is scarce, a matter of life and death, in many other parts of the world. This is directly reflected in the essays on hunger and famine, for example, and on food security and insecurity. It also comes through, we hope, in the way we have approached more

generic topics like eating or cooking, where we have tried not to privilege our own position as Western, middle-class academics. Readers can judge for themselves how far we have succeeded.

Another of our critical friends (Anne Murcott) warned of the ethnocentrism that she felt was inherent to our project, as originally framed, also describing it as fashionable and hodiecentric (excessively concerned with the present-day). We have tried to take these potential criticisms to heart, reshaping the project to address these specific concerns. While the book clearly reflects the concerns of a particular moment—they are "our" keywords, approached from a unique point of view—we have worked hard to take a comparative and historical approach, indicating how these particular words achieved their prominence today and how their meanings may have been quite different in other times and places. We have sought to provide a historical perspective on each of our keywords, examining the specific context in which their contemporary meanings were shaped. Words like "consumer" and "choice," for example, frame the politics of food in a very particular way, a context whose defining influence we attempt to sketch in the relevant essays. In their common usage, we argue, there is insufficient concern for how, where, and when the "modern consumer" was born and how the notion of "consumer choice" is a reflection of our particular marketized economy rather than a disinterested analytical term (cf. Trentmann 2006). When, we might ask, did customers or housewives become consumers and how do these consuming subjects relate to wider political constructions like democracy and citizenship? Similarly, we argue, many of our current food words are ideological rather than strictly scientific or explanatory terms in the sense that they serve particular material interests. Our essays attempt to make this clear through historically informed contextual analysis.

The charge of ethnocentrism is no easier to refute and partly reflects the predominantly Anglo-American nature of our source material. We have sought to guard against this by acknowledging our biases and attempting to identify our specific positionalities (even if we cannot fully fathom the extent of our subconscious prejudices). As authors, we have tried not to write about "us" or "we" without considering for whom we are speaking (preferring to be as specific as possible and to refer to particular times and places). We have actively sought out material from periods and places with which we were initially less familiar (and our critical friends have been very helpful in this regard). But we have also tried to go beyond historical or geographical tokenism, avoiding the kind of ethnographic "butterfly collecting" that Edmund Leach (1961: 5) deplored among some branches of anthropology. Rather than simply adding examples from other times and places, we have tried to identify studies whose particular focus has the capacity to transform our understanding of the "here and now." Good examples of this transformative potential include Richard Wilk's work on Belize (Wilk 2002, 2006), which does far more than adding a specific ethnographic example of culinary difference, using his case study to transform our understanding of the construction of "national" cuisines in general, and James Watson's collection of essays on *Golden Arches East* (1997), which used a series of specific case studies to show how the "same" culinary institution (McDonald's fast food restaurants) have quite different meanings in different places, challenging less critical understandings of this apparently most globalized of brands. In a modest way, too, in writing these essays we have set out to do what Dipesh Chakrabarty (2008) refers to as "provincializing Europe," highlighting the specificity of our source material rather than assuming it to be a universally applicable point of reference. We acknowledge, though, that "decentring" conventional academic knowledge is a long-term political project that will take much time and effort to accomplish.

Finally, then, we might note that a discussion of the current lexicon of food research is of more than academic significance. Other interests are at stake—for example, in recent discussions about Alternative Food Networks (AFNs) where the choice of terms is often highly politicized. So, for example, Sarah Whatmore et al. (2003) ask, pointedly, what is "alternative" about AFNs; James Kirwan (2004) is keen to interrogate the alterity of

farmers' markets and other "alternative" strategies in the UK's agri-food system; while Peter Jackson et al. (2007) explore the appropriation of "alternative" discourse by "mainstream" food producers. The political implications of our choice of food words (how they are deployed and by whom) was emphasized in an article in *The Atlantic Monthly* by James McWilliams (2012), where he suggests that the U.S. agri-food industry is seeking to "manipulate the rhetoric of alternative animal-based systems to its profitable advantage." McWilliams is referring to a specific incident—the annexation by the Center for Consumer Freedom of the "Ethical Butcher" website—but his argument that "language is both cheap and powerful" can be readily generalized. McWilliams concludes that the food movement's buzzwords and catchphrases are easily appropriated to the point where the biggest pig farm on the planet can advertise itself as "humane" and "sustainable." The movement's "fungible verbal lexicon" may, he warns, be its Achilles heel. There is much at stake, then, in outlining a series of food-related keywords, taking us far beyond a purely academic exercise in definition.

FOCUSING ON FOOD

As we have argued elsewhere, food serves as a powerful lens through which to examine wider changes in society (Jackson 2009). It is a subject on which everyone has an opinion, raising questions of inequality and exploitation on a global scale as well as reaching down to what goes on at the level of individual families and households. Food is a subject of serious scientific research and a source of inspiration for art, music, and literature, both high-brow and more popular (Parasecoli 2008). Food issues are confronted in our everyday lives, but they are also the focus of intense philosophical and ethical debate. It is an all-encompassing subject. As Warren Belasco notes, "Food is a strong 'edible dynamic,' binding present and past, individual and society, private household and world economy, palate and power" (2007: 5). Or, as Elspeth Probyn argues,

In eating, we grapple with concerns about the animate and the inanimate, about authenticity and sincerity, about changing familial patterns, about the local rendered global, about whether sexual and alimentary predilections tell us anything about ourselves, about colonial legacies of the past for those of us who live in stolen lands, about whether we are eating or being eaten. (2000: 3)

Alan Warde's sociological account of *Consumption, Food and Taste* (1997) is structured around a similar series of binaries. Based on an analysis of the national Family Expenditure Survey as well as local survey data from Greater Manchester in the United Kingdom and a content analysis of popular magazines, Warde identifies four "culinary antinomies": novelty and tradition, health and indulgence, economy and extravagance, convenience and care, to which we might now add anxiety and pleasure, local and global, safety and risk, innovation and tradition. While seeing these words as mutually incompatible (as implied by the Kantian idea of an antinomy), the interest of social science lies in exploring how these logically separate categories are combined in the practice of everyday life to structure the way people go about the mundane process of buying, cooking, eating, and disposing of food.

Readers will notice that there is no essay on "food" in *Food Words*. So how might we approach this most significant and pervasive culinary keyword? Food, we argue, is simultaneously a source of pleasure and anxiety, having powerful symbolic value as well as both life-sustaining and sometimes life-threatening material properties (cf. Griffiths and Wallace 1998; Coveney 2006). In Claude Lévi-Strauss's oft-quoted phrase, food is "good to think" with as well as (sometimes) "good to eat." This way of thinking has led some critics to argue that food can be understood primarily as a kind of signifying system. In Roland Barthes's words, for example, food is "a system of communication, a body of images, a protocol of usages, situations and behavior" (quoted in Belasco 2008: 15). Mary Douglas's famous essay on "deciphering a meal" (Douglas 1971) could be read in a similar

way, where food plays a semiotic role in the ordering of social life, capable of expressing coded messages about social hierarchy and boundaries of inclusion and exclusion. While Douglas was interested in analyzing food's semiotic properties down to the level of the "gastronomic morpheme" (the mouthful), she also recognized the importance of social context and the embedding of food within a wider network of social relations, which give different semantic categories their meaning. As Douglas's work confirms, semiotic analysis needs to be combined with the ethnographic study of food.

While we insist on the significance of food's social context, however, we should not ignore its material properties. Not only is food rooted in nature, in terms of its agricultural origins, but, as we eat, food is literally incorporated into ourselves and is central to our embodiment and identity. Food sustains our individual and collective lives while simultaneously posing a potential threat to human health and vitality. These ideas have come to inform what is now fashionably referred to as a "materialist turn" in food research (and in the social sciences more generally), as flagged in Jane Bennett's recent work on "edible matter" (Bennett 2007). In this work, Bennett praises recent food research in the commodity chain tradition (which traces commodities along the supply chain "from farm to fork"), arguing that it connects people and places at different points along the chain, giving consumers greater insight into what they eat and highlighting the exploitation of food workers and the greed of agri-business. But, she argues, the "anthropocentric allegiances" of this way of thinking are a significant weakness, figuring food as a resource or a means rather than engaging seriously with its active capacities as vital matter. Let us briefly explore what this might mean in terms of our approach to food's symbolic and material properties.

Bennett is interested in exploring the "force of things," where political agency is understood as a force, distributed across multiple, overlapping human and nonhuman bodies. For Bennett, food is an agent inside and alongside intention-forming, morality-(dis)obeying, language-using, reflexivity-wielding, culture-making human beings. It is capable of generating salient public effects, rather than a passive resource at the disposal of consumers. The active capacities of food as vital matter are central to Allison and Jessica Hayes-Conroy's (2008) work on the "visceral politics" of food (see also Hayes-Conroy and Martin 2010). Like Bennett, these authors are interested in the way bodies "feel" food, arguing that, in the visceral realm, "food links up with ideas, memories, sounds, visions, beliefs, past experiences, moods [and] worries, all of which combine to become material—to become bodily, physical sensations" (Cook et al. 2011: 113). These ideas inform our essays on "anxiety," "body," "emotion," and "materialities" and are an underlying theme in many of the other essays.

As the reference to "culinary culture" in our subtitle implies, food cannot be reduced to individual ingredients or to its purely dietary properties. For what we eat has social as well as nutritional value. Meals are social occasions as well as an opportunity to refuel, with commensality (eating together) marking the boundaries of intimacy and distance. As Sidney Mintz reminds us, a "cuisine" is more than a set of recipes or a series of particular foods. Though sometimes associated with the food of social elites (as in the case of haute cuisine), the word also has a wider application. The recognition of a distinctive cuisine, Mintz insists, "requires a population that eats that cuisine with sufficient frequency to consider themselves experts on it" (1996: 97). The group must have an investment in how particular foods are made and how they should taste: there is a normative or moral dimension to the recognition of a cuisine which renders it simultaneously a cultural and a political act (cf. Appadurai 1988; Narayan 1995). We could, then, easily have extended the range of our culinary keywords to include additional essays on diet and meals, myth and ritual (among many other words).

Readers will also notice that there are separate essays on "race and ethnicity" and on "gender" and "class" rather than a generic essay on "identity," reflecting our uneasiness with much that has been written on this topic as well as our desire to be specific. We have also avoided writing specifically about "culture," reflecting our understanding of this word's limited explanatory value. When authors like Michael Pollan talk about a "traditional food culture" or "how a culture eats" (2009: 89), it is not clear exactly what is meant, and we prefer to speak about specific social and cultural *practices* rather than invoking a more reified notion of culture (see the essay on "practices" for further discussion of this point). Even an astute cultural critic like Lisa Heldke who is fastidious in her use of other terms (such as "exotic" or "authentic"), writes much less guardedly about "culture," referring variously to "a culture's foodways" (2003: 9), "the [culinary] culture being consumed" (2003: 15), "members of a particular culture" (2003: 18), "cultures com[ing] into contact with each other" (2003: 39), "when a culture is so small as to be invisible" (2003: 153)—among many similar examples— all of which, we argue, involve an implicit reification of "culture," which undermines Heldke's explicit interest in exploring the social and political implications of various kinds of culinary exchange.

In delimiting our field of study, we have focused on a range of culinary keywords that encompass the social context of food, its organic properties and complex materialities, and both its domestic (familial) and commercial (industrial) dimensions. We have included an essay on "drinking" that discusses the distinction between eating and drinking, as well as several essays that reflect on the nature of food and the boundaries of the edible, but we have not given equal consideration to the consumption of drugs and other stimulants (somewhat arbitrarily including a discussion of coffee and tea, for example, in the essay on drinking but not much on the consumption of other drugs such as cocaine or tobacco). Some of our keywords refer to specific culinary processes (like cooking, eating, and drinking). Some refer to specific culinary domains (such as kitchens or markets), while others refer to the kind of terminology used to describe or promote particular foods or culinary processes (artisan, convenience, fresh, local, quality, tradition). Some words refer to specific academic fields (such as ecology, nutrition, or more generally "science"), some are technical terms (like aesthetics, governance, or security), while others are the focus of more general discussion (such as celebrity chefs). Some words shift uneasily between domains (like authenticity and exotic) and some are richly ambivalent (like appetite or taste). Others describe particular emotions associated with food and eating (such as anxiety or pleasure). Some are specific to culinary culture (like gourmet or foodscapes), while others have a much wider remit (like time and work, memory and risk, safety and sustainability).

In unpacking this complex field, we have sought to emphasize the connections between production and consumption, though we probably have more to say about the latter than the former. There is no essay on "agriculture," for example, though we cover both "ecology" and "farming." The book also reflects our own research interests, both in its emphasis on the pleasures and anxieties associated with food and in our interest in the myriad ways in which food is embedded within the routines and rhythms of everyday social practice. We have found this a particularly productive way of approaching food (cf. Jackson and Everts 2010) and this is reflected in the way we have approached the writing of *Food Words*.

It may also be worth dwelling briefly on the connections between the two keywords of our title. Though there is no essay on "menus," for instance, they are clearly an important place in which food and words come together in particularly striking ways. Writing in *The Guardian*, for example, Steven Poole (2012) suggests that "foodie" rhetoric has reached a point where some diners enjoy consuming the menu more than the food. Poole draws attention to the extravagant language employed in contemporary menus including "the artifice of breed descriptions, chemistry-set jargon and ingredient rebranding" (2012: 4), where baby scallops "rest" on a parsley coulis, and where meat is accompanied by a foam, mousse or jus. Truly, as Priscilla Ferguson argues, "Cuisine cannot exist without food; nor can it survive without words" (2004: 19).

WRITING *FOOD WORDS*

Given the unique character of *Food Words*, it may be worth explaining the evolution of this project and some of the specific practices involved in its writing. In drawing up the original proposal, we examined a number of comparable projects including Pile and Thrift's *City A–Z: Urban Fragments* (2000), Crang and Thrift's *Thinking Space* (2000), and Harrison et al.'s *Patterned Ground* (2004). These ranged from several hundred short (dictionary-style) entries to fewer, longer essays. Only later in the writing process did we become aware of M.F.K. Fisher's *An Alphabet for Gourmets* (1949), which would have provided another model for us to follow.[6] In the proposal for the book, we provided an initial list of keywords and outlined our aim of writing short, provocative essays on each topic. The publishers encouraged us to be more explicit about our choice of words, and we responded with short (three- to four-line) summaries of each prospective keyword. Reviewers suggested other words that they felt we had neglected and new words kept being added throughout the project.

Members of the writing team all knew each well from working together on the CONANX project. Mostly based in Sheffield in the United Kingdom, we maintained contact with our colleagues in Sweden by e-mail, Skype, and face-to-face meetings at conferences and other events. The project is rooted in our collaborative research experience and this is reflected in the prominence that we give to certain concepts like "anxiety" and in our collective interest in social practice (the "sayings and doings" that shape our experience of the material world) (cf. Schatzki 2002). The writing process was highly collaborative. We began with a provisional list of words and allocated a lead author to each one, inviting others to join them so that some words were coauthored. We then convened a "writing workshop" every few weeks to review and discuss half-a-dozen draft essays on each occasion, repeating the process until all of the keywords were drafted. These sessions were always lively, sometimes disputatious occasions, usually culminating in a drink or a meal, demonstrating the value of commensality in shaping our "community of practice." The actual writing process turned out to be less collective than originally planned as one author usually took charge of drafting each essay, calling on others to suggest references, case studies, and additional data rather than fully coauthoring each piece. All of the essays were discussed by the group on at least one occasion and each essay was subject to at least one round of revisions and later editorial work. Rather than striving for a single corporate style, we encouraged different authorial voices to emerge, identifying each essay with the person who took the lead in drafting it. Though collective in spirit, therefore, each of the essays has some degree of "ownership" and personalization which we have been keen to preserve.

At our editor's suggestion, we developed a set of guidelines to shape the essay-writing process including three "levels" that varied in length from the shortest at around 1,000 words, through mid-length essays of around 2,500 words, to a smaller number of longer essays at around 5,000 words. As well as drawing on our own research, we also strove to provide an overview of other relevant work on each topic, highlighting key debates and pushing the argument forward in the spirit of a critical assessment or intervention rather than simple a review or dispassionate definition. Our guidelines suggested that each essay should begin with a direct reference to the keyword rather than with a lengthy preamble. Essays should have a sense of historical perspective and consider the cross-cultural relevance of the term rather than overemphasizing the contemporary British context. Authors were asked to consider whether the term has a specific historical origin or geographical provenance and how it would have been defined in other times and places. When citing references, we wanted the context to be explicit (e.g., "in DeVault's study of feeding the family in the United States") rather than implying a sense of timelessness and placelessness. We wanted essays to have a critical edge by challenging received ideas and orthodoxies. We encouraged the development of a clear structure and narrative line, including our own research but broadening the scope of each essay to encompass a wide range of other studies. To increase the volume's coherence, we added cross-references to other keywords that received substantial discussion in the current essay and, following Orwell's sage advice, we reminded ourselves to break any of these rules rather than write "anything outright barbarous."[7]

Around half-way through the writing process, we invited Warren Belasco to visit Sheffield to participate in an ESRC-sponsored Festival of Social Science debate on global food security. Warren provided written comments on around half the essays. He participated in one of our writing workshops and attended a meeting with the publishers. His academic input was invaluable in improving the book's international coverage (with suggestions of new examples and additional references). He helped us enhance the book's historical perspective without trying to provide a deep chronology of every word. He also assisted us in redressing the (almost inevitable) emphasis on the global North (given the extent to which contemporary food scholarship is predominantly Anglo-American). In the course of a joint conference session on questions of provenance, another of our critical friends (Richard Le Heron) convinced us of the need to relativize our work still further by considering the intellectual provenance of our keywords. He meant, for example, that an emphasis on "local" food in the United Kingdom might look politically progressive, urging support for more sustainable forms of production and shorter supply chains, generating fewer "food miles." But from the perspective of New Zealand farmers, the turn to "local" foods in the United Kingdom posed a direct threat to their export-orientated livelihoods. The challenge, he suggested, was to try to encompass a more global perspective in thinking about our chosen words and to examine how they invoke a complex geography of interconnection—something we have tried to achieve (as in the essay on "governance," for example).

READING *FOOD WORDS*

In writing these essays, we have imagined an audience of upper-level undergraduates, graduate students undertaking masters- and PhD-level research, and academics with an interest in food studies. Readers may be experts in a particular field, interested in finding out about related ideas and concepts, or students at an earlier stage in their careers, seeking to map out the contours of this fast-moving field. Given the wider popular interest in food, we also hope that general readers will find something of interest in the essays, and we have sought, as far as possible, to write without excess academic jargon.

We envisage that different readers will approach *Food Words* in different ways. Some will simply want to check a particular essay rather than reading more widely. But we have provided cross-references to other essays in the hope that we may tempt even the more purposeful and single-minded reader to extend their search to other keywords. Part of the pleasure in writing the book was in thinking through the connections between words rather than trying to provide one-off stand-alone essays. We have also interspersed the essays with a series of photographs (taken by Angela Meah, a member of the CONANX group), which we hope will stimulate further ideas and connections via a visual as well as a verbal medium. Photographic and video evidence was a key component of the ethnographic aspects of the CONANX research, informing our understanding of the practice of everyday life, where cooking and eating are the kind of mundane social practices that tend to be taken for granted, coming into discursive (as opposed to practical) consciousness only infrequently. Documenting these practices through photography and video methods increases their visibility and helps bring them into the academic spotlight. Some of the photos are keyed directly to the essays that follow; others are less literal and more evocative than referential. Finally, we have also provided a short guide to further reading that suggests a range of alternative sources of information and introductory orientations to the field of food studies, plus a consolidated bibliography that we hope will provide readers with further theoretical inspiration and empirical grounding for your own explorations of the dynamics of contemporary culinary culture.

Notes

1. The CONANX program was funded by an Advanced Investigator Grant from the European Research Council (2009–13). It involved a team of researchers based in the interdisciplinary center of the social sciences (ICoSS) at the University of Sheffield in the United Kingdom and in the Centre for Consumer Science (CFK) at the University of Gothenburg in Sweden. For further details of the project, see http://www.sheffield.ac.uk/conanx.

2. On the emergence of a nameable "sociology of food" in the United Kingdom, see Anne Murcott (2011).

3. Originally intended as an appendix to his study of *Culture and Society* (Williams 1958), Raymond Williams's *Keywords* took on a life of its own as a separate volume. It has subsequently spawned many imitators ranging from Tony Bennett, Lawrence Grossberg, and Meaghan Morris's *New Keywords* (2005) to a special issue of the journal *Social Text* (fall 2009).

4. We started with around forty potential keywords and ended up with just over sixty.

5. Gluck and Tsing's book *Words in Motion* (2009) shares many of our concerns. Writing from the premise that 'words make worlds', the authors trace the social and political life of a series of words (such as community, responsibility and security) as they travel across space and time, moving between continents and from the nineteenth century to the present day.

6. M.F.K. Fisher's book covers the alphabetical range from A (for dining alone) to Z (for zakuski, a Russian hors d'oeuvre), encompassing a wide emotional terrain from caution and innocence to sadness and wantonness. On reading the book, W. H. Auden declared that he did not know of anyone in the United States today who writes better prose, pointing to the first three pages of "I is for Innocence" as proof (quoted in Reardon 1994: 57).

7. In his essay on *Politics and the English Language*, originally published in 1946, George Orwell urged his readers against using metaphors, similes, or other figures of speech that they were used to seeing in print. He advised them never to use a long word when a short one will do. If it is possible to cut a word out, he urged his readers always to cut it out; never to use the passive voice where the active voice can be used; and never to use a foreign phrase, a scientific word, or a jargon word if there is an everyday English equivalent. But, he concluded, "Break any of these rules sooner than say anything outright barbarous" (in Orwell 1970: 169).

A

Advertising © ANGELA MEAH.

ADVERTISING

Advertising as a business practice is crucial to the modern industrial world. While almost all commodities in our daily life are touched by advertising in one way or another, this essay will discuss advertising in relation to food, a commodity of necessity for our existence. It invites the readers to rethink the discourses of food advertising and the wider social and cultural meanings that food advertising draws upon to create powerful narratives to evoke our purchasing desires.

Dictionary definitions describe advertising as the business of persuading people to buy products or services, evoking an age-old tension between those who see advertising as the provision of useful information and those who see it as a more arcane art of persuasion. Advertising has also been described as the "poetry of capitalism" (Paterson 2006: 37), often associated with its ability to create the ("false") needs of consumption. Among various definitions of advertising, the Institute of Practitioners in Advertising provides a useful entry point to probe into the way this practice works: "Advertising presents the most persuasive possible selling message to the right prospects for the product or service at the lowest possible cost" (quoted by Jefkins 2000: 5). Studies of food consumption have established that consumers draw on certain aspects of the symbolic values of food to construct family relations, identities, and social status in connection with their personal taste, convenience, and cost (e.g., De Vault 1992; Yan 1997; Charles and Kerr 1988; Pitts et al. 2007; Takeda 2008; Jackson 2009). Tapping into this, advertisers creatively exploit the social and cultural meanings of food, creating and recreating values based on its symbolic elements.

Like many other marketing techniques, advertising is a controversial topic. There has been much discussion about whether advertising is a benign science providing useful information to prospective customers, allowing them to make more informed choices, or whether it is a more sinister form of "hidden persuasion" taking place beneath our level of conscious awareness (Packard 1957). Some people think adverting is immoral and ugly as it "exploits human weakness through language" (Hoggart quoted in Schudson 1981: 3). This is especially true in the case of advertising to children, who are often considered more vulnerable than adults to advertising's coded messages (Batada and Borzekowski 2008; Mills and Keil 2005; Moore 2006). There have been particularly heated debates among nongovernment organizations (NGOs), governments, industries, consumer groups, and academics about the regulation of advertising for unhealthy food to children (Buckingham 2009; Hawkes 2007), although the outcome of these debates is overshadowed by methodological difficulties in measuring the effects of promotion on consumer behavior or the effectiveness of advertising in general (Hastings et al. 2003).

Historically, food advertising has been envisioned in gendered terms within the context of family life. Mona Domosh (2003) demonstrated how a gendered discourse of food production and consumption contributed to the successful marketing of manufactured food by Heinz in the late nineteenth and early twentieth centuries. More recently, Katherine Parkin (2006) has shown how food advertisements in modern America framed women's role as homemaker, reinforcing the cultural values of family, duty, and affection around food provisioning by women (see also Roger Miller's [1991] work "Selling Mrs Consumer"). The gendered discourse of food advertising is often mixed with other discourses. In addition to the advertising symbol of white women associated with "whiteness," "purity," and "femininity," Heinz's global success was achieved through the construction of a colonial discourse in which civilization was brought to the rest of the world along with manufactured food. Heinz also utilized narratives of "purity" and "freshness" to distinguish themselves from the prevalence of food adulteration at the beginning of the twentieth century, making successful claims about its "pure," "fresh," and "clean" ketchup even though it was highly processed, sterilized, and bottled (Domosh 2003).

The discourse of science and technology in food advertising has also been a strong one, as nutritional attributes and health benefits supported by scientific evidence are a natural selling point for food (Nestle 2010). Advertisements for many food items such as breakfast cereal and infant formula contain many scientific claims about micronutrients and their health-improving functions (Greenaway et al. 2002; Le Heron and Hayward 2002). Being "scientific," which is often associated with being "Western" and "modern," remains a powerful discourse in many parts of the non-Western world (Gram 2007; Moon 2010; Greenaway et al. 2002). In Qian Gong and Peter Jackson's (2012) study of infant formula advertisements in China, for example, "scientific" claims about the benefits of fortified nutrients are a persuasive force for new parents and baby carers to choose formula-feeding over breast-feeding. In particular, after the contamination of infant formula in 2008, the dairy industry in China started to combine discourses of "nature" and "science" in its television advertising to assure consumers about the safety and quality of its product.

Narratives of "purity" and "nature," being "green" and "sustainable," have become prominent with modern food advertising as the agri-food system has experienced an increasing separation of food production and consumption. The distance between production and consumption in the global food chain, as well as the occurrence of "food scares" due to an unsustainable mode of industrial food production, have created an imaginative space for many food and beverage companies to sell their products (e.g., New Zealand lamb, Sainsbury's Woodland chicken) at a premium based on their imagined geographies. Other food manufacturers have managed to "re-naturalize" products such as sugar, a highly processed food additive, in their marketing strategies. Differentiating the "organic," "yellow-tinted and unrefined" sugar from more refined granulated crystal sugar, sugar companies in Florida recreated the value of their products by drawing on public interests in "natural, healthful, and sustainable commodity and production systems" (Hollander 2003: 67–68). The persistent growth of organic foods in the United States also serves as an example of successful food advertising based on the concept of "naturalness" (Dimitri and Oberholtzer 2010). Perhaps the most successful example is bottled water, in which the rich cultural

meaning of water being natural and pure has created $22 billion worth of "pervasive global business" (Wilk 2006: 303). Advertising and marketing not only increased the value of the bottled water substantially, but also, perhaps more importantly, constituted the formation of the material commodity in the first place—turning natural, free water into a commodity. Moreover, through sophisticated management processes such as branding, companies not only create values for their products but also separate them from rival products, giving them unique identities to "devise, stabilize and reproduce" the brand (Arvidsson 2005: 239–44). Evian, for example, has successfully created unique images for its mineral water—"ice-filtered water" from "snow-capped mountains"—and separated it from hundreds of other bottled waters as the only brand available from Cachat Spring in Evian-les-Bains in Western France (Haig 2006: 101–3).

The recent discourse of nature in food advertising is not merely a continuation of the "purity" and "fresh" narrative that Heinz used to distance itself from food-adulteration practices in the early twentieth century. While it is mostly utilized by the food industry to sell products, it also invokes debates among policymakers, academics, and consumers on issues of responsibility, trust, and obligation within the whole global food production chain. The discourse of nature in food advertising also extends to moral aspects of consumption around sustainability, environment, and animal welfare. Social marketing practices—using adverting techniques to change behaviors and improve health outcomes—have been implemented around the world (Cheng et al. 2011). Now $30 billion is spent on food advertising every year (Brownell and Horgen 2003: 103), and 4.5 cents of every food dollar consumers spend is poured back into advertising (Parkin 2006: 2). Despite such vast amounts of money being spent by the food industry, often linked to claims about improving public health, many observers argue that the food environment in advanced industrial countries is becoming increasingly "toxic" (Brownell and Horgen 2003; Adams et al. 2009; Moon 2010; Gunter et al. 2010). While the discourses of food advertising evolve according to changing perceptions of health, body image, eating habits, and other factors, it is important to revisit how advertising shapes our perceptions of the social and cultural meanings of food and the extent to which it affects the way people eat.

See also brands, consumption, media.

Qian Gong

AESTHETICS

Does food have an aesthetic? Or, is food an aesthetic object? For sure, it has visual features and the word "taste"—arguably the most prominent feature of food—not only designates the human ability to perceive the qualities of food but also serves as an analogy for the ability to perceive the qualities of fine art. Food might have good taste, and so might a reviewer of artistic expressions.

Aesthetic issues are at play in relation to many food issues. Commercially, for example, there are concerns about the size, shape, and color of fruit and vegetables: the greenness of beans, the firmness of bananas, and the straightness of cucumbers. These aesthetic issues are of concern to consumers; they are mediated by retailers and have direct consequences for producers. Aesthetics are also at play in many other contexts, including the plating of restaurant food and the display of supermarket goods. It is also possible to discern a personal aesthetics at play within the domestic sphere and at the level of individual consumers, as explored in Elizabeth Mosby Adler's (1981) work on the many ways to eat an Oreo cookie. This essay will, however, concentrate on some of the philosophical issues that are stake in questions of culinary aesthetics and related concerns about taste.

As a concept, aesthetics comes from philosophy and relates to art, more specifically to the judgment of the viewer, the quality of the artwork and the ontological status of art (what is art, and what is it good for?). But throughout the history of philosophy, the gustatory sense itself has come to occupy a low place in the

Western hierarchy of senses, where vision and hearing have been considered the most noble ones (Korsmeyer 1999, 2002). Together with the haptic sense (the sensibility for touch, pain, temperature, movement, and force) and the olfactory sense of smell, taste has been considered a "lower sense," one of the body, a subjective one and therefore inappropriate for rational or aesthetic judgment. This supposed hierarchy and the perception of art that comes along with it is a longstanding Western ideology, dating back some 2,500 years and found among the ancient Greeks. According to Plato, vision and sound are what give us information about the world. These can be shared and rationally estimated together with others; they engage the intellect, while tastes and smells encourage appetite, which in Plato's worldview was primitive, instinctual, and thereby strictly opposed to the rational faculties.

In tracing the historical line of Western taste ideology, Carolyn Korsmeyer (1999) finds a historical point where these already-diverging lines could have converged: the Scottish Enlightenment philosopher David Hume (1711–1776) and his essay "On the Standard of Taste" (1757/2005). For Hume, there is a definite parallel between gastronomic and aesthetic appreciation. This route was, however, not followed through. Instead, gustatory and aesthetic taste is discussed by the German philosopher Immanuel Kant, who instead reinforced the division between taste and Taste. For Kant, smell, taste, and feel are personal, bodily incitements, incapable of reaching to the moral, rational, and aesthetic faculties—those faculties that, by our access to them, make us human. By the end of the eighteenth century, food was disqualified as an acceptable artistic medium.

From the very opening of the book, Korsmeyer's view is simple: food is not art. The reason for this is that art and food simply have different histories, and historical processes are what determine what is art and what is not. Although Korsmeyer tests this thesis throughout the book, at the end she arrives at a similar conclusion: food is still not art, but as food represents, expresses, and exemplifies, food and taste have symbolic functions—and as such, they are aesthetically relevant.

The use of the word taste in the gustatory sense is a valid metaphor for any cultivation of perceptual experience, not only in Western culture. The Western concept of aesthetics is, however, a deeply Eurocentric one, built upon the division of the senses originating from the Greeks and reinforced by Kant. What qualifies the "higher" senses as high and the "lower" senses as low is the ability of the senses to have perceptions of things distant from the subject. Hearing and seeing imply a distance from the body; the objects might well be seen or heard in exactly the same way by others. Smelling, tasting, and feeling, however, are activated in direct contact with other bodies. Among these senses, taste is the most intimate one; it arises when another body is already a part of your own. The Austrian phenomenological philosopher Mădălina Diaconu argues this commonly assumed inability of the lower senses as due to the qualities of the experiences of tasting, feeling, and smelling; the sensory data generated tend to cluster in synaesthetic configurations (meaning that they tend to leak into each other, creating synergy effects together). Hence, it is seldom possible to distinguish exactly what data come from what sensual organ (Diaconu 2006). "Taste" does not exclusively refer to gustatory activity but to experience generated by all the senses together, centering on the mouth and nose.

Diaconu examines art that addresses other senses in order to arrive at an aesthetic inquiry that is able to consider synaesthetic experience, as art today is more and more inclusive of the whole body of the viewing subject and as the creative industries—partly as a response to the visualization of life that followed the information technology (IT) revolution—tend to work toward the lower senses as well, providing an expanded "aesthetization" of the everyday.

The philosopher Yuriko Saito points out that the specifically Western bias of aesthetics that make it difficult to expand it to the "lower" senses is that it "presupposes the institutionalized art world and certain cultural and economic conditions" (Saito 2001: 88). Western aesthetics is closely tied to the idea of art that resides in a specific domain, outside of the everyday. She notes that many

cultures, such as the Inuit and Balinese, do not even have the concept of art. Aesthetics is instead inextricable, integrated, practiced everywhere, in everything done. If Western aestheticians do not aim to exclude such non-Westerners from being able to have a sense of aesthetics at all, then they should try and formulate an aesthetic relating to such things that actually are universally shared. Using the example of the Japanese tea ceremony, Saito shows how expression and communication are integrated aesthetic traits that have to be considered in order to grasp the aesthetic value of this practice. In Western "ocularcentric" aesthetic theorizing, any element of communication is bracketed off, and so is all data outside the visual register, leaving some quite poor theoretical tools for understanding such rich phenomena as the tea ceremony. Hence, Saito calls for a nonvisual aesthetic, one able to take into account not only the richness of integrated cultural phenomena outside or inside the Western cultural sphere, but also the less pleasant consequences of the power relations unavoidably engendered by the aesthetic discriminative capability that is Taste.

When visual media today get more dominant by the minute, aesthetic practices are at play on many levels. Food styling is today an occupational branch in its own right, creating tasteful imagery of foodstuffs for magazines, TV shows, websites, and packaged edibles. As one commentator puts it: "The photograph must appeal to all five senses, but most importantly must be unified into a single, visually appealing image" (Finello 2010). The visual image apparently is not intended to be seen in its artful isolation; on the contrary, it *aims* to create a synaesthetic effect, to engage the whole body of the supposed viewer. This is an aesthetic whose synergetic effects are played out in the field of human appetite and not necessarily as a creation of beauty—still it is undoubtedly an aesthetic effect. Another effect of a visualized and mediatized culture of food was pointed out by Eric Stice and Heather Shaw (1994): that the overall dominant ideal of female beauty was the impossibly skinny body, an ideal propagated by bombarding the public with pictures of extremely skinny models and actresses, professions in which the rate of eating disorders is extremely high. Sheila Lintott (2003) brought this together with Kant's aesthetics, arguing that attempts to control one's own body through excessive dieting was the most intense way that women are encouraged to reach the sublime. Again, aesthetics acts over distance, through food and eating, and into the body.

It may also be that "food" and "taste" are too narrow categories for us to understand the dynamics of a possible gastronomic aesthetics. In aiming for a more universally viable aesthetics—one trying not to bracket off all of reality except that of vision/hearing from the aesthetic event but still not using generalized abstractions such as "food" or "taste"—we might instead talk about *eating*, eating considered a practice in its own right. And, considering that "art" is also a Eurocentric and rather limiting concept, might there also be a more universally useful conception of art to go along with eating considered a practice that might enable us to talk about an "aesthetics of eating"? This seems to be what many writers on the subject are calling for.

One possible way forward might be the route taken by Australian philosopher Elizabeth Grosz (2008). Grosz utilizes a Deleuzian vocabulary to construct an aesthetic so abstract that it actually does not confine itself to the human but still stays within the aesthetic event. For Grosz, aesthetics begins with sensation itself; sensation as a mobilizing force that is neither the property of a given subject or a specific object but a third thing that connects the two—a force in its own right, activated in encounter. For Grosz, gastronomy is "the art of the mouth" (Grosz 2008); an intensity making all organs function together in a specific manner but centering on the mouth and nose in what might be coined an "alimentary event" (Dolphijn 2004), where someone becomes eater and someone (or something) becomes food. Such an aesthetic stays with the event. It might very well go further but does not necessarily take the one-way route into the sublime and isolated realm of fine arts. It comes from somewhere but neither restricts its actors to cultured Westerners, nor excludes the possibly less pleasant aesthetic

forces, such as the visual imagery of those that have self-starved their bodies to sublime beauty.

It pays respect to taste but does not care much for Taste.

See also appetite, body, eating, emotion, packaging, taste.

Jakob Wenzer

ANXIETY

People have been anxious about food throughout human history and in many parts of the world. For long periods and in many places, people have been anxious about food shortages, and in many parts of the world today people still suffer from periodic famines or persistent hunger. These fears are often expressed in the rather sanitized terms of "food security," defined by the Food and Agriculture Organization (FAO) as only having been fully achieved "when all people, at all times have physical and economic access to sufficient, safe and nutritious food to meet their dietary needs and food preferences for an active and healthy life" (FAO 2006a). It is, however, one of the ironies of the modern world that undernourishment and food shortages in the global South have come to be combined with anxieties about overnourishment in the global North, which is often now said to be experiencing an "obesity epidemic." That these two tendencies may be interconnected through the inequalities that inhere within our current agri-food system is suggested by Raj Patel's stark description of the world as simultaneously "stuffed and starved" (Patel 2007).

Contemporary food anxieties in the West have their historical roots in the process of industrialization where fears began to emerge about society's ability to feed its growing and increasingly urban population. In 1798, for example, the Reverend Thomas Malthus proposed that population growth, if left unchecked, was bound to outrun food supply, the former growing at a geometric rate while the latter grew arithmetically. While Malthus failed to foresee the impact of technological change on food supplies, achieved through the relentless intensification of agricultural production, as well as other inventions such as modern means of contraception, his predictions continue to have popular resonance, with Lord Haskins warning in *Prospect* magazine, for example, of "the return of Malthus" (2008).

Although the threat of hunger continued to stalk Western Europe throughout the nineteenth century, erupting periodically and with catastrophic consequences during the Irish Potato Famine of 1845–1852, urban consumers began to experience other anxieties, notably concerning the adulteration of food and drink by unscrupulous merchants who watered down beer and added alum to whiten bread, practices that were largely eradicated by the end of the 1880s through legislative, scientific, and technological interventions (Burnett 1989). According to Ulrich Beck's Risk Society thesis, however, an increasing reliance on science and technology brings both benefits and increased risks. So, while advances in medical knowledge have reduced the incidence of diseases such as TB and while modern methods of risk assessment may have reduced the occurrence of food poisoning, other risks have been introduced into the agrifood system giving rise to their own anxieties.

One of the most notable of these was the outbreak of Bovine Spongiform Encephalopathy (BSE or "mad cow disease"), which decimated the British dairy industry in the early 1990s, leading to an import ban on British beef throughout the European Union and causing a direct threat to public health through the human form of BSE, Creutzfeldt-Jakob Disease (or CJD). BSE was a classic example of Beck's Risk Society Thesis, where threats such as air pollution, radiological hazards, and food contamination are so potent because of their invisibility and the way they are incorporated in our daily lives as "the stowaways of normal consumption" that "travel on the wind and in the water," passing through "all the otherwise strictly controlled protective areas of modernity" (Beck 1992: 40–41). In Britain, the impact of BSE led to the establishment of the Food Standards Agency in 2001 with a clear separation of agricultural interests from those charged with the protection of public health and with a strong emphasis on the role of

independent scientific advice in the governance of food safety. But consumer trust in food was significantly undermined as diseases such as BSE came to be seen as what Charles Perrow (1999) called the "normal accidents" associated with technology.

The occurrence of food-borne illness is, to some extent, an inherent feature of our commercialized food system and its relentless demand for increase choice, described by Claude Fischler (1988) as the omnivore's paradox and later glossed by Michael Pollan (2006) as the omnivore's dilemma. The paradox emerges as a result of our omnivorous human appetite and the fact that we are simultaneously attracted to and distrustful of novel foods. With the constant demand for new products and the ceaseless commercial pressure to innovate, a degree of uncertainty and risk is inherent within our contemporary agri-food system (with examples such as GMOs and nano-foods only the latest in a long line of similar innovations in food supply). Such pressures have given rise to what Fischler termed *les angoisses de l'omnivore*, identifying an important source of contemporary consumer anxieties.

Similarly, as Western consumers have grown more affluent, new anxieties have begun to arise, with food disorders such as anorexia nervosa and bulimia becoming more prevalent. In Susan Bordo's analysis, diseases like bulimia and anorexia are symptoms of a wider malaise associated with the obsessive body practices of contemporary culture (such as the prevalence of dieting and fitness regimes, widespread use of cosmetic surgery and the fashion industry's emphasis on idealized body image). In her "cultural approach" to the body, Bordo (1993) argues that these obsessions are not bizarre or anomalous but logical (if extreme) manifestations of our current anxieties and cultural fantasies. Bordo extends her argument to an analysis of the causes of female eating disorders, which she argues need to be understood not only from a medical or psychological point of view but as "complex crystallizations of culture" (1993: 35).

While the causes of disordered eating are much disputed, sociologists like Anthony Giddens (2006) have suggested that their roots lie in societal factors as much as in the individual's psychological predisposition or family dynamics. Giddens describes bulimia and anorexia as "diseases of affluence," where Western consumers are now faced with a wide range of food from around the world, available year-round, from which they are forced to choose a specific diet. While choice is often held to be a desirable aspect of modern life, Giddens argues that it also contains the seeds of anxiety as the search for identity and meaning become vexed projects of the self, subject to constant monitoring and commercial pressures, and beset with tension and anxiety. Giddens notes that eating disorders have specific class and gender dimensions as well as reflect geographical patterns of relative affluence and deprivation (though these patterns are now changing, Giddens suggests, in response to our increasingly globalized world). One need not subscribe completely to Giddens's argument to acknowledge that contemporary anxieties have both an individual and a collective dimension.

Here, we suggest, the emphasis should be placed on the nature of anxiety as a social condition, albeit one that affects individuals in different ways. While some food fears and anxieties may be experienced on a personal level (such as anxieties related to food intolerances), we propose to focus mainly on the broader sociological, historical and geographical dimensions of anxiety including how anxieties are framed, mediated, and institutionalized; how they spread and are contained; and how they shift between social fields and vary across space and time (Jackson and Everts 2010). Before pursuing that argument, however, we want to consider two more definitional questions: whether anxiety can be distinguished from related concepts such as fear and whether anxiety can be considered a specifically modern phenomenon.

Fear and Anxiety

The word "anxiety" has Anglo-Germanic roots and is derived from a variety of Greek and Latin words describing feelings of constriction or throttling. In contemporary English usage, it has at least four separate meanings: a state of agitation, being troubled in mind, a solicitous desire to effect some purpose, and uneasiness about a coming event (Tyrer 1999: 3–4). Anxiety can be defined as a physically embodied state involving mental and emotional distress combined with a more diffuse sense of uneasiness about a coming event.

The relationship between fear and anxiety has been the subject of lengthy debate. Many authors seek to distinguish between the specific object and rational nature of fear compared with the supposedly irrational nature and lack of a definable object associated with anxiety. Within psychotherapy, for example, treatment often centers on the quest to uncover the underlying reasons for a patient's expressed anxieties on the basis that identifying the object of fear will enable the patient to deal with whatever issue they are repressing. But the distinction between rational fears and irrational anxieties breaks down when viewed sociologically as, for example, when one considers how apparently rational fears (about crime, for example) are often associated with irrational anxieties (based on stereotypical attitudes towards racialized Others, for example). This example is used by the historian Joanna Bourke to advocate that we approach the issue as an empirical rather than a theoretical question. Rather than trying to ascertain whether people in the past were more or less anxious than in the present day, or whether their fears were more justifiable than our anxieties, Bourke (2003) suggests that we treat the question as a kind of "language game," where we pay careful attention to the way that fears and anxieties are expressed both now and in the past, tracing the circumstances and terms in which anxieties are expressed and how they are articulated within wider social relations of power. While no definitive answers may be possible to questions about the different levels of fear among different groups of people, now and in the past, Bourke's work suggests a more contextualized approach to understanding the role of the emotions in modern history rather than seeking to arbitrate between rational fears and irrational anxieties.

Anxiety as a Modern Condition

This essay began by considering the *longue durée* of consumer anxieties about food, seeking to place contemporary Western fears in a longer historical and wider geographical perspective. But there are many observers who describe anxiety as a peculiarly modern condition, arguing that it should be distinguished from related conditions that precede our present-day concerns. Indeed, the modern era has often been described as an "age of anxiety," from the work of W. H. Auden (1947) to more recent analyses of our current economic, social, political, and environmental insecurities (Dunant and Porter 1996). So, too, in Alain de Botton's (2005) analysis of our present-day concerns over social status, anxiety emerges as the flip side of ambition, feeding off our uncertainties about our social standing in relation to those around us.

Within the academic field of food studies, the term appears in the title of several recent works, often without much further elaboration (cf. Griffiths and Wallace 1998; Freidberg 2004; Coveney 2006). For many commentators, it is its pervasiveness as an everyday social condition that distinguishes anxiety as a distinctively modern phenomenon. According to Zygmunt Bauman (2006), for example, anxiety has become a normal, everyday condition of modern society, with more and more people living in a state of constant anxiety: a "time of fears" that threatens our bodies, the social order, and our very survival as a species. Within the medical literature, too, studies have documented significant increases in levels of anxiety and depression among successive generations of children and adolescents. For example, Jean Twenge's (2000) study of birth cohort data showed that the average American child in the 1990s was more anxious than child psychiatric patients in the 1950s. While this may cast doubt on the validity of the measures used and their robustness in assessing change over time, attempts have been made to link these changes to the increasingly competitive nature of American society during the twentieth century (cf. Dorling 2009).

For many authors, then, "It is now a matter of sociological common sense to identify ourselves as living through a period of acute insecurity and high anxiety…the brute facts of anxiety appear to be almost beyond dispute" (Wilkinson 2001: 42). So, too, for Rollo May, "The evidence is overwhelming…that men and women of today live in an 'age of anxiety,'"

occupying a state of "nameless and formless uneasiness" (1950: v). Wilkinson has, however, questioned whether the presumption that we are living in a qualitatively new or different "age of anxiety" can be substantiated (Wilkinson 1999). He asks to what extent our present-day anxieties about the environment and climate change, the resurgence of nationalism, or the demise of communism differ in a qualitative way from the anxieties of earlier historical periods.

A case can certainly be made that anxiety lies at the heart of modern society, with writers such as Georg Simmel describing the links between anxiety and urban living, notably in his essay "The Metropolis and Mental Life" (1903). Max Weber provides an account of the process of disenchantment that accompanies modernity. Emile Durkheim examines the nature of anomie and Marx highlights the centrality of alienation to modern life. But it was not until Freud's writings on the psychology of the unconscious mind that anxiety became a central concept of contemporary social theory. As several observers have noted (e.g., May 1950; Wilkinson 2001), it is only with the rise of psychotherapy that anxiety truly enters the theoretical language of social science.

For Freud, anxiety was a normal fact of everyday life rather than a peculiar psychological affliction. Freud saw the increase of anxiety as an inevitable response to the evolution of civilization, which had been achieved through the "sublimation of instinct" (1930: 63). In his later work, Freud (1936) debated whether anxiety was a cause or a result of repression. Psychoanalytical theories of anxiety cover a wide range of approaches from Freudian notions of repression, sublimation, and projection to John Bowlby's ideas about attachment and separation, also encompassing Melanie Klein's work on persecutory and depressive anxiety and Wilfred Bion's discussion of the containment and modulation of anxiety (see Emanuel 2000 for a useful review). These diverse approaches are united in their sense that human beings often struggle to tolerate uncertainty and deal with ambivalence and that anxiety is a defensive response to as-yet-unrecognized threats to the self. Psychoanalytic theories suggest that feelings of anxiety and dread are rooted in the unconscious and that childhood experiences may lay down powerful psychological templates that recur in different guises later in life. In many cases, psychoanalytical theories posit a link between food and anxiety (via notions of disgust and the transgression of bodily boundaries, for example), suggesting a connection between our sexual and culinary appetites (as explored by Probyn 2000 and others).

Anxiety can also be considered as a modern condition through its association with existential philosophy. In his study *The Concept of Anxiety*, for example, the Danish philosopher Søren Kierkegaard (1844/1980) describes anxiety as an internal condition of the human being rather than as something that intrudes on the individual from outside. Anxiety is a condition that attracts and repels; we are pulled into it at the same time as we are terrified by it. In modern society, where belief in God is no longer a given, individuals must face up to their own mortality, recognizing their own position in the world and taking responsibility for their own fate. Indeed, for Kierkegaard, the experience of anxiety is freedom's actuality (1844/1980: 42). According to Kierkegaard, this process involves a number of stages, from ignorance and purposeless, seizing of this or that opportunity, through becoming thoughtful and responsible individuals, to the realization that everything is grounded in nothingness which opens up the possibility of true faith (grounding the human being in the eternal). Anxiety is therefore intrinsic to our being in the world, and while it can lead to inaction and paralysis, it can also be a spur to creativity and freedom. For, as Kierkegaard argued, "Whoever is educated by anxiety is educated by possibility" (1844/1980: 156). Elaborating this idea, recent commentators have argued that anxiety is not something to be abhorred or stamped out, for "a world without anxiety would be a grey and boring place that would lead to frustration and torpor" (Tyrer 1999: 1) or, as Renata Salecl suggests:

> While anxiety is today perceived as something one needs to be able to control and hopefully in the long run get rid of ... it is almost forgotten that philosophy and psychoanalysis discussed anxiety as an essentially human condition that may not

only have paralysing effects, but also be the very condition through which people relate to the world. (2004: 15)

Like Kierkegaard, Nietzsche identified a similar series of stages as characteristic of our spiritual development, beginning from a belief in ideals, passing through a phase in which we destroy those beliefs before accepting the nothingness that gives way to a new, childlike way of affirming life. Between the realization that all meaning is relative and the last stage lies the transition that Nietzsche called nihilism. It is the realization that humans have no purpose in the world apart from those they craft themselves, that the world is indifferent toward human life and that death is inevitable. While this might be seen as a cause for desperation, Nietzsche saw it as the beginning of a glorious new age where human lives are free from prejudice and traditional biases.

A similar trajectory can be traced in the work of Martin Heidegger. In *Being and Time* (1978), for example, Heidegger analyses angst as a phenomenon that is at the heart of understanding the human condition. For Heidegger, anxiety is experienced as a sudden awareness of nothingness, revealing the relativity of meaning to the individual. In the face of anxiety, individuals realize meanings are unstable and relative; that we create meaning ourselves. It is our being in the world that produces meaning and death is the end of meaning. According to Heidegger, the anxious person realizes the relativity of meaning and recognizes the inevitability of his or her own mortality. These philosophical ideas have direct application to our understanding of modern food-related anxieties.

Anxiety As a Social Condition

According to Peter Jackson and Jonathan Everts (2010), anxiety events such as "food scares" go through a number of more-or-less predictable stages, commonly involving a threat to our health and well-being (the recognition of our own mortality) and/or a threat to our established ways of making sense of the world (the threat of meaningless). Food scares can be approached as events that rupture the fabric of our everyday lives, disrupting our established routines and confusing our normal ways of making sense of the world until a new mode of understanding is put firmly in place. Analysis of such events, Jackson and Everts suggest, involves the identification of subjects and objects of anxiety, their successful resolution requiring the elimination of one or the other (or both). So, for example, with the threat of avian influenza spreading to human populations across Europe in the spring of 2009, the objects of anxiety can be identified as the infected and vulnerable birds that were eliminated in a very literal sense so that people were no longer subject to the virus. In this case, the subjects of anxiety (potentially infected human beings) disappeared together with the object, with the particular strain of the virus also being found to be less virulent than had been feared.

This theory of social anxiety also draws attention to the "framing" of events by particular communities of practice such as the media and government agencies, food manufacturers, and retailers. So, in the case of avian influenza, one could point to the role of medical science in identifying the strain of virus, to epidemiologists and others who attempted to predict its spread and estimate the likely number of victims, but also to the various governmental agencies, from the World Health Organization to national and local governments, who sought to control the outbreak, to the media who reported on the emerging crisis. Significantly, too, one might note how the issue became "racialized" as authorities in one country (e.g., the United States) sought to place the blame for the outbreak in other places (e.g., Mexico), where food safety and health systems were alleged to be of lower quality. So, too, in the case of swine flu, the Egyptian government ordered the killing of all swine stocks that were kept by the Koptic minority, inflaming religious tensions, while many Asian countries stopped importing pork from the United States and Mexico, fearing that the consumption of meat posed a threat to human health (Johnson 2009). In the United States, meanwhile, the farming lobby stressed that there was no evidence to associate swine flu with pork consumption, blaming the media for creating "false" anxieties. While swine flu is still framed as an emerging pandemic with potentially fatal effects, it has already had real

consequences not only for infected individuals but for societies and economies in general.

As we have argued elsewhere (Jackson et al. in press), anxiety can be located in the social insofar as it is a shared experience that results in some discernible action by significant numbers of people. Anxieties are also social insofar as they involve associations or connections with other entities causing them to spread out over space and time. So, for example, when "food scares" lead supermarkets to withdraw goods from the shelves, consumers are drawn into a social condition of anxiety whether or not they are anxious at a personal level. In the language of actor-network theory, anxieties have the capacity to engage and enroll more and more elements (Latour 2005). The question of whether individual feelings can be transmitted or shared with others is, however, the subject of intense debate. In her recent work on the transmission of affect, for example, Teresa Brennan (2004) suggests that emotions such as depression or anxiety can be transmitted between individuals through a process of constant communication between individuals and their physical and social environments.

Developing these ideas, Wilkinson (2001) defines anxiety as a complex combination of affective experiences, bodily reactions, and behavioral responses. While anxiety may be experienced as a personal condition (such as a fear of the dark), Wilkinson maintains, its incidence can be exacerbated by "social predicaments and cultural contradictions." To quote Wilkinson in full: "Anxiety is conceived not so much as a personality defect but, rather, as a function or consequence of the social predicaments and cultural contradictions in which individuals are made to live out their everyday lives" (2001: 17).

A useful way of thinking about the social dimensions of anxiety is suggested by Sheldon Ungar's attempt to identify the specific sites of anxiety associated with environmental, nuclear, chemical, and medical threats. Ungar sees anxiety as a response to uncertainty and ambivalence where concerns about public safety lead to an exaggerated response akin to a contemporary "moral panic" (Ungar, 2001; Cohen 1972). Commenting on Ungar's argument, Sean Hier (2003) suggests that the sites of social anxiety are converging with discourses of risk, frequently containing a strongly moral dimension which he describes in terms of the "moralization of risk." Hier goes on to identify a growing tension between the "techno-scientific rationalities" of expert systems and what he calls the "social rationalities" of everyday living. The gap between these different rationalities is a fertile ground for the development of social anxiety, as might be illustrated in terms of the gap between expert advice and popular understandings of food safety (cf. Beardsworth's [1990] work of food scares that describes the spiraling and amplification of anxieties and draws attention to the ambivalent role of "experts").

Methodologically, then, the recognition of anxiety's social dimensions suggests a parallel with Rachel Pain and Susan Smith's (2008) recent work on the geopolitics of fear and everyday life, where they argue that fear is a social or collective experience rather than an individual state, embedded in a network of moral and political geographies. Pain and Smith refer to the materialization of fear, highlighting its methodological significance:

> Recognising the materiality of fear means that there are tracks and traces between the different lives of those who seek to control fear and those whose lives are pervaded by it. It is possible to follow the materialisation of certain fears into local landscapes; and it is important to show how everyday practices might be inspired by this, might tolerate it, could ignore it, will certainly pose alternatives, and may well have other, more pressing, 'things' to contend with. (2008: 13)

Following the "tracks and traces" of food-related anxieties has rich potential as a field for future research. And, as we have argued elsewhere (Jackson and Everts 2010), approaching food-related anxieties through the analytical lens of current theories of practice (Warde 2005) may also be a particularly fruitful avenue to pursue.

Anxiety and Theories of Practice

At the very least, practice theory provides a vocabulary for analyzing food scares and related anxieties seen in terms of events that rupture the fabric of everyday life, examining how they are framed and mediated by different communities of practice, how they become institutionalized to varying degrees, intensifying and spreading to different sites or being contained and dissipating over time. Theodore Schatzki (2002) draws attention to the "doings and sayings" that underpin social life, including the way that such practices become routinized and institutionalized to varying degrees. He also refers to the teleoaffective structures or emotional resources that underpin social life, which he defines as "a range of normativized and hierarchically ordered ends, projects, and tasks, to varying degrees allied with normativized emotions and even moods" (2002: 80).

Social practices can be defined as "a routinized way in which bodies are moved, objects are handled, subjects are treated, things are described and the world is understood" (Reckwitz 2002: 250). More specifically, practice theory emphasizes the skillful performance of social life, the practical knowledge (or "know-how") and learned behaviors that underpin our everyday actions. It is this sense of tacit understanding that anxiety threatens to undermine where people feel unable to deal with the threatening situations in which they find themselves. Where once science and technology may have been looked to for the solutions to social problems and environmental crises, science itself may now be a figure of suspicion. Rather than the Enlightenment replacing fear and superstition with rationality and scientific knowledge, such fears have been displaced to new sites of anxiety which can be equally troubling as the role of magic or witchcraft in the Middle Ages. As historian Joanna Bourke suggests, harmful microbes and bacteria are equally capable of evoking fear as the evil spirits they replaced; scientists are potentially as destructive as sorcerers (Bourke 2003: 112).

A practice-based approach reaffirms the nature of anxiety as a necessary or normal part of the human condition, not as some exceptional state associated with individual phobia or personal pathologies. How, then, do practice-based theories understand the emotional and affective not as an individual "possession" but as a social practice? According to Andreas Reckwitz, "Wants and emotions…do not belong to individuals but—in the form of knowledge—to practices" (2002: 254). "Knowledge" can, of course, take many forms, from technical expertise to lay understanding. It can be explicit or implicit, codified or tacit, and, as previously argued, the gap between lay and scientific knowledge can be particularly fertile ground for the growth of social anxiety. Theories of practice offer a valuable way of demystifying this process, demonstrating that anxiety is not some free-floating mental activity; it is embedded in specific (often complex) doings and sayings. Anxieties are embodied and social, practical and practiced. Like other social practices, they are routinized, collective, and conventional in character.

Practice-based theories are well-suited to understanding this kind of routinized behavior and offer a powerful alternative to the model of autonomous individuals making informed choices that prevails in much consumer research and in government rhetoric about the sovereignty of individualized "consumer choice." Practice theory also suggests an alternative to current ways of thinking about behavior change at a highly individualized level, consistent with the neoliberal agenda of promoting the "responsibilization" of citizen-subjects. In this sense, the promotion of social anxieties can serve particular political or commercial ends, and we need a critical vocabulary such as is provided by practice theory to resist this tendency.

In focusing on food-related anxieties and their social as well as their individual character, we run the risk of exaggerating the extent to which modern-day consumers are beset with anxieties, paralyzed by fear and incapable of exercising agency in their decisions about what and how to eat. While there is much evidence to support the lack of consumer trust in food across Europe (Kjaernes et al. 2007) and survey evidence confirms the persistence of consumer anxieties about food, we should also acknowledge that food remains a source of pleasure for many consumers. Indeed, it is the balance between pleasure and pain, desire and dread, fear and fascination that makes food such a potent source of emotional investment as well as underpinning its political significance and potential for commercial exploitation.

See also pleasure, practices, risk, security.

Peter Jackson

APPETITE

Appetite is a complex word, encompassing medical, biological, social, and cultural aspects. Like taste, it involves both physiological and sociocultural dimensions. Quoting from the mission statement of the academic journal *Appetite* gives some idea of this range and complexity, covering behavioral nutrition and the cultural, sensory, and physiological influences on food choices and the intake of food and drink. The journal also covers normal and disordered eating and drinking, dietary attitudes and practices, and the bases of human and animal behavior toward food. Its disciplinary range encompasses psychology and neuroscience as well as the social and behavioral sciences.

The academic study of appetite also has deep philosophical roots which can be traced back to the Platonic distinction between reason and appetite which maps on to the distinction that Descartes drew between mind and body. For Plato, bodily appetites must be satisfied, but they also need to be controlled in order that reason may prevail as the proper governor of the soul. From Plato, too, we derive the modern tendency to distinguish raw appetite from a trained and discerning palate. Unlike most philosophers who eschewed the bodily pleasures of food, associating it with gluttony and sexual excess, Epicurus wrote about food as a source of modest pleasure, alongside friendship, freedom, thought, shelter, and clothes. (According to Alain de Botton [2001: 56], Epicurus's own diet consisted mainly of bread, water, vegetables, and olives.) Following in this philosophical vein and seeking to transcend the conventional distinction between mental and manual labor, Lisa Heldke (1992) develops the idea of food-making as "thoughtful practice." Inviting us to breach the separation of knowing from doing and treating theorizing as a kind of practice, Heldke holds out the promise of a more responsible and respectful approach to food.

The significance of these distinctions becomes clear when one considers so-called eating disorders such as anorexia nervosa and bulimia. The word anorexia is of Greek derivation, referring literally to the negation of appetite. Associated with bodily self-image, it is most prevalent among adolescent girls and is ten times more prevalent in women than in men (cf. Bordo 1993; Sobal and Maurer 1999a, 1999b). It is a serious illness with the highest mortality rate of any psychiatric disorder. Patients with anorexia have an obsessive fear of gaining weight. But, far from losing their appetite, Bordo (1992: 33) insists, the typical anorexic is haunted by her appetite. Experiencing a constant desire for food, anorexics fear that once they start to eat they may not be able to stop. Many engage in bouts of binge eating, subsequently purging the body by enforced vomiting (the medical condition known as bulimia). Bordo (1993) also explores the relationship between hunger and ideology, arguing that the popular media's obsession with ultrathin female bodies places an "unbearable weight" on young woman to conform to the relentless imagery of thinness in contemporary celebrity culture.

Strong parallels are often drawn between our culinary and sexual appetites. So, for example, anorexic girls often starve themselves to the point where their menstrual cycles are interrupted or cease altogether, the suppression of their culinary appetite paralleling the Augustinian denial or suppression of one's sexual appetite. While Augustine was haunted by the "slimy desires of the flesh" (quoted in Bordo 1992: 33), anorexics are haunted by the constant desire for (and dread of) food. In what Bordo (1992: 34) describes as an anorexic "metaphysics," a typical fantasy involves their total liberation from the bodily prison, a desire that Plato and Augustine would both have recognized.

A connection between culinary and sexual appetites is also often made outside of the sociomedical realm of disordered eating. Elspeth Probyn's exploration of carnal appetite is a good example where she explores the common vocabulary of "touch and timing" as the source of sensual pleasure, arguing that "the sensual nature of eating now constitutes a privileged optic through which to consider how...the relations between sex, gender and power are being renegotiated" (2000: 5–7). Food has, of course, long been associated with the rhetoric of care and the preparation and eating of food are highly sensual and deeply gendered practices. Probyn concludes her account of the relationship between eating and sex with a reflection on the ethical possibilities that eating and sexuality offer when practiced with care, restraint, and good timing (2000: 64). But there are many other explorations of carnal appetite that show less restraint, such as the pervasive imagery of food advertising and the so-called gastro-porn that constitutes the stock-in-trade of the popular food media.

Vegetarianism provides another way of connecting our various human appetites, as in Carol Adams's exploration of the sexual politics of meat where she draws a parallel between the objectification of women and the objectification of animals (see also Fiddes 1991). When animals are killed for food, Adams argues, the once-living creature is rendered invisible, becoming the "absent referent" of food advertising, referred to as pork rather than pig or beef rather than cow. Her analogy between food and sex culminates "when the male-defined consumer eats the female-defined body": animals and women become objects to others who act as subjects (Adams 1990). Based on this premise, Adams argues that vegetarianism and feminism should be in deeper conversation with each other.

Probyn draws a further parallel between the way food and sex have been commodified as appetites have become jaded and consumers have become increasingly blasé in the face of ever greater choice (2000: 83). She speaks of the way markets are "cannibalized" and of the way consumers are "hungry for difference," paralleling bell hooks's argument about "Eating the Other" (hooks 1992). As Probyn's account of anorexia reveals, eating and sex can both elicit powerful emotions of shame and disgust when we find ourselves in "incongruous proximity" to the object of desire/dread (2000: 132). But Probyn also suggests that feelings of shame and disgust can be productive of community, calling on others to witness our pulling away as a plea to establish common ground (2000: 131).

One might also reflect further on the pleasures as well as the anxieties provoked by our human appetites. In her analysis of the ambiguities of contemporary food advertising, for example, Susanne Freidberg (2010: 478) discusses the way that notions of natural and healthy, pure and fresh, refer simultaneously to the physical or material qualities of food and to ideals for living and eating well.

All these examples suggest that the study of human appetite is a richly provocative field. It has stimulated philosophical debate, prompted medical research, called forth arguments for social change, and evoked fascinating parallels with other sources of pleasure and anxiety. As Probyn argues of food and eating in general, our appetites bring together "a cacophony of feelings, hopes, pleasures and worries, [orchestrating] experiences that are at once intensely individual and social" (2000: 3).

See also body, eating, hunger, pleasure, sex, taste.

Peter Jackson

ARTISAN

According to the American Cheese Society, the word "artisan" (or "artisanal") refers to goods that are produced primarily by hand, in small batches, with particular attention to the traditions of the cheesemaker's art, using as little mechanization as possible (quoted in Paxson 2011: 116). As this definition suggests, the term is usually applied to particular products and to specific forms of manufacture. So, for example, the School of Artisan Food in Nottinghamshire (United Kingdom) focuses on pies and sausages, jams and chutneys, beers, ales, and cider and offers courses in baking, butchery, brewing, and cheesemaking. The School's website (School of Artisan Food 2011) admits that there is no single definition of the term but talks about goods that are produced by nonindustrialized methods

using techniques that have been handed down through generations and are now in danger of being lost. The term also refers to particular ethical dispositions such as understanding and respect for raw materials, knowing where ingredients come from, and being concerned about the environment. Artisanal food is spoken of in terms of mastery and craft production, involving an historical, experiential, and intuitive understanding, acquiring skills, such as dexterity and savoir faire, from experienced practitioners, emphasizing hands-on and tacit forms of knowledge rather than learning by rote or from the book. This definition of artisanal food also emphasizes taste (in both senses of the word: sociological and physiological) and the pleasures of direct bodily experience (tactile, sensuous, caring), often thought to be lacking in more industrialized forms of food processing and commercial manufacture, caricatured as overly standardized, bland, and uniform.

As in Richard Sennett's work on the craftsman (2008), artisanal production has particular class and gendered connotations. Sennett's craft producers are cabinet-makers and metalworkers, not hairdressers or florists. Craft production emphasizes pride in one's work as its own reward, acquiring skill, using tools, and demonstrating knowledge of particular materials. Artisanal production has much in common with the kind of craft skills described by Tim Ingold, where workers have a feel for what they do and where their movements are continually and subtly responsive to their materials (2000: 357). Learned via long apprenticeships and protected through trade associations and guilds, accounts of artisanal production often suggest that the status of craft work is being eroded through the deskilling and alienation of labor. A common narrative suggests that, as the distinction between makers and users grew with the Industrial Revolution, producers became increasingly divorced from consumers, until such time as artisanal work is being partially revalued in the form of industrial heritage, often involving a thinly veiled nostalgia for "the world we have lost" (Laslett 1965). In contemporary usage, artisanal products often involve elements of the folksy or contrived—a "modern pastiche," according to

Paxson (2011: 122)—failing to acknowledge the extent to which much of what now passes for tradition may, in fact, be quite recently invented (Hobsbawn and Ranger 1983).

Indeed, many of the qualities attributed to artisan food are now being appropriated by large-scale industrialized food producers, sold through high-street supermarkets rather than through local independent stores or farmers' markets. The distinction between alternative and mainstream forms of production is becoming blurred as supermarkets and their suppliers seek to capitalize on the recent turn to local, quality food (Goodman 2003; Jackson et al. 2008). As Suzanne Freidberg (2003) remarked in the context of the advertising-saturated markets of the global North, food is increasingly being "sold with a story"—and artisanal production is an appealing way of narrating the distinctive qualities of food for an audience that has become suspicious of industrialized methods of food manufacture.

The blurred boundaries between artisanal and industrialized forms of production are explored in Polly Russell's (2003) research on British culinary culture. In her life-history interview with Stephen Hallam, managing director of Dickinson and Morris—a company that has manufactured pork pies since 1851—the tensions between the firm's commitment to tradition and authenticity and the increasing automation involved in mass production are sensitively explored. Reflecting on this process, Stephen Hallam attempts to reconcile the inevitability of technological change with his own personal sense of commitment to artisanal production and craft skill. He admits that raising the pastry case by machine, the mechanical deposition of the meat, and the automated securing of the lid is a compromise, while the crimping of the pie crust and the glazing of the top is still done by hand. He insists:

> You can't substitute that technical knowledge, that knowledge with the hands, the eyes, the nose. You will smell a pie baking and your nose will tell you if something's wrong. Now you tell me a machine that can do that…As long as you still embody the essence of the heritage, there's nothing

amiss to using technology to assist you with that. (quoted in Russell 2003: 211)

Hallam is well aware of the commercial significance of heritage and authenticity. The company's website proclaims the fact that Dickinson and Morris is "the oldest pork pie bakery and the last remaining producer of authentic Melton Mowbray pork pies based in the town" (Dickinson and Morris 2012). But he also acknowledges the disjunction between the public presence of the company's shop in Melton Mowbray (Ye Olde Pork Pie Shoppe, staffed by women in starched white aprons) and the fact that most of the company's pies are manufactured in a large-scale bakery in nearby Leicester:

> To a lot of people, Dickinson and Morris is just the pork pie shop and they believe all the packets of pork pies and sausages you see in the supermarket on shelves come from the shop but in reality they can't. We don't have the space, it's impossible. So we utilise the resources of our sister companies and divisions in the group…And the branded products, i.e. all those that are in supermarkets, come from the pork pie bakery facility on the outskirts of Leicester. (Russell 2003: 216)

For Hallam and others like him, the artisanal quality of the product is about "embodying the essence of the heritage" rather than insisting on a particular mode of production or direct connection to a specific place.

This flexible notion of artisanal practice is taken up by Heather Paxson in her discussion of the art and science of cheesemaking in the United States, where she argues that the artisanal nature of "handcrafting" involves a balance of aesthetic creativity and intuition combined with accurate measurement, meticulous record-keeping, and scrupulous hygiene. Paxson (2011: 116) describes this process in terms of "synaesthetic reason" (bringing together cross-sensory apprehension with reasoned analysis), arguing that artisanship combines quasimystical elements with an acknowledgement of market-based tastes and conventional understandings of acceptable retail form.

While most definitions of artisanal production stress its hand-made and small-scale nature with minimal use of mechanization, recent research suggests that these distinctions are rarely tenable in practice. Among "artisanal" cheesemakers, for example, those who claim the label employ varying degrees of mechanization, producing cheese on a variety of scales and selling it through a variety of channels. This has led some researchers to claim that the label "artisan" cannot be used to distinguish particular types of food, methods of production or kinds of worker. According to Joby Williams, for example, none of these qualities truly defines the artisanal. Rather, she suggests, on the basis of her ethnographic work with cheesemakers in Britain and the United States, the nature of artisanal production lies in a particular ethical disposition toward the materials with which cheesemakers work. This "ethic of regard" (Williams 2011) entails a respect for the vitality and unpredictability of the raw materials involved in the process of manufacture, extending from the cheesemaker to the retailers (*affineurs* and specialist cheesemongers). From this perspective, artisanal is defined through specific practices and ethical dispositions rather than inhering in specific products or modes of production. In this sense, we might argue, artisanal production has not been destroyed by industrialization. Rather, its performative and aesthetic dimensions can be remobilized and reappropriated in different contexts. As with the related concepts of authenticity and tradition, the artisanal is a complex and contested term whose meanings need to be traced through their usage in practice.

See also authenticity, taste, tradition.

Peter Jackson

AUTHENTICITY

While in most spheres of life, "authenticity" is considered an overwhelmingly positive trait, providing one of the philosophical foundations for exercising ethical judgment (cf. Trilling 1972;

Taylor 1992), the term is regarded much more skeptically by food studies scholars and in relation to other arenas of cultural production. This skepticism arises, in part, from the frequency with which restaurants and food products make claims about their authenticity in promotional materials. There is scarcely an Indian restaurant in the United Kingdom that does not advertise itself as "authentic," while even the most international brands insist that they are "the real thing" ("Coca-Cola *is* Coke"). Given such indiscriminate use in commercial circles, many food scholars have questioned the academic value of the term. In an early essay on culinary authenticity, for example, Arjun Appadurai (1986b) expressed his doubts about whether the term should be applied to culinary systems at all, recognizing its normative dimensions and ahistorical nature.

At its simplest, authenticity refers to something that is factually true. By extension, the word is also used to refer to something, such as an artwork, whose provenance is considered genuine or verifiable (and here one immediately enters the contested terrain of claim and counter-claim). Authenticity may also refer to questions of sincerity and intent (as with an "authentic" musical performance that may perhaps depart in detail from the circumstances in which it was composed provided that the performer remains faithful to the spirit of the original). While some accounts of authenticity lament the way that contemporary consumer culture has substituted the virtual for the real, resulting in what James Gilmore and Joseph Pine call "toxic levels of inauthenticity" (2007: 43), others accept that authenticity is a social construction rather than a verifiable fact (cf. Van Leeuwen 2003; Vannini and Williams 2009). So, for example, in Richard Peterson's (1997) study of Country and Western music, authenticity is seen as something that is fabricated through continual renegotiation between adherence to tradition and creative interpretation or musical innovation.

Besides its centrality to studies of culinary culture, authenticity has also been debated at length in the field of tourism studies. Here, the notion that tourists travel in search of authentic experiences has given way to a more reflexive understanding of how many tourists are willing, in effect, to suspend their disbelief, acknowledging that many of the people and places they encounter have been staged for their pleasure and entertainment. This idea if often associated with the notion of "staged authenticity," put forward by Dean MacCannell (1973) and elaborated in John Urry's work on the "tourist gaze" (1990). Commenting on MacCannell's work, Barbara Kirschenblatt-Gimblett and Edward Bruner (1992: 303) argue that "authenticity is not given in the event but is a social construction." From this perspective, the analytical focus shifts from judgments of authenticity to questions of authentication: "Who has the power to represent whom and to determine which representation is authoritative?" (1992: 304).

This approach has been widely employed in studies of culinary culture (e.g., Lu and Fine 1995; Cook et al. 2000; Molz 2003). To take one recent example, Heng-Chang Chi and Peter Jackson (2011) have examined the performance of authenticity in Thai restaurants in Taiwan focusing on décor and signage as well as ingredients and dishes. They suggest that a variety of authenticating strategies are used by different kinds of restaurant, drawing on a range of culinary imaginaries to appeal to different market segments, from Thai migrant workers to tourists and business people with cosmopolitan tastes. Only in the latter case, involving the most "upmarket" restaurants, is the language of authenticity regularly used, reflecting the marketing strategy of the Thai Ministry of Commerce, which, in 2006, introduced its "Thai Select" trademark to promote "authentic Thai cuisine" abroad. The certification is designed to assure customers *that delicious Thai cuisine is being served in a pleasant atmosphere, and with a famous Thai smile. It's not just a meal; it's a journey into Thai culture*" (cited in Chi and Jackson 2011). The use of the word "select" clearly designates the restaurant's status, serving as a marker of social distinction and good taste in the sense outlined by Bourdieu (1984). Thai Select restaurants must use genuine Thai ingredients and their chefs must have a Thai Cuisine Training Certificate issued by the Thai government. While other restaurants may be more "authentic" in the sense of serving the kind of food that is familiar to Thai migrants from their homeland, such restaurants rarely feel the need to advertise their authenticity.

Chi and Jackson's research demonstrates that claims to authenticity are readily challenged in practice. While some restaurant proprietors insisted on the authenticity of their dishes and on the Thai origins of their ingredients, others accepted that their food had been adjusted (in terms of the intensity of spices, for example) to suit the taste of their Taiwanese clientele. Some even admitted that popular dishes such as Jaioma chicken are rarely if ever served in Thailand, having been created for the emerging market for "Thai" food in Taiwan. While many proprietors, particularly of upmarket restaurants, insisted on the authenticity of their food, there were exceptions such as the owner of the Thai Hey restaurant. Asked whether his food was authentic, he replied with refreshing candor: "Authenticity? Is my cuisine authentic? Are you crazy?" His clear admission of the constructedness of "Thai" food in Taiwan—heavy with irony and self-deprecation—contrasts sharply with the Thai Select brand and its insistent claims to culinary authenticity.

The contested nature of authenticity claims has created a demand for legislative intervention whereby certain products and methods of manufacture seek to guarantee their distinctiveness through legal means. The use of labels such as Appellation d'Origine Contrôlée and the Italian equivalent Denominazione di origine controllata (DOC) are examples of such initiatives. Their economic and cultural significance is explored in Jonathan Nossiter's 2004 film *Mondovino*, which addresses the homogenization of wine production worldwide, contrasting the fortunes of single, small-estate producers with large, multinational producers such as Robert Mondavi, focusing on the role of influential wine critics such as Robert Parker and jet-setting wine consultants such as Michel Rolland.

Authenticity claims are now so common within culinary culture that it is possible to identify a number of recurrent themes. Within contemporary American food writing, for example, Josée Johnston and Shyon Baumann suggest that common criteria of authenticity include "simplicity" (hand-made, small-scale, lacking pretention), personal connection to specific people or places (including the work of named individuals), historicism and tradition (including "age-old" or "timeless" methods of production) as well as more general claims like closeness to nature (natural, organic, etc.), sincerity, honesty, and integrity (2007: 179). Johnston and Baumann also highlight a central tension within authenticity claims that access to such "simple," "traditional," or "artisanal" foods is often restricted by price or by its relative lack of availability in mainstream commercial channels. Instead, they point out, "Authentic food items are primarily accessible to cosmopolitan, upper-middle-class individuals with ample grocery budgets who are capable of extensive global travel" (2007: 188).

Through their connections to the "exotic," authentic foods are often marked by their rarity or relative obscurity as explored in Jon May's research on the consumption cultures of a gentrifying neighborhood in North London where one of his informants expressed her desire for "a little taste of something more exotic" (May 1996), where the use of the word "little" serves as a marker of cultural distinction. Similarly, in Sharon Zukin's (2008) work on New York farmers' markets, markers of culinary authenticity also serve as a means of social exclusion for those who do not share the gourmet tastes and select consumption practices of the gentrified middle classes.

Like Zukin, Johnston and Baumann suggest that authenticity and exoticism are a means for contemporary foodies to legitimize their culinary tastes and that these strategies enable them to negotiate the ideological tension between democracy and distinction (2007: 169). They suggest that this process involves the valorization of cultural forms from outside the dominant Western cultural canon whereby consumers can demonstrate a cultural openness to multiple ethnic and class cuisines while simultaneously constructing criteria for maintaining social and cultural distinctions. An alternative reading is offered by Meredith Abarca (2004), writing in the context of Mexican-American cuisine, where she argues that authenticity can be deployed in a more strategic way as an act of culinary resistance by "cultural insiders." Abarca

warns, however, that this kind of "planned authenticity" can become a kind of culinary straitjacket, forcing people to work within a narrow set of cultural and economic boundaries (2004: 5). Sylvia Ferrero makes a similar argument about Mexican food businesses in Los Angeles, showing how Mexican business people can claim authenticity and draw on their cultural capital in the authentication of Mexican food terms and culinary practices but that this strategy is not without its risks, restricting their movement into wider food markets where their claims to authenticity have less traction.

Jackson's comparative work on the advertising strategies of two Indian curry sauce manufacturers in the United Kingdom sheds further light on these issues. In one case, Patak's emphasizes the company's family links to India and the embodied authenticity of its culinary skills, inviting its customers to "Share Patak's passion for India." In the other case, one of Patak's rival companies, founded in London in 1869, makes a less geographically specific claim about its culinary authenticity. Sharwood's, who makes Thai and Chinese as well as Indian cooking sauces, invites its customers to "Stir up some passion," under the slogan "It's half the world, it's Sharwoods" (Jackson 2002). While both companies claim to be passionate about the authenticity of their products, they are branded in significantly different ways.

These ideas are taken further in Lisa Heldke's (2003) analysis of the "exotic appetites" of people, like herself, who she describes as "food adventurers." Heldke questions whether (and under what circumstances) it is possible to consume the food of other cultures in a respectful manner, avoiding the cultural imperialism that is often associated with the practice of culinary appropriation. Her answer is complex and contingent, arguing that "sometimes eating in an ethnic restaurant actively supports and advances colonialism, and sometimes it does not" (2003: 5). Heldke challenges the easy acquisitiveness with which other kinds of food can be appropriated by food adventurers, suggesting that such attitudes often derive from a position of economic and racialized privilege that fails to acknowledge its own specificity. So, for example, she argues that the United States is often assumed to be culinarily neutral, a beige backdrop against which other cuisines can display their difference. "Our" food is assumed to be ethnically unmarked and culturally mainstream, she argues, while "theirs" is regarded as exotic and excitingly alternative. Heldke challenges the colonizing impulses and assumed universality of contemporary American culture. Her project involves a philosophical investigation of the quest for novelty and exoticism, leading her to reject the very idea of culinary authenticity as both confused and confusing (2003: 24). Rather than debating whether curry is "authentically Indian," for example, she seeks to advance a more nuanced understanding of culinary culture in which aesthetic and ethical judgments inform each other, rejecting notions of culinary purity and timelessness and examining more closely the specific circumstances in which the borrowing of food may be injurious to those from whom it is borrowed. Her book provides a thoughtful exploration of how respectful culinary interchanges might take place (2003: 59), where ethnic difference is not simply regarded as a resource for one's own use. A more ethical approach to culinary difference, she suggests, would involve a greater sense of self-questioning and a more contextual understanding of food's agricultural origins.

See also artisan, brands, exotic, provenance.

Peter Jackson

B

Body © Angela Meah.

BODY

Combining the concepts of "body" and "food" in social science indexes inevitably generates a huge number of hits about compulsive eating, obsessions with slenderness, and bodily objectification, particularly the objectification of the female body. In this essay, some influential studies in this strand of research will be briefly discussed. The essay will also argue that such studies say more about our time and prevailing cultural ideals than about possible, and maybe more intriguing, ways of combining food and body in research.

In contemporary popular culture, the body appears as the Western world's major renovation project (Featherstone 2000; McRobbie 2009; Dworkin and Wachs 2009). Understood as private property, the body becomes an object in which everyone can invest in order to increase its market value and therefore something that can be almost endlessly transformed and reshaped. This is done by the help of exercise and body modifications, ranging from piercing, plastic surgery, and the use of implants. Food and eating also play an important role. This can be witnessed in a never-ending row of diets and health and super foods supposed to strengthen the body, defend it against diseases, and prolong its life. An interesting phenomenon is the range of products and procedures for detoxing, from the intake of herbal mixtures to bowel rinsing (colonic irrigation). The idea is that the body is impure, not just in visible terms of physical contamination but also in terms of an inner invisible intoxication of the blood, intestines, lymphatic system, and deeper layers of the skin, resonating with Mary Douglas's (1966) famous theories of purity and danger.

The view of the body as an object in the making and the duality of mind and body that can be witnessed, for example, in the detoxing debate, where the poisonous body needs to be rescued by the sensible mind, attracted new interest in the 1980s. Postmodernists regarded identity increasingly as something created by consumption and technology, generating visible signs on the body (see, for example, Featherstone 1982; Turner 1984; Featherstone et al.

1991/2001). The desired individualization and cultural modernization, where society became less and less tradition-bound, created a growing market for identity projects based in the body. These researchers also pointed to the paradox that the realization of individuality went hand in hand with mass consumption and homogenized body ideals. To use the body in the quest for identity required a readiness to relate to the body as an object and a willingness to shape it from an idealized image of what a body should be and express.

A number of influential feminist writers (e.g., Bordo 1990, 1993; Probyn 2000) have shown that the mind/body dualism supports gender inequality by associating men with the exalted, controlling mind and women with the lowly body subject to control. Such attitudes, it has been argued, have delayed serious attention to food and eating, which is considered as something feminine and secondary (Curtin and Heldke 1992; Korsmeyer 1999). The mind/body dualism also meshes with the need of consumer capitalism to sell products because the body, especially the female body, is constantly defined as an object to be worked on and improved by buying things. In her book *The Anthropology of Food and Body* (1999), Carole M. Counihan reveals the cultural underpinnings of these ideologies. There is nothing "natural" about the pursuit of thinness. Medieval Europeans, for example, defined the body as a site of fertility, decay, and holiness. They controlled, disciplined, and even tortured their bodies to come closer to the divine, whereas Victorians reinforced women's subordination by defining the female body as weak, sickly, and without legitimate desires. In her own study of medieval Florence, Counihan describes how men and women developed a positive and active relationship to their bodies by enjoying eating and self-nurturance. In their belief that the body gave legitimate gustatory pleasures and simultaneously represented and reenacted the family, Florentines defined the body as an active agent of a person's self, not a passive object to be molded into an abstract commodity of beauty. Florentine women were empowered by the way their culture defined the body as a social product out of their control—the result of family heritage and habits—rather than as an imperfect demonstration of individual moral failings. They were also empowered by the active and agentic definition of the body prevailing in their culture, which emphasized doing—working, having children, making food, wearing beautiful clothes—rather than having a perfectly sculptured body (Counihan 1999: 188).

An interest in the active body resonates well with another strand in the sociocultural theorizing of the body focusing on bodily movements and techniques. Already in 1934, Marcel Mauss had published his famous article about the techniques of the body. His point was that the body is marked by the techniques it is practicing. It learns implicitly the culturally established ways to move, making recourse to others and using gaze and gestures that exist in a certain era and social group. Mauss referred to the way the French use spades, how Maori women talk, how English boys hold their elbows at the table, and the walk of American girls to illustrate this point (Mauss 1934/1973). Picking up from this, Pierre Bourdieu (1990) developed his celebrated theory of habitus and hexis, where he argues that social structures and cultural schemes are incorporated and function as generative dispositions behind bodies' schemes of action. Through injunctions such as "sit up straight" or "don't hold your knife in your left hand," fundamental cultural principles are inscribed on the body and guide its movements.

Another similar, but less socially anchored, theory is Maurice Merleau-Ponty's about the lived body in his book *Phenomenology of Perception* (1962, originally published in French in 1945), generally considered one of the classics of phenomenology. In this book, Merleau-Ponty argued that existence in the world is something that humans first and foremost experience through the body, through looking, listening, and touching, as acquired cultural, habit-based, forms of conduct. The body "knows itself" by virtue of its active relation to the world. Another characteristic of the body according to Merleau-Ponty is its double character of being always visible as well as seeing, tangible as well as touching. The body is "flesh": a generative body of being and becoming that touches, sees, hears, smells, and tastes both itself and other flesh and becomes aware

of itself in that process. The flesh of the body is part of the "flesh of the world," connecting all bodies to each other and to the history of humankind. All human beings consist of the same organic components. This means that differences in status, beliefs, or values are not what fundamentally construct a human. Instead, it is the individual subjective body that both creates and is created in an historic, cultural, and situational world and also carries other bodies' and organisms' stories as part of itself. This is, of course, a theory that opens up exciting horizons for research into the link between food and body.

The phenomenological theories of Merleau-Ponty have gained increasing attention following the interest in theories of practice. In her overview, Kirsten Simonsen (2010) argues that the most significant consequence of Merleau-Ponty's theories for practice theory is his principles of intercorporeality, the way body-subjects-objects are always at the same time visible-seers, tangible-touchers, audible-listeners, and so on. But, Simonsen argues, it is important to appreciate that humans do not only perceive another body in its materiality: they are also affected by the meaning of its appearance. They do not only contemplate the communications of the other; others affect them, and they respond to them (Simonsen 2010: 223). This not only applies to human bodies but to the meetings of different kinds of bodies, such as human bodies and foodstuff.

Needless to say, there are a number of studies highlighting the embodied character of food and eating, such as the Kalymnian's tactile skills in preparing and shopping for food in David Sutton's Greek studies (2001); the grilling, microwaving, shallow frying, and casseroling in Frances Short's study of British households (Short 2006); or the sensual knowledge and artistic expressions reflected in the stories of working-class Mexican and Mexican American women in Meredith Abarca's book *Voices in the Kitchen* (2006). Memories of past meals are stored in our bodies and become an integral part of our identities. As Sutton reminds, we are not only what we eat but what we ate as well (Sutton 2001: 7). An interesting aspect of the materialization of food and body is found in art: from the fruit faces of sixteenth-century artist Giuseppe Arcimboldo (Strand 1999) to the provocative paintings of skulls and dead animals by Damien Hirst; video installations and performances, such as Carole Schneemann's *Meat Joy* of men and women celebrating the flesh by rubbing raw fish, chicken, and sausage, as well as wet paint, onto their bodies; and Carol Adams's depictions of women's body parts expressed through ads for the breasts, legs, and thighs of chickens and turkeys (Adams 2003).

It has been argued that the "corporeal turn," which introduced the concept of "embodiment" and the material turn, giving birth to material culture studies, was followed by a "sensory turn" in the late 1980s and 1990s (Howes 2003). Leading researchers in this field, such as David Howes in *Empire of the Senses* (2005), Constance Classen (1993), and Mark Smith (2008), argue that members of a society "make sense" of the world or translate sensory perception into a particular worldview and, moreover, that in all cultures the senses are organized hierarchically with vision at the top. There are a number of prominent examples related to food, such as Lisa Law's studies of Philippine women in Hong Kong and Shanghai eating "pinaket" or "adobo" with their hands, exuding the aromas and textures of "home" (Law 2001); Nadia Seremetakis's study of how the memory of a no-longer-available peach generates a phenomenological space in which public culture is understood and played out (Seremetakis 2005); and Lisa Heldke's meditation on her first contact with "Thai ginger" (Heldke 2005). Yet the overall impression is that there are surprisingly few examples of food studies in this field, probably due to the prominence given to vision. There is still a lot to be done in this field for food culture scholars.

One of the most prominent examples of both the embodiment of childhood food memories and the sensory properties of food is Marcel Proust's tale of the madeleine cake bringing back the memory of childhood teas at aunt Leonie's, when putting a piece of it into his mouth as an old man. As he poetically observes:

> But when from a long distant past nothing subsists, after the people are dead, after the things are broken and scattered, taste and smell alone, more fragile but more enduring, more unsubstantial, more persistent, more faithful, remain poisoned a long time, like souls, remembering, waiting, hoping, amid the ruins of all the rest; and bear unflinchingly, in the tiny and most impalpable drop of their essence, the vast structure of recollection. (Proust 1913/1922: 50–51)

The permeability of the body, including the way entities passing through the body transform bodies as well as foodstuff, has intrigued many researchers. In an interesting article, Annemarie Mol (2009) introduces the tasting body as a main character in this drama. Her problem is how to theorize pleasure in such a way that it does not appear to be inherently selfish and politically suspect. The solution, she argues, is to turn to the body. "Citizens," she states, are defined as willing to serve the "common good," while "consumers," by definition, allow themselves to have "pleasure" and follow the whims of their bodily desires. It is this "naturally given lust" that is the problem. What is needed, she argues, is a body that is not just understood as interested in one kind of good (pleasure) but in various goods at the same time (such as health or fair trade), a body that is sensitive and attuned to its surroundings. The trick, Mol argues, is to focus on the tasting body. Taste is embodied but not innate; it has to be acquired by tasting good food while absorbing the linguistic repertoires that help to fine tune the tasting (Mol 2009: 271). The model that emerges is the eater, who has carefully acquired the skills of juggling the lust for bodily pleasure with the desire for the common good. The eater does not anymore need to silence her body but has learned to listen to it. The eater, Mol argues, "does not judge from the outside, but (selectively) opens up to the world that she tastes. She does not take safe distance, but allows herself to be altered by what she tastes" (Mol 2009: 278).

Mol shares an interest in the eating body with Elisabeth Grosz (1998). According to Grosz, eaters do not observe from a distance but are mixed up with their surroundings. Eating is a physical activity. Eaters get to know the world by tasting it, chewing on it, even partially absorbing it. As Grosz explains: "Bodies reinscribe and project themselves onto their sociocultural environment so that this environment both produces and reflects the form and interest of the body" (1998: 42). The body is what is acted on and what acts back.

A similar model of how to understand the interplay of body and surroundings is offered by Bruno Latour, who presents a concept of the body as an "interface" that is effectuated in its encounters with surrounding entities. In his essay "How to Talk about the Body," he argues that "to have a body is to learn to be affected, meaning 'effectuated,' moved, put in motion by other entities, humans or non-humans" (Latour 2004a: 205). To make his point, he exemplifies with the training of people to work in the perfume industry. Here, bodies learn to discriminate odors, and noses gets trained to smell and distinguish between an ever-more-subtle range of fragrances. Bodies, Latour concludes, constantly transform through engagements with other entities, whether human or nonhuman. The body acts as an interface that "leaves a dynamic trajectory by which we learn to register and become sensitive to what the world is made of" (Latour 2004a: 206). Influenced by actor-network theory, other writers on the body (for example, Berg and Akrich 2004; Berg and Mol 1998; Mol 2008) share the tendency to pay attention to the way specific sorts of bodies are created in collaboration with other things—medical technologies, discourses, and so on—such that the body becomes "the empirical result of practices with those various things" (Berg and Akrich 2004: 3).

Studying risk management, the interconnectedness of bodies and technologies becomes obvious. To curb risks, technical equipment is used in more and more areas to control and regulate not just the food but also the body: the measurement of blood pressure, cholesterol content in the blood, how many steps you take a day, how high your heart rate is during jogging—all intended to prevent disease and early death. Risk assessments are made, for example in relation to food intake during pregnancy, that can have major consequences for women's ability to trust their

bodies. Despite practices of affect modulation by governmental agencies (Milne et al. 2011), conceptions of worst-case scenarios generate anxieties that something is wrong with the expected baby (Brembeck 2011).

Finally, an interesting way to understand the body in relation to food is Elsbeth Probyn's suggestion of "alimentary identities" (2000). Inspired by Gilles Deleuze and Félix Guattari, Probyn argues that we are "alimentary assemblages, bodies that eat with vigorous class, ethnic and gendered appetites, mouth machines that ingest and regurgitate, articulate what we are, what we eat and what eats us" (Probyn 2000: 32). This is the body emerging in Deleuzian studies of foodscapes (e.g., Dolphijn 2004). According to Rick Dolphijn, foodscapes are processes where elements relate to each other and generate relations and affect, including food, eating, and bodies. Bodies, argues Dolphijn accordingly, are not defined by their genus or species, by their organs and functions, but by "what they can do, by the affects of which they are capable" (Dolphijn 2004: 17). This means that matter never *is* food; it *becomes* food, just like the eater never *is* the eater; "it becomes the eater whenever the matter has the capacity and the ability to be affected in that particular way" (Dolphijn 2004: 17). In a reversal of Proust eating the madeleine, Dolphijn asks if we can be really sure that it is Proust eating the cake, and not the other way round, the madeleine consuming Proust.

Exploring the food-body connection in more depth seems to be one of the most exciting and rewarding tasks for future food studies.

See also consumption, eating, foodscapes gender, memory, practices, risk, taste.

Helene Brembeck

BRANDS

Upon entering a food store, what immediately surrounds consumers is not first and foremost an environment dominated by food staples. It is one of brands. Brands mediate our relationship to food; brands dominate the visual field in the public space, and sometimes brands even become a synonym for a product, an attitude, or even a lifestyle. Often, brands are almost transparent. Without thinking much of it, brands are invested with trust, thereby letting them take the place of a personal sense of judgment. Both campaigning author Naomi Klein (2000) and branding researcher Douglas Holt (2002) have made the point that brands invade people's life-world, colonizing the visual and sonic registers that people share through media and public spaces. The terms they use associate the practices and logics of branding with war: through a set of maneuvers, a territory that rightly belongs to someone else is taken over and exploited.

Not every analyst or commentator utilizes a vocabulary explicitly borrowed from warfare. Within the academic field of marketing, the lexicon is quite the reverse. Here, words like trust, relations, and comfort are used. Such variables are, according to this discourse, actually crucial to the emergence of a successful brand and one of the important tasks of brand management. David Aaker (1991, 1996) uses the term "brand equity" to designate the specificity of a given brand, claiming that brand equity has a measurable marketing effect that comes with a given product compared to the effect that the same product would produce without the brand attached to it. This prompts brand managers to attempt to map consumer preferences in order for them to create strong, preferably emotional, connections to the brand name, a bond not necessarily associated with any specific product (Aaker 1996). This process includes work on such things as creating a *brand identity*, how to make this identity adaptable to different and changing environments, how to attach a specific expressive aesthetic to it, making it easily recognizable—all this in order to create loyalty, awareness, associativity, and perception of quality among consumers. Subject to successful brand management, leverage is created that extends beyond individual products and can be attached to new products through a process of brand extension (Farris et al. 2010).

This vocabulary of branding builds not on antagonistic power relations but on the metaphor of *reciprocal personal relations* (and quite a cozy relation at that, building on mutuality, equality, and the possibility of choice). The customer is supposed to choose a product of a specific brand at the expense of another, which may be otherwise equal in quality, basing the decision on *trust* for the brand. And the techniques of brand equity management are not a haphazard construct. They are an invention based on insights from the history of branded products throughout Western capitalism.

Historically, branding was tied to the early industrial era and to processes of *standardization*. When food begun to be mass-produced, packaged, and distributed to remote localities, some kind of promise was necessary to ensure consumers that these eatables from distant locations upheld the same or higher quality standard as similar food that was locally produced—and that this quality was a constant feature of the brand. Mass production was what made this promise possible. In the same way that consumers earlier invested trust in local producers such as specific farms, bakeries, and butchers, they were now prompted to invest trust in the supposed uniformity of vacuum-packed foodstuffs from a specific producer. (Of course, trust in a specific butcher also involves personal judgment involving the eye, the nose, and the mouth.) The origin of modern-day brand culture lies in the conditions of the food market around the turn of the twentieth century and developed during the World War years. According to Adam Arvidsson (2006), brand management practices then took a leap during the 1950s and 1960s with the expansion of media technologies. At this time, the motif of standardization for the sake of health security came to be foregrounded by new advertising strategies grounded in academic discussions of psychological theories and the cultural value of goods. A new, more active consumer emerged. This tendency was intensified in the 1970s. With the new information and communication technologies of the 1980s and 1990s, according to Arvidsson, brands became for contemporary informational capitalism what the factory was to the industrial era.

At this point, we are back with the critics of modern-day information capitalism. Arvidsson's main thesis is that the essential feature of brand management has remained the same from its birth and consists in finding ways of putting public communication to work. Maurizio Lazzarato (1997) coined the term "immaterial labour" to designate all the labor put into producing aesthetic, emotional, and social qualities associated with goods, or to produce, reproduce, and modulate the conditions under which this might happen. This labor, many commentators (e.g., Cova and Dalli 2009; Lury 2004; Hardt and Negri 2004) argue, is mainly carried out by those who use the commodities—consumers. Being such an important part of the modern individual's life-world, Celia Lury (2004) argues that brands are the new media objects. They constitute a common resource for otherwise scattered individuals. In the world of new information and communication technologies, they are a common world, making up the communal frame of reference in relation to which you can feel, look, and be whoever you are, wherever you are.

According to protagonists of the paradigm of brand equity, this shared world is a matter of new creative communalities, resulting in a situation where everybody wins—producers, customers, and marketers. To its critics, it consists in unpaid labor carried out without the possibility of consent. Notwithstanding who you listen to, upon entering a contemporary supermarket in order to buy the next week's consumables, the fact remains that brands are, through different kinds of packaging, physically mediating your contact with the things that you are about to put into the mouths of yourself and your loved ones, requiring the kind of confidence that earlier in history fell to our personal sense of smell, taste, and vision.

See also aesthetics, emotion, packaging, trust.

Jakob Wenzer

C

Cooking © Angela Meah.

CELEBRITY CHEFS

Celebrity chefs are reported to "have attained pop star status on a par with Hollywood actors, and their numbers are growing at the same inflationary rate as the programs they host" (Versteegen 2010: 448). Celebrity chefs cannot be easily defined under a single set of criteria. The word "chef" itself is derived from the old French *chef de cuisine* and means "chief," originally referring to the head chef only. Some celebrity chefs such as Gordon Ramsay, Marco Pierre White, or Anthony Bourdain can be considered chefs in this respect. Such chefs are not necessarily filmed in their capacity as kitchen managers but are nonetheless recognized by their professional histories. Other "celebrity chefs," such as Nigella Lawson or Julia Child, have never commanded brigades of professional cooks and made it to the television screens as cooks for other reasons. The umbrella term, "celebrity chef" is, then, rather a misnomer: to be a celebrity chef you don't have to have been a chef. Celebrity chefs can be understood as a diverse collection of individuals who are famous for cooking or talking about and presenting cookery via various kinds of media. Perhaps the most important of these has been television, which is almost always accompanied by supporting cookbooks and, in many cases, websites and other branded goods.

What, though, is "celebrity"? Chris Rojek suggests that celebrity can be crudely defined as impact on public consciousness involving "the attribution of glamorous or notorious status to an individual within the public sphere" (Rojek 2001: 10). The cooking itself and its particular cultural appeals to notions of novelty or normality may form one of the means by which an individual can gain such notoriety or glamour. Celebrity chefs can be (with various gradations) "mold breakers" of cuisine or can be seen to "ride" or reinforce existing culinary trends. Celebrities who are famous for other reasons can also become celebrity chefs, such as Sophie Dahl, whose fame as a former model is recognizable alongside her fame as a cook and food writer.

Celebrity chefs have arguably been in existence for a very long time. One popular author argues that the late Antonin Carême might be considered the first of their kind (Kelly 2005). Indeed, it is now possible, given the term's popular currency, to trace back through history, pinpointing "celebrity chefs" of their day. Although such arguments are tempting, it seems likely that the celebrity chefs of today had their advent somewhat more recently as cooks-cum-cookbook-writers. Roger Dickinson (in press) notes the appearance of Julia Child and later Martha Stewart in the United States as the likely precursors of a string of celebrity chefs producing written and televisual cookery material. In the United Kingdom, Dickinson (2011) cites Margeurite Patten, Philip Harben, and Fanny Cradock as examples of the early, more instructional, format of the genre. Delia Smith is arguably the most influential UK celebrity chef to date in terms of her recognition for teaching culinary skills with a popular reputation for producing reliable recipes "that work." Conversely, Keith Floyd, who was screened in the early 1980s, became notorious for his alcohol consumption on-screen rather than the strength or achievability of his recipes. Whilst much has been made of Floyd's drinking on television, perhaps one should ask whether there is a peculiarly British or indeed Western relationship to alcohol that rendered this noteworthy or shocking in the first place. The fact remains, however, that interest was as much on Floyd as a personality as on Floyd as a chef. Indeed, many celebrity chefs are known as much for their personal behavior and demeanor as for their recipes.

Floyd's programs were also notable for the practice of cutting to shots of the local scenery or agricultural practice in addition to footage of him cooking. A continuing practice of blending instructional cookery with travel- or documentary-style entertainment exists today in numerous forms. For example, celebrity chefs have been visualizing a narrative of "farm to fork," albeit in partial ways, for some time. The idea continues today in a revamped "shock tactic" form as celebrity chefs such as Jamie Oliver, Hugh Fearnley-Whittingstall, and Gordon Ramsay host programs explicitly detailing the life, and more importantly, the uncensored death of animals raised for food.

According to Heinrich Versteegen (2010), Britain is a "special case" in terms of the proliferation of celebrity chefs, food programs, and the implied prominence that they hold for British audiences. Where these chefs base their programs around a UK context, they can be seen to address two key concerns, namely those that surround the association of food with place and the associations of food with social class. Celebrity chefs play a diverse role in the associations they make between food and place. Sometimes one sees a potentially parochial celebration of place and food through the likes of Rick Stein (British Food Heroes, etc.), whereas at other times one sees the potential denigration of people and place as "expert" chefs pass judgment on the culinary practices of those in a given locale.

Rebekah Fox and Graham Smith (2011) have documented how mainstream newspapers debated Oliver's role in producing and reinforcing class- and place-based stereotypes that could be directly traced to the consumption of "junk food" by some people in Rotherham, South Yorkshire. However, it is unlikely that such stereotyping could have occurred without a level of audience recognition of a well-worn stereotypical characterization of the "north" and of the "working classes." As Fox and Smith (2011) point out, much of the debate in the mainstream press pertained to whether or not Oliver was delivering an accurate representation of Rotherham. The potential danger, it seemed, was that Oliver could be seen to hold up Rotherham as an example of what certain politicians were touting as "Broken Britain" (Hollows and Jones 2010). Depictions of monetary poverty were being placed alongside depictions of moral bankruptcy, and nowhere was this more apparent or striking than with the photographs of the "sinner ladies" passing "junk food" through the fence of Rawmarsh comprehensive school in defiance of recently introduced initiatives to improve the quality of school meals.

Celebrity chefs have also opted to use place as a way to celebrate food, enjoyment, and the mixing of cultures. Sometimes these places are "far flung" and "exotic"; at other times, they are "local" and closer to home. David Bell and Joanne Hollows (2007) refer to the way that

Oliver emphasizes his "Italianicity" in a way that allows him to maintain, anecdotally at least, a strong "Essex boy" screen persona. As celebrity chefs are seen to travel on television, Bell and Hollows argue that they can provide the audience with a form of virtual travel. Celebrity chefs, then, can be seen as virtual tour guides, providing people with the opportunity to experience mediated culinary trips. From Elizabeth David's celebration of Mediterranean cooking to Claudia Roden's introduction to Middle Eastern food, celebrity chefs have provided a vision for a kind of cosmopolitan lifestyle based on how to eat and enjoy oneself when abroad, as well as how to incorporate those influences in domestic settings.

These celebrity chefs traverse the bridging point between the vicarious affordances of the travel documentary and the traditional cookery show. However, they also show and tell partial and selective stories about the people, places, and foods in their programs. This partiality can undoubtedly support consumer fantasies (Ketchum 2005) that position particular ways of cooking, eating, and sharing food as better or worse than others. An argument can be made that sees the celebrity chef as a kind of salesperson, operating under a mediated veneer, where ultimately their role is to stimulate consumer spending as much as consumer appetite (see Hansen 2008). When celebrity chefs openly endorse or advertise a company, whether it is their own or that of a supermarket, they can be directly characterized as salespeople (Byrne et al. 2003). Here we see celebrity chefs in a role that much more neatly conforms to the original etymology behind "chef" because they literally preside over the presentation of food. In many cases, celebrity chefs are overseeing the presentation of food imagery to a potential consuming public and are the figureheads for particular culinary aesthetics, both on the plate and on the screen.

Celebrity chefs teach us about more than how to cook and what to eat; it is also possible to conceive of celebrity chefs performing other kinds of "public pedagogy" (Rich 2011). If this is true, then one has to wonder what it is that celebrity chefs are effectively teaching. Celebrity chefs may well have a desire to help us cook (M. K. Goodman et al. 2010b), but they can and do teach us other things too. In

chef actually *is* may be determined by a potentially infinite range of producing and consuming relationships.

See also consumption, media, space and place.

Nick Piper

CHOICE

When thinking about choice in relation to food, it is impossible to ignore availability, and modern supermarkets have excelled in making a wider choice of foods available to many consumers, particularly in the global North. But consumers can only choose a food item or meal when it is available to them, and availability is not just an issue of absence or presence but also requires certain capabilities in order to make something available for selection (including purchasing power). It also requires a desire for the food. The act of choosing food places the "choosers" at the end of a variety of processes that have produced the food item and placed it before them.

From the above assertion, it follows that "choice" is far from straightforward and is not synonymous with decisions made over a shopping trolley in well-stocked supermarket aisles. For Raj Patel, "Our choices are not entirely our own because, even in a supermarket, the menu is crafted not by our *choices*, nor by the full range of apples available, nor by the full spectrum of available nutrition and taste, but by the power of food corporations" (2007: 2). Patel is pointing toward the institutional context of choice, the organization of rules, decisions, and actions that work to guide the food choices we make. These ongoing, almost invisible, decisions over product lines are not the only steers on food choice. The periodic emergence of "food crisis" events, such as outbreaks of BSE, salmonella, or E-coli and crop failures, can quickly reconfigure the choices people make and the choices available to them. Routines of purchase—in effect, the settlement of choice decisions—are unsettled in these circumstances, provoking new questions about safety, risk, and the price of food.

Despite these complexities, choice over food is most often associated with the act of purchasing food. Once food items or meals have been selected for purchase, there are additional choices to be made over the storage, cooking, and eating of food. It is the purchase of food items that has preoccupied much thinking about food choice, in particular food purchasing in supermarkets. However, as suggested above, choice cannot be reduced to the purchase action alone. In a highly cited study, Tanis Furst et al. (1996) carried out intercept interviews in supermarkets, stopping shoppers in order to ask questions about their purchase decisions. The authors were not only interested in the purchase action but also identified three major components of food choice: life course, influences, and personal system. They suggest that life course—encompassing past experiences, present activities, and future plans—is an underlying steer on food choice and should be explicitly considered. By introducing life course, attention is drawn to the importance of social relations, suggesting that an individual person does not act without the influence of history and shared experiences. Such interaction occurs in addition to, and in relation with, the institutional steering of choice alluded to by Patel.

In focusing upon supermarkets as the principal arena of choice, one can take a radically different point of entry to the notion of choice by considering the emergence of the shopping trolley or supermarket cart. Catherine Grandclement (2009) considers that the trolley/cart allowed the creation of fluidity in the development of the supermarket, but that this process was not straightforward and linear. Before the trolley/cart, the selection of food items was limited by the effort required to carry them in the newly created self-service shops. Choice was therefore limited not only by the presence of items in the supermarket but also by the possibilities of the technical apparatus of shopping. The advent of the basket carrier, followed by the telescopic trolley/cart, and ultimately the ever larger nested trolley/cart used today proceeded along with the expansion of product varieties and the ownership of motor vehicles and domestic appliances such as the refrigerator and freezer units.

Questions about the institutions, histories, and technologies of choice suggest that conceiving of choice as a pure expression of individual autonomy is highly suspect, some would say ideological. A sustained treatment of this proposition was presented in 2010 by Lawrence Busch at the World Congress of Sociology in Gothenburg. In his paper, Busch considers how values have been conceptualized as properties pertaining to individuals, a move that suggests that autonomous individuals come together through customs and laws to produce social interactions. One outcome of this process, according to Busch, is that choice has become regarded as a universal good, allowing individuals to express their values in the marketplace. However, it is possible to consider this differently by proposing that individual choices emerge from shared (social) values. Busch suggests that the identification of the autonomous consumer is not wrong, in that it does identify how choice is represented and conducted in contemporary life, but that as an analytical strategy it fails to consider that the autonomy of individuals is the outcome of these very performances. Busch argues:

> It is precisely because (1) values are assumed to be individual in character and merely equivalent to tastes or preferences, (2) that these values are not considered alterable by policy makers, (3) that people's desires are taken to be identical to what is good for them, and (4) that bargaining is rampant but hidden (although with respect to consumers the sellers clearly have the edge), that "the market" performs as it does. (Busch 2010, no pagination)

The centrality of choice has certainly influenced policy decisions pertaining to food and health. As an example, concerns over rising levels of obesity and diet-related diseases, such as hypertension, type 2 diabetes, and cardiovascular disease, are now prevalent in intergovernmental policy (WHO 2003), UK policy (Department of Health 2010; Scottish Government 2008; Welsh Assembly Government 2006), and UK government futures analysis (Foresight 2007). The latter report suggests,

There are opportunities for interventions by the food industry through reformulation of existing products and innovation to provide healthier options. Unless physical activity increases to boost energy demands, dietary habits will need to be reformed to meet the nutritional needs of a largely sedentary population. (Foresight 2007: 49)

The policy approach in the UK focuses on product reformulation, public information campaigns, and proposed changes to portion sizes. Changes to portion size, the creation of healthy options (explicitly advertised as such), and the use of information campaigns are all dependent upon the individual consumer making the "correct" choices. However, encouraging manufactures and retailers to reformulate products to contain less salt, sugar, and fat, without explicitly informing the purchaser, suggests that consumers cannot always be relied upon to make the right choice. Indeed, reformulation is acknowledged by UK policy-makers as being more effective than providing alternative products and conducting advertising campaigns (see also Thaler and Sunstein's [2008] influential argument about the politics of "nudging" consumer behavior toward socially desirable outcomes and the debate about "choice editing").

The dislocation between conceptualizations of appropriate food choices and the context in which action takes place has been discussed by Peter Jackson (2010) in terms of differing forms of rationality. Providing expert advice on which food choices will lead to better health outcomes may follow a different rationality from the behaviors of a family with a low household income. While some affluent consumers may seek the presumed health benefits of new product categories, it is often financially poorer members of society who are identified as pursuing the "wrong" food choices, a situation regarded by Julie Guthman and Melanie DuPuis (2006) as symptomatic of a malfunctioning food system dominated by "debilitated" food.

The rapid increase in the international trade in food products has exposed many people to new forms and categories of food. These new choices are a consequence of expanding international supply systems and are imbued with meanings and values that go beyond the novelty of new taste sensations. As Peter Jackson et al. (2009b) discuss, the accumulation of meaning as some commodities are transformed into food products ensures that choice is mediated by more than price (as in the case of chicken), whereas for other commodities, meanings are "forgotten" or only remembered selectively (as in the case of sugar). The specificity of particular commodity chains requires a differentiated notion of choice as applied to certain products. Further, the development of meanings and values around food can give rise to different allegiances among different groups. For some consumers, brand loyalty strongly influences choice and can be rooted in the life course, habit, or emotional attachment. In a similar way, consumers may seek out so-called alternative food networks to ensure their purchases are locally sourced and to engage in interaction with food producers and other like-minded people. Ethical concerns about labor and animal welfare can also provide a steer on food choices.

Clearly, choice is about more than the purchasing decisions of autonomous individuals. As Busch insists, while the performance of choice may suggest that this is so, paying attention to the activities of choice reveals a much more complex set of interactions. Importantly, where a person lives, their life course, and their social status and income have defining influences on the choices available to them. This is as true of food as other areas of social life, but few things are as critical to human well-being as what a person eats.

See also commodities, consumption.

Richard Lee

CLASS

In his account of eating and taste in France and England since the Middle Ages, Stephen Mennell (1985: 17) argues that, compared to national, religious, or other differences, class has been overwhelmingly the strongest influence in shaping the history of food. Noting the persistence of nutritional variations in food consumption by social class, Mennell documents how, throughout European history, people have used food to climb the social ladder and to push other people down. This essay will explore both aspects of Mennell's argument, examining differences in food consumption between social classes and tracing how food serves as a marker of class in social judgments of taste. Following Pierre Bourdieu (1984), this essay aims to show not only that there are systematic social differences in diet but also that food is routinely used as one of the means of reproducing class-based identities.

As Mennell's work shows, class distinctions have been a feature of European culinary culture from the Middle Ages to the present day and these distinctions have always been freighted with political and moral significance. In medieval and modern Europe, food was often scarce and subsistence crises were frequent. Harvest failures led to steep increases in mortality, with wide variations by locality and class (Mennell 1985: 26–27). As late as 1828, Richard Cobb (1970: 215) notes, the fear of a dearth of food, especially among the lower classes, remained a powerful threat to public order in France.

Even before food supplies became more secure as a result of developments in transport and technology, distinctions of taste were being made along class lines. Writing about the science of "good-living" in 1822, for example, Launcelot Sturgeon distinguished between gluttony ("a mere effort of the appetite") and the development of a "refined and discriminating taste" ("the peculiar attribute of the palate"). While such distinctions were socially constructed, they reflected material differences in consumption patterns by social class. So, for example, Friedrich Engels drew attention to the significance of dietary variations in his study *The Condition of the Working Class in England in 1844*:

> The habitual food of the individual working-man naturally varies according to his wages. The better paid workers,

especially those in whose families every member is able to earn something, have good food as long as this state of things lasts; meat daily and bacon and cheese for supper. Where wages are less, meat is used only two or three times a week, and the proportion of bread and potatoes increases. Descending gradually, we find the animal food reduced to a small piece of bacon cut up with the potatoes; lower still, even this disappears, and there remain only bread, cheese, porridge, and potatoes, until on the lowest rung of the ladder, among the Irish, potatoes form the sole food. (1845/1969: 105)

More subtle class distinctions were at play in some of the classic cookbooks of the nineteenth century, such as Isabella Beeton's *Book of Household Management* (first published in 1861), which provided advice to anxious middle-class consumers regarding the social graces of etiquette and table manners as well as more prosaic information about what and how to cook (with or without the assistance of domestic servants).

Class differences in diet were still starkly apparent when George Orwell visited Wigan and other towns in northern England in the 1930s. Having made detailed observations of working-class consumption, he noted, "The basis of their diet ... is white bread and margarine, corned beef, sugared tea and potatoes" (1937: 88). Asking rhetorically if it would not be better if they spent more money on wholesome food like oranges and brown bread, he concluded that "no ordinary human being is ever going to do such a thing." No doubt reflecting his own prejudices as well as his self-consciously "lower upper-middle class" position, he continued:

The ordinary human being would sooner starve than live on brown bread and raw carrots ... A millionaire may enjoy breakfasting off orange juice and Ryvita biscuits; an unemployed man doesn't ... When you are unemployed, which is to say when you are underfed, harassed, bored and miserable, you don't *want* to eat dull wholesome food. You want something a little bit "tasty" ... Let's have three pennorth of chips! Run out and buy us a twopenny ice-cream! Put the kettle on and we'll all have a nice cup of tea! (1937: 88)

Lamenting the working-class taste for processed vegetables and tinned milk, Orwell noted the willingness of middle-class observers ("parties of Society dames") to give shopping lessons to the wives of the unemployed. Orwell quotes a communist speaker in London, deploring such condescension: "First you condemn a family to live on thirty shillings a week, and then you have the damned impertinence to tell them how they are to spend their money" (1937: 92). Yet Orwell felt able to criticize the lack of a "proper [dietary] tradition" that led people to "pour muck like tinned milk down their throats and not even to know that it is inferior to the product of the cow" (1937: 92).

Social condescension regarding the domestic skills of the poor has a long history. In 1845, for example, Alexis Soyer had no hesitation in criticizing the "General Ignorance of the Poor in Cooking" in his book *A Shilling Cookery for the People* (quoted in Mennell 1985: 227). Similar attitudes persist to the present day, resurfacing in the public debate that followed Jamie Oliver's attempt to "teach a town to cook" in the TV series *Jamie's Ministry of Food*. Reviewing the first episode, Felicity Lawrence concluded that the show confirmed the enduring truth that "our diet today is as much about class as it always has been ... Food, and real people's experience of it, is still all about class" (Lawrence 2008). Quoting research by Tim Lobstein, Lawrence outlined the close links between diet, health, and social class in contemporary Britain:

Mothers from low-income groups are ... more likely to have children of low birthweight, who, in turn, are likely to suffer poor health and educational prospects as a result. Working-class families have more dental disease and more childhood eczema and asthma. They are more likely to suffer from obesity, both as children and as adults. They have higher rates of raised blood pressure, thanks to excess salt in their processed diets. They are more likely to suffer diabetes, heart disease, vascular disease and strokes. They suffer more cancers of the lung, stomach and oesophagus. They have more cataracts caused by poor nutrition than those in other classes. (Lawrence 2008)

But Lawrence went further than Oliver or Orwell in probing the reasons for poor people's questionable dietary choices. When you are on a low income, she argued, you buy the kind of food that fills you up most cheaply. From this perspective, what may seem like ignorant choices to a middle-class observer may in fact be quite rational as filling up on fats, processed starches, and sugars is the cheapest way to get energy from food. According to Lobstein's research, 100 calories of broccoli cost 51 pence, while 100 calories of frozen chips only cost 2 pence. Fresh orange juice cost 38 pence per 100 calories, while the same amount of energy from sugary orange squash cost just 5 pence. The decision to serve children processed or convenience foods rather than fresh fruit and vegetables may also reflect a concern that these "healthier" options will simply go uneaten, exacerbating contemporary concerns about food waste (Stuart 2009). A more complete examination of class-based differences in cooking and eating patterns would also need to pay closer attention to the domestic routines and work rhythms of different households (as outlined in Jackson 2009).

Studies of so-called "food deserts" (residential areas that have low levels of retail provision) also question the adequacy of models of individualized consumer choice as explanations for variations in diet. Separate studies of Leeds and Glasgow have been undertaken (Wrigley et al. 2003; Cummins and MacIntyre 2002) showing how the lack of retail investment in these areas can have significant consequences in terms of residents' access to a range of adequate and affordable food. Research has also questioned whether geographical proximity to a supermarket is an adequate explanation of people's food choices. Based on research in Portsmouth (UK), Jackson et al. (2006a) found that notions of access and convenience involve cultural judgments about value and taste rather than being simple reflections of cost or geographical distance, while Wrigley et al. (2002) questioned the impact of improved retail access on diet, following the arrival of a major supermarket in a former "food desert," suggesting that consumption practices are socially embedded and highly routinized, not amenable to rapid change.

Bourdieu's (1984) work on the way that judgments of taste serve as markers of class distinction remains a sociological classic, as applicable to the study of culinary culture as to other fields of consumption (see also Bennett et al. [2009] for a later application of Bourdieu's ideas in the United Kingdom). Following Bourdieu, we should not be surprised that the relationship between class and diet is often cast in moralistic terms. So, for example, the depiction of a working-class mother feeding her children kebabs on her living room floor (in *Jamie's Ministry of Food*) or the image of working-class mothers passing "junk food" to their children through the railings at Rawmarsh school in Rotherham (dubbed "sinner ladies" in the tabloid press) provoked a strong reaction from the viewing and reading public. In their analysis of the moral panic that these issues provoked, Fox and Smith (2011) describe the public reaction in terms of "class disgust." The fact that middle-class viewers may derive a sense of guilty pleasure from such feelings of schadenfreude is less often noted (though see Piper 2011). Ambivalence about social respectability is also at the heart of Skeggs's (1997) ethnographically informed account of contemporary formations of class and gender which, she argues, involve subtle processes of identification and dis-identification.

Despite a long-term convergence of diverse class-based food consumption patterns in Britain, significant differences in eating habits persist. These differences are revealed in Mark Tomlinson and Alan Warde's (1993) discriminant analysis of Family Expenditure Survey data for the period 1968 through 1988. In 1968, the "unoccupied" class showed a preference for tea, fish, jam, cocoa, and flour; the working class exhibited a preference for beer, bread, potatoes, and cooked meats; while the middle class showed a preference for eating out and for processed fruit, frozen vegetables, wine, coffee, spirits, and fruit. These patterns showed relatively little change by 1988 except that the "unoccupied" class had added sugar and eggs to their preferences and the middle class had developed a taste for manufactured potato products. Their analysis also suggests that a preference for eating meals outside the home and the choice of alcoholic drink (beer, wines, or spirits) remain powerful predictors of social class even when income differences are held constant. While most research has focused on the nutritional aspects of dietary inequality, Tomlinson and Warde's work highlights the importance of the symbolic significance and sociological dimensions of food choice.

The political discourse of class underwent a significant shift in Britain in the Thatcher years (1979–1997) with its emphasis on a service-based "enterprise" economy. Later, in the era of New Labour, a concern for "social exclusion" came to replace the language of class across much of Europe, broadening the definition of poverty and placing greater emphasis on social inequality (Wilkinson and Pickett 2009). Meanwhile, in the United States, a different debate about class ensued after the Second World War, with the emergence of the blue-collar middle classes seeking what Warren Belasco (2007: 192) called the "basic accoutrements" of a middle-class lifestyle such as kitchen appliances, the latest convenience foods, and an occasional dinner at a family restaurant. As the blue-collar middle class was squeezed by deindustrialization from the mid-1970s, the racialized nature of class divisions in American society were starkly revealed, with black and Hispanic minorities clearly overrepresented among what William Julius Wilson (1987) called "the truly disadvantaged." Recent figures on food insecurity reveal the persistence of these class- and race-based divisions, with 14.5 percent of U.S. households reported to be food insecure for at least some time during 2010, including 5.4 percent (or 6.4 million households) with very low food security (Coleman-Jensen et al. 2011). The same report notes that black and Hispanic households had substantially higher rates of food insecurity than the national average.

More obliquely, recent research shows how well-intentioned initiatives such as farmers' markets and community-supported agriculture schemes remain socially exclusive in class terms as well as being racially coded in their tacit appeal to white middle-class consumers. So, for example, Rachel Slocum has documented the "whiteness" of farmers' markets in Minneapolis (Slocum 2007) while Julie Guthman has shown how student-led alternative food practices in Santa Cruz, California, "lack resonance" with low-income African American communities, leading her to conclude that "current [food-related] activism reflects white desires more than those of the communities they putatively serve" (2008: 431).

Finally, we should also note that class-based (and racialized) divisions are all too apparent in relation to food production as well as in highly stratified cultures of consumption. From Bill Friedland et al.'s pioneering work on the role of capital, labor, and technology in the U.S. lettuce industry (Friedland et al. 1981) to current work on the recruitment of East European fruit-pickers by agricultural gang-masters in the United Kingdom (Scott and Brindley 2012), stark divisions of labor are all too apparent in the routine work of food production, processing, and packaging. And while affluent urban consumers indulge their taste for local, quality, and organic food ("yuppie chow" in Guthman's [2003] memorable phrase), they often seem more interested in the environmental conditions in which their food is produced than in the labor conditions being endured by those who pro-duce it. Food production, it seems, is no exception to the all-too-pervasive, barely hidden injuries of class (Sennett and Cobb 1972).

See also choice, consumption, taste.

Peter Jackson

COMMODITIES

Karl Marx once famously remarked that a commodity appears at first sight to be a "very trivial thing" but that further analysis showed it to be of bewildering complexity, "full of metaphysical subtleties and theological niceties" (1867/1976: 163). This is decidedly the case when it comes to food, a range of commodities whose origins in nature are frequently obscured and whose properties are often fetishized through the use of marketing terms like natural, wholesome, fresh, pure, and healthy. While commodities appear to be associated unequivocally with modernity (associated with industrial capitalism, marketized exchange, and mass consumption), their continued fetishization reminds us that the boundaries between modernity and tradition, sacred and secular, are easily blurred. So, too, when Walter Benjamin (1936) wrote about the diminishing "aura" of works of art in the age of mechanical reproduction, he could as easily have been speaking about food and other commodities in the industrial age.

Commodities are usually defined as goods that are produced for monetary exchange. In Marx's terms, they have exchange-value as well as use-value. Conventionally, too, commodities are distinguished from gifts, the former being part of the market economy, the latter subject to nonmonetary forms of exchange (Carrier 1990). But the distinction blurs as soon as one recognizes that gifts impose obligations (as argued by Mauss 1925/1970) and that things move in and out of the commodity form, rather than permanently being unambiguously in one state or the other (cf. Kopytoff 1986). While one may be able to speak about a long-term process of *commoditization*, where over time more things enter the commodity form (including formerly uncommodified goods and services such as health care, the arts, and education), *commodification* is a more uneven process as things follow their "social lives" (Appadurai 1986a), entering and leaving the commodity form. So, for example, money might be exchanged for a range of ingredients that are then baked into a cake that is given to a friend or loved one. Alternatively, it might be sold for profit or taken to a cake sale and sold for charity. Thus emerges Arjun Appadurai's celebrated invocation to "follow the thing," for the meaning of things is inscribed in their forms, their uses, and their trajectories: "It is

things-in-motion that illuminate their human and social context" (1986a: 5).

These ideas have been taken forward in studies of commodity chains, circuits, and networks. Such studies have sought to trace the passage of commodities along the supply chain, from farm to fork or plough to plate in the case of food, attempting to identify the points at which value is added and profit extracted. There are many studies in this vein, from Bill Friedland et al.'s pioneering work on the U.S. lettuce industry (*Manufacturing Green Gold*, 1981) to Sidney Mintz's anthropological history of the global trade in sugar (*Sweetness and Power*, 1985). There are many studies of single commodities, from French beans (Freidberg 2004) and tomatoes (Barndt 2002) to exotic fruits such as papaya (Cook 2004) as well as (somewhat fewer) comparative studies that seek to trace the commodity-specific cultures of consumption associated with different products (see www.followthethings.com for constantly updated ideas, debates, and examples). Some analyses have a "vertical" orientation, drilling down to expose the hidden labor that goes into the manufacture of particular products, following Marx's metaphor of "unveiling" the commodity fetish. One such study is David Harvey's (1990) analysis of the South African grapes which lie mutely on the supermarket shelves, unable to speak of the exploitative conditions in which they were produced. Other studies seek to trace the "horizontal" connections between things as they travel across space, their meanings being displaced as objects become entangled in different contexts of use (cf. Cook and Crang [1996], drawing on Thomas's [1991] work on entangled objects).

The metaphor of commodity chains has been criticized by those who question their linearity, arguing instead for commodity circuits or networks, with a different spatial logic and temporal dynamic (cf. Reimer and Leslie 2004). While commodity chains have been criticized as a "chaotic conception" by academic observers (Jackson et al. 2006b), the metaphor remains sufficiently compelling and politically salient that the term has proliferated among campaigners and policy-makers, urging producers to improve workers' labor conditions and to reduce or eliminate waste along the commodity chain.

Nor is the process of commodification limited to physical objects, as other things ("the sizzle *and* the steak") are subject to marketization. For example, coffee shops trade on their appeal as sociable environments as much as on the quality of their cappuccino, with Starbucks alleged to have succeeded by selling "everything but the coffee" (Simon 2009). Indeed, Sharon Zukin (1995) speaks of entire neighborhoods in New York City being "gentrified by cappuccino" while Jonathan Morris (2007) writes about the "cappuccino conquests," describing the way that Italian-style espresso-based coffee drinks have taken over the market in specialty or gourmet coffee in the United Kingdom. Indeed, some entrepreneurs have taken the concept of brand extension to extremes, selling a lifestyle rather than a specific product, to the point where the company logo may be more valuable than the goods to which it is attached (the Nike swoosh may be a case in point or McDonald's golden arches).

The commodification of various kinds of cultural difference has been a notably feature of Western capitalism in recent years, with the promotion of "ethnic" food through notions of authenticity and exoticism, for example (as described by Heldke [2003] and others). Jonathan Rutherford (1990: 11) has noted how "capital has fallen in love with difference" (cf. McGuigan [2009] on the evolution of "cool capitalism"). In such cases, the commodification of difference usually involves a process of abstraction and appropriation whereby goods are branded, stereotyped, spectacularized, and aestheticized. Critics of the commodity form such as Naomi Klein (2000) have focused on the "web of brands" that pervades the modern world, though, ironically, the No Logo movement that was spawned by her book has now become a kind of brand itself with its own website (www.naomiklein.org) and logo. The apparent ineluctability of the commodity form has led some authors such as Michael Taussig to suggest that, rather than resisting or admonishing the fetish quality of modern commodity culture, we should work on the surfaces of commodities, "getting with the fetish"—submitting to its powers and channeling them

in revolutionary directions (1992: 122; see also Taussig 1980). There can surely be no better illustration of Marx's argument that the commodity is an elusive and subtle thing whose analysis demands urgent attention.

See also brands, markets.

Peter Jackson

CONSUMPTION

In mainstream economics, consumption conventionally refers to the final use of goods and services by a consumer until the point of disposal. Consumption is simply where things end up after all the interesting activities that take place in factories and markets. As has been shown by Richard Wilk (2004), generally a hydraulic relationship is implicated. The economy is often visualized as a system of plumbing, but the wells, pumps, and piping are considered the interesting part and consumption is just water going down the drain. There are interesting hydraulic theories that give consumption a more prominent role in this process, like Avner Offer's (2006) argument about the commitment devices consumers gradually develop to handle the constant flow of consumer goods. But basically, regarding consumption as the inevitable and dependent end product of production leads mainstream economists to think that consumption needs no analysis. Whatever is pumped forth naturally just drains away.

In media and public debate, however, consumption is not so neutral—a simple effect of what is happening in the production sphere. Consumption is a highly moralized topic; it is good or bad, right or wrong. Today, consumption is generally considered as bad. It is about overspending, overeating, destruction of natural resources, mountains of sugar, our bodies clogging up inside, brimming over their borders. Not long ago, by contrast, consumption was seen as a good way of obtaining pleasure, individuality and identity, even a key way of becoming human. There are a number of robust histories of the rise of consumer culture, such as the broad global and historical overviews by Frank Trentmann (2006) and John Brewer and Frank Trentmann (2006), and for the United States, seminal books by (among others) Lizabeth Cohen (2003), Daniel Horowitz (2004), and Jackson Lears (2009). Trentmann, in particular, insists that "consumers" did not emerge on their own but in "dynamic relations with other social actors and agencies" (2006: 14), building on Raymond Williams's (1976) argument that "consumer" indicates a more abstract figure in a more abstract market, compared to "customer," which always implied some degree of regular and continuing relationship to a supplier. In this essay, however, the point of departure will be the shifting and moralized understandings of consumption and a model bridging the production-consumption divide will be suggested.

As first pointed out by Mary Douglas in her seminal work *Purity and Danger* (1966), almost every aspect of consumption is laden with moral value and meaning, so that attitudes and values toward consumption are shaped by moral and often religious values that have very little to do with the act of consumption itself. This makes the moral discourses about consumption that we are hardly aware of, but that steer our way of thinking, an appropriate starting point in an excavation of the concept of consumption. This will be done by following in the footsteps of Richard Wilk (2004). With the help and guidance of George Lakoff, Wilk argues that basic-level concepts are often grounded in direct bodily experiences like pain and hunger that all humans share. In addition, hundreds of "primary metaphors" that we use both in reasoning and as the basis for action are grounded in common everyday experiences, sometimes so common that they give rise to metaphors that arise spontaneously in many cultures around the world. Furthermore, within a single culture there can be conflicting and contending metaphorical systems, which also inform and structure quite distinct models of moral behavior, gender roles, attitudes, and so on. So these metaphors have real power; they help people visualize complex situations and find actions that seem consonant with their more fundamental beliefs.

Returning once again to the basic economic model, dividing the economy into a productive sector, a market, and a household or domestic sector with flows between them, Wilk argues that the basic metaphor is the life cycle: birth-life-death, or, in terms of consumption, production-use-discard. Raw materials exist in nature, are taken up by humans, and are modified into artifacts, which are used until worn out, and then discarded. The life-cycle metaphor, Wilk suggests, tells us that consumption is like senility, loss of energy, decline in value, and ultimately death and disappearance. It leaves all the activity, value, and economic growth on the production side, while consumption is a passive process of decay and even waste. Just as in life, any growth must be followed and eventually balanced by decline: production has to be balanced with consumption or the entire system is unstable. The "magic of the market" in neoclassical economics creates just this balance, at least in the imagination.

If the life-cycle metaphor is lurking behind conventional economic models, there are two other metaphors that play a prominent role in the blaming of consumption as the root to all evil, according to Wilk: Consumption-as-Fire and Consumption-as-Eating. Burning is historically the first English usage of the verb consume, attributed to the Wyclif Bible in 1382, in a biblical passage where a sacrifice "with fier shal be consumyd" (Leviticus 6:32). Fire is still a powerful metaphor for consumption that destroys completely, leaving behind nothing useful. We all recognize sayings like "people have money to burn," "fortunes go up in a puff of smoke," or that today's hectic lifestyles cause total "burnout." Fire, of course, has a dual nature—both destructive and useful. Likewise, consumption can run out of control and become wanton gluttony or excessive luxury leading to corruption and ruin, while at the same time it is the "daily fuel" that keeps the "human engine" going, the center of social life and domestic commensality. As Barbara Czarniawska and Orvar Löfgren (2012) show in their studies of the generation and managing of overflow, it is not the equilibrium that is the problem, it is when things brim over, like the waistlines of millions of people today, that consumption turns toxic and threatening.

Fire has a will of its own, and we are often helpless before it. The eating metaphor, on the contrary, puts the human at the center, with the impersonal forces of the economy and nature providing the fuel and carting away the waste. Eating is a complex prototype, rooted in human bodily experience. The prototypical scenario is hunger: finding and preparing; chewing and swallowing; digesting and excreting. Because of the power of the Consuming-as-Eating metaphor, the physical sensations of eating are associated with those experienced in other kinds of consumption, particularly those associated with shopping. If you cannot get enough food, you are constantly hungry and you feel a nagging need, which can only be satisfied by consuming (see Belk et al. 1997). Similarly, the bodily experience of being satiated, full of food, relaxed, and lazy is extended to other acts of consumption, so that enough shopping should satisfy needs for a while, make people comfortable and satisfied, and no longer in need of more consumption, just as John Kenneth Galbraith in *The Affluent Society* (1958) said that once each American family got a small house, a car, and basic appliances, their needs would be fully satisfied. But, as Wilk comments, Galbraith did not recognize that even after the most sumptuous meal, people still get hungry (Wilk 2004: 18).

While the fire metaphor puts the blame on consumption as a force that simply takes hold of our bodies and souls, like an infectious disease spreading across the world, the plague of our time, the Consumption-as-Eating metaphor puts the blame on consumers who do not have enough character to withstand the pull of consumption and its swirls of desire, pleasure, and lust. Overspenders and overeaters become bad specimens, derelicts. It is up to humans to act as regulating valves in the flow of goods from production and markets. This is, in fact, Offer's suggestion (2006). We need to learn techniques to manage our deficient self-control, like norms, knowledge, pride, and shame or get help from society. Likewise, American historian Gary Cross (2002) maintains that consumption for the sake of their children serves as valves for parents' desire to consume, regulating the ambivalence between the idea of children as creatures to be protected from commercialism, and, at the same time, as recipients of consumer spending. Shopping for children means preserving the innocence of childhood and yet also the possibility of spending for the sake of evoking delight in children.

Wilk even suggests from his American experience that the Consuming-as-Eating metaphor comes to regard wealth as fat. Americans, he argues, "extend the same ambivalence they have towards food and gluttony to money, wealth and the rich. Rather than being evil, the rich are more likely to be seen as victims of the temptations offered by goods and glitz, as if they were at a giant Las Vegas smorgasbord" (Wilk 2004: 20). As long as consuming is eating, it is hard to imagine any mass movement toward metaphorical anorexia and a more sustainable consumption. Maybe Wilk's observations are specifically rooted in American culture and harder to recognize from a European or Nordic perspective where Lutheran modesty and temperance have been the model, or a restrictive everyday divided by outbreaks of excessive drinking and eating on festive occasions. It is, however, not hard to see why many critics of the global economy draw on the fire and eating metaphors in their arguments about consumption. They tell us that the inevitable result of consumption is ashes and waste, of little and no value, stinking and filthy. To say that resources are being eaten up, that consumerism is a raging fire or a greedy beast, gives visual and visceral force to messages about the state of the planet and its resources. Neither is it hard to see why some food researchers want to rescue food studies from the raging force of consumerism and instead place it in culture, gastronomy, and the culinary arts.

This metaphorical exercise gives us a useful tool to understand the debate about consumption in the wake of the new environmental awareness at the beginning of the twenty-first century due to the climate crisis, resonating with the environmental debate of the 1960s and 1970s. But just stepping a few decades back, to the 1980s, consumption then seemed somehow to transform from basically bad to intrinsically good. Consumption was associated with pleasure, happiness, freedom, and so on, at least in the eyes of many social scientists and cultural critics inspired by postmodernism, and food and eating were indeed a part of this. Advocates of postmodernism insisted that production was driven by consumer demand and gave production a subordinate position. The customer "was king." This in turn depended on the supposed ability of consumers to experience a continual desire for goods and services. In this respect, it was their affective states, most especially their ability "to want," "to desire," and "to long for" and their ability to experience such emotions repeatedly, that were thought to underpin the economies of modern societies. An extraordinary value was attached to individualism in conjunction with the emphasis placed on the right of individuals to decide for themselves which goods and services to consume.

Consumption moved from the field of economics and commerce to the field of culture. Consumer culture studied meanings and relations to artifacts and most of all their relation to identity-building. In this terrain of meanings, discourses, and representations, consumption as activities in the marketplace transformed into consumerism as an overarching ideology or ambience that colored modern life. Speaking specifically about trends in food practices, leading researchers, such as Colin Campbell (1989), Mike Featherstone (1991), and Alan Warde (1997), implied that individuals—by making use of the wide-ranging and ever-changing products on offer in a modern consumer society—were regularly engaged in the process of recreating themselves. This was made possible because, as Stuart Ewan and Elisabeth Ewan put it: "Today there are no ... rules, only choices" (1982: 249–51). At the same time, it was commonly suggested that individuals had little choice but to behave in this manner since what Jean-Francois Lyotard (1979) had called "grand narratives" were no longer credible, with the direct consequence that there was no longer any firm cultural anchorage for the individual's sense of identity. For Jean Baudrillard (1983), it was not the products themselves, but their sign-values, expressed in, for example, advertising, branding, and the media, that mattered, resulting in a state of hyperreality. Everything was a copy or a simulacrum

(a copy of a copy) and what was fake seemed more real than the real.

Colin Campbell (1989) among others remarked that individuals appeared to be defining themselves almost exclusively in terms of their tastes in music, literature, the arts, food, and drink, together with leisure-time pursuits. He suggested that this was because these tastes were what defined individuals more clearly than anything else, and that their "real identity" was to be found in their special mix of tastes. For Pierre Bourdieu, Featherstone, and Warde, taste and consumer desire were social phenomena and the result of struggles in different class groups. Bourdieu (1977), for example, regarded taste a key mechanism in social reproduction. Through the habitus, the individual exhibited taken-for-granted preferences about the appropriateness and validity of his or her taste in art, food, holidays, hobbies, and so on. Lifestyle was highlighted as a related concept and was pinpointed by Dick Hebdige (1979) among others as characteristic of modern consumption: through lifestyle, consumers were seen to achieve a more stylized awareness. Hebdige argued that as a member of a particular lifestyle grouping, individuals actively used clothes, the home, food and drink, music, film, and so on in ways that indicated their taste or sense of style. This activity was seen as a central life project; it was what life was all about. Bourdieu found these groupings in "the new middle classes," and in particular in service and white-collar professions concerned with the production of symbolic goods and services in tourism, journalism, publishing, cinema, fashion, and advertising. While the old bourgeoisie based its life on a morality of duty, the new middle-class groups urged a morality of pleasure as a duty. This new "fun morality" was observed and described in the United States by Martha Wolfenstein (1951) and is similar to what Featherstone four decades later referred to as a calculating hedonism, a hedonism in which the individual strategically moved in and out of control, enjoying the thrill of the controlled suspension of constraints.

This new use of consumer goods such as food and drink and the increased stylization and aestheticization of the self gave members of the middle classes new roles as "cultural intermediaries" (e.g., Featherstone 1991; Lash and Urry 1987)—a concept that has also been the focus of a range of studies loosely grouped under the banner of "cultural economy" (e.g., DuGay and Pryke 2002). The postmodern world also gave experts a new role. The old-time role of the experts who told consumers what they needed and who gained their authority primarily from an institutional role had been rejected, while their place had been taken by "gurus": people who help you discover what it is you really "want" or "desire" (cf. Giddens 1991; Featherstone 1991). This could be witnessed today in the burgeoning output of cooking shows, celebrity chefs, food magazines, and home styling and makeover experts. The link between food and consumption was basically choice: the right to choose what foods to buy for pleasure, for distinction, or for exploring and expressing your "inner self."

The idealist ideology at the heart of postmodernism reached its most extreme form in Campbell's (2004) claim that consumers do indeed create their own reality. Wants are emergent constructs, he argued, the products of a psychological trick on the part of consumers, producing desire where none previously existed. Consumers are themselves responsible for creating the necessary conditions for their consumption experiences. Personal experience and experience alone—largely in the form of wants and desires—constitutes the highest authority. Reality consists of mind and spirit rather than matter. Consumption—basically our wishes and desires—is all there is; we live in a "consumer civilization" (Campbell 2004: 42). This position could not be any further from the all-powerful hand of the market.

This "magical" philosophy brings us close to a world driven by consumption metaphors. Although there is no denying that ideologies, discourses and representations, wants and dreams are integral parts of consumption and the way we see ourselves as consumers, this antimaterialist stance only brings us part of the way in an excavation of consumption that is certainly not made of dreams alone. It is no wonder that researchers embarked on a search for what had been missing in consumer research, most notably materiality and the more mundane or trivial forms of consumption such as cooking and provisioning that are more routine than reflective exercises. Material culture studies and theories of practice both challenge the conventional social science emphasis on discourse and representation. A material culture perspective brought materiality back into consumption studies rather than emphasizing imaginary dreams and desires, while theories of practices focused on flows of events, performances, and "doings."

The basic tenet of material culture studies is that people relate to each other socially through the mediation of things. Material culture is defined as the study of these person-thing relationships, the study of things or objects in use (Lury 1996). Human-object relationships have been an issue in anthropology ever since Bronisław Malinowski's (1922) interest in the Trobriand Islanders' exchange of shells in the Kula ring and the building of seagoing canoes to transport them. In the late 1980s, this interest was reinvigorated by Daniel Miller in his thesis that consumption is the dominant context through which people relate to the world of goods (Miller 1987). Material objects, in Miller's view, are cultural forms not just in the sense that they mirror or reflect the social relations within which they are embedded. Material culture has a constitutive character, objectifying social relations (Miller 1998a).

In theories of practice, the emphasis is on the myriad daily rituals that reproduce our everyday lives: taking a shower, washing clothes, cooking, and so on (Shove 2003; Shove et al. 2007). Practices require performance for their existence and this performance involves a diverse range of technological procedures, objects, competencies, and practical know-how. Applied to the field of consumption, Alan Warde understands consumption as a nexus of practical activity and its representations ("doings and sayings"), which become coordinated by understandings, procedures, and engagements (Warde 2005: 134). Eating practices such as grabbing a sandwich for lunch "on the go" are organized by understandings of eating (e.g., the metaphor food-as-fuel for the body), by procedures for eating (using a takeaway, not sitting down), and by engagements in eating (to get it over and done with). In both material culture and practice-based approaches, the link between food and consumption was broadened to include routine material interactions with foodstuff.

No doubt, theories of material culture and practices are necessary companions in an endeavor to grasp what food consumption is all about. But understanding consumption in terms of consumer culture or sets of integrative practices does not seem enough. We need to find ways to incorporate production and retailing, including the work of technicians, economists, and marketers, in our analysis—a manoeuver that has proved to be hard for many cultural researchers, who are convinced that "the market" is as cold as everyday culture is warm.

In an attempt to overcome the strong polarization between production and consumption, the authors of *Commercial Cultures* (Jackson et al. 2000) moved to an understanding of commerce and culture as complex but integrated forms where culture often turned out to be the product of commerce and vice versa. In his book *A Theory of Shopping*, Miller (1998b) offers a great example of this hybridization brought about by a complete reversal of the traditional binary understanding of consumption. The cultural component, the gift, appeared in its most calculating aspect, while the market behavior of provisioning served as the main proof of love and generosity among the London housewives studied. Another example is presented by Jackson et al. (2009b) in a study of the moral economy of two contrasting commodities: chicken and sugar. Following these commodity chains, the authors show how the manufacture of meaning along the chain had direct commercial consequences. Rational decisions were highly susceptible to ethical and moral concerns. Just as consumption is always an economic as well as a cultural process, the authors show how production is always a cultural as well as technological and economic process. Production is imbued with ethical and moral issues negotiated by a range of actors at different points along the supply chain.

In a similar manner, the CONANX researchers explore the procedural geographies of social anxiety among the full range of actors: producers, retailers, consumers, legal authorities,

and the media, uncovering practices for managing or "attuning" anxiety among all of these actors (Jackson and Everts 2010; Milne et al. 2011). This is a big step from the postmodern understanding of anxiety in terms of the kind of ontological insecurity or existential angst that could only be cured by consumption. For postmodern consumers, overspending was a response to a psychological urge to cure feelings of meaninglessness and insecurity in the late modern age. For us, it is more interesting to look at how social anxieties work: where they occur, how they develop, who they involve, and how they are dealt with.

A similar example, referring once again to Lakoff, is Eivind Jacobsen's (2004) study of the different tropes by which we understand the meaning of food. Food-as-culture places food in the framework of the everyday to be understood through the categorizations, identities, and relationships of everyday life. Food-as-nature approaches food through the framework of farming and is associated with plants, animals, and agriculture. Food-as-commodity sees food in terms of (lowest) price, sourcing, efficient logistics, standardization, and mechanization of production carefully supervised from sanitary and food safety points of view, where raw materials are mixed and processed and given new identities as branded products. In such an analysis, the same piece of meat may appear as biodynamic at the farmers' market (food-as-nature), as a fillet of beef Provençale at the gourmet restaurant (food-as-culture), or as a Big Mac at the fast-food restaurant (food-as-commodity). Hence, food is and will always be genuinely hybrid, a socio-natural mix (cf. Jacobsen 2004).

Bruno Latour (1988) and other actor-network theorists (ANT), such as Michel Callon (1986a, 1986b) and Madeleine Akrich (1992), suggest that the agency of nonhumans is often as powerful as that of human actants. Nonhuman actants appearing in ANT studies range from microbes and scallops to transit systems and aircraft. Carefully applied actor-network studies give actants like fragrances, taste buds, intestinal glands, microbes, and refrigerators their rightful place in the history of food consumption. Moreover, the humans and nonhumans of ANT are intertwined in sets of relations that amount to networks in which it is difficult to identify precisely where the agency for action lies. Developing these ideas, the authors of *Little Monsters* (Brembeck et al. 2007) found ANT an attractive companion in their attempt to understand consumption since this heterogeneous body of work really proves to be open to all kinds of combinations. Entities that in conventional approaches are taken for granted, such as consumers, goods, and companies are here brought under the spotlight. Consumers are no more to be understood as naked choosing subjects; instead, they are made up of complex assemblages, together with other people, goods, and companies. Agency is a question of capabilities that arise within these new combinations, out of a network, not stably residing inside a given actor. With Bruno Latour, it appeared less necessary to rehearse the divide between disembodied markets and humans as consumers; it became more interesting to look at humans and nonhumans interacting, making up new entities with fleeting permanency, networking in a continuous flow. In the book, consumption is explored as a number of connected networks involving goods and transactions of value. Networks with different bases, linking actants across traditional divides like the state, the market, and everyday life; networks or assemblages that were more or less firmly or loosely coupled and that were organized with different objectives in mind: they could be about making everyday life bearable, getting dinner on the table every day for the family; for companies, they could be about making people buy your products; for activists, they could be about enrolling others to sustainable ways of producing and consuming. These networks or assemblages could be about me and my stuff or be global and involve millions of potential actants.

This rhizomatic model of consumption may be the best way to understand the new forms of collaborative consumption that are spreading across the world. Collaborative consumption is basically about sharing, bartering, lending, trading, renting, gifting, and swapping, redefined through technology and peer communities (Botsman and Rogers 2010). New ways of interacting between humans and things, new meanings and identities, new economic models, new

modes of political activism are emerging out of these new aggregations of people and things, discourses, and materialities. In organizations such as Landshare (which connects those who have land to share with those who need land for cultivating food), food co-ops, and resource-sharing networks like the American Replate, the British Patch Match, or the global network Windowfarms, value is created out of shared and open resources, and the relationship between physical ownership and self-identity is undergoing a profound change. Consumption and production get blurred and are not meaningful to separate. It is no longer possible to decide exactly where agency lies. Activities are emanating out of intermingled networks in motion.

This essay argues that metaphors, desires, representations, and dreams are part of what constitutes consumption, and so are materialities, technologies, and practices. We must, however, do away with the production-consumption divide once and for all. Consumption is best studied as the many related activities of networks of human and nonhuman actants. Just like production and retailing, consumption is what emerges out of these activities, as consumers, producers, retailers, and food itself go through a process of "becoming" in these encounters. Food and consumption are forever connected. There is really nothing "natural" about putting a piece of bread in your mouth or drinking a glass of wine. Such acts are just the peak performance emanating from the coproduction and co-consumption of a myriad of actors connected by networks spread across time and space. It is simply our choice of framing that decides what activities and which actors are to be included, and where the temporal and spatial boundaries are to be drawn.

See also choice, eating, moral economy, pleasure, practices, shopping, taste.

Helene Brembeck

CONVENIENCE

Convenience is often invoked within the business and marketing literature as an explanatory term in accounting for consumer behavior whether in relation to the popularity of convenience foods (like baked beans), the attraction of convenience stores (compared to larger-scale supermarkets), or the preparation of ready-to-eat convenience meals. When examined more closely, however, and especially when viewed from a historical perspective, it can readily be argued that the word has very limited explanatory value in contemporary food studies.

While it might be argued that an apple is a perfect example of a "convenience" food—small and portable, nutritious, cheap, and ready to eat—the term is usually applied to processed foods that have been manufactured for mass consumption. Indeed, Warren Belasco describes convenience as the food industry's primary product emphasizing how the concept implies a degree of privilege, choice, and discretion that is not available to many of the world's poor (2008: 55–57). As a marketing category, convenience foods are usually defined as commercially prepared food, designed for ease of consumption, and typically include (frozen or chilled) ready-meals; confectionery, snacks, and beverages (ready to eat or drink "on the go"); processed meat and cheese; and canned goods (such as soup or baked beans). The category also often includes takeaway foods such as pizza and other so-called "fast food," with an implicit (often moralized) comparison with other kinds of food, lovingly cooked from scratch using fresh, raw ingredients.

A report by the Future Foundation, commissioned by Domino's Pizza, predicted a 70 percent growth in the takeaway and convenience food sector in the United Kingdom over the fifteen-year period to 2015 (Future Foundation 2006). Associated with increased female participation in the labor force and with a decreasing amount of time spent in the kitchen, convenience food is often criticized for contributing to the alleged decline of the "family meal" and associated with deficit models of cooking and parenting skills (see Murcott 1997; Jackson 2009). Because of associations with excess packaging and food waste, and with nutritional concerns over the amount of saturated fats, salt, and sugar in many convenience foods, such foods are often described pejoratively as "junk"

food. To gain some critical purchase on these highly emotive issues, it is useful to adopt a more historical perspective.

Using the previous definition of commercially prepared food, designed for ease of consumption, the earliest mass-produced convenience foods included condensed milk, commercially available from the 1850s, as well as a range of canned goods, such as Heinz baked beans, first sold in the United Kingdom in the 1880s. While food has been preserved for domestic consumption for centuries, including salted meat and pickled vegetables, experiments in bottling and canning food on a larger scale date from the 1820s and were largely driven by the need to feed military forces on the move. Nicolas Appert's experiments with preserving cooked food in glass jars were inspired by the Napoleonic Wars, and the production of canned pork and beans was prompted by the needs of the U.S. army during the American Civil War in the 1860s. During the First World War, the British army largely subsisted on tinned foods such as corned beef and Maconochie's Irish stew. Companies like H. J. Heinz and Nestlé then seized the opportunity to sell tinned goods to the public, utilizing technological breakthroughs such as the invention of the double-seamed can in 1888, which increased the shelf life of food by providing an airtight seal (see Shephard [2000] for a history of food preservation).

The early development of mass-produced convenience foods was aimed largely at the urban poor. By the 1950s, however, the ideology of "convenience" had spread to middle-class consumers for whom it was associated with the aura of liberation, freedom, and choice: "Faced with the trade-off between craft satisfactions and push-button, pre-wrapped wizardry," Belasco argues, "consumers generally chose the latter" (2007: 53). How such developments impacted the lives of women has been fiercely debated. On the one hand, new domestic technologies promised to liberate women from the drudgery of household chores, while, on the other hand, the rejection of convenience might be seen as a reassertion of female competence and control. Many such "conveniences," however, redefined the standards of cleanliness and order required in bourgeois households, making *More Work for Mother* (Cowan 1983) and leading to a sense that housework was simply *Never Done* (Strasser 1982). Elizabeth Shove's (2003) work on the social organization of normality provides further evidence of the way that new domestic technologies (like washing machines or dishwashers) may reduce the labor required for routine tasks without necessarily saving time. Other devices (such as freezers and microwave ovens) may reorder the time spent on domestic work rather than reducing the overall amount of time spent on such tasks (Shove and Southerton 2000; see also Warde [1999] on the spacing and timing of convenience food).

One consequence of these dilemmas has been the emphasis in food marketing on making convenience as guilt-free as possible: overcoming the conflict between craft and convenience. So, for example, Laura Shapiro (1986) has documented how women's magazines pitched convenience to female consumers as a way of addressing their marital anxieties, reducing the drudgery of domestic labor, and providing more time to be sexually appealing to their husbands. Belasco goes further, suggesting that the invention of the TV dinner in the 1950s promised to release women from the kitchen "so they could snuggle up to their husbands on the couch as they watched even more perfectly feminine TV wives avoid the kitchen altogether" (2007: 157). The 1950s is also the period identified in Harvey Levenstein's (1993) social history of eating in modern America as the "golden age of food processing" in which food marketing sought to replace home cooking using raw ingredients, cooked from scratch, with more convenient (processed) food (cf. Inness 2001; Parkin 2006). Closer to the present-day, there is evidence from the United Kingdom of how some mothers attempt to manage their children's food choices in order to conform to the conventions of serving "proper food" while embracing the convenience of the ready-made, using an internal hierarchy whereby only some convenience foods are considered to be "junk" (Carrigan et al. 2006).

From this comparative and historical perspective, convenience emerges as an ideology—a set of ideas that serve particular material interests—rather than as an explanatory term with significant analytical value. Yet the term is widely employed in studies of retailing and business where it is used to describe and sometimes to explain consumer behavior. In this literature, convenience is used as an explanatory variable whereby people choose particular goods or shop at particular stores because it is "convenient." By contrast, empirical research with consumers in Portsmouth (UK) has demonstrated the wide range of meanings that are associated with the term (Jackson et al. 2006a). The survey phase of this research project revealed that, in working-class neighborhoods, distance, accessibility, and price were the factors most frequently given by consumers to explain their choice of store, while in richer areas, quality and service were regarded as the most important factors. However, convenience was mentioned as one of the top three reasons for store choice across all neighborhoods (Clarke et al. 2006). Evidence from focus groups and ethnographic work at the household level allowed the researchers to probe the meaning of "convenience" in more depth and detail, avoiding the homogenization of different factors like "convenient parking" or "convenient hours." At one level, convenience simply refers to physical accessibility, measured in terms of distance or travel time from people's homes. But convenience can also relate to the ease with which shopping at a particular store can be combined with other commitments (such as dropping off or collecting children from school). For other respondents, "convenience" was related to the frequency of shopping trips, the availability of monetary or other resources, the range of services provided, as well as more subjective notions of quality and freshness or the crowdedness of a specific retail environment. Smaller stores were also described as more "convenient" than supermarkets in terms of meeting consumers' immediate needs for midweek "top-up" shopping. In all these cases, words like convenience and accessibility, value and quality have complex meanings that vary according to different personal and household circumstances. Understanding their meaning requires us to relate consumers' at-store behavior to the domestic context in which their consumption choices are embedded. Indeed, consumer "choice" is rarely an individualized decision and words like "convenience" remind us of the need to understand the domestic routines and household rhythms within which consumer practice is conducted.

In other times and places, street hawkers and mobile vendors have supplied the need for "convenience" food, consumed on the move or during short breaks in the working day. Such unregulated modes of food provisioning have often been seen as a threat to modern city planning, expressed through concerns about hygiene and cleanliness, public health, and food safety (McGee 1973). Banned in colonial Singapore, for example, street vendors were moved indoors to mall-like hawker centers, similar to the experience of Bogotá's illegal street traders, who sacrificed income for improved working conditions following their relocation to government-built markets (Donovan 2008). Nor are these issues confined to "Third World" cities in the global South, as mayor Rudolph Giuliani's much-publicized campaign against unlicensed food vendors in New York City vividly reveals (*New York Times* 1994). In each case, it seems, what' constitutes "convenience" is contingent, contested, and context-dependent.

See also choice, practices, technologies, time.

Peter Jackson

COOKING

The activity of cooking has come to occupy an increasingly ambiguous place in our use of language. Adrienne Lehrer (1969), for example, draws attention to three levels of generality of the word "cook." The first implies the act of "preparing a meal," which belongs in the field of household tasks (itself a list that is hierarchical: cleaning the toilet, ironing, gardening). The second differentiates "cooking" from "baking." Although Lehrer emphasizes the semantic distinction that "baking" refers to products that can be found in bakeries, female participants contributing to Angela Meah and Matt Watson's (2011) study of domestic food practices differentiate between everyday cooking as a practical responsibility that must be fulfilled,

while "baking is fun." However, the third meaning is perhaps the most commonly used understanding: "The application of heat which produces irreversible change in the object (food) cooked" (Lehrer 1969: 40–41). The word "cooking" is clearly loaded and gives rise to a series of questions regarding who does it; for whom; on what occasions; and how do they feel about it? And, against a backdrop of discourses alleging the "decline" in cooking in the United Kingdom (see Short 2006; Meah and Watson 2011), what actually "counts" as cooking? These are some of the questions addressed in this essay.

The "Raw" and the "Cooked"

No discussion of cooking would be complete without an acknowledgement of Claude Lévi-Strauss's (1969) suggestion that the act of cooking represents a form of "civilization." That the "cooked" is perceived, in some cultures, to be superior to the "raw" is reflected in Tim Oakes's (1999) discussion of eating the food of ancestors in a Chinese frontier river town. Oakes points out how Chinese settlers in this region drew upon "a food orientated way of making sense of the other" (1999: 129). Thus, according to the imperial continuum, the indigenous Miao people of this region were *sheng* ("raw"), occupying the zone of "cultureless savagery," and only achieved *shu* ("cooked") status via exposure to Chinese civilization through land appropriation and marriage, whereby the "barbarians" would be taught to cook proper Chinese meals in order to observe the necessary food rituals of the ancestors (1999: 129–131).

While the anthropological and sociological literatures abound with examples of one cultural group displacing the traditions and practices of another via processes of colonial expansion, Angela Heuzenroeder (2006) attempts to problematize notions of an exclusively unilateral flow of knowledge and skill from a dominant culture to those who are perceived as being technologically less advanced. Indeed, she illustrates some of the ways in which early German-speaking settlers in South Australia were influenced by Aboriginal culinary practices. For example, Aboriginal skills in finding food and water are reported as having proved invaluable to the settlers in the process of adjusting to an unfamiliar landscape. However, drawing upon Norbert Elias's *The Civilising Process* (2000) and Lévi-Strauss's "culinary triangle" of raw, cooked, and rotten, Heuzenroeder reports the limitations of European culinary adaptation, highlighting that to adopt the Aboriginal practices of smoking or cooking their food directly over heat (roasted, on the side of nature), without a vessel (a cultural object) in which to contain it, would involve abandoning centuries of tradition—and "civilization"—something they were not prepared to do (2006: 36).

Who Cooks, and Under What Circumstances?

Over the last 100 years or so, culinary practices have become increasingly mediated by the incorporation of cultural objects, such as pans, and open-fire cooking has gradually been replaced with ovens, hobs, and microwaves. These developments were concomitant with the transfer of domestic cooking to women. Of course, many accounts of domestic cooking produced over the last twenty or thirty years (see, for example, Charles and Kerr [1988], reporting on the United Kingdom; DeVault [1991], on the United States, and Giard [1998], on France) highlight the denigration of women's cooking as part of the routine activities that constitute the business of "feeding the family." These mundane, everyday acts of care in the private domain of the domestic home are contrasted with the professional *male* kitchen, located in the public arena. While Sherrie Inness (2001) reports that, at different points in the twentieth century, for some Americans this was the only context in which it was acceptable for a man to be in the kitchen, Tony Coxon (1983) suggests that—in the United Kingdom—it was only "womenless" men who could be seen "stepping up to the plate." Others have highlighted that where men have been involved in domestic cooking, this has frequently been based on their establishing "sovereignty" over particular routines or types of events: weekend breakfasts, Sunday dinners, and barbecues—a particularly "masculine" form of outdoor cooking (Adler 1981). Where men have been visible in traditional accounts of domestic cooking, this

has largely been through the lens of women, who have been reported as being dismissive of men's contributions, describing their outputs as "snacks," as opposed to "proper" meals (Charles and Kerr 1988) and relegating their activities to more inferior mealtimes (not the main meal) (Murcott 1983a).

These hierarchies beg the question of what counts as "cooking," and by what processes has it become pertinent to ask this question in the first place? Increasing concerns about nutrition and food safety, for example, have converged with anxieties about the "impoverished state of domestic cooking," which now contribute to a common part of public discourse in the United Kingdom (Short 2006), with parallel concerns reflected in public health campaigns in the United States. Whether reported in academia (Griffith and Wallace 1998), or the media, or highlighted by an increasing number of celebrity chefs, a perception of the erosion of skills held by previous generations has emerged over the last ten to fifteen years. Among a range of contributing factors—including women's increased labor force participation—the wider availability of "convenience" foods and the effects of technologies are cited as culpable in deskilling cooking in the kitchen. Indeed, while Luce Giard (1998) has suggested that electromechanization transformed the cook into an "unskilled spectator who watches the machine function in her place" (1998: 212), Cynthia Cockburn and Judith Ormrod (1993) quote a home economics teacher, contributing to their study of household technologies, who speculates that microwave manufacturers and producers of the ready-meal have combined to "usurp the traditional housewife's skills" (1993: 147).

Accounts regarding the alleged "deskilling" of cooking have been provided by Frances Short (2006) and Angela Meah and Matt Watson (2011), while Joanne Hollows and Steve Jones (2010) have noted—in relation to the recent work of TV chef-cum-moral-entrepreneur, Jamie Oliver—that this accusation functions within a wider discourse of "class pathologization" (2010: 308), appealing to populist discourses within which it is assumed that it is socially and economically excluded populations who are least able to cook. This pathologization of certain social groups is not, however, a recent phenomenon. Concerns about the dearth of cooking skills among the "lower" classes in Britain can be traced back at least 200 years, when calls were first made for the poor to be educated in the basics of cooking (Lang et al. 2009). Likewise, in the United States, Katherine Leonard Turner (2006) reports the work of Boston philanthropists in the late nineteenth century who sought to "teach the city's poor and working class how to cook nourishing food with little money" (2006: 14). Their efforts were undermined by a failure to acknowledge—among other things—the cost of fuel for cooking and that (immigrant) workers' time could be better spent earning wages than producing meals at home, hence providing a market for bakery products, delicatessen food, and ready-to-eat foods bought and consumed outside the home at saloons, small restaurants, pushcarts, and stands (2006: 14).

What is "Cooking"?

The verb "to cook" is limiting in itself if we adopt the popular understanding of the word espoused by Lehrer since it includes only food that has been transformed by heat. By that rationale, does cooking include the heating up of beans in a microwave and their arrangement on some toast but not the preparation of a complex salad dish with a subtle homemade dressing made from a selection of fresh ingredients? Does it include the heating of a frozen pizza but not elaborately prepared sushi? An English roast dinner but not Greek salad or an Italian one made with cured hams? Or, as Short asks, can it only apply to the preparation of fresh, raw ingredients prepared "from scratch" (2006: 7)? Does cooking only apply to the performance of skills, the display of knowledge, and an understanding of food and ingredients assumed to pass via a hierarchy of gerontocratic authority (Steinberg 1998)? Importantly, Short draws attention to the apparent failure among those lamenting the deskilling of cooking to unpack the meaning of phrases such as "cooking ability," "culinary knowledge," "traditional cooking skills," and "assembly skills" (2006: 7). Indeed, as Elizabeth

Silva (2000) points out, the introduction of innovations such as ovens has not eliminated complex assessments and judgments required on the part of the "cook." Knowing when a cake or joint of meat is done does not hinge on manual abilities but, as Short observes, on cognitive, perceptual skills that prompt the appropriate action (2006: 8).

Further considerations in the understanding of cooking *practices* include shifting food tastes and preferences and ever-changing guidance regarding what we should eat and how it should be prepared. Salads, raw vegetables, and fruit are increasingly advocated as the cornerstone of a healthful diet as consumers are made increasingly aware of the impact of heating food on taste, on nutrients, and, ultimately, the impact on ones' health.

In the way that cooking knowledge and skill is valorized as a moral benchmark of care and domestic competence is embedded an implicit assumption that, at some point in the past, our mothers and grandmothers *did* know how to cook, that they executed care of the family through their efforts in the kitchen, and that they had acquired their knowledge via embodied experience and a form of cooking apprenticeship (Sutton 2006: 97), through observation and an engagement in the kitchens of their own childhoods. These scripts of the past clearly reflect a valorization of "traditional" cooking practices associated with a golden era of cooking, during which the "family meal"—reportedly now also in decline (see Murcott 1997)—was the cornerstone of family life. But *when* was this era, and for whom was it a reality? While Meah and Watson (2011) problematize assumptions about both the knowledge and skills possessed by a now-dead generation of British women, as well as limitations in the way in which feeding can reflect caring, Shapiro reports on the United States at the turn of the twentieth century, documenting the emergence of the domestic science movement, which saw "traditional" approaches to cooking displaced by science and technology, the latter having gained "the aura of divinity" (1986: 4) during this period. Indeed, exponents of this approach specifically eschewed "tradition," including the intrafamilial, inter-generational transfer of cooking knowledge: "As they saw it, domestic science would recast women's lives in terms of the future and haul the sentimental, ignorant ways of mother's kitchen into the scientific age" (Shapiro 1986: 9). It would seem that—in the United States at least—early twentieth-century modernity brought to cooking practices a rejection of more tacit understandings of food and taste in favor of something more precise, more reliant on instruction and guidance, and involving less judgment or experience from the individual. Shapiro suggests that, by the 1950s, domestic science had not only brought with it culinary regimentation but also intellectual and imaginative collapse. In *Something from the Oven* (2004), Shapiro points toward the role of the food industry in attempting to facilitate the reconstitution of the model housewife into someone who "mindlessly surrendered to packaged foods whenever they beckoned" (2004: 5) and dreamed of a "frozen food utopia" (2004: 11). However, as Katherine Parkin (2006) points out, such women were not characterized by food advertisers as neglectful wives and mothers but as demonstrating love and care. Shapiro (2004) concludes that the "housewife's dream" of a life free of cooking was not widely shared beyond food industry exponents in 1950s/1960s America. Indeed, in the absence of independent research, it could not be confirmed that American women "loathed" cooking (2004: 44) as was suggested at the time. Moreover, the response to Julia Child's efforts to demystify French cooking via *The French Chef*, first televised in 1963, indicates that "cooking had roots so deep and stubborn that even the mighty fist of the food industry couldn't yank all of them up" (2004: xxii).

Over a decade into the twenty-first century, the food industry has not only failed to weaken these roots, but a further shift in the way that cooking has been conceptualized has, in fact, widened the appeal of cooking in many parts of the global North. Not only has this challenged those who suggest that wealthier nations are constituted by time-poor, convenience-orientated individuals who no longer know how (or are not inclined) to cook, but cooking has been reconstituted as a recreational, leisure activity (as variously reported by Roos et al. 2001; Holden 2005; Short 2006; Aarseth 2007; Swenson 2009; Cairns et al. 2010). Indeed, writing in France, Jean-Claude Kaufmann (2010) makes a distinction that "there is cooking and there is *cooking*," the latter being understood as representing something more creative, rather than a chore. The advent of "recreational" cooking—including male television chefs "performing" it—has had particular appeal to a male constituency. Indeed, Hollows (2003a) indicates that cooking has become a "cool" *masculine* lifestyle activity (2003: 230), while Rebecca Swenson (2009) suggests that that television has been particularly instrumental in invoking a sense of "masculine domesticity" which—in a significant break with the past—has given men a place at the stove (2009: 47), albeit one still largely occupied on their own terms.

See also gender, kitchens, skill.

Angela Meah

D

Drinking © Angela Meah.

DRINKING

Drinking has been going on throughout human history, but it doesn't just happen. As a child, it is one of the very first and most essential tasks to be achieved. Yet, even from this very early stage, drinking is a complicated issue, not least because drinking milk could also be considered eating, although it is more commonly referred to as "feeding." The implication of another person (in this case usually a mother) forms part of the enduring sociality of drinking extending well beyond the mother-child scenario. The 2008 infant formula scandal in China demonstrated how grave the consequences of such interconnections can be, as toxic melamine was added to the product resulting in multiple infant deaths (Gong and Jackson, 2012). Such extreme events render the human interdependence involved in drinks and drinking visible and palpable, highlighting the preoccupation with health credentials that applies to certain drinks such as baby milk.

The study of drinking is often divided into discrete categories based on the properties of the beverages in question. For example, "drinking" is very often a social as well as academically used byword for alcohol consumption. There is an expansive literature from the well-established field of alcohol studies that this short essay cannot hope to synthesize. It is notable that alcohol is often researched in conjunction with, or published alongside, other research on a range of other drug-containing drinks such as caffeinated beverages (Reissig et al. 2009). Their pathological potential is of obvious interest (e.g., Wilcox et al. 2004), which is in turn linked to a need to understand the particular kinds of "uses" they might have in different ways, from "recreation" (Williams and Parker 2001) to "self-medication"(Carrigan and Randall 2003). Understandings of the potentially damaging nature of drinks and the morality of drinking are worked up by lay and expert audiences and form a long tradition of coupling scientific understanding of alcohol with normative claims made for its use in society alongside other kinds of drink.

The cultural significance of alcohol consumption is well-charted territory in the anthropological literature, where scholars have tracked the various rituals and rules that surround the imbibing of ethanol-based drinks. Whilst these generally all "go down" the same way, the practices required to get a drink require a detailed knowledge and competence in local customs—see Charles O. Frake (1964) for the case of Subanan in the Philippines, for example. The Social Issues Research Centre publication "Passport to the Pub" documents how tourists of multiple nationalities encountered difficulties, broke rules, and often struggled to get a drink in an English pub. Both of these examples also highlight the extent to which alcohol holds a central place in social spaces where a degree of intoxication is customary.

Campbell (2000) documents the way that masculine rituals such as one-upmanship continue to play a part (specifically the phallic one) in drinking practices in rural New Zealand. Here, as with the former examples, the surrounding behaviors, rules, and customs are of great importance to the way drinking is understood. That British people say "going for a drink" is significant in attaching primary public significance to the physical act of drinking rather than, say, talking with a friend. However, to say "Do you fancy going for a talk?" doesn't imply the prospect of alcoholic intoxication in the same way that "Do you want to go for a drink?" suggests the prospect of both drinks and conversation. Drinking, then, is rarely just drinking as the practices that surround it and are supported by it become wrapped up under seemingly tacit social codes.

Speaking of rituals, the practices of tea and coffee consumption, though by no means necessarily adjoined or mutually exclusive practices, are important in cultures that support alcohol use as well as those that do not. Consider, for example, the Swedish practice of *fika* (taking a coffee break with colleagues, friends, or family, often accompanied by a cinnamon roll or cookie) or the German ritual of *Kaffee und Kuchen* (coffee and cake). David Grigg finds that although most countries have established practices of tea and coffee drinking, "typically one predominates" (2002: 283). Whilst a good deal of attention is lavished upon alcohol consumption, Grigg reminds us that alcoholic beverages are not the most commonly consumed drinks in most countries. Historically, tea and coffee have been conceived of in benign terms by many, particularly the temperance movement, as they are seen as good alternatives to alcohol. Despite this, it is also the case that scholars and consumers alike are now casting a more critical eye on the potentially exploitative relationships involved in tea and coffee production and consumption. Fair trade tea and coffee are now a common alternative, not to alcohol but to other teas and coffees, which are considered less fairly produced or traded in one way or another. The list of so-called fair trade products extends at least as far as wine now, though could there be fair trade water or fair trade baby milk powder? Boycotts of Nestlé products by pressure groups such as Babymilk Action (www.babymilkaction.org) suggest that the prefixing of fair trade status to such drinks would be in bad taste for some, particularly as it could add value to a product that is not as beneficial for infants as breast milk.

Whilst ritual and custom are important in social analyses of drinking, symbolic projection or fetishization of the product cannot entirely replace the materiality of the actual liquid. Distinctions such as hard (alcoholic) and soft (nonalcoholic) drinks, sports drinks and energy drinks are amongst many descriptions that hinge on a drink's physical properties of some kind. They are a reminder of the tendency to attribute discrete functions to different drinks. However, the function and effect of a beverage beyond its immediate personal impact is often ambiguous.

Some drinks have reached such notorious and ubiquitous symbolic status that there is a temptation to assume they have a powerful significance where perhaps they do not. Miller (1998c) for example, cautions against the tendency to assume that a certain "sweet black drink" automatically functions as the hegemonic capitalist soft drink of choice. Indeed, Miller's empirical work reminds us that choosing what to drink is conditioned by market forces interacting across related scales, both local and global. Cristina Alcalde (2009) draws similar attention to the way Inca Kola operates within "local hegemonic discourses" in Peru that are racially hierarchized. In a sense, one can

read the success of Inca Kola as a blow against corporate monopolization or coca colonization and yet, in another way, Alcalde points out that local processes are themselves often routed in and productive of relations of subordination. These racial hierarchies may also be territorializing and even more insidiously so for their familiarity and embeddedness within a given social system.

A prominent ideological critique of certain drinking practices (e.g., drinking cola of various kinds) is that the experience is far enough removed from the exploitative economic effects of its purchase to render the practice as innocuous or unproblematic. To an increasing extent, the practices of drinking and choosing what to drink are interrogated, marketed, and self-consciously enacted as moral and ethical processes. Cola, and perhaps more prominently coffee, can be consumed according to a range of ethical banners that carry overtly normative baggage. Michael Goodman et al. note, for example, that the "good food" revolution can include "foods defined variously as healthy, low carbon, fairly traded, local, organic, free range, cruelty free, natural and/or slow" (Goodman et al. 2010b: 1782). Most of these categories also apply to drinks of various kinds, although the notions of "free range" and "cruelty free" are not, as yet, being used in conjunction with ethical claims about the production and consumption of specific kinds of drink.

Clive Barnett et al.'s (2005) paper on "consuming ethics" highlights the idea that a route to more ethical consumption might involve the assumption of responsibility. A version of this argument is manifested in the discourse that situates alcohol abuse as a problem of individual choice. Reminders to "drink responsibly" are also reminders that the drinking subject is a socially, culturally, and governmentally regulated one. James Kneale (1999) refers to the ways in which the nineteenth-century public house was constituted as a space in need of regulation and supervision. Different modes of drinking—either "perpendicular" or seated in "secretive" compartments—were, he argues, sources of concern as they were seen to promote heavier and therefore perhaps more vice-laden drinking. James Kneale and Shaun French (2008) have noted changes in the way "problem drinking" has been represented at various times. For example, they note that it can be represented through maps of clusters or through individual psychological accounts. The former are amenable to those who wish to highlight that availability is the main driver of alcoholism, as mapping makes the link between supply and consumption visible; the latter emphasize problem drinking as a personal pathology where individual contributions to the maps are largely the result of more complex motivational processes that can be accounted for by supply-side arguments.

On the opposite end of the intoxicative spectrum lies water. As a drink, it is highly regarded for its health-giving properties, and it is an absolute necessity for life. Water is a substance that, as a drink, becomes prominent in the conscious mind only when there is a deemed to be a lack of it. In contrast to alcohol, it is often the lack of water that causes hardships, tensions, and conflicts (Gleick 1993). Water drinkers in most parts of the global North are fortunate in having a selection of predefined sources of water available at the current time of writing. One of these, bottled water, is a source of huge controversy, where groups oppose its use on environmental grounds but where its use as a commodity is actually defined by sound cultural logics that respond to a lack of clean municipal supplies in some places (Wilk 2006a). Bottled water, then, does not mean the same thing to all people in all places, just as tap water is only a choice for some.

This brief and necessarily partial essay demonstrates the importance of a culturally and politically sensitive approach to understanding how and why drinks, and those who thirst for them, have such a complex history.

See also consumption, eating, moral economy.

Nick Piper

E

Eating © Angela Meah.

EATING

In an anthropology of eating, Peter Farb and George Armelagos (1980) point out that while all animals "feed," humans alone "eat." Whatever our social, cultural, or geographical location, human beings engage in the practice of eating in different ways, performing a range of routines and rituals around the food we consume and the context in which meals take place. Indeed, Farb and Armelagos point out that much can be learned from a society and its culture through an examination of eating. From the industrialized world to the global South, eating encompasses almost the entire life-course: from conception to death and all the calendrical and social markers in between.

But what *is* eating? Dictionary definitions suggest that it represents the start of the alimentary process which begins with the insertion of food into the mouth to be chewed, then swallowed, from whence it will make its journey through the gastrointestinal tract, nutrients (and toxins) being absorbed along the way, with waste products eliminated in due course. If, however, we were to run an Internet search, the distinction between "eating" and "feeding" become more clear. Pages of links are returned for discussions concerning either eating disorders (including methods of how to speed up the alimentary process) or obesity. Seen in this light, eating is constructed as a "problem," and one of extremes: restraint and excess, with pleasure and anxiety working in tension with each other (Coveney 2006). Indeed, eating can be said to invoke feelings of disgust and shame (Probyn 2000). Issues of food security and hunger also highlight the fact that, globally, nourishment is unequally distributed (Patel 2007). This essay will not focus on any of these extremes. Rather than focusing on Western public discourses which problematize eating, this essay will extend our understanding of what "eating" can mean to different people in different contexts. Among other things, it explores the function of eating beyond its nutritional contribution to the self, highlighting how eating is implicated in identity formation and its role in connecting us to the past and to others, via memory, ritual, and experience.

"We Are What We Eat"

Wherever Western consumers turn, there appears to be some cautionary reminder that "we are what we eat." Not only is food necessary for human nutrition and development, but the *right* type of food is held to be important to achieve particular outcomes. There are diets that help promote weight loss and fat reduction, which emphasize the elimination of refined sugars, fats, and starchy carbohydrates. For other individuals, the aim might be to gain muscle, to which end protein consumption is the key, and, depending on their discipline, athletes will maintain complex regimes balancing slow-release carbohydrates with protein for strength and muscle mass. For most people, however, everyday eating practices are largely dictated by hunger, time, cost, convenience, availability, and personal tastes and preferences, as well as those of others. At particular points in their lives, individuals may become more conscious of eating (or avoiding) particular things. In industrialized countries, women planning pregnancies may increase their intake of foods rich in folic acid, while expectant mothers may follow injunctions to avoid particular foods, such as soft cheeses and seafood. Farb and Armelagos (1980) note that Mbum Kpau women in Chad will avoid eating meat from particular animals prior to, and during, pregnancy in the belief that this will help avoid painful deliveries and reduce the risk of birth defects in babies. Children require calcium-rich diets to help the development of strong bones; individuals with anemia may consume food that is iron-rich; certain vegetables may be eaten for their antioxidant properties, while patients undergoing or recovering from cancer treatment have been known to eat calcium-rich diets to counteract the effect of drug regimes known to leach calcium from the bones. Particular foods are believed to have an impact on mood, on organ function, and on the skin. Another relatively recent development has been the claim that individuals of specific blood types have genetically evolved to require particular types of diet, and failure to adhere to these may result in a predisposition to certain health conditions (D'Adamo and Whitney 1998). Clearly, people eat for nutritional reasons, be it to satiate hunger, for health or for performance—both mental and physical. However, eating fulfills more than purely functional requirements; indeed, it operates as a practice on a range of levels from the sensory and the personal to the social and cultural with implications for subjectivities (see Mol 2008).

Eating as Sensory Practice

Separating the "problems" and risks associated with eating from its other dimensions opens up the possibility of a much wider understanding of its role for the individual and the wider social and cultural contexts in which people move between and eat in. While concerns about food safety, nutrition, and obesity represent constant "background noise" in public discourse, in Europe at least, food and eating continue to be associated with pleasure (Eurobarometer 2010), not least the sensory delights associated with buying, preparing, smelling, and ultimately experiencing the textures, tastes, flavors, aftertastes, and surprises accompanying each mouthful of food that individuals allow themselves to enjoy. With the reconstitution of cooking and eating as lifestyle choices, the sensuality of food and eating has become ever more apparent and Mary Eberstadt (2009) observes that it has become difficult to talk about food without invoking sex (see also Beck 1993; Lukanuski 1993; Jaivin 1998; Crumpacker 2007). The elision of eating and sex has been usefully explored by Elspeth Probyn (2000), and it would seem that the sight of celebrity chefs sucking their fingers, licking spoons, and engaged in a "real food orgasm" (Probyn 2000: 6) has released Western viewers' taste buds from the closet. Importantly, Probyn argues that eating has become a privileged optic through which to consider the negotiation of identities. Although she was alluding to the relationship between sex, gender, and power, we might suggest that identity has always been inscribed through what and how we eat, albeit implicitly.

Eating as Identity Practice

That identification is "never a final or settled matter" (Jenkins 2004: 5) is confirmed by the case studies presented by Gill Valentine (1999), writing in the United Kingdom, who illustrates how practices around food and eating shift at different points in the life-course and in response to the different environments and people encountered along the way. Valentine provides several examples of the circumstances in which "decisions" to become vegetarian are made and unmade, reminding us that where "moral" eating practices are concerned, such decisions are often marked by "conscientious inconsistency" (Safran Foer 2009: 9). Our practices are in flux with our identities and the opportunities available through which to live them out. In families, for instance, decisions about what to eat are made pragmatically and shaped by factors including cost, time, and convenience. Consequently, in the same way that Valentine highlights the power that a child can have in altering the eating practices of an entire household through a decision to renounce meat, so too do Angela Meah and Matt Watson (2013) illustrate the ways in which morality and ethics are sometimes superseded by cost and convenience, their British participants demonstrating a range of practices that enable ex-vegetarians and ethical omnivores to "feel nicer about eating meat."

Citing a 1978 newspaper article, Stephen Mennell reminds us, "The truth is that with food, as with sex or religion, different people like different things. *It is not a moral issue*" (1985: 1). He suggests that what is really at issue is a matter of *taste*, something that is "culturally shaped and socially controlled" (1985: 6). Invoking Claude Lévi-Strauss's (1969) ideas about "the raw and the cooked" and the so-called "civilizing" processes implicated in the latter, conflict abounds in relation to the position of various cuisines within the culinary hierarchy, and the linking of food to human behaviors has resulted in a range of national stereotypes, British "reserve" apparently owing to an "unimaginative diet" (Farb and Armelagos 1980: 2). Interestingly, Mennell observes that "mankind has always liked the food he was accustomed to" (1985: 4). While this may have been true in the past, one impact of globalization has been the explosion of food choice and availability. Indeed, contradicting Mennell, Lisa Heldke suggests that the gourmet food craze in the United States has been spawned by "boredom with our own foods" (2003: xxi).

While some Western consumers have sought to appropriate new eating adventures through their engagement with other cuisines, described by Heldke as "cultural food colonialism" (2003: xvi), for those who find themselves displaced from their own cultures via processes of migration, the practices surrounding eating and feeding take on particular significance. Indeed, Valentine observes that food, more than language, becomes a way of imagining cultural identity (1999: 519) and thus becomes a key marker in identification. Not surprisingly, particular anxieties can be invoked in response to perceived threats of a loss of cultural identity, and, among older people, traditions concerning food are often the last outpost to be surrendered in the process of cultural assimilation (cf. Gabaccia 1998; Ray 2004). Drawing on Pierre Bourdieu's concept of habitus (the collective schemata of experience and perceptions that predisposes individuals' social and cultural practices), Oscar Forero and Graham Smith (2011) illustrate the experience of older Ukrainian migrants in Bradford. Although claims are made regarding the "authenticity" associated with "traditional" foods, they report that Ukrainian cookery has borrowed ingredients and dishes from a range of neighboring culinary traditions. There is, in fact, little that makes the dishes prepared by British Ukrainians distinctively "Ukrainian." The significance of these dishes lies not in their strict adherence to ancient recipes. Rather it is "through family and the social rituals that the oldest generation of the diaspora pursued so emphatically [that] these dishes became a powerful symbol of the lost nation" (2011: 84). Conversely, for those of a younger generation, partaking of the foodways of their new home can be interpreted as symbolic of the process of assimilation. Writing on the experiences of South Asian young people in the United Kingdom, for example, Marie Gillespie suggests that eating what is described as "English" food represents both a way of feeling or appearing to be part of the wider society and culture (1995: 198) and one way they can express independence from their parental culture. This is also noted by Valentine, who reports

the significance for her South Asian Muslim participants of maintaining a link with "homeland". This link is most meaningfully maintained through family foodways, which include the consumption of particular kinds of South Asian dishes while seated on the floor for those meals consumed within the home.

For those who experience cultural displacement, eating has increased salience in the struggle for identification, be that in maintaining an existing identity or developing a new one. Writing in the United States and within the psychological tradition, Kim Chernin highlights how, for some people, the shift from one culture to another can induce painful ruptures that have profound psychological consequences extending across generations:

> My mother was born in Panama ... A big woman, like me, but we didn't think she was fat. Then we came here [United States]…right away the whole family enrolled themselves in some diet group. That was what my father wanted. I was 14 years old…A big woman, but now she thought it was fat. And all this was part of preparing me to become an American, to take part in this society. She wanted me to be a typical American girl. And that meant slender. And that meant diet. And that meant not cooking or eating the way we ate in Panama. (1986: 5–6)

This excerpt, from a therapeutic consultation with a client presenting with an eating disorder, illustrates the ways in which the exterior map of the body and the internal map of the self can converge and clash when familiar norms around which eating practices are constituted are ruptured in a new cultural context.

Eating as Social Practice

Thus far, we have focused on the personal aspects of eating: on the different ways in which what we eat constitutes who we are both organically and in terms of different dimensions of identification. But no discussion of eating would be complete without acknowledgement of it as a profoundly *social* practice. Eating does more than nourish bodies and sate appetites. As

Probyn observes, it "brings together a cacophony of feelings, hopes, pleasures and worries, as it orchestrates experiences that are at once intensely individual and social" (2000: 3). Whether one is eating at home (see Valentine 1999; SIRC 2006), eating at a fast food outlet, or "dining" in a restaurant (Finkelstein 1993), the most significant satisfactions derived from eating are largely associated with the sharing of food or the occasion (Warde and Martens 2000: 206). Indeed, Mary Lukanuski points out that food is prepared with the expectation that it is shared. Not only is the prospect of dining alone a situation at which many people balk, but, she writes, "Eating alone is a stigmatized behavior since it defies the expectations we have of eating" (1993: 119). Nonetheless, while shared mealtimes may be an ideal that is valorized as integral to the process of "doing family," reporting on the United Kingdom, Nickie Charles (1995) suggests that family meals can prove to be a "battleground" for all concerned, while in France, where shared eating is imagined to be an important part of social life, the harmonious family meal has been described as a "frail skiff" (Muxel 1996: 66), in which discipline may be imposed via expectations of table manners by older generations, enabling generational and gender differences to be reproduced (see Kaufmann 2010 for more on family meals).

These scholars all report from the context of the industrialized world, but the social significance of eating is no less salient in the countries of the global South. Anthropological studies of eating in "simpler societies," such as those reported by Farb and Armelagos, suggest that "eating is associated with initiation and burial rites, the role of the sexes, economic transactions, hospitality and dealings with the supernatural—virtually the entire spectrum of human activity" (1980: 1). Indeed, food and eating are particularly important in marking the transition between life-course positions. For example, the transition from single to married status by Hindu men and women is marked by the bride and groom feeding each other five bites of a sweet food. Among the Trobrianders of New Guinea, eating does not take place to satisfy hunger but out of social necessity. The giving of food is seen as a virtuous act, and the man who distributes large amounts of food is,

therefore, a "good man." Likewise, in a range of rituals, food is offered to the spirits to encourage their participation. Farb and Amelagos also observe that the simple act of sitting down together to eat can convey important statements about a society, giving the example of the birth of the civil rights movement in the United States which began as a dispute about the rights of African Americans to sit at lunch counters with white people. This was an important right since, in North American society, people customarily only sit down to eat as equals. Indeed, recent history is littered with examples of individuals who have made political statements via a *refusal* to eat (see for example, suffragettes in the United Kingdom, Ghandi in India, political prisoners in Northern Ireland, and, more recently, detainees at Guantanamo).

Eating as Remembrance

In many cultural traditions, eating does more than nourish; it also helps people remember (Safran Foer 2009: 12). As illustrated above, in some circumstances and contexts, the role of eating and the practice of sharing food is pivotal to maintaining important links to a cultural heritage that might otherwise be subsumed (see Field 1997; Sutton 2001). Thomas Adler (1981) and Deborah Lupton (1994) report the place of shared eating within memories of food and how these frequently reflect particular family dynamics, routines, rituals, and social relations, providing a lens through which to remember loved ones, including those who are now deceased. Indeed, reflecting upon his grandmother's challah, Steven Steinberg (1998) highlights how this bread was "like no other," representing a connection both to his grandmother and his ancestors—a link that was lost with his grandmother's death, since the recipe died with her. While memories of eating are often recalled with fondness, this is not always the case. Jenny Hockey and colleagues (2007), for instance, illustrate how particular foods can become associated with experiences of domestic violence, leading to long-standing aversions.

"Eating" encompasses a wide range of meanings across a range of social and geographical contexts. That it is not simply a question of satisfying hunger and fuelling the body is evident. If we look beyond the way eating is problematized within Western discourses of diet and restraint, it is clear that eating plays a role in both nourishing the body and the self. Eating is implicated in processes of identification, in connecting us to the past, and in facilitating and maintaining familial, social, and cultural connections. As Jack Goody (1982) put it, eating is a way of placing oneself in relation to others.

See also drinking, hunger and famine, memory, pleasure, sex.

Angela Meah

ECOLOGY

As a branch of biology, ecology comprises the scientific study of the relationship between plant and animal organisms and their environment. The term was coined in 1866 by the German scientist Ernst Haeckel. Ecological thinking was further developed in the 1930s when crop physiologist Roy Clapham coined the term "ecosystem" to describe the relationship between plants and other organisms living in a particular area, an idea that was later refined by the pioneering British ecologist Arthur Tansley (1935). Ecological ideas have, however, escaped their scientific origins to inform all kinds of environmental movements, including organic farming and the growth of various other "alternative" food networks. When thinking ecologically about food, the key message is to emphasize the web of relationships within which food is suspended, encompassing both the natural and the social world and linking modes of production with cultures of consumption.

Ecology is one of the few food-related words to appear in Raymond Williams's *Keywords* (1976), where he demonstrates the common linguistic roots of the words "ecology" and "economy," both of which originated around concerns about household management before developing their respective application to the study of natural habitats and the wider political-economy. Significantly, Henry David

Thoreau (1854) maintained this root connection by labeling the first chapter of *Walden*, his account of life in the woods, "economy" while, as late as 1931, H. G. Wells referred to economics as a branch of ecology: "the ecology of the human species" (quoted in Williams 1976: 111).

In *Appetite for Change*, his history of how the counterculture took on the U.S. food industry, Warren Belasco argues that the word "ecology" was not much used before the environmental crisis of the late 1960s, when it was "lifted from the dusty academic shelves of abstract scientific definition" to become "a powerful breathing consciousness [including] all things about life, death, and survival that no radical could avoid" (2007: 21). Belasco traces the origins of ecological thinking back to the work of the Diggers who campaigned for the abolition of private property in mid-seventeenth-century England. As it reemerged in the late 1960s, however, ecological thinking received renewed inspiration from Rachel Carson's *Silent Spring* (1962), which exposed the environmental damage caused by DDT and other pesticides, and from successive editions of Wendell Berry's *Whole Earth Catalog* (first published in 1968). Belasco also notes that Frances Moore Lappé's *Diet for a Small Planet* sold almost two million copies within ten years of its first publication in 1971, becoming *the* vegetarian text of the ecology movement (Belasco 2007: 56). Following the occupation of People's Park in Berkeley on April 20, 1969, environmentalists were further energized by nationwide "teach-ins" and Earth Days, and mobilized by groups with agendas as diverse as the Sierra Club and Friends of the Earth. Belasco concludes that by the late 1960s, ecology had broadened its appeal from "a baroque branch of biology into an interdisciplinary embrace of the whole earth" (2007: 25), developments that were given further impetus by the Club of Rome's influential study of *The Limits to Growth* (Meadows et al. 1972).

Today, ecology retains its central focus on human relations with the natural world but has come to be associated with a range of environmental and social movements promoting sustainable development, organic farming, and ethical consumption. The idea of tracing a product or a person's "ecological footprint," for example, is one way of attempting to estimate the environmental costs of an industrial process or consumer lifestyle. Contemporary debates about political ecology also serve to remind us that the agricultural and the sociological are fundamentally interconnected (Bennett 2009; Latour 2004b; Peet and Watts 1996).

The promotion of more ecological modes of production, such as organic farming, has also provided commercial opportunities to the food industry. In Norway, for example, certain products are marked with the label "Økologisk," indicating food that has been produced according to comprehensive standards regarding ecology, resources, and ethics, and without the use of artificial fertilizers and other chemicals. Similar products are certified by The Soil Association in the United Kingdom and by the USDA in America. Such "ecological" products often command a higher price than conventional products, reminding consumers that organic farming entails what Belasco describes as "a supervigilant, labor-intensive manipulation of nature in non-destructive ways," without which nature would mean "plagues, pestilence and famine" (2007: 117).

Words like organic, natural, and ecological have been readily appropriated in food marketing where strict definitions are all-too-easily subordinated to sales and principles to profit. As a result, organic producers have had to fight a constant battle to validate their claims and to verify that their methods are genuine, with their opponents seizing on any lapse in regulatory standards, eager to expose every last example of food fraud and bogus advertising (see, for example, *The Observer* 2005; *Macleans* 2007). In 2009, for example, the UK Food Standards Agency became embroiled in a dispute with The Soil Association over whether organic food had greater nutritional value as well as being environmentally less damaging than conventional food (*BBC News* 2009). In the claims and counterclaims that ensued concerning how the available scientific evidence should be interpreted, it became clear that ecology has become a deeply politicized field with high stakes in ethical, environmental, and commercial terms. In this context, the fact that Wal-Mart is now a major retailer of organic foods in the United States could be seen as a triumph for

the "mainstreaming" of ecological thinking or as confirmation of the ideological capture of the original ideas behind the environmental movement (see, for example, *Organic Consumers' Association* 2006). A similar ambivalence might be felt towards the U.S. supermarket chain Giant (owned by the Dutch conglomerate Royal Ahold), whose website boasts that the chain has more than 500 products in its Nature's Promise range, representing "what nature intended and nothing more" (Giant Food 2011). For further discussion of the commercialization of organic production, see Samuel Fromartz (2006).

Thinking ecologically about food reminds us, in Wendell Berry's words, that "eating is an agricultural act [ending] the annual drama of the food economy that begins with planting and birth" (Berry 1992: 374). Berry makes this point to counter what he calls the "cultural amnesia" about food's agricultural origins, which he associates with today's "passive and uncritical" consumers (1992: 375). Advancing a food politics that is more ecologically rooted, Berry insists that we need a food aesthetics and a food ethics, points that are regularly and systematically obscured by contemporary food advertising that denies the connection between food and farming, disguising the hard work that lies behind the gleaming products on the shelves. William Cronon makes a similar point in his environmental history of Chicago where he argues that the meatpackers were deliberately encouraged to forget that "eating was a moral act inexorably bound to killing" (1991: 256). Such amnesia may also reflect a more general reluctance among the American public to acknowledge the deplorable and unsanitary conditions in which the slaughterhouse workers toiled. So, when Upton Sinclair forcefully reminded them of these facts in *The Jungle* (1906/1965), his readers were more concerned about the impact of food safety violations on their personal health than they were about the welfare of those who worked in the industry, effectively ignoring the fundamental ecological principle that everything is connected to everything else.

See also science.

Peter Jackson

EMOTION

What and how people eat is deeply intertwined with their emotions—what Jack Barbalet describes as "an experience of involvement" that makes something matter to us and that "registers in [our] physical and dispositional being" (2002: 1). Such experiences are not necessarily conscious, nor indeed may they necessarily be labeled as emotions. They include instant reactions, such as anger, fear, or joy, but also ongoing states, such as calmness, satisfaction, regret, or anxiety.

Selecting, preparing, and eating food are "intensely emotional experiences that are intertwined with embodied sensations and strong feelings" (Lupton 1996: 36). Indeed, Lupton argues that the relationships "humans" have with food and eating are subject to the most powerful emotions experienced in any context" (1996: 34). Food choices are affected by and affect people's feelings and emotional states. In psychological studies, links between eating and emotion are well-established. According to Michael Macht (2008), emotions affect the motivation to eat; how much and how fast people eat; how they experience, taste, and chew food; and the foods they choose. These effects vary across emotional states. For many, boredom is associated with increased appetite, while sadness is linked with a disinclination to eat or eat as much. Some people's response is different again, as reflected in the propensity of some "emotional eaters" to binge-eat sweet, high-fat foods in response to negative emotions.

However, emotions are not only individual states, but are socially, culturally, and historically embedded. In different cultural contexts, emotions are explained and expressed in radically different ways. Similarly, the relationship between food and the emotions extends beyond individual psychologies. For example, while people vary in their individual understandings of the foods associated with particular emotional experiences, as in the case of sadness and "comfort food" or joy and celebratory foods, these tastes are culturally contingent. Although there is an expanding body of research on emotion and affect across the social sciences (see, for example, Anderson and Harrison 2006; Barbalet 2002; Bondi 2005; Thien 2005; Thrift 2007), emotions have received relatively little attention in sociocultural studies of food, often being subsumed within discussions of memory. Yet this obscures the potential of work on emotions to contribute to understanding the role of food and eating in constituting the human subject. This essay explores the place of emotions in thinking about food as well as thinking about how food is central to exploring emotional attachments to place. The essay considers how food is used in the expression of emotions and introduces an intersubjective approach to the study of food and emotions that is continued through an engagement with recent theorizations of affect.

Emotional Boundaries

Emotion is often negatively positioned in opposition to reason, as a feminized personal "gut" experience (Lupton 1996; Thien 2005). The "civilizing process" described by Norbert Elias (2000)—the development of table manners and the regulation of consumption—involved the management of emotions and of the gluttonous, animalistic loss of control associated with them. For George Orwell, "One of the effects of safe and civilized life is an immense oversensitiveness which makes all the primary emotions seem somewhat disgusting" (in Miller 1997: 177). Yet food is inextricably emotional. It forms the subject of human feeling, and has a sensory and symbolic effect on the emotions involved in food choice and social life. For example, the physiological effect of alcohol is to relax, exhilarate, and dull the senses. However, the emotional effects of alcohol are produced through its symbolic association with relaxation, the boundary between work and leisure, and our expectations that it will raise the spirits (Lupton 1996). Similarly, the physiological and sensory qualities of chocolate are rendered more potent by its association with feelings of indulgence and desire. These feelings are reinforced by advertising that plays on chocolate's connotations of romance, love, and seduction.

The contrast between emotion and reason is particularly evident in debates over the introduction of genetically modified (GM) crops. In a speech to the Royal Society in London in 2002, the UK prime minister, Tony Blair, described a visit to Bangalore. He recounted how a group of academics told him of their "astonishment" about how British debates about GM crops had become "completely overrun by protesters and pressure groups who used emotion to drive out reason" (Blair 2002). Blair's comments reproduced a Cartesian opposition between emotion and rationality, crystallized in the description of one GM foods researcher that "the scientists think and the public feels" (quoted in Cook et al. 2004). Arguments both for and against the introduction of agricultural biotechnology are often reduced to popular distinctions between scientific reason and popular sentimentality, emotion, and intellectual vacuity (Wynne 2001). These emotional responses are not even entirely owned by the public, but rather are prompted and manipulated by the "scaremongering" media. Despite research that describes the range of knowledges drawn on in public discussions of biotechnology (Marris et al. 2001) and studies that highlight the importance of emotion in motivating and enabling scientific research itself (Barbalet 2002), the equation of emotionality and ignorance persists (e.g., Sheldon et al. 2009).

Emotional opposition to GM food varieties is characterized as based on a visceral "yuk factor" (Burke 1998). This draws attention to the best-studied emotional experience associated with food: disgust. Work on disgust highlights the processes through which cultural norms of consumption are established and through which edibility is defined. The experience of disgust highlights the cultural specificity of emotional experiences, events, and displays as it is prompted by different foods and eating experiences that relate to differing cultural norms of "good food." Disgust combines both sensory and symbolic aspects of emotion. It is one of thirty-two basic emotions listed in Charles Darwin's *The Expression of the Emotions in Man and Animals* (1872). As William Miller (1997) points out, by the time Darwin was writing, disgust in English was closely linked to distaste:

The term "disgust," in its simplest sense, means something offensive to the taste. It is curious how readily this feeling is excited by anything unusual in the appearance, odour, or nature of our food. In Tierra del Fuego a native touched with his finger some cold preserved meat which I was eating at our bivouac, and plainly showed utter disgust at its softness; whilst I felt utter disgust at my food being touched by a naked savage, though his hands did not appear dirty. A smear of soup on a man's beard looks disgusting, though there is of course nothing disgusting in the soup itself. I presume that this follows from the strong association in our minds between the sight of food, however circumstanced, and the idea of eating it. (Darwin in Miller 1997: 1)

Darwin's interest in disgust reflected its rise in importance as other emotions were "civilized" (Elias 2000). However, despite its increasing importance, disgust received little subsequent attention until the 1990s (Miller 1997; Rozin et al. 2008), led by Paul Rozin, for whom the expression of disgust derives from the evolutionary emergence of a food rejection emotion associated with the protection of the body from food-borne pathogens. In this form, it is a visceral response of revulsion. However, over time, Rozin argues, disgust has subsequently become associated with protecting the soul from contamination and harm, and less with taste. Disgust extends beyond purely sensory properties of food to incorporate symbolic or ideational characteristics. For example, George Orwell's classic commentary on social class in Britain in *The Road to Wigan Pier* dwells at lengths on his disgust, as in his description of the Brooker family:

Mr Brooker was a dark, small-boned, sour, Irish-looking man, and astonishingly dirty. I don't think I ever once saw his hands clean. As Mrs Brooker was now an invalid he prepared most of the food, and like all people with permanently dirty hands he had a peculiarly intimate, lingering manner of handling things. If he gave you a slice of bread-and-butter there was always a black thumb-print on it. (1937: 6)

For Orwell, disgust at the British working class was a major barrier to democratic socialism, and reasserted boundaries between the bourgeoisie and the proletariat. While Orwell's comments are easily dismissed as snobbery, Miller (1997) argues that it represents an extended consideration of the importance of disgust to our most common social orderings. As Mary Douglas (1966) famously pointed out, what is conceived of as disgusting or "dirty" is not universal, but is the product of cultures of classification. Disgust acts to police the boundaries of these classifications and the limits of the self, by distancing it from Others, whether those of social class or gender, or of race and ethnicity, as in Darwin's concerns about the "naked savages" of Tierra del Fuego. Thus, Lupton (1996) describes how, in the West, Chinese cuisine is routinely described as disgusting and vice versa. Similarly, insects and grubs are commonly consumed throughout the world—and, indeed, hopping insects meet the strict Levitican dietary criteria of edibility—yet are often considered "disgusting" in Europe and North America (Schiefenhövel and Blum 2007).

Food and Affective Relations

Disgust lies at the heart of systems of consumption, conduct, and manners associated with ensuring the integrity of individual, political, social, and moral bodies. Work on disgust suggests the importance of food in forming, maintaining, and expressing emotional attachments. Practices of growing, cooking, and eating food are a key site for the expression of care, love, and desire, and also of anger, hate, and fear. The preparation of family meals "is redolent of emotional caregiving" (Lupton 1996: 49) and is freighted with meanings of security, comfort, and love. However, the time-consuming practices of home cooking may also result in resentment and anger, nor are they the only uses of food to express love and care—as the purchasing of "junk food" as treats suggests.

The emotional experience of food and eating is important in understanding connections between people and place. For example, Kalissa Alexeyeff (2004) discusses the transportation of food by migrant Cook Islanders as they travel back and forth to New Zealand. Cook Islanders have migrated to New Zealand in significant numbers since the 1920s. More than 60,000 now live there, compared to fewer than 20,000 in the islands themselves. Alexeyeff highlights the role of food in sustaining links between the islands and the diaspora, drawing attention to how it materializes affective relations. For example, she describes the trauma for a Cook Island woman when customs officials quarantine her food, as "this food represented the love (uro 'a) of her family for her; the best gift they had to give her" (2004: 69). Homegrown food represents the "bounty of home," both that of food and of loving relationships, and is carried in phenomenal quantities—one respondent carries over 200 kilos of food carefully prepared in such a way that it will pass New Zealand biosecurity import inspections. As described elsewhere, food is inextricably linked to memory, nostalgia, and the emotional experience associated with times lost. However, Alexeyeff also describes how returning Cook Islanders bring large quantities of food back to New Zealand with them, including buckets of KFC (fried chicken), which are distributed immediately to family on arrival. The gifting of food is thus associated with the commemoration of home and with the reassertion of affective values (cf. Mauss 1923/1990). Alexeyeff (2004) concludes that these material movements of food gifts create an "affective surplus" within an "economy of love" that incorporates notions of home, homeland, and kin.

Lupton (1986) also draws attention to the use of food in the expression of anger, including the poisoning and contamination of food and its use to "get even" with those we loathe. She uses the example of Peter Greenaway's The Cook, the Thief, His Wife and Her Lover, in which a man kills his wife's lover and she retaliates by cooking the corpse and serving it to her husband. Similarly, Shakespeare's Titus Andronicus achieves revenge on his enemy Tamora by serving her a pie containing her sons, which she unwittingly eats. The dramatic use of food to express anger, hate, or revenge resonates with urban legends, anxieties, and rumors about food, as in tales of the use of contaminated fried chicken by the Ku Klux Klan to cause sterility among black men (Fine and Turner 2001) or late 1970s concerns about "Halloween sadists" giving children poisoned candy or apples with razor blades hidden in them (Best and Horiuchi 1985).

More prosaically and more grounded in empirical observation, Paul Stoller and Cheryl Olkes (1989) describe the ability of food to convey anger and displeasure in their ethnographic work with the Songhay of West Africa. Stoller and Olkes's "sensuous" approach aims to capture the arrangements of senses and emotions, which they suggest is lacking from traditional ethnography. This allows them to focus on the ability of the material qualities of food to convey emotion, not only on its symbolic meanings or the verbal or physical expressions associated with emotional states. During their research, Stoller and Olkes stayed with a Songhay healer and his family. They describe how the presence of European guests meant the provision of high-quality sauces to accompany food, prepared by the healer's daughter-in-law, Djebo. On departure, the researchers offered gifts to the family and describe how Djebo's dissatisfaction with the gift, and anger with the researchers, was materialized in an inedible sauce.

Representing the Emotional and Visceral Materialities of Food

Food serves as an effective medium for the expression of love or anger through its material ability to affect, playing a role in the constitution of the consuming subject. This draws attention back to the sensory experience of food, as captured in Michael Pollan's description of the capacity of potatoes to absorb emotion and meaning alongside flavor:

> You can smell the cold inhuman earth in it, but there's the cozy kitchen too, for the smell of potatoes is, at least by now, to us, the smell of comfort itself, a smell as blankly welcoming as spud flesh, a whiteness that takes up memories and sentiments as easily as flavors. (Pollan 2002: 241)

While drawing attention to the ability of food to absorb sentiment as well as memory, Pollan's prose also draws attention to the perennial problem of capturing and representing the affective qualities of food. This is emphasized in Marcel Proust's celebrated description of the madeleine, perhaps the most famous piece of emotional narrative in Western literature. In *Swann's Way*, the first volume of *À la recherche de temps perdu*, the narrator describes how eating a madeleine induces "exquisite pleasure," but expresses the frustration of his attempts to capture and articulate the experience:

> No sooner had the warm liquid mixed with the crumbs touched my palate than a shudder ran through me and I stopped, intent upon the extraordinary thing that was happening to me. An exquisite pleasure had invaded my senses, something isolated, detached, with no suggestion of its origin. And at once the vicissitudes of life had become indifferent to me, its disasters innocuous, its brevity illusory—this new sensation having had on me the effect which love has of filling me with a precious essence; or rather this essence was not in me it *was* me. I had ceased now to feel mediocre, contingent, mortal. Whence could it have come to me, this all-powerful joy? I sensed that it was connected with the taste of the tea and the cake, but that it infinitely transcended those savours, could, no, indeed, be of the same nature. Whence did it come? What did it mean? How could I seize and apprehend it? (Proust 1913/1922: 48)

Proust's description of the madeleine "points us to the emotional charge of the moment of consumption for keying…associative memories" (Sutton 2001: 84). However, it also points to the problems of capturing the emotions prompted by or associated with food, whether in research or fiction. The difficulty of capturing the emotional content of foods points to the limits of representation and highlights the potential value of more-than-representational approaches to the study of food. Here, it is worth considering the relationship between studies of emotion, which often concentrate on states of being experienced by individuals, and the intersubjective, relational conceptualization of affect.

Food and Affect

Building on Baruch Spinoza and Gilles Deleuze, work on affect expresses dissatisfaction with representational or structuralist methods of researching, capturing, and depicting the world. It concentrates on arenas that do not necessarily lend themselves to representation, such as dance or music. Studies of affect reemphasize the body and its interactions, considering the embodied and unconscious or precognitive aspects of experience. Within this work, affect is not considered as a property of individual bodies alone, but as emergent from encounters. Affects are thus "in-between" bodies, between subjects and objects, with each affected by the other. This is captured in Bruno Latour's (2004a) discussion of "learning to be affected." For Latour, "To have a body is to learn to be affected, meaning 'effectuated', moved, put into motion by other entities, humans or non-humans" (2004a: 205).

A growing body of work positions affect within contemporary forms of biopolitics and the exercise of biopower. For Nigel Thrift (2007) and William Connolly (2002), the radical openness of bodies posited by an interactional theorization of affect creates new opportunities for manipulation. Thrift argues that affect has become a key political technology for the instrumental and strategic manipulation of "motivational propensities" through which populations are "primed to act" (2007: 26). In Connolly's discussion of the neuro-politics of affect, the media, and particularly television, plays an important role in the "formatting of perception." In the case of food, the power and influence attributed to the media in the communication of affect is readily observable in discussions of scaremongering related to GM foods or in concerns about the communication of emotions through marketing and advertising. For example, Katherine Parkin's (2006) analysis of food advertising in the United States in the twentieth century emphasizes its role in "selling" the emotions of love and care associated with food and in creating and playing on the gendered anxieties associated with their appropriate expression.

Attributing such a powerful role to the media in the communication of emotion returns us to the diagnoses of the problems with

GM food's publics described above. However, the case of GM and similar food scares also emphasizes the limited influence of the media in shaping public anxieties (Macintyre et al. 1998). While "affect modulation" may have displaced previous disciplinary regimes, its effects are unpredictable (Clough and Halley 2008), and analysis of food risk communication emphasizes the need to nuance "hypodermic" models of mediated affect (Milne et al. 2011). However, when extended beyond a narrow focus on the media, the communication, manipulation, or modulation of affect represents a potentially fertile site for the development of more-than-representational research on food.

For example, Nigel Thrift (2007) proposes that the manipulation of "propensities" also takes place through the design and production of space and the recombination of biology and culture. Here, the material qualities and sensory experiences of food and eating come to the fore in the use of food smells such as vanilla, chocolate, or candy floss by fragrance companies to create feelings of reassurance and calm, or in the smell of baking bread that is used by supermarkets to stimulate appetite and encourage purchasing, or even in the brewing of fresh coffee by house vendors to invoke positive emotions among potential buyers (Lupton 1996). Such approaches speak directly to the consumer's body by drawing on the cultural associations of key memories and emotional states. Hence, Allison and Jessica Hayes-Conroy (2008) argue:

> Addressing the visceral realm—and hence the catalytic potential of bodily sensations—has the potential to increase political understanding of how people can be *moved* or *mobilized* either as individuals or as groups of social actors. (2008: 469; original emphasis)

This approach aims to recombine questions of mind and body separated in contrasts between emotion and reason, and bring together biological and social experience. Hayes-Conroy and Hayes-Conroy (2010) suggest that understanding how different bodies feel food, food environments, and food practices differently can contribute to understanding, and potentially to extending, participation in food-based social movements such as Slow Food or school garden programs. They suggest that the motivation to eat healthily depends upon not just the ability to access local, affordable food supplies or on knowledge of food, but also on emotional impetus, upon the

> *articulated bodily capacity to feel* a certain level of comfort, excitement, affection, pride, and so on, for what she/he is eating. This articulated capacity is influenced by geographic and economic and intellectual forces, but it is also always more than the sum of these. (2012 : 6)

To capture this, they build on work in political ecology to suggest the need for research to attend to the structural, material, and epistemological complexity of bodily practices. In turn, their work suggests the value of research that explores the visceral politics of food, particularly how power in food systems is experienced, expressed, perpetuated, and challenged through affective milieux and the technologies and practices through which this is accomplished.

See also body, memory, pleasure, risk, sex, taste.

Richard Milne

EXOTIC

Referring literally to things that originate from outside, modern Western ideas of the exotic took on their current meaning in the first half of the nineteenth century where, through the discourse of Orientalism (Said 1978), the term "exotic" became virtually synonymous with the Middle East. Though now with a wider geographical reference, Edward Said's work demonstrates how constructions of the exotic, whether in art, literature, or food, are inherently relational in the sense that they reflect back on those who use the label as much, if not more, than on those whose cultural practices are so described.

Notions of exoticism are commonly opposed to ideas of the familiar and the mundane. So, for example, in his essay "On the Exotic,"

Alain de Botton begins by describing his sense of wonder at the subtle differences between airport signs in London and Amsterdam, though he quickly concedes that these differences would not conventionally be described as "exotic." Instead, he suggests that the word is more readily attached to "snake charmers, harems, minarets, camels, souks and mint tea poured from a great height into a tray of small glasses by a mustachioed servant" (2002: 70). Engaging with Victor Hugo's *Les Orientales* and Gustave Flaubert's fascination with Egypt, de Botton suggests that what we find exotic abroad may be what we hunger for in vain at home. Evoking notions of longing and desire, the connections between the exotic and the erotic have a long history, which, as George Rousseau and Roy Porter (1990) show, can be dated back to the European Enlightenment.

Similar ideas run through much recent work on "exotic" food. So, for example, Ian Cook's work shows how constructions of the exotic (such as the "sweet delight" of Jamaican papaya) have been used in the marketing of tropical fruit (Cook 1995; Cook et al. 2004), while Jon May (1996) has shown how middle-class consumers in North London talk eagerly about their desire for "a little taste of something more exotic." Describing her frustration at being asked to cook stereotypically "exotic" Caribbean food for "a European crowd" (rice and peas, ackee and salt fish, curried goat and mutton), Rosamund Grant challenges such stereotypes and insists that the "exotic" always reflects a particular point of view:

> I hate being seen through the eyes of Europeans. I don't like defining myself through the eyes of somebody who's white or is European. I have my own definition of myself and I think that is really important for me, you know, as a black woman to make an impression in that field [culinary education] 'cause this is my field, you know. And because I suppose there's a lot of passionate feeling left over from slavery and the impact of slavery and migration and displacement and all that kind of stuff...so it does irritate me when people talk about 'exotic food', you know, exotic through whose perspective,

is it mine or somebody else's? (British Library 2012)

Constructions of the exotic (in food or music, for example) can be a source of celebration or a subject of critique. So, for example, in Claudia Roden's (1974) attempt to introduce British readers to the joys of Middle Eastern cooking, she describes such foods as rich and exotic, exciting and seductive, while others have been much more critical of the deployment of these culinary tropes. Writing about the recent popularity of Asian Dub music in Britain, for example, John Hutnyk asks why bands such as Asian Dub Foundation and Fun^Da^Mental became "flavour of the month" in the 1990s, arguing that they provided "seasoning for transnational commerce" (2000: 3). Hutnyk is deeply critical of the way that exotica is deployed through music, suggesting that the term frequently involves a misrepresentation of more complex cultural forms, "blind to its own hypocrisy," as when Fun^Da^Mental was described by music critic Simon Frith as "an Asian Public Enemy," demoting the group to a "place of mimicry, imitation and derivative decay" and conveniently forgetting how European cultures might also be described as derivative in their appropriation of tea, coffee, sugar, chocolate, potatoes, balti restaurants, and a host of other cultural borrowings (2000: 213–4).

Graham Huggan highlights the paradox that notions of exoticism depend on proximity as well as perceived distance. It is the availability of exotic artifacts, he argues, as well as their apparent distance that renders them exotic (1994: 26). Exotic food should be sufficiently different to be alluring but familiar enough to avoid what Lisa Heldke describes as "dangerous weirdness" or "just plain disgusting" (2003: 127). Frequently, then, the exotic has to be tamed or domesticated before it can be consumed: sanitized and controlled while retaining elements of difference and potential danger (cf. Heldke's [2003: chapter 4] discussion of the machismo involved in eating exotic animals, close to extinction in some cases).

Heldke's "ruminations of a food adventurer" in *Exotic Appetites* (2003) provide a thoughtful and extended engagement with notions of exoticism and authenticity. Heldke shows how the quest for culinary difference can turn into a form of cultural colonialism, calling for a greater respect in our encounters with "exotic" food (requiring changes in attitude and action, character and conduct). Without such a critical orientation toward culinary difference (the new, the obscure, the exotic), she argues, food can become simply a resource or raw material in the process of cultural domination (2003: 7). Heldke provides a detailed critical account of the process of cultural appropriation where "yesterday's new exotic cuisine becomes tomorrow's supermarket special" (2003: 13), documenting the "domestication" of the exotic where what was once perceived as strange is rendered familiar, recognizable, and under control (2003: 19). Accepting that culinary boundaries are porous, Heldke nonetheless questions who has the right to alter a recipe or to record it as their own, contrasting conditions of duly acknowledged borrowing with inadequately credited stealing (2003: 133). Reflecting on Claudia Roden's inscription of "traditional" Middle Eastern recipes, for example, Heldke raises difficult questions regarding culinary ownership (2003: 138).

There is clearly much cultural capital to be derived from the pursuit of exotic food, tied closely to ideas of culinary authenticity. As with authenticity, constructions of culinary exoticism frequently imply a position of unexamined privilege where "our" food is considered mundane and unexceptional, while "theirs" is excitingly different and exceptional. The search for novelty and distinction in saturated markets can also lead to an exoticization of the familiar as with the "rediscovery" of traditional or heritage foods. The regionalization of British cuisine, including dishes such as Lancashire hot pot or Bakewell pudding could clearly be interpreted in this vein (Cook et al. 2000), while it might also be suggested that the growing popularity of "local" and homegrown food represents a new form of exoticism. As with all such distinctions, constructions of the exotic clearly represent the differential power of those who define and those who are subject to definition.

See also authenticity, local-global, provenance, sex, tradition.

Peter Jackson

F

Farming © Angela Meah.

FARMING

Farming encompasses a wide variety of organized land- or marine-based activities intended to produce food and other materials for domestic consumption or for sale through a market mechanism. As a result, farming has deeply significant implications for humans. However, the food produced from farming is not only consumed by humans. Some is intended for consumption by livestock (which, in the case of silage, may not be recognized as food by humans), while crops and livestock are targets for hungry animals and debilitating pathogens. In addition, farming shapes the ecology and aesthetics of the rural environment to the point where, in many countries, the farmed landscape has a cultural value that rivals or exceeds its economic significance.

Understanding the traditions and future of farming was conceptualized as part of a wider "agrarian question" by Kautsky in the late nineteenth century, seeking to address the role of the peasantry and family farmers in the process of capitalist development. Similar questions remain pertinent today in the context of the globalization of food supply chains (Goodman and Watts 1997). Over recent decades, farming systems have been subject to a process of intensification and industrialization as a result of technological and other innovations. Farming practices have adapted to various forms of mechanization, described by Harry Schwarzweller (1971) in a European context as the "tractorization" of agriculture, while Jan Douwe Van Der Ploeg (1985) and Frank Vanclay and others (2006) have written on the differentiation of farming practices within particular regions and sectors. Tracing the transition from farming to biotechnology (Goodman et al. 1987) or from farming to agribusiness (Whatmore 2002a) highlights the way that traditional images of the "family farm" are being superseded by technological developments and the commercialization of biological processes. Important differences remain, however, between production sectors (such as dairy or arable farming, for example) and between commodity systems (such as cereals or fruit and vegetables).

The variety of farming systems and practices found across the world has been reviewed by Alec Duckham and Geoffrey Masefield (1970), drawing upon examples such as the mixed farms of Sweden, the rice farms of Malaysia, the collective kibbutz of Israel, and the forest farming systems of the Democratic Republic of Congo. Duckham and Masefield deployed extensive data on moisture regimes, soils, vegetation, ecology, farm work, and social and economic factors, the latter category focusing on demographic data. This kind of system-level approach contrasts with sociological and anthropological work on farming practices that explore how farmers develop indigenous agricultural knowledge (e.g., Richards 1985), while Michael Carolan (2006) has explored how farmers adjudicate between competing knowledge claims. Work in rural sociology and human geography has also focused on the subsumption of agriculture within wider circuits of industrial and finance capital, as well as on the dynamics of family farming and the reproduction of agricultural labor (Whatmore et al. 1987). Sarah Whatmore's (1991) work also reminds us that farming is a highly gendered activity, challenging casual references to the "farmer's wife," especially in light of the diversification of on-farm economic activity in the United Kingdom and elsewhere in the global North, where women's work may be responsible for generating the majority of farm income.

In other parts of the world, discourses of food sovereignty have sought to defend small-scale farming from incorporation into larger circuits of capital, with advocates such as Amartya Sen (1981) calling for the implementation of a human rights approach to individual entitlement to safe, nutritious, and culturally appropriate food; the promotion of access to land, water, genetic, and other natural resources; mainstreaming of agro-ecological production; and the promotion of policies that tackle the effects of subsidized exports, food dumping, artificially low agricultural prices, and other negative elements of the agricultural trade model (Blandford et al. 2011).

While states take a keen interest in the governance of farming activity, international systems for steering agriculture and the trade in agri-food commodities have been particularly conspicuous since 1945. Examples include the development of the Common Agricultural Policy (CAP) in Europe and the increasing spread of international trade agreements from the failed International Trade Organization to the General Agreement on Trade and Tariffs (GATT), the Blair House Accord (1992), and the increasingly fraught (and stalled) negotiations of the WTO. Such international policies are deeply contested, with the role of farming featuring prominently in successive rounds of negotiation and reform. In the case of the CAP, for example, reforms have seen a move away from the direct support of agricultural production toward the wider agenda of rural economic development (Lowe and Ward 1998) and multifunctionality (Potter and Tilzey 2005).

The internationalization of regulations and guidelines also has other impacts on farming practices. For example, the management of animal and plant diseases in the interests of improving biosecurity has become an important preoccupation of governments, agri-business, and farmers (Mather and Marshall 2010). Private quality standards also have significant impacts on the ability of farmers to access markets and can require fundamental changes to farming practices (see, for example, Stefan Ouma's [2010] work on the impact of GlobalGAP on Kenyan horticulture).

In the current context of increasing global concern for future food security, governments are focusing on the need to increase agricultural productivity, given a finite or declining resource base in terms of available farm land, with "sustainable intensification" regarded by many as a preferred policy option. A recent Foresight report on the future of food and farming by the UK government concluded that there was a compelling case for urgent action in reforming the global food system (Foresight 2011). The report recognized that improving agricultural productivity was a key factor in ensuring that there is adequate global access to food but argued that this needed to be accomplished in an environmentally sustainable way (using fewer pesticides and less damaging artificial fertilizers, for example). Farming is clearly about much

more than producing food as cheaply and efficiently as possible. In increasingly urbanized societies, farming is (among many other things) a unique way of life, an occupation of great cultural significance, and a means of (re)producing a socially valued landscape.

See also ecology, governance, security, sustainability.

Peter Jackson and Richard Lee

FOODSCAPES

Differing from most of the food-words discussed in this volume, the term foodscape is one that has not worked its way into everyday vocabulary. Neither is it a very well-known concept in food studies research. Within those contexts where it is used, its usefulness and possible areas of application will be discussed. One thing, though, they all have in common—paralleling Arjun Appadurai's (1996) discussion of related terms such as ethno-, techno-, finance-, media- and ideo-scapes—is that they all touch upon food's spatiality.

Perhaps the most obvious quality of the term is its similarity to the word landscape. That word, of course, is integrated within everyday vocabulary. Its meaning, however, is not clear-cut either. Is a landscape the view of a slice of land as seen by a spectator, or is the landscape there whether anyone watches it or not? This same question also applies to the academic discussion of the nature of a foodscape. There are at least four different uses of the word, each with its distinct area of application, spanning a number of different disciplines.

To the Canadian anthropologist Anthony Winson, a foodscape refers to "the multiplicity of sites where food is displayed for purchase and where it may be consumed" (Winson 2004: 301). This is a *seen* landscape, one where informed consumers move around in a landscape containing different kinds of food; some of it is healthy food, called "real food" by Winson, and some unhealthy, referred to in Winson's polemical vocabulary as "pseudo-food." Hence, the concept of foodscape is here one that can be used in analysis of equality in food distribution and access; it is primarily a political and humanist concept especially useful for comparative analysis of fieldwork at different locations.

A related conception of foodscapes concerns the spatial distribution of foodstuffs over a rural or urban surface (Cummins and McIntyre 2002). Here, the viewer is subordinated and socio-geographical aspects are more prominent. For Pauline Adema, for example, the foodscape is a tool for analyzing issues of identity in a society becoming more and more globalized (Adema 2006). Food is also constitutive of identity, either ethnic (Ferrero 2002) or personal (Bugge and Almås 2006). This variant of Winson's notion has social implications as well as political ones.

A totally different conception of the term relates to the visual features of food itself. Jeffrey Sobal and Brian Wansink (2007) claim that the term should be restricted to "the view of a particular food object, as seen in the sum appearance of the food's visual features" (Sobal and Wansink 2007: 11). They exemplify some research conducted from this position with analyses of subjects such as the eater's judgment of portion size (Harnack et al. 2004), how the shape of the food influences the eater (Krider et al. 2001), or the eventual correspondence between nutritional content between food and the same food's chromatic properties.

Perhaps the most imaginative conception of foodscapes, however, comes from the Dutch philosopher Rick Dolphijn (2004). Dolphijn is influenced by the seventeenth-century materialist, nonhumanist philosopher Baruch Spinoza, for whom human bodies and human perceptions have no preeminence over those of any other entity. Hence, for Dolphijn, eating itself has to be explained from the encounter where one entity becomes "food" and the other becomes "eater," what Dolphijn calls "alimentary events." The foodscape is, consequently, a concrete topology made up by such encounters in the course of such alimentary events. This foodscape is constantly moving; it is created and recreated continually.

In a recent report on young people's habits of eating out or eating away from school, Dolphijn's abstract use of the term foodscapes is borrowed and used to designate a "population of eating practices" (Wenzer 2010) in order to make it analytically manageable. Here, the alimentary events are themselves the result of something prior to them: the practices that order the events. Eating seldom occurs spontaneously; it is, in the world of humans at least, circumscribed by habits, traditions, customs, and other practices governing its different forms. Practices are what regulate the ways in which some concrete bodies are over-layered with and get taken up by other bodies, as happens with food when it is eaten. Hence, the practice of "eating at McDonald's," with all the actors, habits, expectations, materials, and techniques it encompasses, is what regulates the event when some actors become eaters and others food. In this example, McDonald's can itself be considered a foodscape, making humans into "hamburger eaters" and hamburgers into "people-food."

Yet another use of the term comes from sociologist Torbjörn Bildtgård who proposes that a "mental foodscape" is a shared imaginary map or geography of food, pertaining to places the researcher's informants would like to go in order to eat good food (Bildtgård 2009). These ideas could be extended to include the symbolic links between food and place—such as the association between "America" and fast food. They are also relevant to Ellen Desjardins's (2010) work on the relationship between people's "personal food environments" and dietary quality in Waterloo, Ontario. A link could also be made to urban planner Kevin Lynch's classic book *The Image of the City* (1960) in which the author examined how spatial information was perceived and organized by users as they made their way through cities. These users formed cognitive or mental maps of cities where the elements of landmarks, nodes, paths, edges, and districts conformed in common and predictable ways in these mental maps.

The term foodscape might therefore act as a suggestive approach to how the world is theoretically "materialized," bringing it back to the stringy, messy network of entities that comprise it. Foodscapes are never alone—in cities, they overlap with other scapes and populations among the concrete blocks of the suburbs and the bourgeois esplanades of the city centers, they move with the trams and the pedestrians navigating the streets and lingering with those resting in the parks and the cafés, all at the same time.

See also aesthetics, eating, local-global, practices.

Jakob Wenzer

FRESH

Words like "fresh" and "natural" are deployed in food marketing and similar contexts in an almost uniformly positive way. They are examples of the kind of "warmly persuasive" terms (like "community") that never seem to be used unfavorably (Williams 1976: 76). Linking fresh and natural in the context of modern agri-food systems is, however, somewhat ironic as what is sold as "fresh" frequently depends on a whole series of technological innovations, such as refrigeration and air freight, that are anything but natural.

The industrialized production of freshness is at the heart of Susanne Freidberg's "perishable history" of fresh produce, whose development she relates to our uneasy appetites for modern living, including the anxieties and dilemmas of industrial capitalism and the culture of mass consumption (Freidberg 2009: 3). Freidberg argues that freshness involves both positive and negative features, signaling the inclusion of vitamins, minerals, and other healthy ingredients like fiber, and the absence of excess salt and other harmful additives. Her discussion of freshness leads into an analysis of the demand for "local" food, with all its paradoxes and contradictions. She notes, for example, that in the United States the supermarket giant Walmart has begun to promote local produce, including apples and melons, from the customer's own state, and that, for a variety of social and political reasons, it is now easier to be a locavore (dedicated to eating locally) in Berkeley, California, than in Burkina Faso (2009: 279–81).

Definitions of freshness are, of course, complex and contested. According to the U.S. Food and Drug Administration, for example, the use of the label "fresh" is not permitted on frozen, heat-treated, or chemically preserved goods with the significant exception of pasteurized milk. Strict adherence to these rules has, however, led to the emergence of categories such as "fresh-frozen" and to the advertising of irradiated salads as fresh. As one might expect, uncertainty over the meaning of freshness has proven to be fertile ground for food marketers. Freidberg quotes a lobbyist for the American Fruit Juice Council who argues that freshness is a "state of being" rather than a simple measurement, albeit one that is frequently produced through highly intensive technological interventions. "Theirs," she continues, "was an industrial freshness: mass-produced, nationally distributed, and constantly refrigerated. Far from a natural state, it depended on a host of carefully coordinated technologies, from antifungal sprays to bottle caps to climate-controlled semi trucks" (Freidberg 2009: 2).

As Freidberg argued in her previous book, *French Beans and Food Scares* (2004), perceptions of freshness are only one of several desirable features in fruit, vegetables, and other produce that is grown abroad for consumption in distant markets. Perfectly edible food can be rejected by supermarket buyers and other "middlemen" because it does not meet their exacting requirements in terms of shape, color, size, or a host of other aesthetic properties. Fruit and vegetables are among the most demanding foods in the modern supermarket sector in terms of their need for high levels of labor input and the amount of intensive care required at every stage of the supply chain, from field to fork.

For these reasons among others, access to fresh foods such as vegetables, meat, and fish has historically been regarded as a luxury. The perishability of these foodstuffs limited their availability and increased their value. As with seasonality, the preservation of freshness came to be seen as a problem to be overcome as societies strove to subordinate nature to human will (Morgan et al. 2006: 9). While freshness and seasonality are now being marketed as part of a return to "tradition," where consumers are in harmony with nature, other readings of society's vexed relationship with nature are equally if not more plausible as the demand for year-round supplies of "fresh" produce has led to the widespread application of artificial pesticides and chemical preservatives. From this perspective, "freshness" stands at the intersection between scientific concerns about food safety and more subjective judgments of quality and taste (as revealed in the contested history of food labeling, for example).

As previously noted, milk represents a particularly interesting case in the industrial production of freshness. Represented as "nature's perfect food" by generations of American nutritionists (DuPuis 2002), the production of "fresh" milk on an industrial scale involved all kinds of human interventions in the food chain, from the domestication of cattle to the use of artificial growth hormones such as Bovine somatotropin (now banned in many countries). The mass consumption of milk depended on the elimination of bacteria through heat treatment and pasteurization. But pasteurization kills both harmful and harmless bacteria, leading to intense debates about the consumption and regulation of so-called "raw" milk (see http://www.realmilk.com). Milk is, indeed, an excellent example of what Jane Bennett (2009) refers to as "vital matter," whose agency is distributed among a range of human and nonhuman forces. And, as Peter Atkins's historical research reveals, milk's "liquid materialities" have generated a series of complex political and legal interventions in the name of food safety and public health, involving a highly moralized discourse of purity and danger (Atkins 2010).

As societies urbanized, milk travelled further to market, increasing the dangers of spoilage and infection (associated with diseases such as typhoid, diphtheria, scarlet fever, and tuberculosis), justifying its description by some contemporary commentators as "poison from the countryside" (Freidberg 2009: 208–10). Despite these concerns, milk gradually came to be seen as wholesome and nutritious, a process charted by Melanie DuPuis (2002) in her study of how milk became "America's drink." Historically and in many different national and cultural contexts, milk's whiteness added to its allure as an apparently pure, natural, and healthy product. But milk still provokes fierce debates about animal cruelty, genetic engineering, and antibiotic

residues, to say nothing about the controversies that have raged over infant formula (Nestle 2002) or the development of "mega dairy" farms with herds of several thousand cattle (*Daily Telegraph* 2011a). Despite recent dietary concerns about the implications of consuming full-fat milk, milk sales have not decreased significantly, being deflected into increased consumption of semi-skimmed and low-fat varieties, and global demand is increasing rapidly as higher levels of meat and dairy consumption serve as markers of modernity in "emerging economies" like China and India.

Some foodstuffs seem to defy the common equation of freshness and quality. The best quality beef will be carefully aged (and so not "fresh" in the way the term if routinely defined). Good-quality cheese is painstakingly matured and wine may be aged in the barrel or in the bottle to achieve a level of complexity and depth of taste that is lacking in younger "fresher" wines. But these are the exceptions that prove the rule, and the antonym of fresh (stale) is never regarded as a virtue in food (though words like "vintage" are often used to command a premium).

Finally, and notwithstanding its many positive connotations, the demand for freshness has also contributed to current concerns about food wastage. In his campaigning work to expose the "global scandal" of food waste, for example, Tristram Stuart reports on a sushi outlet in London where trays of freshly prepared prawn, salmon, swordfish, and tuna are disposed of every day as shelves are refilled until just before closing time to avoid the appearance of empty space (Stuart 2009: 17–18). Similarly with freshly made sandwiches, Stuart argues, overordering is standard practice across the retail sector, leading to high volumes of waste when supply regularly exceeds anticipated demand. As all these examples suggest, something as apparently positive as "freshness" clearly has a darker side, and, while consumers will frequently pay a premium for what they perceive to be fresh food, its production often involves serious hidden costs.

See also advertising, innovation, labeling, local-global, technologies, tradition.

Peter Jackson

G

Gender © ANGELA MEAH.

GENDER

"Gender" differs from "sex" in that while the latter refers to the physiological and biological characteristics that define men and women, gender refers to the socially constructed roles, behaviors, activities, and attributes that a given society considers appropriate for men and women (WHO 2012). "Gender," therefore, has different implications across a range of social, cultural, and geographical contexts.

When discussing gender in relation to food, the resounding narrative is one in which the dominant voice is a largely white, Anglo-centric, pro-feminist one, focusing on the normative positioning of food within the domain of women and depicting women's domestic engagement with food as "oppressive," derided, and underappreciated. While feminists have, undoubtedly, had grounds for criticism regarding domestic distributions of labor, women's relationship to, and perceptions of, food-work cannot be fully understood if viewed via the optic of those focusing exclusively on industrialized nations. Nor should it be argued that women's—and men's—relationship to the kitchen, and related spaces in which responsibilities concerning food are distributed, has remained immutable since second-wave feminists first spoke out against that plight of "captive wives and housebound mothers" (Gavron 1966). This essay challenges those discourses that emphasize the oppressive and "drudging" character of food-work by making visible the experiences of a range of minority ethnic women—largely but not exclusively in the global South—for whom the activities surrounding the growth, acquisition, preparation, and distribution of food in the domestic context can represent opportunities to demonstrate creativity and skill, as well as accruing value within families and communities, and increasing opportunities to express resistance and power. Additionally, the essay also explores the impact that the reconstitution of cooking as a "leisure" activity—through which the door has been opened, enabling men's entry into the kitchen—has had in the alleged "democratization of domesticity" (Meah and Jackson, 2013) in industrialized countries. In presenting a more nuanced, culturally and geographically inclusive picture, this essay contributes to a revisionist history of food-work.

The Feminist "Food-Gaze": Perspectives from the Global North and South

The identification of quotidian domestic food provisioning as the exclusive preserve of women has, perhaps unsurprisingly, led many contemporary Anglo-American feminists to balk at the idea of commenting on either kitchens or cooking (see, for example, Ruth Hubbard's response to an invitation to contribute to Arlene Avakian's collection *Through the Kitchen Window* [1997: 5]). Where women's relationship to food has come under feminist scrutiny, it has tended to emphasize issues such as eating disorders and the victimization of women which, according to U.S. food historian Barbara Haber (1997), reflects an "intellectual framework that sees food and its preparation as fraught with conflict, coercion and frustration." Indeed, "kitchens and cooking have become symbols of subservience, rather than pleasure and fulfillment" (1997: 68). Commenting on the role of food advertising in shaping gender roles in modern America, historian Katherine Parkin (2006) notes that cooking is represented as something done in the service of others; women should not find gratification in eating and it is considered "morally wrong" to indulge oneself (2006: 37). In spite of the efforts of contemporary food writers, such as Nigella Lawson, in encouraging women to engage with food as a source of pleasure and to cook and eat for the self, as opposed to deferring to the tastes and preferences of others (Hollows 2003b: 184), the focus of feminist scholarship on eating disorders is illustrative that women's engagement with food—at the level of eating—continues to be characterized by issues of guilt, shame, disgust, and restraint (see Probyn 2000; Julier 2004).

But not all women, or even all people, have the opportunity of overeating or the choice of undereating. In those areas of the global South most harshly affected by the multiple burdens of poverty, disease, poor healthcare, and food insecurity, daily life is all too often

characterized by the absence of quality nutrients. While the British women reported by
Ann Oakley (1974), Anne Murcott (1983b) and
Nickie Charles and Marion Kerr (1988), and
the American women reported by Marjorie
DeVault (1991) may have experienced frustration, lack of fulfillment, and even resentment
toward the everyday activities that constitute
"feeding the family," it is unlikely that their burdens, or those of subsequent generations, will
have included fetching water, gathering wood,
grinding grains, and drying and pounding cas-
sava, in addition to washing, breastfeeding,
caring for children, looking after the home,
and cooking, *in addition* to subsistence farming, such as the Kenyan and Tanzanian women
reported by Adnan Hyder and others (2005).
Such experiences are not uncommon in male-
headed households across sub-Saharan Africa
and are reflective of what the authors suggest is
a "pervasive triad" of food insecurity, gender inequity, and ill-health among women (2005: 328)
whose food-work is part of the informal economy and therefore remains invisible. As with
women in other parts of the world, they are also
responsible for the health, nutrition, and development of their children, but while women in
industrialized countries may be frustrated by
children who have fussy or inconsistent tastes
(see Meah and Watson, 2011, for example), for
these women, limited resources, poor access
to water, poor health (not least in the context
of high levels of HIV-infection), and limited
decision-making authority in the distribution
of household food resources represent everyday
challenges. Reporting on other parts of Kenya
and also in Malawi, however, Eileen Kennedy
and Pauline Peters (1992) indicate that where
women *do* have decision-making autonomy—
for example, in female-headed households—it
can have a significant impact on their children's
health. Although these households are among
the poorest, levels of malnutrition among pre-
school children were reported as being lower
than those recorded among children living in
male-headed households. In both countries,
women tend to allocate a higher proportion-
ate expenditure on food than men do and, in
the case of Malawi, it is suggested that lower
levels of child malnutrition are attributable to

women's tendency to allocate a higher proportion of food calories to their children (1992:
1082), reflecting their predisposition toward
nurturing and care.

Across a range of cultural contexts, food-
work has been inextricably bound with notions
of womanhood, care, and love, something that
food advertisers in the United States have not
shied away from commodifying (Parkin 2006: 1).
However, although meals may be willingly "gifted"
as part of women's contribution to the domestic
economy of a household, and mealtimes can represent a space in which ideologies about "family"
are celebrated and reproduced, these practices
can also be experienced as sites of contestation
and anxiety for women, men, and children. In
the United Kingdom, Nickie Charles (1995)
observed that mealtimes can become a "battleground," particularly where the dining table is regarded as a site for the socialization of children,
while tension over the choice of food can—in
some circumstances—only be avoided by the
deference of women to the tastes and preferences
of their partners and/or children (see Charles
and Kerr 1988; DeVault 1991; Brown and Miller
2002). Globally, everyday meal preparation can
be seen as an illustration of how the mundane
can be used as "an interpretive framework for the
extreme" (Hockey et al. 2007: 140), with mundane memories of food providing a lens through
which to recall acts of conflict or violence. For
example, Ketu Katrak (1997) reflects upon her
lack of enjoyment of the food of her childhood
in India since it "tasted of the conflictual relationship my parents shared," her mother's culinary
accomplishments being "snuffed," all too often, by
her father's "critical palate" (1997: 264–7). In the
United States, one of Carole Counihan's Chi-
cana participants talks about having "learned to
make rice the hard way" (2005: 210), while Jenny
Hockey and others report a British woman who
had been forced, by her husband, to eat an entire pan of spaghetti Bolognese after having been
judged to have "got it wrong" (2007: 139). More
extreme forms of violence are documented in
India, where the kitchen has been a site of a very
specific form of violence against women: dowry
murder by fire. Here, women work on kerosene
stoves, with tins of fuel held in reserve. It is not
uncommon for women to be doused in fuel and

set alight, the highly inflammable nature of the liquid, open flames, and dangling saris enabling incidents to be passed off as "accidents," while simultaneously destroying the evidence (Oldenburg, cited in Abarca 2006: 25).

Presented with this range of evidence, it is perhaps not surprising that food has been conceptualized as part of women's oppression, or as a burden from which they need to be "liberated." However, speaking from within women's studies in the United States, Avakian (1997) has argued that feminists need to look at meal preparation again. Although women's contribution to food-work has undoubtedly been taken for granted in many social and geographical contexts, cooking, she argues, "is more complex than victimization … If we delve into the relationship between women and food we will discover how women have forged spaces within that oppression" (1997: 6). Avakian's edited collection *Through the Kitchen Window* includes interesting and useful insights that facilitate a more nuanced perspective on how food can be, and has been, conceptualized by her contributors. The next section examines alternatives to the anti-cooking refrain that has characterized much white Anglo-American scholarship on food.

Entrapped or Empowered? Ethnically "Other" Women Performing Agency through Food-Work

Resistance to the intellectual and cultural imperialism that has characterized much feminist writing of the Other is not new within postcolonial literature (Meah 2001). Writing in New Zealand, Linda Tuhiwai Smith (1999) has challenged scholars undertaking research with indigenous (or ethnically Other) populations to employ decolonizing methodologies that facilitate an epistemology from the ground up. Drawing upon this type of methodology, Mexican American Meredith Abarca (2006) highlights the importance of not imposing our meanings on others. One such imposed stereotype is reflected upon by Helen Barolini who, growing up as an Italian American, felt constrained by the image of Italian women

as a "silent, submissive [and] stuck in the kitchen … [a] benighted drudge and simple stirrer of sauce" (1997: 228–234), an image she felt compelled to distance herself from. However, in reconnecting with her family's culinary traditions via her mother's stories of her own youth, Barolini attempts to transform "the so-called women's room (the kitchen) from a holding pen into what it really is—an embassy of cultural tradition" (1997: 109). Likewise, Abarca reexamines foodways and their meanings among working-class Mexican and Mexican American women, whom she identifies as "co-theorists." In *Voices in the Kitchen*, she reveals that food-work can be reconstituted as something other than mandatory labor performed in the service of others (2006: 23). For many of the women she spoke with, cooking is seen as a celebration and affirmation of their talent, knowledge, and identity, acknowledging their resourcefulness and as performances of affection. Echoing Daniel Miller's (1998b) observations about women who "make love in supermarkets" via performances of thrift and care through mundane acts of shopping for their loved ones, one woman explains: "It's a way of showing love" (Abarca 2006: 24).

Abarca observes that when the kitchen is conceptualized as a space rather than a place, it "can represent a site of multiple changing levels and degrees of freedom, self-awareness, subjectivity and agency" (2006: 19), it is the social interactions that unfold within it that defines its significance. Her arguments build on those presented by African American critics such as bell hooks (1990), who says of her own memories of "homeplace" that "houses belonged to women, were their special domain, not as property, but as places where all that truly mattered in life took place—the warmth and comfort of shelter, the feeding of our bodies, the nurturing of our souls" (1991: 41). Similarly, Marvalene Hughes (1997) writes that for African American women, cooking is not coterminous with oppression, routine, or drudgery, but is an expression of love, nurturance, creativity, and sharing, which became a route through which to escape the painful realities of racist oppression. Gloria Wade-Gayles recalls how her mother "moved in majesty within our small kitchen, her woman's room" a kitchen-temple in which she "prepared sacrifices for family rituals" (1997: 95–96). Where the food-work undertaken in white employers' kitchens may have been characterized as oppressive, Wade-Gayles suggests that in their own kitchens, many women like her mother "converted what might have been a demand into a desire, a responsibility into a joy, a task into a talent" (1997: 96–97). In these spaces, women worked, served, thought, meditated, and bonded with one another. Here, she argues, "Women experienced influence, authority, achievement and healing" (1997: 97).

These reflections facilitate a way of finding alternative readings of food-work and the spaces in which it is undertaken. For minority women in the United States, the kitchen can represent a haven from the dominant culture and a private space in which ethnic, cultural and feminine identities are affirmed and a sense of belonging and freedom achieved (see also Supski [2006] writing about the experiences of migrant women in postcolonial Australia, and Pascali [2006] reporting the practices of North American Italian immigrants). But what of the experiences of those indigenous to the global South? While our earlier observations highlight very specific structural challenges presented by poverty and lack of resources, as well as cultural restrictions that can limit the agency of many women, particularly in the African context, this essay will now explore a range of examples in which traditionally gendered tasks, or spaces, have been used as resources in performing creativity and resistance, as well as mechanisms of survival and empowerment.

Gendered Gastro-Politics in the "Third World" Kitchen

Because farming is seen as a masculine preserve, not least since men are largely responsible for overseeing livestock management and the public activities that take place in markets, the notion of a patriarchal pastoralist has proliferated in the sub-Saharan context. However, increasing anthropological interest in the role of women in pastoral societies has revealed some interesting nuances that challenge the validity of claims of male power in this context. For example, writing about the Samburu of

Kenya, Jon Holtzman (2002) highlights how, at the age of fourteen, Samburu boys are initiated as *moran* or "bachelor warriors." Holtzman observes that the identities of Samburu men are intricately bound to their relationship with women as food providers. Once initiated, the bachelor warrior is prohibited from consuming food which has been seen by women, and this does not change until he marries and becomes an elder, thereby entitling him to access food produced by his wife (2002: 265–66). Drawing upon Arjun Appadurai's (1981) notion of "gastropolitics," Holtzman highlights the role that Samburu women, both as mothers and as wives, play in the everyday domestic politics of food allocation in the household. Unlike the women cited by Hyder and others (2005), who lack decision-making power in distributing food, Samburu women are presented as "gatekeepers of the family larder" (Counihan, cited in Holtzman 2002: 269); neither these women, nor those of the Nuer in Southern Sudan, defer to men as "breadwinners," and among the latter, cooking can be used to express resistance to male authority (Holtzman 2002: 272).

Similarly, Elsbeth Robson (2006) reports that by looking at the organization of food, assumptions about the relative position of women and men among the Muslim Hausa of Northern Nigeria are challenged. In this context, public spaces belong to men, while domestic space is the domain of married women. While the Muslim seclusion of married women may be deemed questionable from an Anglo-American perspective, seen from an insider's standpoint it is not without its advantages, not least since it protects women from unwanted male attention. As much domestic cooking takes place outdoors in communal spaces, and given the multigenerational and polygamous organization of these spaces, women are, in fact, less socially isolated (however, close proximity to co-wives can also lead to competitiveness and jealousy). Although women cook primarily for domestic needs, they are not excluded from entrepreneurial activity and consequently cook for the market, their produce being sold by unmarried girls who are permitted to inhabit the public domain. While men are only "apologetic and temporary visitors" (Robson 2006: 670),

Hausa women exercise considerable power over what is prepared and when, how it is distributed and to whom. In this context, food can be used as a mechanism to express reward and exercise retribution.

Elsewhere in the South, women's quotidian food-work is also seen as active in reconstituting distributions of power at a public level. In Latin America, for example, women's participation in social movements has a well-established history, women frequently representing the vanguard in community activity. Kathleen Schroeder (2006) identifies the link between community kitchens and the empowerment of women in Bolivia and Peru, particularly for women of indigenous origin. Community kitchens are typically organized by women who are community leaders and already heavily involved in, and influential within, their communities. Lauded as training grounds for entrepreneurial development, they are promoted as invaluable since they help develop skills that can be transferred into entrepreneurial activity, which could be used to the advantage of individual households (see Wardrop [2006] for a South African example of women's entrepreneurial cooking activities). While women's participation in these kitchens can reduce social isolation and provide an opportunity for informal networking by facilitating access to the kind of information and support required to help improve material well-being, Schroeder also notes that the kitchens can reinforce the marginalization of women already on the fringes of their communities. Moreover, they rely on the volunteer labor of women already burdened with demanding work/family obligations, and their successful implementation is premised on the assumption that women's time is infinitely elastic.

Drawing upon her work with two pre-Hispanic communities in Xochimilco and Octopec, just outside Mexico City, Maria Elisa Christie (2006) specifically challenges the antikitchen refrain of Western feminism and questions the assumption that kitchens are a site of social isolation and oppression for women. Rather than representing a domestic jail in which women are secluded in the performance of unpaid and undervalued work, Christie explores women's control over *kitchenspace* (both indoor and outdoor spaces for food preparation), a space that younger men complain they are excluded from, except to be fed. In both these communities, women are historically recognized as playing an indispensable role in food preparation, particularly around the many fiestas and community celebrations that take place, and this provides women with a meaningful role in community life. Christie argues that the embodied knowing bound up in women's knowledge and practices concerning food has, contrary to how it is perceived in industrialized countries, "enhanced women's sense of their capacities as transforming agents, opening up spaces in which to reshape women's familial and societal position" (Matthee, cited in Christie 2006: 655). Importantly, Christie reminds us,

> As long as feminists look for women's participation and power in places where they are not, and ignore the less visible, accessible or 'desirable' places where they are, research is more likely to reflect our own ideological positions than the reality of women's lives and spaces around the world. (2006: 659)

"Democratizing" Food-Work in the Global North

Thus far, this essay has attempted to present an alternative view with which to challenge the idea that kitchens, and the activities that take place within them, serve only to reinforce particular gendered roles and responsibilities, through which "status is confirmed and exclusion practiced" (Floyd 2004: 62). In this next section, interest shifts back to the industrialized global North, where the demarcation of certain domestic activities as "masculine" and "feminine" has become blurred in recent years with the dismantling of the "standardized biographies" that once traced our progression through life (Giddens 1992). Sex, parenthood, and cohabitation have increasingly been uncoupled from marriage and more diverse family forms have emerged, resulting in an increase in the number of reconstituted families, solo living, and house-sharing (Smart and Neale 1999; Allan et al.

2011). In the United Kingdom, for example, the "nuclear" household with two parents and their dependent children living under the same roof is no longer statistically the norm and domestic roles have subsequently required reconceptualization (Jackson 2009). At the same time, however, individuals' engagement with physical and emotional spaces outside the home has facilitated a reconstitution of their relationship to activities that take place within it. Consequently, Debbie Kemmer (2000) has argued that not only should empirical research on food shift its lens from particular household types (such as the nuclear family with dependent children—see Murcott [1983b]; Charles and Kerr [1988]; DeVault [1991]), but that research agendas should move on from the gendered assumptions of the past, through which men have been excluded, thereby undermining their contribution to food-work and further reinforcing the identity of cooking as a feminine task.

Given that research in the United Kingdom (Sullivan 2000), the United States (Bianchi et al. 2000), and Australia (Baxter 2002) indicates that the gap between women's and men's contribution to cooking is the housework domain that has witnessed the greatest narrowing, it would seem that food-work has become a vehicle through which distributions of power have potentially become more diffuse and open to negotiation. In spite of men's increased participation in the kitchen, an explicit examination of cooking and feeding practices has been conspicuously absent in the burgeoning sociological literature on masculinities and men's shifting relationship with the domestic sphere (see, for example, Popay et al. 1998; McMahon 1999; Segal 2007; Gorman-Murray 2008). Although conventional ideas about what is and is not strictly "women's work" might be shifting (Swenson 2009), Alice Julier and Laura Lindenfeld (2005) highlight that there have been very few academic analyses of how ideologies surrounding women, men, and food are changing, and—until recently—there has been a "lack of research based on men's own accounts of involvement in 'food-work'" (Metcalfe et al. 2009: 95). Indeed, while some have focused on the stereotypically masculine environment of the commercial/professional kitchen, men's accounts of their

activities in domestic spaces have remained a neglected area. While the work undertaken by Alan Metcalfe and others (2009) moves on from those widely cited studies of domestic feeding noted above, the emphasis is on men who have fathering roles. Where, then, does that leave those men, of all ages, who are "womanless" (Coxon 1983) or do not, or no longer, have childcare responsibilities—gay men, students, singles, coupled but living alone, house-sharing, separated/divorced, widowed, or caring for elders or partners—who increasingly make up the male population? And how has their engagement with the kitchen shifted—if at all—with the advent of consumer-based living that has provided fertile ground wherein cooking has been reconstituted not only as a recreational, leisure activity (Roos et al. 2001; Holden 2005; Short 2006; Aarseth 2007; Swenson 2009; Cairns et al. 2010), but as a "cool," masculine lifestyle activity (Hollows 2003a: 230)? While the television has been particularly instrumental in invoking a sense of "masculine domesticity" that has given men a legitimate place at the stove (Swenson 2009: 47), what this might also have done is leave the kitchen feeling unfamiliar or unhomely for some women, particularly when the practices associated with professional kitchens are transferred into the domestic context. Have women therefore lost whatever power they had in the kitchen? And does men's participation in the kitchen render them "unmanly" as earlier studies implied (Charles and Kerr 1988; Cameron 1998)?

Some of these questions have begun to be addressed via empirical work undertaken in the United Kingdom by Angela Meah and Peter Jackson (2013). Where previous research on domestic food-work has been limited largely to interview data, questionnaires, and/or diaries, which rely on reports of what takes place and are then "used as proxy for studies of what actually *does*" happen (Murcott 2000: 78 [emphasis added]), Meah and Jackson report on data collected via a combination of qualitative and ethnographic methods, including life history interviews, provisioning "go-alongs" (Kusenbach 2003), and videoed kitchen tours and meal preparation. Of the twenty-three participants contributing to Meah and Jackson's multigenerational household study, seven were men, five of whom were observed in the kitchen. A significant departure from those studies that have focused on families with dependent children, household types represented in this research included retired couples where the husbands were the principal cooks, a lone male and an all-male house-share.

Findings from the study facilitate a more nuanced understanding of food-work undertaken within a socially and geographically specific area in the United Kingdom (South Yorkshire and North Derbyshire). The authors illustrate that conflict over food is not an experience entirely owned by women and can also be witnessed in households where there are no female occupants. For example, echoing Kristin Natalier's (2003) findings concerning the distribution of domestic responsibilities in all-male households, one participant complains about his housemates' failure to do their "fair-share" in keeping the kitchen clean: "I'm not your fucking dinner-bitch!" was his indignant response. In deferring kitchen responsibilities to him, this man's housemates also appear to reflect an assumption that some men "behave as though they were husbands even in the absence of women who might act as wives" (Natalier 2003: 265). In conditions where "everybody is doing masculinity, and masculinity is linked to dominance," Natalier asks, "is anyone oppressed?" (2003: 263). Ethnographic and observational work with this particular participant suggests that the answer is yes.

As Swenson notes, television has played an important role in reconstituting how cooking is perceived, the competitive approach of many programs in Australia, the United Kingdom, and the United States recasting food preparation as "sport," with chefs as "athletes" rather than "cooks" (2009: 36). Seen in this light, the kitchen is no longer women's "homely," feminized domestic space, but a "stadium" in which culinary battles are fought, with specialized knives, gadgets, and tools serving as equipment to aid "performance." In the same vein, Meah and Jackson use their observational work to compare how women and men set about preparing garlic. They report that men's displays took place amidst much "bashing" and engagement with pseudo-professional knife skills,

while women tended to be more understated in their performances. They note that women participants appeared to be discretely getting on with the everyday business of preparing a household meal, while male participants seemed to be engaged in culinary displays that exhibited their flair and skill. In one household, a retired woman expressed anxiety about her perceived lack of skill relative to that of her husband, whom she felt had taken cooking "to a much higher level," thereby raising awareness of her own skills deficit (cf. Short 2006).

A frequent claim made of men who engage in cooking is that they do so out of choice, rather than through a sense of duty and obligation (Swinbank 2002). This is confirmed by the retired male participants contributing to Meah and Jackson's study, who reverse the "server" and "provider" ideology (Kerr and Charles 1986) of the past, since it is their wives who continue to work outside the home while they engage with food as a hobby in retirement. However, they also report that it is a younger man, with a very young child, who most strongly reinforces claims that, where a woman is present, men continue to be selective in how they contribute to food-work. This man indicates that preparing food that a toddler will eat is simply not "challenging" enough, therefore leading him to defer responsibility for his three-year-old's meals to his partner: "in the first year or two years it was such basic cooking that it almost wasn't very interesting for me."

To some extent, the familiar albeit "oppressive" domain in which women have undertaken the routine business of feeding the family—begrudgingly or otherwise—has become one in which they can feel alienated and marginalized. Thus, as Avakian and Haber (2005) observe, women are not only engaged in a public struggle for equal power with men but have simultaneously lost influence in the private domain. Meah and Jackson provide a range of examples via which women have potentially been marginalized in "their" space as they have made room for men. At a basic level, this might be through the incorporation of items which are literally too heavy for women to lift easily. In other circumstances, conflict may ensue in designing a kitchen for both male and female users. A more common example, however, is the tension arising over the mess created during the process of men's culinary creativity. The authors consequently question whether—as with the advent of technologies intended to reduce women's domestic labor—the irony of men's increasing involvement in cooking is that it may simply create "more work for mother" (Cowan 1983).

Conclusion

This essay has sought to challenge conventional accounts of the relationship between gender and food. It has attempted to reconceptualize the relationship between women, men, and food in ways that not only account for the diversity of experience in those contexts in which women continue to be identified, or identify themselves, as "servers," but that also reflect the changing social and structural conditions that have enabled (or required) men to become more actively engaged in food-work. The essay has attempted to create a more nuanced account of the relationship between gender and food, through which distributions of power are more diffuse and more complex, than those presented in more conventional or culturally myopic analyses. Following Christie (2006), the essay has aimed both to make visible the spaces and activities through which minority women and those in the global South experience autonomy and power, and express creativity and resistance, and also to look for and make visible the presence of men who may also experience conflict, struggle, power, praise, and frustration.

See also cooking, kitchens, pleasure, sex.

Angela Meah

GOURMET

Originally referring to the refined taste of French wine brokers and later extended to other aspects of haute cuisine, the word "gourmet" often now has a somewhat pejorative connotation, denoting a snobbish obsession with French cuisine (Trubek 2000). Any person who enjoys the pleasures of fine food and luxury dining can be described

as a gourmet, while the word can also be used adjectivally to describe particular kinds of food or eating establishments. The idea of gourmet food seems to have emerged in the context of the first restaurant guides such as the *Almanach des Gourmands* that appeared in Paris in the early nineteenth century, beginning an association between food and the media, further marked by the launch of *Gourmet* magazine in 1941 and later associated with the rise of the "celebrity chef." Indeed, Julia Child's book *Mastering the Art of French Cooking,* which introduced American readers to French gourmet food, spawned one of the first such TV shows, *The French Chef,* originally broadcast in 1962.

While it is now distinguished from related words such as "gourmand," referring to people who are devoted to eating excessive quantities of rich food, gourmet retains some of its moralizing undertones, as implied in the term "gourmandize," referring to the unrestrained enjoyment of good food. Compared to the excessive appetites of the gourmand, however, or the undisciplined consumption of the glutton, gourmet food tends to emphasize smaller quantities of high-quality food, exquisitely prepared, as in the case of nouvelle cuisine, for example.

Stephen Mennell (1985) provides a masterful account of the emergence of gastronomy in eighteenth- and nineteenth-century France, associated with pioneering figures such as Alexandre-Balthazar-Laurent Grimod de la Reynière (1758–1838) and Jean Anthelme Brillat-Savarin (1755–1826). In Mennell's account, gastronomy was as much literary as a culinary accomplishment, as illustrated by the Michelin guides in France and the *Good Food Guide* in the United Kingdom, providing further evidence of the double orality of food (taste and talk).

The reverence for French cuisine (described by some in terms of "sacralization") has been challenged by the increasing popularity of food from other countries and different national traditions as, for example, in the rise of "foodie" culture in the United States. According to Josée Johnston and Shyon Baumann, the word "foodie" can be applied to anyone with a special interest in food, lending itself not just to an interest in what people eat but "how foodies talk about food, write about food, use food in public culture, and how food operates as a source of status and distinction" (2010: 31). Particularly in the American context, Johnston and Baumann talk about the democratization of gourmet food as a range of other influences began to challenge the dominance of French culinary culture. Among these factors, they note the impact of Elizabeth David's (1950) celebration of Mediterranean food, promoting the art of everyday "peasant" cooking and introducing new flavors and ingredients to British readers following the austerity of wartime rationing, and the rise of the American "counter-culture" that, as Warren Belasco (1989) has shown, first took on and was then rapidly appropriated by the mainstream food industry. The diversification of food cultures in the United States challenged the hegemony of French food, with the celebration of various ethnic and regional cuisines (such as Creole and Cajun as well as Italian, Chinese, Thai, and Mexican food). Foodies and other "culinary adventurers" (Heldke 2003) were quick to take up these "exotic" foods as a mark of their cultural distinction and social capital, with critics noting how "foodie" culture in the United States remains exclusive, affluent, and white (Dickinson in press).

Johnston and Baumann (2007) show how the twin themes of democracy and distinction can be applied to the history of gourmet food writing. These tendencies also apply to other aspects of contemporary food culture such as the rise of so-called gourmet coffee and ice cream, popularized by franchises such as Starbucks and brands like Häagen-Dazs. A similar process has occurred in the United Kingdom, with celebrity chefs such as Jamie Oliver repudiating the authority of haute cuisine in favor of a more simple style of cooking, stripped down to the bare essentials, as recognized in the title of his first book and TV series, *The Naked Chef* (2000). Jamie Oliver's cooking was "naked" in the sense that it was a stripped down version of restaurant cooking, avoiding the social pretensions of the professional chef or gourmet (described by Oliver as "poncey") and relying on the "bare essentials" of the kitchen larder. Oliver outlines his approach to cooking as being "for normal people who want short cuts and tips ... It's for anyone who is interested in cooking tasty, gutsy, simple, commonsense food

and having a right good laugh at the same time" (2000: 11). While Jamie Oliver's approach is, in some respects, the antithesis of the professional chef, his work is often criticized for celebrating the pleasures of cooking while denying the labor involved. What might seem like a democratization and demystification of cooking—refusing to privilege the world of haute cuisine and the authority of the professional chef—nonetheless assumes a privileged position, located within the domestic space of the kitchen but not defined by its routine demands and responsibilities (cf. Hollows 2003a). In this respect, then, celebrity chefs like Jamie Oliver represent a modern version of the classic conundrum of the gourmet, whereby the enjoyment of cooking and the pleasures of food seem inescapably caught up in social distinctions of class and taste.

See also celebrity chefs, exotic, pleasure, taste.

Peter Jackson

GOVERNANCE

Governance is frequently distinguished from government, the latter referring to the power and rule of the state, the former to the regulatory role of various state and nonstate mechanisms (see, for example, Jessop 1995; Stoker 1998). A shift from government to governance has frequently been associated with the rise of neoliberalism as is the case with food where a "new architecture" of food governance has been identified (Lang et al. 2009), associated with the rise of all kinds of nongovernmental structures and processes. As Tim Lang and others maintain:

> Governance implies more indirect, softer forms of direction from the state than command and control, and reflects collaborative outcomes, involving a wide range of actors often from the private sector, as well as from government bureaucracy, as much as deliberate interventions by the state. (2009: 75)

Food governance is a fine example of these tendencies, illustrating the increasing role of the private sector in setting industry-wide standards and policies which, while voluntary in terms of their legal status, frequently exert considerable power along the supply chain, often working to the benefit of larger producers and to the detriment of smaller ones.

Food governance is particularly problematic because of the way food-related issues crosscut conventional boundaries of government. In England and Wales, for example, the regulation of agricultural production and the maintenance of environmental standards is the concern of the Department for Environment, Farming and Rural Affairs; the promotion of "healthy eating" is a matter for the Department of Health; the regulation of food safety is overseen by the Food Standards Agency; and the promotion of an economically efficient agri-food sector is the concern of the Department for Business, Innovation and Skills. Different arrangements apply in Scotland and Northern Ireland, indicating the significance of multilevel governance within the United Kingdom, further complicated by international-level, European-wide, and local jurisdictions for other food-related concerns such as the Global Agreement on Tariffs and Trade (GATT), the EU's Common Agricultural Policy, and environmental health inspections, which operate at Local Authority level. This "variable geometry of governance" (Barling et al. 2002) has evolved from the interplay of competing political interests as well as in response to specific food and farming crises such as the BSE epidemic, which led to the breakup of the former Ministry of Agriculture, Fisheries and Food.

These multiple, sometimes competing, layers of government have been further complicated by the involvement of a range of nongovernmental actors. In part, this is a response to the restructuring of the global food industry, where longer supply chains regularly cross national boundaries and where food retailing has become increasingly concentrated in a relatively small number of large corporations (including the major supermarket chains). As neoliberalism has called for a rolling-back of state regulation, its place has been taken by new forms of governance, often including and sometimes led by these key corporate players. Moving into the spaces vacated by the withdrawal of the state, the

major supermarket chains have developed their own "voluntary" initiatives to ensure the quality and reliability of food supplies, committing their suppliers to a specified set of standards. While voluntary in theory, however, the imposition of standards and certifications has led to a marginalization of small farmers and retailers who cannot afford to pay the costs of market entry, exacerbating social inequalities across the global marketplace (cf. Busch 2000). This has led critics such as Doris Fuchs and others (2011) to question the democratic legitimacy of private food governance initiatives in terms of their participation, transparency, and accountability. Similarly, Emelie Peine and Philip McMichael have criticized the turn to governance for its close associations with the process of globalization, arguing, "The historical context for this extended meaning of governance is the deterritorialization of space, through the deepening of market relations" (Peine and McMichael 2005: 19).

The number of such governance initiatives is increasingly rapidly with Fuchs and others (2011) listing the following prominent examples: the British Retail Consortium's Global Standard for Food Safety; the International Food Standard (led by a federation of food retailers); Safe Quality Food (owned by the Food Marketing Institute); the Global Food Safety Initiative (led by a group of international retailers); the Global Partnership for Good Agricultural Practice (GlobalGAP, known as EurepGAP until 2007); the Marine Stewardship Council; and the Ethical Trading Initiative (formed by a group of UK trade unions with the participation of numerous charities and high-street retailers). While such initiatives can have positive effects in terms of increased food quality and safety, pushing up environmental standards, and improving labor conditions, these benefits are by no means certain and can have an adverse impact in terms of public accountability and democratic legitimacy.

New systems of governance have also emerged from the development of new trading blocs and international institutions. Richard Lee (2009) examines the case of the *Codex Alimentarius*, an intergovernmental organization jointly administered by the UN Food and Agricultural Organization and the World Health Organization (WHO). Lee argues that the formal partners to the *Codex* are involved in the negotiation and settlement of international food standards, which are referenced by the WTO, giving them a quasilegal status in regulatory terms. He also shows how a range of nongovernmental agents are involved in the *Codex* deliberations, focusing particularly on the contested role of scientific expertise in the process of policy-making.

Based on his analysis of the agri-food sector in New Zealand, which has experienced two decades of neoliberal reforms, Richard Le Heron (2003) demonstrates the emergence of new corporatist and managerial dimensions in contemporary food governance. Examples include the systematic introduction of private standards in different food commodity chains, a drive to improve contract arrangements between farmers and agribusiness, the reworking of biosecurity regulations, new forms of regulation to meet environmental risks, and the establishment of a Royal Commission to investigate the impact of genetic modification. Many of these initiatives work through the arenas of audit, contract, ethics, and policy involving calculative practices such as benchmarking, best-practice, and harmonization, which, Le Heron argues, reassemble the state in various guises in order to enable New Zealand agri-food businesses to participate more effectively in the globalizing world food system.

Also focusing on New Zealand, Hugh Campbell (2005) examines the impact of a specific form of international food governance (EurepGAP). Implemented by an alliance of European food retailers, NGOs, producer organizations, consumer groups, agri-industry representatives, and scientists, EurepGAP comprises a system for auditing food safety and agricultural sustainability aimed at ensuring good agricultural practice among fruit and vegetable suppliers to the European market. While it is virtually invisible to European consumers, Campbell argues, EurepGAP's audit process has a series of unintended consequences for food producers in other parts of the world, including New Zealand, which, through its monopolizing tendencies, Campbell likens to the reinvention or reinscription of colonial food relations.

Susanne Freiberg's (2004) work on French beans and food scares shows how different governance regimes in France and Britain impact differentially on producers in Burkina Faso and Zambia, while Qian Gong and Peter Jackson (2012) examine the impact of the infant formula scandal of 2008 on the reform of food safety regulation in China, as well as its impact on consumer confidence and parenting practices.

Food governance issues are also relevant outside the commercial mainstream, applying to so-called alternative food initiatives including organic, local, and ethical forms of production. The regulation of such schemes frequently relies on nonstate actors both in terms of certification and enforcement. The key questions then become who is included and excluded from such processes and what inequalities are created as a result (Higgins et al. 2008). Here, too, as in the conventional sector where schemes like HACCP (Hazard Analysis and Critical Control Points) are now widely applied, there is a growing penetration of private rules, conventions, and market forms of regulation. Frequently relying on various kinds of labeling to protect their "alternative" status and/or to secure a premium price, Julie Guthman (2007: 457) argues that such schemes often end up conceding the market as the locus of regulation and may even have the paradoxical effect of creating markets where none existed before.

Summarizing the current state of play surrounding food governance, Terry Marsden argues:

> It is clear that, through the haze of food scares, the emergence of alternative food networks and the public anxieties surrounding GMOs ... there is a significant shift in those agencies and actors who wish to have a say and stake in the new food politics and governance systems. (2000: 27)

Yet it is also clear that these privately regulated systems of food governance are increasingly dominated by retail capital.

See also labeling, safety.

Richard Lee

H

Hunger © Angela Meah.

HUNGER AND FAMINE

Though famine has a very particular meaning, the related idea of hunger can be used in both a physiological and a metaphorical sense. Hinting at its complexity and relativity, hunger can refer to a physical lack of food, whether in terms of quantity or quality, and to a more general sense of desire or yearning (when we hunger for something or someone). Though often used interchangeably, words like hunger, famine, starvation, malnutrition, and malnourishment all have specific meanings whose precise definition is freighted with political implications.

Hunger can, of course, be applied to a whole range of circumstances, from a chronic condition of near-starvation to the much less urgent dietary needs of those of us whose next meal is only a few hours or minutes away. According to the latter definition, we may all experience hunger several times a day while, on a different timescale, UK gardeners are prone to speak of a "hungry gap" each spring when there is a shortage of fresh produce to eat. Hunger clearly varies in intensity and its form is radically different in different times and places. Hunger is conventionally divided into its chronic form (which currently affects over one billion people worldwide who regularly suffer from an insufficient diet) and its acute form (which receives more media attention and is frequently described in crisis terms). Globally, patterns of hunger and malnutrition are dynamic and show substantial seasonal and annual shifts. While the majority of hungry people live in Asia (where China, India, Pakistan, and Bangladesh account for the highest absolute numbers of chronically malnourished people), hunger is also extremely widespread in sub-Saharan Africa (where, according to Young [2010: 62], its incidence exceeds 35 percent of the population in fifteen countries).

Famine is a more specific condition, its onset subject to official definition, signaling the transition from a "humanitarian emergency" to a "humanitarian catastrophe" in terms of the language used by the United Nations. The UN definition of famine is confined to circumstances in which at least 20 percent of households face extreme food shortages, acute malnutrition is experienced by over 30 percent of people, 2 deaths per 10,000 people occur each day, and people have access to less than 4 liters of water and 2,100 calories of food per day. So, for example, almost a million Ethiopians are thought to have starved to death during the 1984 famine in the Horn of Africa despite a large-scale mobilization of government aid and charitable donations. That such events are highly politicized is demonstrated by the fact that the U.S. Treasury withheld food aid when famine was declared again in Africa in 2011 because of fears that such donations might "materially benefit" terrorist organizations (*Daily Telegraph* 2011b).

While the immediate and underlying causes of famine are much disputed, Frances Moore Lappé and others (1998) do an excellent job of challenging many of the "myths" surrounding conventional explanations of world hunger. They challenge the view that there is simply not enough food to go around. They dispute the argument that famines result from natural causes, like droughts and floods, that are beyond human control. They critique the assumption that hunger results from a simple imbalance between population growth and finite resources leading to "too many mouths to feed." They pose an alternative to the stark choice between feeding the hungry and protecting the environment, challenging the view that technological innovations such as a second Green Revolution will provide a once-and-for-all solution to world hunger. They question whether social justice and increased agricultural productivity are inevitably in tension, doubting whether market mechanisms or "free trade" can be relied upon to resolve the hunger problem. They champion the ability of poor people to bring about social change and question whether increased foreign aid is a panacea for world hunger. They challenge the view that the prosperity of the global North depends on its ability to import cheap goods from the global South ("we benefit from their hunger"), and they question whether ending hunger can only be achieved by curtailing people's civil liberties, concluding that hunger is a result of powerlessness and a lack of effective democratic rights.

Indeed, many have argued that the incidence of hunger corresponds to a lack of political power, resulting from institutional failure and a lack of democratic accountability rather than from a lack of overall food resources. Such accounts emphasize the political economy of hunger (Drèze and Sen 1991) rather than accepting the argument that hunger results from environmental causes or other natural disasters (that may exacerbate existing conditions but that are not in themselves a sufficient explanation for its occurrence). Writing in this tradition, Nobel prize-winning economist Amartya Sen has argued that famine results not from a general lack of food but from people's differential accessibility to vital resources and restrictions on the capability of the most impoverished to feed themselves (Sen 1981). Sen helped (re)define the question of food security by focussing on issues of food sovereignty, defined as the right of peoples to healthy and culturally appropriate food, produced through ecologically sound and sustainable methods, and the right to define their own food and agriculture systems (Food Sovereignty 2011).

The political economy of hunger has also been emphasized in many accounts of specific famines. The Great Famine in Ireland, which caused the death of over a million people between 1845 and 1849 and led to another 1.5 million to emigrate to the United States, is often explained as a natural disaster caused by an epidemic of potato blight. But it must also be acknowledged that Ireland was a net exporter of food throughout these years and that potato crops were devastated elsewhere in Europe without having such catastrophic effects. As one observer wrote to the British prime minister in 1846:

> For 46 years the people of Ireland have been feeding those of England with the choicest produce of their agriculture and pasture, and while they thus exported their wheat and their beef in profusion, their own food gradually deteriorated ... until the mass of the peasantry was exclusively thrown on the potato. (John Hale, letter to Lord Russell, cited in Woodham Smith 1962)

Similar arguments can be applied elsewhere in the British Empire as explored in Michael Watts's (1983) account of the "silent violence" affecting northern Nigeria, where colonial capitalism exacerbated the famine conditions experienced in nineteenth-century Hausaland, undermining the moral economy of the peasantry and making them more vulnerable to famine throughout the twentieth century.

It cannot also escape notice that the world is currently experiencing conditions of widespread "over-nutrition" in the global North, commonly referred to as an obesity epidemic, at the same time that it continues to experience chronic "under-nutrition" in many parts of the global South. So, for example, Brian Halweil and Lester Gardiner (2000) refer to the current global situation as simultaneously "underfed and overfed," while Raj Patel (2007) refers more starkly to the world being both "stuffed and starved." The vulnerability of the global economy to sudden shocks, which can have catastrophic effects in terms of exacerbating world hunger, was highlighted by the 2007–08 spike in agricultural commodity prices, which resulted in an additional 75 million people being pushed into conditions of severe hunger worldwide (FAO 2008), causing UN secretary general Ban Ki-Moon to declare that the world was facing the worst food crisis in a generation (*The Guardian* 2008).

Hunger and famine are terms used both to describe current global inequalities and as analytical terms invoked to explain those conditions. Both words are deployed within academic social science and by those who campaign for social change. It is no surprise, then, that their use is so deeply contested and highly charged. The relationship between the science and politics of food is starkly revealed in Dana Simmons's (2008) account of the transition in "starvation science" from the colonies to the metropole as a medicalized interest in starvation and death morphed into a population science interested in nutrition. Hunger has also been used as a political weapon as in Mahatma Gandhi's twenty-one-day hunger strike in protest against the British authorities in India during the 1930s and the republican hunger strikes during the Troubles in Northern Ireland in the 1980s. Meanwhile, the symbolic appropriation of hunger can be illustrated in numerous ways from the Hungry Generation, a literary movement in 1960s Calcutta, to the feeding of "emotional hunger" described by those experiencing eating disorders such as anorexia.

See also appetite, eating, moral economy, nutrition, security.

Peter Jackson

Innovation © Angela Meah.

INNOVATION

The ubiquity of innovation as a mantra for the betterment of economic and social conditions suggests that to innovate is to do great things. Being innovative with food, however, is not always so welcome.

An indication of this skepticism toward commercial innovation can be found in a study across six European countries by Luis Guerrero and others (2009), who examined consumer responses toward innovation and changes to traditional food products. Interestingly, they comment on the difficulty of talking about innovation owing to it being an abstract concept. For consumers in this study, innovation invoked notions of novelty, variety, processing and technology, origin and ethnicity, and convenience. The innovations that met with the most approval involved novel forms of packaging and did not alter the (traditional) foodstuff contained within. Changes to the sensory properties of foods were less popular, with innovations involving flavor and taste regarded as undermining the properties of traditional products.

A focused treatment of approaches to food innovation and consumers has been undertaken by Klaus Grunert and others (2008). It is worth unpacking their approach and argument, as they consider a range of relevant research trajectories. Their focus is upon "user-driven" innovation, which they define as "a process towards the development of a new product or service in which an integrated analysis and understanding of the users" wants, needs and preference formation play a key role." (2008: 590). Such an orientation is not new; as they note, contemporary articulations of fork-to-farm emphasize the primacy of consumers. Likewise, reverse food chain thinking has become established as a policy concept (Wolf 2002). In paying attention to the development of food products, Grunert and others (2008) suggest that three main research streams are involved in analyzing and producing user-driven innovation: understanding user preferences, innovation management, and interactive innovation. However, the relevance of these streams is related to the type of innovation being undertaken and the

level of engagement with mass markets. They also identify three types of food innovation: in-house food processing (arm's length from users) and retailer-led and whole chain innovation (including primary production).

Understanding *user preferences* is regarded as necessary for innovation in mass markets, which involve minimal personal interaction between consumers and company employees tasked with innovating products. Grunert and colleagues (2008) argue that articulations of latent needs and the formation of preferences are important to establishing user preferences, in particular through quality perception. They juxtapose individual, psychological perspectives with "contextual factors," involving practices of daily life such as the family meal. While advanced methodologies have been developed to explore (and construct) food preferences, innovation proceeding on this basis is characterized as incremental innovation.

Under the *innovation management* research stream, the authors suggest that a "proactive market orientation" or a "learning orientation" is advocated to encourage more radical forms of innovation. Whole chain forms of innovation are regarded as being typical of this learning orientation, as new developments in one area of primary production and manufacturing are integrated upstream and/or downstream. "Cross-functional" teams are viewed as important groups in this process, operating across traditional boundaries of expertise.

The third stream of research identified by Grunert and others involves *interactive innovation*. Interactive innovation can involve collaboration between companies, and the authors suggest, "When a manufacturer develops new products in close cooperation with an industrial customer we may still call this user-oriented innovation due to the fact that the user's needs play a key role" (2008: 597). The heterogeneity of consumer demands, they argue, has required cooperation across supply chains and an associated reliance upon knowledge sharing and trust. They also recognize that innovation is conducted through networks. Among various approaches to innovation networks they note the relevance of actor-network theory to innovation, suggesting that this perspective has not yet been widely applied to the food sector.

There are, however, other treatments of interactive innovation. The association between innovation and food has been considered by Kevin Morgan and Jonathan Murdoch (2000) and Gilles Allaire and Steven Wolf (2004). The former examine the distribution of knowledge in networks and the implications for innovation, suggesting that the agri-food sector is rarely considered as an "innovative" area of economic activity. They state:

> The major innovations in production, processing and retailing that have so changed the food sector almost beyond recognition in the post war period have largely been ignored by those concerned with the knowledge-based economy. (Morgan and Murdoch 2000: 162)

For Allaire and Wolf, agri-food innovation is defined as the "knowledge creation underlying the introduction and diffusion of food products" (2004: 432) and they consider the coherence and diffusion of information structures associated with innovation paradigms. They note:

> It appears that the separation between conception of technologies and production, which was the essential engine of agricultural productivism within a linear model of innovation, has been replaced by a more recursive process of innovation in which production is adapted to markets through continuous strategies of differentiation. (2004: 434)

For both sets of authors, it is the relationship between innovation, forms of agricultural production, and other domains of the food sector that is of particular interest. These connections have been appreciated by other specialists, and in the early 1980s UK agricultural economists were emphasizing the importance of such change across the agri-food sector, with Jim Burns suggesting: "Production of food does not just take place on farms, and there is an important need to view the whole chain, and understand the nature of the elements and connections in order to appreciate the total impact of economic and technical change, and of policy decisions" (Burns 1983: 16).

Morgan and Murdoch suggest that the routines of particular forms of agricultural production are located within the institutionalization of recognizable knowledge practices. In the case studies they present, these knowledge practices are not institutionalized on an internal basis within agriculture but instead evolve through distinctive networks typical of "conventional" and "organic" UK agriculture (which they acknowledge to be stylized categories or Weberian ideal types). In particular, they focus upon "localized" and "standardized" knowledge within networks, suggesting that conventional agricultural innovation networks emerged through the transfer of knowledge and competency to input supply companies and their agents.

In a similar way, Allaire and Wolf (2004) discuss an approach to food innovation that regards the decomposition of materials (knowing more about biochemical processes) and information (knowing what customers want to buy) as a desirable step, to be followed by recomposition and the construction of new products. They term this a "logic of decomposition" approach and contrast it with a "logic of identity" approach to innovation. The logic of identity turns on the information structures dealing with the translation of local resources into distinctive food products which are then subject to identification and marketing procedures and give rise to a diffusion of products imbued with local/regional identities.

In sum, both these papers set out to understand the innovation processes at work across mainstream and niche areas of the agri-food sector, in line with increasing attention to the "quality-turn" in food (Goodman 2003, 2004). Similarly, Roberta Sonnino and Terry Marsden (2006) have discussed alternative food networks as innovations, an identification that draws attention to the social and material processes comprising innovation.

Given the recognition of networks of innovation across the food sector, it is possible to locate analyses from a variety of starting points. Alison Blay-Palmer and Betsy Donald (2006) have examined innovation through the lens of small, medium, and multinational food manufacturing companies with operations in Toronto. Focusing upon three companies with diverse characteristics and that are involved in the production of a variety of products, they note how a multinational firm became locked into incremental product innovation based upon small changes to ingredient composition for mass-market foods. For their small- and medium-sized case-study firms, a different focus was evident, comprising an emphasis on diverse and exotic foods, and working to ensure products were associated with desirable qualities. The authors suggest that for large, branch-plant companies the setting of regulations and standards is an important area for influencing innovation, while smaller firms focus their efforts upon sourcing and niche-market development.

The relationship between standards and innovation in food has been examined from other perspectives. Alessandro Stanziani (2007) has taken forward the notion that innovation in food might come to be defined as undesirable through definitions to be found in standards in an analysis of the wine, butter, and milk markets of late-nineteenth- and early twentieth–century France. In particular, he considers how some innovations came to be considered as adulteration, carrying the negative connotations of fraud and poisoning. Importantly, the characterization of a food as "luxury" or "basic" is the outcome of institutional processes that result in the stabilization of acceptable and unacceptable forms of innovation.

The acceptability of innovations in food—as defined within standards—is an outcome of negotiation over knowledge claims. Richard Lee (2012) examines two case studies of standard-setting that have implications for food innovation, one involving the agreement of a definition for dietary fiber in the *Codex Alimentarius* Commission, the other an examination of efforts by the UK government to implement reductions in the saturated fat content of foods through voluntary guidelines. In comparing these two cases, Lee suggests:

> Although governance techniques have an impact on the form innovation takes, often these techniques operate on the basis of knowledge claims that have been produced according to controversial histories and have been deployed in the

production of particular food products. The two case studies demonstrate that knowledge claims are active constituents of the governance process and that the closure and stabilization of a controversy is related to the means by which interested groups can negotiate complex issues through a governance technique. (2012: 88)

Paying close attention to the material properties of food and the role they play in steering innovation is regarded as an important analytical orientation *and* as a means of exciting interest from those groups (such as food scientists and technologists) engaged in innovation.

Of course, the style of enquiry discussed above is not the only one. In a study of the Danish agri-food industry, Kostas Karantininis and others suggest that innovation "is the commercialization of an innovative idea" (2010: 112). Specifically, they examine the role firm organization and vertical integration (the incorporation of different economic activities into one firm) play in innovation, concluding that both have a significant influence. They acknowledge that the history of organizational analyses of innovation originates in the work of Joseph Schumpeter (1943). For Schumpeter, sectors of economic activity can never remain stationary as

> the fundamental impulse that sets and keeps the capitalist engine in motion comes from the new consumers' goods, the new methods of production or transportation, the new markets, the new forms of industrial organization that capitalist enterprise creates. (1943: 83)

In another econometric analysis also citing Schumpeter, Christoph Weiss and Antje Wittkopp (2005) examine the influence of retailer market power upon innovation in food manufacturing, suggesting that innovations pose a much greater challenge to firms than competitive pricing policies implemented for existing products. They assert that retailer buying power limits innovation in food manufacture. From a different perspective, Gernot Grabher and others (2008) have discussed "co-development" practices involving iterative producer-customer relationships. They assert that too much emphasis has been placed upon innovation occurring in sites of production, with too little regard for the mediation of innovation by consumers. The co-development approach is said to differ from previous inductive (bespoke development for an individual customer) and deductive (market research) interpretations by focusing on the interactions between producer groups, customer groups, and others in the ongoing development of products. They note the example of the Consumer Channel of Kraft Foods in developing consumer communities, though from a UK perspective the commercial actions of this U.S. firm have not necessarily fostered a community dialogue (BBC 2011).

Within some food commodity chains, the quest for innovation has assumed an influential position. In an account of the governance of trade in fresh vegetables between the United Kingdom and Africa, Catherine Dolan and John Humphrey suggest:

> Innovation has become a key source of power and security in the supply chain. Suppliers who assume responsibility for product and packaging innovation greatly increase their value to the supermarkets and minimize their risk of substitution. (2001: 164)

While, in their study, innovation is undertaken in collaboration between UK supermarkets and African-based exporters, the failure of an innovation is a greater burden for exporters. The result is a concentration of innovation among those who can accept the risks, further restricting the market. A similar process occurs for the growers of vegetables, with the distribution of innovation processes influenced by the size of enterprise. However,

attempting to adopt innovative processes may not be in the interest of small- and medium-sized enterprises if quality can be established on a different basis.

In focusing on innovations within the agri-food system, one should not neglect the role of consumers in shaping technological developments, whether through the way such innovations are appropriated and deployed in the home or in the way that domestic innovations shape commercial systems of provision. Innovations in refrigeration exemplify these complex interactions, as explored by Elizabeth Shove and Dale Southerton (2000). Innovation, therefore, remains a subject for debate and a topic for analysis, especially when conceived of as a domain where the material and the social interact, or are "mangled," to use Andrew Pickering's (1995) concept. Rather than speaking of innovation in generalities or marketing mantras, the specific characteristics of the changes brought about by innovation should be explored and explained. It is easy to be carried away by the possibilities of innovation and Mary Earle (1997) ends a measured article on food innovation by suggesting:

> The greatest innovation will be the development of new food sub-systems within an integrated global food system. There is the opportunity to create a global food system that will provide adequate food for all, without causing the diseases of excess. (1997: 175)

While the ethical concerns of this vision can hardly be denounced, a more fully integrated global food system may not be such a plausible or desirable outcome.

See also safety, science, technologies.

Richard Lee

K

Kitchens © Angela Meah.

KITCHENS

According to Terence Conran, "The kitchen mirrors more effectively than any other room in the house the great social changes that have taken place in the last hundred years" (1977: 1). The kitchen is often identified as the domestic space in which "home" is most strongly located. It is also a space where household gender relations are played out, producing and reproducing gender-based subjectivities. As with any other space, the home itself has come to be regarded as deeply contested, not least since it is a principal source of self-identity for both men and women (Munro and Madigan 1999; Blunt and Dowling 2006). Not surprisingly perhaps, feminist scholarship undertaken in the 1960s and 1970s drew attention to the condition of the "captive wives" and "housebound mothers" (Gavron 1966) who would never realize their full potential until they shrugged off the shackles of domestic oppression (Friedan 1963; Gavron 1966; Greer 1970; Oakley 1974). For these scholars and many who followed, rather than providing a "haven in a heartless world," the family home could also be represented as "the locus of oppression, ranging from the frustration of women who find themselves tied to a narrow domestic role, to those who are victims of sustained violence" (Munro and Madigan 1999: 108). Seen from this perspective, the kitchen emerges as a key site in which power is deployed within the home. Conversely, however, revisionist histories of the kitchen that have emerged from the global South, and also second wave feminists commenting on the experiences of migrant populations in the United States (see for example, Avakian 1997; Barolini 1997; Hughes 1997; Wade-Gayles 1997; Abarca 2006), have provided insights into the potential of the kitchen to afford women power that they may be unable to access in other domains. This essay will explore how kitchens have been conceptualized in both academic and popular understandings within and *outside* of the Anglo-American tradition, examining how power is distributed within the spatial dynamics of the kitchen, along with the shifting gendered subjectivities afforded by individuals' changing relationship with this domestic space over the last century.

A Brief History of the Modern Kitchen: Designing Kitchens, Designing Women

The domestic kitchen has become identified as a space of routine and ritual, one that both inscribes and reinforces particular gendered roles and responsibilities and one in which "status is confirmed and exclusion practiced" (Floyd 2004: 62). Indeed, it has been argued that the kitchen represents an arena in which "First and Third World inequalities are 'brought home,' a recess repellent to middle-class woman and domestic worker alike" (Floyd 2004: 62). But the history of the modern, fitted kitchen and women's relationship to it is, as June Freeman (2004) illustrates, a complicated one. Its origins lie in the United States, with Catherine Beecher's (1869) early visions of the "principles of domestic science" and "good kitchen management" which, ironically, she saw as taking place within, and structured by, a religious moral framework (cited in Freeman 2004: 27–28). However, it would be another fifty years before American journalist Christine Fredericks would pick up the mantle of scientific management and, equipped with evidence from her own time-and-motion experiments, would use it to call for the professionalization of housework. However, since Fredericks remained "politically superficial," Freeman argues that her ideas were never adopted as part of any feminist campaign for the liberation of women from the perceived oppression of the kitchen, and were—conversely—vulnerable to conservative appropriation (2004: 100). Indeed, criticisms of the kitchen as a locus of oppression challenged the "industrialization" of the domestic kitchen on the basis that it was a site of production, in which women became "workers." However, while these criticisms originate with socialist feminists during the 1960s, feminist utopians in the United States had called for "kitchenless" houses, characterized by the "socialization of domestic work," as early as the mid-nineteenth century (Hayden 1978: 275).

And following the First World War, the movement to transform domestic kitchen spaces accelerated with women architects and designers at the forefront of efforts to improve efficiency and rationalize the design of kitchens in both the United States and United Kingdom (see Hayden 1978; Llewellyn 2004).

It is perhaps no surprise that the demand for greater domestic efficiency coincided with economic depression "which caused educated women to become their own cooks and housemaids" (Peel 1933: 125). The kitchen, and associated activities, was no longer the exclusive domain of working-class women employed as cooks and maids and relegated to the rear of the house beyond public view; it was, therefore, in middle-class women's interests to create a space that was less isolated, more accessible, and more efficient. Here, as elsewhere, more work is needed to distinguish the experience of different groups of women, which varied significantly by social class.

A number of scholars, reporting on differing contexts, have commented on kitchen design in the years following the First World War and up to 1960, a period characterized by a drive toward nation-building, with domesticity core to this objective (Lloyd and Johnson 2004: 254). Mark Llewellyn (2004), for example, discusses the British kitchens designed by Elizabeth Denby and Jane Drew between 1917 and 1946; Kirsi Saarikangas (2006) focuses on the modern kitchen in Finland between the 1930s and 1950s, while Justine Lloyd and Lesley Johnson (2004) are concerned with Australian kitchens between 1940 and 1960. Each author highlights the emphasis placed on functionality and how this was translated in practical terms. Although the domestic would remain unchallenged as women's domain, the application of time-and-motion principles, the prioritization of the working triangle (see Johnson 2006 for variations on this), and masculinist values—namely those associated with industrialization—infiltrated the way in which kitchens were designed. Llewellyn points out that Elizabeth Denby, for example, envisaged

> an efficient worker-housewife, whose role in the kitchen was paralleled with that of

the factory worker. Her routinized tasks and ruthlessly efficient working space left no room for feminine qualities of nurture and care…The scientific management of this space had created a value-free laboratory wherein women were masculinized. (2004: 53)

This theme is echoed in Saarikangas's observations of the Finnish case, where

> the repetitive and monotonous model of factory work performed alone on the assembly line was transferred to the modern kitchen. With superfluous movements reduced, household work could be performed standing in one place. (2006: 164)

Given the reassignment of housework to now servantless women, this period also witnessed a relocation of the kitchen from the margins of the household to a more central location within it, albeit still closeted from other spaces in the house. Saarikangas depicts early modern Finnish kitchens as tiny spaces within which was confined the messy business of "sanitary labour" along with the person who performed it (2006: 165). This, however, would give way to more open designs, which facilitated greater fluidity between the kitchen, eating, and leisure spaces. But in opening up kitchens and putting housework on show, this spatial openness also increased the pressure on women to achieve and maintain particular standards of hygiene and cleanliness. Moreover, the creation of more open-plan spaces also transformed kitchens into a panoptican-like space (Johnson 2006: 128), enabling mothers to keep an eye on the children while preparing a meal but, as Llewellyn observes, further reinforcing women's feminine subjectivity as mothers and, therefore, principally responsible for childcare. Thus, the kitchen is not only designed *for* women but also serves to *design* women themselves.

Writing in the United Kingdom, Daniel Miller (1988) notes how different households in London actively appropriate and transform the standardized space of the domestic kitchen in radically different ways. Starting with the identical interior space and kitchen design provided for them by the state, former council tenants eagerly seized the opportunity to redesign their kitchens as soon as they were able to buy their homes from the local authority in the 1980s. Susie Reid (2002) provides similar evidence from the former Soviet Union of the "de-Stalinization" of consumer taste in kitchens and other domestic spaces during the Khrushchev era as the Cold War began to thaw.

Saarikangas observes that while minimalistic, laboratory-like designs lent themselves to achieving an appearance of cleanliness, this also left them devoid of any feminine features (2006: 168–69). In the Australian context, however, while it was acknowledged that functionalism envisaged the kitchen to be a "laboratory for food preparation," home magazines, such as *Australian House and Garden*, also illustrated that the modern kitchen could be a space that was "invested with pleasure," demonstrating the "'glamour' possible in ordinary housework in the right setting" (Lloyd and Johnson 2004: 264). Indeed, Lloyd and Johnson cite a 1948 volume of the magazine: "Colour, too, has made the kitchen of today one of the most liveable rooms in the house. Daring and colourful kitchen setups are commonplace. The color does a lot for the housewife's morale too!" (2004: 267). Also writing on Australia, Sian Supski (2006) comments on the experiences of postwar immigrant women. Acknowledging the currency of functionalism and efficiency, these women are reported as offering resistance to laboratory or workstation-like designs in their feminization of the kitchen through use of color, pink being a notable example. Thus, these women can be seen as affirming their agency, on the one hand, but also conforming to stereotypical notions of femininity on the other (Supski 2006: 139).

Subverting Patriarchies through the Spatial Politics of the Kitchen

The standpoint offered by Supski is one of ethnically Other women attempting to define for themselves a settler identity in postcolonial Australia (cf. the other contributions to a special issue of *Gender, Place and Culture* [2006] where "modern," "hybrid" and "global" kitchens are variously reported and reflected upon). Supski's account, along with those originating in (or reporting on) the global South, contributes to the development of a revisionist history of the housewife (Supski 2006). Indeed, reporting the experiences of immigrant women in New Zealand, Robyn Longhurst and others (2009) suggest that rather than representing a source of oppression, women's activities within the home enable them to remain connected with their "homeland." Indeed, Alison Blunt (2005) points toward the spatial politics of home in which ideas about household, nation, and diaspora intersect. She argues that lived experiences of home intersect with identity and belonging in politically significant ways which both shape and reproduce wider ideologies, values, and material cultures, as well as everyday practices.

These ideas resonate within Supski's work. For her women participants, the kitchen was not a site of oppression but represented "home" and was a place of safety, comfort, and belonging, and a space through which they could define their various identities as wives, mothers, and home-builders, as well as resist dominant patriarchal discourses. Likewise, global scholarship has increasingly acknowledged that far from existing as an unproblematized site of women's oppression, the kitchen also has liberating potential. For Katy Bennet (2006), the traditional Dorset farmhouse kitchen is a site through which gender roles are both remade and subverted, while in South America, the community kitchen has become a site of cultural resistance for some women (Christie 2006), offering opportunities for local development and empowerment (Schroeder 2006), or for Muslim Hausa women in Nigeria, a private space away from men in which they are both confined *and* empowered (Robson 2006). All these examples illustrate the use of the domestic kitchen to resist patriarchal and cultural constraints. As Janet Floyd (2004) observes, while the kitchen may historically have been perceived as the seat of women's oppression, conversely, it has also emerged as one which offers improvisatory and rebellious potential (2004: 61).

Locating Men in Cooking Spaces

Of course, the domestic kitchen is not the only space in which food preparation takes place. Not surprisingly, those who have reported on professional kitchens indicate that male dominance in this sphere is no less "oppressive" in character than the domestic kitchen. Indeed, J. D. Pratten (2003) has pointed out that professional kitchens are renowned for their machismo and sexism, an observation reinforced by women in the industry (see Roche 2004). However, the demarcation between professional and domestic has become blurred over the last ten or fifteen years as television has made the world of professional chefs more visible. As Jonathan Deutsch (2005) and Rebecca Swenson (2009) have noted, the proliferation of food-related cooking programs in the United States in particular has inspired some men to become more than just recreational "burgermeisters" (Deutsch 2005: 92), while the conventions employed by broadcasters simultaneously uphold existing gender binaries: men's cooking is competitive or leisurely, while women's cooking remains domestic work (Swenson 2009: 42).

In the United Kingdom, where some food programs have attempted to bridge the gap between the professional and the domestic, Joanne Hollows (2003a, 2003b) has highlighted some of the contradictions wrought by television chefs, such as Nigella Lawson, who have attempted to reconceptualize the kitchen for both men and women: cooking can be indulged in by women for the self, and not just in "service of others" (Murcott 1983a); meanwhile, Jamie Oliver has appealed to men by demystifying cooking, refusing to privilege the world of haute cuisine and making cooking "cool." Both presenters distance their culinary activities from the pressurized world of the professional (male) kitchen by inviting audiences into their homes for an intimate view of "home-based" cooking.

While a number of scholars have commented on men's predilection for particularly "masculine" forms of cooking (outdoors and with fires), which invoke memories of campfire cooking in boyhood (Adler 1981) or which can be seen as an extension of their interest in outdoor activities such as hiking, hunting, and fishing (Aarseth

2007), the broadcasting of Oliver's programs has meant that television has become particularly instrumental in invoking a sense of "masculine domesticity," which has given increasing numbers of men a place at the stove (Swenson 2009: 47). If the kitchen has been interpreted as historically constituting "femininity" for women, conversely, the current reconceptualization of kitchens as "democratized" spaces is understood to have opened up possibilities for a wider range of masculinities. Writing in Australia, for example, Glendon Smith and Hilary Winchester (1998) observe that cooking can represent an opportunity for men to escape from the pressures of work-based masculinities, while, in the United States, Deutsch (2005) reports on the negotiation of identities among male cooks in an urban firehouse.

Crowded Kitchens

Research by Angela Meah and Peter Jackson (2013) draws attention to the implications of the "crowding" of the domestic kitchen as men have increasingly become involved in domestic cooking. They suggest that in reconstituting its gendered dynamics, men's engagement with the kitchen has led to it emerging as an increasingly contested space. Where once the domestic kitchen was considered an exclusively female preserve, a space over which women had control (wanted or otherwise), encouraging increasing numbers of men into this space has had the effect of making kitchens "uncanny" for women, particularly when the practices associated with professional kitchens are transferred into the domestic context. As Ken Gelder and Jane Jacobs explain, "the uncanny" is a process by which the familiar becomes unfamiliar (*Unheimliche*): it is an "estranging experience" (1995: 182) where space works on place to make it unhomely.

The "crowding" of domestic kitchen space is reflected in the tensions reported among some of Meah and Jackson's participants while negotiating the design and equipping of a kitchen. In one household, the kitchen was ergonomically designed with a male cook's needs in mind, including the selection of a cooker, which his wife not only found difficult to operate but was also physically excluded from its use since some of the detachable griddles were too heavy for her to lift. Described as a "proper bit of kit," the appliance was an industrial-quality French cooker, which enabled the (male) cook to feel good about using it. This recalls Elizabeth Shove and others' observation that things are "consumed not for their own sake, but for what they make possible" (2007: 22). This cooker enables the male domestic cook to exhibit flair and competence, demonstrating how objects can actively configure their users (2007: 23). As Thomas Adler observes, "Special cooking gadgets proclaim the special cook" (1981: 48). However, Megan McArdle (2011) has noted the paradox that the more money American consumers spend on their kitchens, appliances, and cookware, the less time they actually spend in or with them.

As Vamie Oliver distances himself from the pressures of the professional kitchen in *The Naked Chef*, the acquisition of an industrial-quality cooker enables Meah and Jackson's participant to take his culinary activities to "another level." Likewise, another male cook makes the observation that "you can learn a lot from the professional kitchen," highlighting the benefit of open wall units with everything visible and within easy reach.

In an interesting and ironic addendum to architectural debates concerning kitchen design, Meah and Jackson's study makes visible both the tensions between gendered notions of form and functionality and the continuing relevance of the location and proximity of the kitchen in relation to the wider spatial dynamics of the household. Indeed, a male participant laments his wife's refusal to consider opening up their separate kitchen and dining spaces into one large, open-plan space, which would become the "hub of the house." Her reason, to "keep the kitchen mess in one space." Indeed, dealing with the aftermath of messy male cooks appears to be one of the consequences experienced by women following the "democratization" of the kitchen.

While providing a historical account of the design history of the modern kitchen which, some Anglo-American feminists argue, *designs women* by reinforcing feminine subjectivities, this essay has also made visible revisionist accounts of the kitchen. In looking beyond the experiences of Anglo-American women, the alleged oppressive character of the kitchen can be displaced by hearing the stories of those women, both from migrant populations in the global North and those indigenous to the global South, who have demonstrated the potential of the kitchen to be used as a subversive and empowering space. Moreover, in the decades that have passed since second wave feminists first drew attention to the plight of "captive wives and housebound mothers" (Gavron 1966), the spatial dynamics of home have changed irrevocably. However, while women may now spend less time in the kitchen than their mothers or grandmothers and men may spend proportionately more time there than their fathers or grandfathers, and not just on a "festal" basis (Adler 1981), male engagement with the kitchen still takes place largely on their own terms, as a lifestyle choice, leaving persistent inequalities regarding the distribution of tasks associated with cooking. One may therefore question the extent to which power has genuinely been redistributed, and for whose benefit.

See also cooking, gender, skill, space and place.

Angela Meah

L

Labeling © Angela Meah.

LABELING

In North America, Europe, and beyond, debates about labels for nutritional content, country of origin, fair trade, food miles, expiry dates, and the presence of genetically modified ingredients go to the heart of key issues in contemporary food systems. Yet it is only rarely that labeling itself receives direct critical attention in social science research. This essay draws on research that has examined debates around nutrition labels, date/expiry labels, and the labeling of genetically modified ingredients among others. It argues that while existing research explores the politics and comprehension of labeling, work is needed that brings these strands together to examine the assembly of labels from diverse expertises, materials, and assumed roles, responsibilities and behaviors of actors within food systems.

In the late nineteenth century, labels on packaged foods were introduced by manufacturers to make claims about the qualities of their products, subsequently becoming a focus and instrument of food policy. In the United States, the 1906 Pure Food and Drug Act prohibited food labels from bearing statements that were "false or misleading in any particular", an injunction that remains central to labeling guidelines around the world, as for example in recent EU regulations on health claims and in the international *Codex Alimentarius*. The development of the labeling system was closely associated with political, social, geographical, and material changes in food during the twentieth century. In particular, the use of labels and the turn to "reading food" (Frohlich 2011) has been both necessitated and facilitated by the growth in sales of prepared, packaged foods whose quality, constituents, and freshness are not readily assessed, and that emerge from globally extended networks of production and transport.

Food labels embody particular constructions of the roles of government, the food industry, and consumers concerning their responsibilities for healthy, safe eating. They take a variety of forms, from simple symbols to complex ingredient lists and have differing aims, audiences, and histories; they can be positive,

as in the case of health claims, or negative, as in warning labels. According to Tim Lang and Michael Heasman (2004: 203), labels are the "war zone" in which the concerns, claims, and counterclaims of consumers, activists, regulators, and the food industry are expressed and contested. On one side, labels are denounced as insufficient, opaque, and misleading, as in Felicity Lawrence's exposé of production practices in *Not on the Label* (2004) or Marion Nestle's discussion of nutrition labeling (Nestle 2002). On the other, industry bodies such as the Food and Drink Federation argue that labeling regulations are unnecessarily restrictive or burdensome—for example in relation to nutrition and health claims or origin labeling (Food and Drink Federation 2011a).

The development of labeling systems reflects the history of food regulation systems more generally, having moved from a focus on protecting consumers from fraud to enabling rational consumer choice—and possibly on to consumer disciplining (Frohlich 2011). The role of labels is reflected in descriptions of food labeling by governments and food industry bodies:

> Food labeling is an important means of providing essential information to consumers on the composition of products and the methods of storage and preparation etc. and identifying the manufacturer or other responsible business. (Food and Drink Federation, 2011b)

Similar definitions of the role of labeling are widely held, within and outside government. Labels are conceptualized as the medium through which information about food qualities is provided by manufacturers or governments, and through which practices associated with social, ecological, and individual responsibilities are promulgated. In turn, the nature of this information changes to reflect changing practices. For example, fresh food labels that once informed (mistrustful) consumers that they were purchasing cold-stored food now tell them the conditions under which they should cold store themselves (Freidberg 2009). Mikael Klintman (2002) shows that both pro and anti sides within debates on genetically modified

(GM) food labeling cleave closely to a similar "informational" model of labeling, whether insisting that consumers need information about the presence of GM ingredients or in arguing that such information is misleading.

The circulation of information about food through labeling redistributes responsibility in areas such as food safety—once informed, consumers are expected to take into account storage and preparation methods, avoid food containing allergens, or eat food that is low in saturated fats. As explored in the following sections, this distribution of responsibility forms part of the heated politics of food labeling and involves the attribution of particular roles and characteristics to the consumer.

Labeling and the Politics of Food

The use of labels has become an increasingly important feature of the politics of food. In their book *Food Wars* (2004), Lang and Heasman describe the arena of food labeling as consisting of a series of ongoing battles being fought among the government, consumers, and food industry. In the course of these battles, roles and responsibilities are distributed through the food chain and relations of power and capital congeal around standards and certification schemes.

The application of voluntary labeling and certification schemes has received significant attention within research on food systems, including in areas such as organic labeling (2004), marine certification (Constance and Bonnano 2000), carbon labeling (Morgan 2010), provenance, and heritage (Bessière 1998). Many of these labels incorporate promises of social change that extend (or co-opt) the values of alternative food movements based on direct interactions between actors. They also enable new distinctions to be made that may otherwise be undetectable, such as that between organic and nonorganic, creating market differentiation (Guthman 2007).

In contrast, mandatory labeling regimes have been less studied, despite the prominence of debates about which labels should or should not be required by law, the ubiquity of such labels, their stated importance to consumers (Grunert and Wills 2007), and their role in distinguishing national regulatory regimes. International nonbinding *Codex Alimentarius* standards suggest eight mandatory labels: the name of the food; the list of ingredients; net contents and drained weight; the name and address of the producer or distributor; the country of origin; lot identification; date marking and storage instructions; and instructions for use. However, as the case of expiry date labeling illustrates, heated local debates surround about the boundaries of mandatory labeling.

Although some form of date marking is included in the *Codex*, significant variation in labeling systems exists. The diversity of approaches to date labeling illustrates that whether and in what form labels become mandatory is deeply embedded in local political cultures and in the political, moral, and technological economies of food systems. For example, in the United Kingdom, the introduction of open (consumer readable) labeling systems was driven by pressure from a variety of "consumer representatives" in the face of long-standing industry and government protestations about the unmanageable complexity of regulating foods through the production chain (Milne in press). This led to the opening up of coded industry systems, as described by Marks and Spencer's technologist Norman Robson in an interview for the British Library's "Food Stories" archive:

> We'd done a lot of work on this cherry Genoa cake, and when you make it you make it in a big slab, because to make it smaller affects the quality of it … So, what we did was to build in to the sheets of film a coloured strip, and the colour represented the day on which the girl cut and wrapped the cake, and then the store would know when the cake was cut and wrapped and hence they received it, 'cause they always received it on the same day as it was cut and wrapped, and how long they'd got to sell it. And that was really the starting point for real control. And the magic word was "Progby." Purple, red,

orange, green, blue, yellow. Six days of the week. And if you wrapped it on a Monday, you had film with a purple streak in it, and so it went on. And that was the first real attempt, certainly for us, to label a perishable food with the date of packing.

Interviewer: But there was no indication on that that would tell the customers to eat within a week or two days or … ?

No, there wasn't initially, but customers started asking questions and so we told them. And we issued a little ticket which was put on the display explaining what the coloured strip was … Because you really need to come clean with customers. They spot these things and they ask questions and you should answer them … But I mean that was the beginning, as I say, of this freshness story and this dating business that's now so terribly important. (quoted in Milne in press)

Richard Milne describes how the regulatory introduction of date labels required and supported the introduction of new forms of discipline within food systems, including clearly defined lines of traceability and safety devices such as HACCP (Hazard Analysis and Critical Control Point) plans. However, over time the labeling system has become the focus of criticisms about food safety and waste, which have transformed labels from tools of consumer protection to instruments of consumer discipline.

Similar examples of the politics of mandatory labeling are provided in the case of GM crops and front-of-pack (FOP) nutrition labeling. In the late 1990s controversy around the introduction of GM crops was accompanied by widespread calls for the application of labels to produce containing GM ingredients. As in the development of date labeling regimes for food in the United Kingdom, or the labeling of fresh food (Freidberg 2009) and trans fats in the United States, significant consumer support exists for the mandatory labeling of GM foods. In both Europe and the United States, this has been mobilized by consumer organizations (Einsiedel 2002; Klintman 2002). However, only the European Union has moved towards mandatory labeling systems.

Like the labeling of GM crops, the provision of nutritional information about prepacked foods lies at the boundary of the labeling system and is widely supported by consumers (Malam et al. 2009). In the European Union (from 2012), the United States, and a number of other countries, basic nutritional labels are mandatory, generally in the form of a standardized nutrition information box (Frohlich 2011). However, in recent years, concern has been expressed about the ability of these labels to effectively communicate essential information about food in light of rising obesity levels. This has prompted moves to present consumers with simple, FOP information about key nutritional characteristics.

In the United Kingdom, the Food Standards Agency adopted a color-based "traffic light system" in 2006 which highlights total fat, saturated fat, sugar, and salt content on the front of food packages. Similar systems have been proposed in Australia and New Zealand, and in 2010, the U.S. FDA launched a consultation on rationalizing front of pack labeling. The initial reporting of the FDA consultation supported the UK Food Standards Agency's argument for the introduction of single standards for labeling. However, in both Europe and the United States, such labeling schemes are voluntary and their format remains open. Label designs have proliferated, arguably creating more confusion than they solve.

The proliferation of FOP designs reflects the political economy of labeling and the ability of powerful interests to adapt voluntary systems for their ends. Despite considerable pressure on the part of consumer organizations, new food labeling regulations introduced in Europe in 2012 still incorporate no requirement for FOP labeling or standard design. Indeed, it is only in Thailand that FOP labeling has become mandatory.

Klintman's (2002) analysis suggests that a focus on the informational content of labels can reinforce existing food market structures and relationships within them. Unni Kjaernes and others (2007) point out that for regulators and consumer groups, labels are seen as a means of increasing transparency, opening up the contexts of food production or the contents of foods themselves to scrutiny. However, the ability of industry actors to adapt labeling systems to their own ends distorts this transparency, as exposés of production practices such as Lawrence's *Not on the Label* reveal. Indeed, Julie Guthman (2007) argues that the labeling and accreditation of organic produce is complicit in incorporating it within neoliberalized food markets, erecting new barriers to entry into these markets. Labeling of organic products may thus reflect and reinforce arrangements of power that producers originally hoped to counter or expose.

Using Labels

As commonly conceptualized, labeling relies on the effective use of labels by consumers to make consumption decisions. Quantitative research suggests that consumers are generally positive toward receiving more information about food through labeling and that people generally make use of the mandatory labels discussed above, particularly concerning price, date, quantity and ingredients (Grunert and Wills 2007). Labels are more commonly read by female consumers and those with higher levels of education and socioeconomic status (Malam et al. 2009). However, consumers may use labels less than they suggest, particularly on products they purchase regularly, when buying food as a treat, or when short of time (Guthrie et al. 1995; Malam et al. 2009). Furthermore, while labels such as expiry dates or quality marks are valued by consumers, their use may not coincide with that intended by the labeler (Grunert and Wills 2007; WRAP 2011). For example, consumers are regularly accused of mistaking "best before" labels (intended as a marker of food quality) for "use by" labels (intended as a marker of food safety), and there is further confusion about "display until" labels (intended for use by retail managers rather than consumers themselves).

Much research on labeling is conducted under the aegis of, or is orientated toward, specific policy or commercial concerns related to labeling. Thus, studies of nutrition, date, or warning labels are primarily concerned with identifying which labels are understood and which are not, rather than how labels are used. This reflects the framing of labels as an essential conduit of information between regulators,

the food industry, and consumers. Within this framing, consumer use of labels is conceptualized as that of rational actors concerned with the maximization of value and minimization of risk. While there are undoubtedly problems with understanding labels, the nonuse or misuse of labels becomes a problem of ignorance which itself becomes the target of further interventions aimed at educating and disciplining consumers to act as they should. Xaq Frohlich (2011) suggests that this involves a reframing of labels' audience, within which labels become tools of education as well as media of information, associated with prompting self-discipline among unruly consumers.

However, the diagnosis of consumer ignorance in the face of information is not clear-cut. Rather, labels are interpreted, understood, and reworked in local social and cultural contexts (Eden et al. 2008; Kjaernes et al. 2007; Green et al. 2003). Trust in provisioning systems and the actors that inhabit them are central to how consumers make sense of information about food safety and other characteristics of food (Kjaernes et al. 2007). In addition, the information contained within labels is encountered and interpreted within the spaces and times of the everyday routines and practices and individual biographies associated with consumption. For example, date labels may be used to assess freshness while shopping but may be less used when cooking or in the home, where concerns about waste may take precedence, particularly among older groups (Milne 2011; WRAP 2011).

Opening the Black Box

Consumer understandings and use of labels occurs in the context of consumption routines and among the contested politics of labeling. However, consumers do not simply represent the end point of the labeling process. As date, nutrition, and GM food labeling suggest, assumptions about consumer knowledges, tastes, and behaviors are integral to the construction of food labels.

Susanne Freidberg's (2009) description of the regulatory discussions surrounding the labeling of food as "fresh" in the United States introduces the complexity of labeling systems:

Could freshness be measured? Should it be de fined by taste or by internal qualities? Did the agency need another term to describe foods that were processed but "fresh-like"? How much information about a product's freshness did consumers need or want on a label? And finally, if the FDA redefined the legal meaning of "fresh," who would profit or lose out? (2009: 2)

The definition of a label involves not only "calculation," even if appropriate metrics are available, but also a series of qualitative judgments that introduce new relationships between products that were previously separated—in the case of fresh food, between "fresh" but pasteurized milk and juices subject to the same treatment that could not be labeled as fresh. These establish consumers, their informational demands, and their tastes as an essential component in the formulation and application as well as reception of labels. For example, the perceived problems for the food industry of the requirements of EU regulations on health claims in food labels are accentuated by the important influence of health claims on consumer demand. In turn, this has created demands for new forms of evidence related to the effects of food that create new links between the testing of foods and pharmaceuticals.

Similarly, debates over date labeling in the United Kingdom have focused on how such dates could be accurately established and on whether they would reflect and/or shape consumer taste, including whether "date-conscious" consumers would create unnecessary food waste (Milne in press). Later, concerns about food safety following the scares of the 1980s crystallized in the questioning of the accuracy of labels, as the responsibilities of consumers were offset against those of labelers. Milne describes how, in early 1989, the National Consumer Council argued that although consumers had a duty to observe date marks, they "need to know the degree of risk, if there is any, of food contamination. They need consistent and reliable information. They need to know that research is adequate" (in Milne in press). The introduction and refining of the date labeling

system required the redefinition of the end of food, the point at which it ceases to be edible.

Consequently, understanding how labels are defined, how they function, and how they incorporate the complex socio-technical networks associated with food production and consumption requires further work to "open the black box" of labeling (Eden 2011). This means examining the processes of qualification and calculation that go into the classification and labeling of foods as "fresh," "organic," "fair trade," or "perishable." It involves examining the politics of expertise involved in the production of food labels and of the delineation of the required content and form of mandatory labeling, and analysis of the incorporation and mobilization of consumers within labels themselves. Such an approach would capture the two-way communication implied in Sally Eden's (2011) description of labels as "boundary objects" and enrich and deepen a discussion of labels that often remains blinded by the importance of information and the (in)ability of consumers to use it.

See also advertising, packaging, responsibility, safety, trust.

Richard Milne

LOCAL-GLOBAL

Food is one of the most obvious avatars of the globalization of trade and culture. Historically, the majority of the food consumed by the bulk to the world's population was "locally" produced and exchanged. The rarity of nonlocal produce was reflected in the value of products such as spices in Europe and played a significant role in spurring exploration and commercial expansion from Marco Polo onward. As described in Sidney Mintz's classic *Sweetness and Power* (1985), the production of sugar in the Caribbean was heavily implicated in the global imperial projects of the United Kingdom and in changing British tastes in consumption. Since Columbus arrived in 1492, the Caribbean has "always been entangled with a wider world ... caught up in skeins of imperial control, spun in Amsterdam, London, Paris,

Madrid, and other European and North American centers of world power" (Mintz 1985: xv–xvi).

Nonetheless, until the late nineteenth and early twentieth centuries, global trades in produce, dairy, and meat were inhibited by the inability to preserve and transport fresh food over long distances. Now, it seems, Western consumers can have "the world on a plate" (Cook and Crang 1996). Commodities, cuisines, ingredients, and even chefs circulate around the globe, enabled by networks of refrigerated transport, telecommunications, and global travel. The globalization of food-supply chains has allowed the spatial resolution of many longstanding problems related to scarcity, seasonality, and scale. Food can more easily be transported to where it is needed, particularly urban centers of industry and commerce. A cook in London may use a French recipe to produce a dish assembled from green beans grown in Kenya and meat farmed in Argentina, while a resident of New Delhi can order "Italian" pizza from the American company Dominos. However, this process has raised concerns about the homogenization of global cuisines, the power of transnational agri-food corporations, and, increasingly, the governance of food safety in spatially distended networks of food supply.

Globalization and "McDonaldization"

Recently, historical processes of globalization have acquired new forms and meanings and have become synonymous with criticisms of the homogenization, "McDonaldization" (Ritzer 1998) or "Coca-colonization" (Hannerz 1992) of food and culture. Globalization—of food, business, and industry—has become a defining discourse of contemporary societies. It indicates a process of ever-closer global integration, which breaks links with nation states and creates what newspaper columnist Thomas Freidman (2005) (in) famously described as a "flat" world in which no areas are unaffected. This is commonly represented by companies such as McDonald's, Coca-Cola, or the coffee chain Starbucks.

Founded in 1950s California, McDonald's now has over 30,000 restaurants worldwide and is the archetypal global food business. In turn, its globality is mobilized within marketing that brings together McDonald's customers as a "global family." As Elspeth Probyn suggests, "The Big Mac preceded the internet in bringing us all together … extending an ethics of care into the realm of global capitalism and creating its consumer as a globalized familial citizen" (2000: 35). However, the global "McDonald's family" is not always a happy one, nor is the "ethic of care" it seeks to promote always evident. The company has become a focus for campaigns critical of contemporary forms of globalization, most famously in France, where José Bové of the *Confédération Paysanne* demolished a McDonald's under construction in Millau as a protest against the antidemocratic nature of global trade rules. In Italy, Arcigola protests against the opening of a McDonald's restaurant chain in the Piazza di Spagna in Rome prompted the emergence of the Slow Food movement.

Criticisms of globalization draw on a tradition based in Theodor Adorno and Max Horkheimer's (1944/2002) influential critique of the commodification of culture and the emergence of a culture "industry" involved in the production of uniform cultural goods. Similarly, in talking about food, globalization is accused of eroding the diversity of local consumption cultures, imposing a standardized, "place-less" cuisine in a "flood of standardization" (Petrini 2004: 28). For Jonathan Murdoch (2005), McDonald's is characteristic of food networks that extend across space but are not grounded in specific places. These networks are associated with standardized, specialized forms of production associated with economic standards of quality based on efficiency, competitiveness, and price. They enable the process for cooking a burger or an apple pie to be maintained across every McDonald's branch, producing consistent, standardized food.

While criticism of McDonald's highlights its role in "flattening" culinary culture, it also forms part of wider, sustained critiques of the globalization of agri-food systems that emphasize its role in perpetuating economic, social, and environmental inequalities (see, for example, Patel 2007). For example, controversy around the introduction of GM crops has focused not only on questions of safety and environmental risk but also on issues of global equity and the control of the food supply. European opposition to genetically modified crops linked organizations such as the Confédération Paysanne with international antiglobalization movements, drawing associations with activists such as Vandana Shiva to illustrate the global inequalities reproduced by biotechnological agriculture. It drew attention to the implication of agricultural science with the distribution of wealth and resources between the global South and North, and provided an alternative definition of the problems of the new technology that moved debate in countries such as France away from dominant risk framings (Heller 2007).

Localization

Critiques of globalization have been accompanied by a revalorization of "local" food associated with variety, heritage or tradition, quality or reduced environmental impact (Bessière 1998; Murdoch et al. 2000). The "local" has become a point of resistance to the logic of global capitalism and is often seen as a good, progressive, and desirable counterpoint to inexorable globalization (Hinrichs 2003; DuPuis and Goodman 2005).

For its proponents, a turn to "local food" reconnects production and consumption, providing solutions to economic, social, and ecological concerns (see also Heldke's [2003] rhetorical question about the desirability of going "home" to eat). Locally sourced food may be seen as safer and better quality than industrial food. It may also be seen as a response to concerns about "food miles" and the environmental impact of global agriculture. Local food movements are also associated with rural development and tourism—as in the case of cheese production in South Wales (Murdoch et al. 2000) and food heritage in southern France (Bessière 1998)—or with achieving improved, sustainable nutrition in cities, as in the "edible cities" of New York or Toronto (Friedmann 2007). In contrast to the distant market relations associated with global agriculture, it is also suggested that "the 'local' will manifest high levels of social capital and relations of care—in short, a more moral or associative economy" (Hinrichs 2003: 36).

In these terms, local consumption may serve as a "totem" that enables consumers to think about local social relations (Winter 2003). Localism thus represents a powerful tool for responding to the problems of the contemporary food system. In this context, the local food or locavore movement continues to expand and has attracted high-profile support from prominent food movement figures such as Alice Waters, Michael Pollan, and Michelle Obama, whose support for "community gardens" included planting a White House vegetable patch.

However, as Clare Hinrichs continues, the unreflexive adoption of localization is a "perilous trap." "Local" scales are not inherently more equal or communitarian than global ones, and local food movements are inherently heterogeneous, bringing together different forms of agriculture and a range of consumer views that incorporate a broad spectrum of political motivations for supporting local food (Weatherell et al. 2003). In the case of the Iowa local food movement, Hinrichs (2003) points out that localization is a strategy by agricultural producers under pressure from imports and wary consumers. This "defensive localism" is associated with conservative parochialism and exclusion rather than an inclusive ethic of social and environmental care. Similarly in the United Kingdom, Michael Winter (2003) describes how support for local food was associated with the protection of local farming interests following the effects of foot-and-mouth disease. In other contexts, localism may be adopted instrumentally to protect regional or national food industries in the face of international competition, as in the case of EU geographical origin marks. "Local" concerns may thus conflict with wider responsibilities associated with the expression of a global ethic. However, this is not to discount the potential of "reflexive localism" (DuPuis and Goodman 2005), which, as Hinrichs (2003) argues, can lend itself to diversity as much as conservatism and to the pursuit of equality and social justice.

How Global is Globalization?

So far, this essay has discussed the global and the local as opposing poles. However, a growing body of work suggests that globalization is not as smooth a process as either proponents (like Thomas Freidman) or critics would suggest. For example, Richard Wilk (2006b) traces the different relations between the local and the global in the emergence of Belizean cuisine, from the British "high colonial" era, in which a Bourdieuian hierarchy of taste drove middle-class consumption of "foreign food" and highbrow tastes for foreign forms of food preparation, to the construction of specifically Belizean food culture. What is now "local" Belizean food incorporates earlier phases of industrial food consumed by the first European settlers and a constant mixing with the cuisines of immigrants to Belize and of Belizeans living in North America, through which the "taste of home" is constructed.

Doreen Massey (1995) points out that concerns about globalization always depict it as starting elsewhere and as ungrounded in specific localities. Instead, she suggests that the global should be approached through the local, revealing the existence of multiple globalizations. Describing processes of "indigenization," "glocalization," or "creolization," Arjun Appadurai suggests, "At least as rapidly as forces from various metropolises are brought into new societies they tend to become indigenized in one or another way" (Appadurai 1996: 198).

Chapters in Wilk's edited collection *Fast Food/Slow Food* similarly trace the complex mixings and unexpected juxtapositions of the local and the global in locations as distant as Mali and Moscow, describing how processes of localization and decommodification are constantly at work as people take global raw materials and cook with them. Indeed, the work collected in James Watson's (1997) *Golden Arches East* describes the indigenization of menu and meaning at McDonald's, the archetype of globalization, in East Asia. For example, Emiko Ohnuki-Tierney (1997) describes the local adaptation of the company's menu in Japan, including the introduction of teriyaki burgers. Although, as Carlo Petrini (2004) argues, this by no means constitutes the "localization" of McDonald's, Ohnuki-Tierney also shows how McDonald's restaurants have come to be defined as a utopian space by representing an idealized, classless America to Japanese youth living in a hierarchical society. Like

McDonald's, Coca-Cola has become a target of resistance to U.S.-led globalization, as through explicitly "anti-coca-colas" such as Mecca Cola or the Iranian Zam Zam Cola (Ram 2007). However, it also enjoys a complex relationship with "local" consumption that is not reducible to Americanization, as among Punjabi youth in London who appropriate Coca-Cola, not as a symbol of Americanization but as a means of distinguishing their identities from those of their parents (Gillespie 1995). Cola drinks have thus provided an excellent lens through which to study global/local relations or how "globality is itself a localized image, held within a larger frame of spatialized identity" (Miller 1998c: 184). Building on this earlier work, Cristina Alcalde (2009) focuses on Inca Kola, the only cola drink to outsell Coca-Cola in its national market. She examines how Inca Kola maintains an identity as distinctly Peruvian and as globally viable, suggesting this occurs through the production of a distinctly Peruvian globalization that distinguishes the drink from the American/global identity of Coke. However, she shows that the relationship between the global and the local depends on which "local" one uses to approach the global. In its name and presentation, Inca Kola links itself with the historical identity of Peru and the pre-Colombian indigenous population. Yet Inca Kola's representations of national identity also exclude contemporary indigenous populations. The global image of Inca Kola thus represents a locally hegemonic homogenized, white-mestizo, urban version of Peru's "national flavor."

"Global" Space?

Distinctions between McDonald's and alternative food movements should not be drawn solely on their prima facie "global" or "local" character but how they are orientated toward, and constructed across, space. For example, although emergent from the 1986 protests, the Slow Food movement set out not to directly oppose McDonald's but to provide a heterogeneous alternative globalization that "create[s] networks of communication among diverse realities" (Petrini 2004: 28). Murdoch (2005) suggests that the spaces of Slow Food are "topological" networks, contrasting them with the "topographical" concepts of well-ordered space that characterize fast food and McDonald's. Topological spaces of food link local to nonlocal processes, such as the Slow Food movement, constructing a network that flows from the local to the global while not being easily classified as either. However, the conceptualization of the local within the spaces of Slow Food and related movements appears static. Alcalde's work on Inca Kola (2009) emphasizes that the globalization of foods involves movements of people as well as things. The co-migration of people and their foods and the consequent changes in the places they move to as well as those they leave is considered in work that describes the transnationalism of contemporary food systems. This work emphasizes the reciprocal transformations and continuous circulations of people, money, goods, and information involved in economic globalization. Philip Crang and others (2003) concentrate on the movements of goods, people, ideas, and capital within a space of networks and circulations that contrasts with static and restricted notions of the local or the all-encompassing, homogenizing global. Such an approach reveals connections and disconnections across global supply chains and demonstrates how "foreign" food can transform the consumption patterns of so-called "host" societies. For example, Peter Jackson and others (2009b) explore how the moral geographies of sugar production were established through their relation with the historical geographies of imperialism, commerce, and slavery, and how "Indian" foods have become indigenized as a core part of the national British diet.

Although globalization is not solely a U.S.-led phenomenon, it is often things that originate in Europe and North America that come to be considered global (Ohnuki-Tierney 1997), particularly brands, such as Coca-Cola, McDonald's, or Starbucks. While ostensibly demonstrating the "flatness" imposed by the food industry, the dominance of Western food companies and cuisines highlights the unevenness and inequalities of globalization. Work that emphasizes the transnational connections between communities and cuisines is valuable in understanding this unevenness and shaping how research approaches the ethics, quality, and safety of food in the global food system.

See also authenticity, exotic, provenance, space and place.

Richard Milne

M

Markets © Angela Meah.

MARKETS

Markets are places where goods are exchanged for money or traded via other means such as bartering. Many of the world's oldest markets were food markets, associated with the spice trade at the points where long-distance trade routes crossed (Turner 2005). As well as being a physical place for the exchange of goods, however, markets also have a more abstract meaning as in references to financial markets or futures markets, which are only loosely connected to specific places such as the New York Stock Exchange on Wall Street or the International Financial Futures Exchange in the City of London. In this more abstract sense, "markets" can refer to entire financial systems, as in the idea of the capitalist market economy, as well as to highly localized places for the exchange of food and other goods.

Conceptually, then, markets can refer to abstract systems of economic exchange as well as to specific places for the buying and selling of goods. Markets can also refer to the demand for particular goods (as in questions about whether a market exists for this or that product); they can refer to the social or geographical range of such demand (as in estimates of the extent of a particular market); and they can refer to the operation of a particular form of economic logic (as in arguments about the nature of "market forces" or the operation of the "free market").

In his work on the wholesale fish market in Tokyo, Theodore Bestor distinguishes between markets as abstract institutions or processes and the marketplace as a localized set of social institutions, transactions, social actors, organizations, products, trade practices, and cultural meanings that occur in a specific geographical place (2004: 20). Writing about fresh produce markets in France, Michèle de la Pradelle criticizes the tendency to turn markets—the physical and institutional spaces in which buyers and sellers meet and engage in trade—into mere manifestations of the Market—the abstract set of transactions that occur around a given category of goods (2006: 2). Neil Fligstein and Luke Dauter also try to sidestep the distinction between actual markets "on the ground" and abstract conceptions of the Market, arguing:

> Markets imply social spaces where repeated exchanges occur between buyers and sellers under a set of formal and informal rules governing relations between competitors, suppliers and customers ... [which] operate according to local understandings that guide trade, define what is produced and provide stability for buyers, sellers and producers. These marketplaces are dependent on governments, laws and larger cultural understandings supporting market activity. (2007: 18)

Christian Berndt and Marc Boeckler also insist that markets "do not simply fall out of thin air, but are continually produced and constructed socially [through] dense and extensive webs of social relations" (2009: 536). Markets, they argue, are comprised of "bundles of practices and material arrangements [that are] always in the making" (2009: 565).

Food markets are often celebrated for their exuberance and sense of embodied pleasure (smelling, touching, and squeezing the produce, for example), in contrast to the more clinical experience of supermarket shopping. Turning this distinction on its head, Clifford Geertz argues that the bazaar economy in North Africa is "the nearest thing to be found in reality to the purely competitive market of neoclassical economics" (1979: 198). Examining the Moroccan *suq* as both a cultural form and an economic institution, he defines it as "a place where half-commercialized tribesmen meet supercommercialized shopkeepers on free if somewhat less than equal grounds" (1979: 129). These tensions between the operation of abstract markets and the routines and rituals of actual markets in practice have been the subject of intense study. In her celebrated ethnographic account of an outdoor food market, for example, de la Pradelle refers to the "embodied and emotional pull" of the Provencal market in Carpentras (2006: 2) and to the "symbolic magic" of the market produce (see also de la Pradelle 1995). But she also argues that market traders and shoppers collude in exaggerating the difference between the alternative and the mainstream, with many of the fruit and vegetables on sale in the market being identical to those on sale in nearby supermarkets, having been produced industrially and bought from the same wholesale markets in Avignon. For every account of the sensual pleasures of the marketplace, it seems, there are parallel and opposing accounts of food adulteration, misrepresentation, and dodgy dealing (Wilson 2008). Jonathan Everts and Peter Jackson (2009) make a similar argument about the extent to which modernity and tradition might be better thought of as moments in all kinds of shopping experiences rather than being associated respectively with supermarkets and cornershops as they are commonly conceived.

Since Karl Polanyi's classic work on *The Great Transformation* (1944/1957), it has been widely recognized that the economic exchange of goods is always embedded in social relations of reciprocity and trust, giving rise to notions of the cultural or moral economy (cf. Dixon 1999). Relatedly, there have been widespread concerns about the "marketization" of social life (as described by Çaliskan and Callon 2010 among others). Writing in this vein, de la Pradelle (2006: 1) laments the fact that "market society" no longer seems to need its street markets and stall-holders, having developed other forms of distribution that better satisfy its demands for rational efficiency and profit. These concerns have underpinned a revival of various "alternative" forms of food provision in Europe and North America, defined in terms of their alterity to the conventional retail sector and the dominance of the supermarket economy (cf. Hinrichs 2000; Kirwan 2004). Concerns have, however, been expressed about the extent to which farmers' markets and similar ventures exhibit a form of social exclusion in their appeal to affluent middle-class urban consumers. Based on her observation of farmers' markets and food co-ops in Minneapolis-St Paul, for example, Rachel Slocum (2007) talks about the unexamined "whiteness" of such places. This argument might also be applied to the kind of "fine foods" market described by Ben Coles and Philip Crang (2010) in the case of London's Borough Market and to Sharon Zukin's account of the Union Square farmers' market in New York City (Zukin 2004). Taking these arguments

further, Roza Tchoukaleyska (2009) describes how a busy North African food market in Montpellier in the south of France was forcibly relocated to make room for a more genteel books and antiques (*brocante*) market, ostensibly driven by the logic of urban revitalization but possibly also concealing a murkier politics of gentrification and racialized displacement, played out through arguments about the food market's questionable standards of hygiene and the alleged criminality of the market traders.

Finally, we might note the way that different kinds of markets come together as when financial speculation on international food markets drives up commodity prices, which, in turn, exert an upward influence on supermarket food prices. The main supermarket chains are now themselves involved in financial speculation, which can result in increased food insecurity among the most marginalized in society. In all these ways, markets can provide a lens through which to examine the links between the smallest scale of individual markets and stall-holders and the global scale of agri-food markets.

See also commodities, moral economy.

Peter Jackson

MATERIALITIES

"Materialities" is a word that embraces and invokes a range of ways of thinking, which together can cast distinctive light on the ways in which the matter of food matters. The word is one of those pieces of academic jargon that can be upsetting. After all, "materialities" refers to the same stuff as "materials": the stuff that conventionally is understood to provide both the grounds for possibility and the background for social life. What is gained by adding "ities" into "material"?

Different intellectual traditions inform thinking on materialities. What they share is a problematization of the way in which the material has been framed in the carving out of intellectual space for the social sciences. At least since Émile Durkheim, the "social" has been predominantly understood as distinct from the material, the physical character of the nonhuman world figuring only as passive backdrop, limits, and substrate for the human activities and relations that comprise the object of social scientific inquiry (Breslau 2000; Latour 2000). By contrast, for different traditions informing understandings of materialities, the material is part of the social. Whether in providing a carrier for social meanings, relations, and power, or as active participants in the making, shaping and reproduction of the social, the material is understood as part of the social. It is the different senses in which material things are understood as more or less active participants within the flow of human action, rather than as mute and passive background, that justifies the use of the term "materialities." There is probably no better class of materials than food for exploring the value of the different approaches to understanding materialities.

Debates over the priority to be given to the material in shaping social life are nothing new. Philosophical debates between materialism and idealism echo down the millennia. To condense complex traditions of thought into a couple of lines—for the materialist, matter is the primary substance of all things including those phenomena we take to be social or mental; for the idealist, ideas form or underlie reality. Food easily figures as a bone of contention in the territory between these two poles of thought. On one hand, the physical reality of food is clearly inseparable from its meanings, symbolism and cultural purposes. On the other hand, the inability of even the most radical idealist to carry on producing reality without eating something has long placed a limit on the tenability of any pure idealism.

However, the intellectual landscape in which food studies emerged in the late twentieth century can be argued to have itself fractured about the idealist/materialist divide. On the one hand, agri-food studies were established in a materialist tradition; specifically, the historical materialism identified with Marxist approaches. Meanwhile, attention to the cultural roles of food, particularly in relation to consumption, was established in academic fields defined by prioritization of discourses and representations. What defines contemporary approaches to materialities, however, is a broad position that repudiates any simple delineation between idealism and materialism, or the dualism of culture and nature on which such delineation is premised.

The academic field of material culture studies maintained an interest in material things in relation to culture throughout the twentieth century. Material culture has its roots in archaeology and anthropology. Archaeologists interested in reconstructing long-past cultural phenomena are compelled to rely on their material remains. Food seems to fit poorly into this purpose for paying attention to materials, thanks to its putrescibility. However, both the relatively durable wastes from foods in the favored archaeological empirical focus of the midden—such as animal bones, seeds, and chaff—and the many artifacts associated with collection, storage, preparation, and consumption of food have been assiduously examined by archaeologists, as a means of reconstructing past relations around the cultural roles of food (Gilbert and Mielke 1985). From the nineteenth century, anthropology has paid attention to the role of material things, not least around food, in the production and reproduction of social relations, roles, and meanings. The centrality of the stuff of food and the specificities of its materiality figure in the fundamental categories of structural anthropology, evident in the first volume of Claude Lévi-Strauss's *The Raw and the Cooked* (1969). Food was a key focus when anthropologists started turning their gaze upon the cultures of Europe and North America in the later twentieth century. For example, Mary Douglas (1971) "deciphered" meals through an analysis of her own household's food practices and rituals, and, later, food and the practices of feeding the household figured in Daniel Miller's groundbreaking application of material culture approaches to the exploration of contemporary UK consumption (Miller 1998a).

As material culture approaches spread from anthropology into other fields of social science, food has continued to figure amongst the range of commodities whose social lives (Appadurai 1986a) have provided much of the focus for attention. For example, human geographers drew upon material culture approaches to effect a "rematerialization" of their field (Jackson 2000), following the discipline's preoccupation with discourses, texts, and images in the wake of the cultural turn. Key works in this reorientation of the discipline have focused on food, such as Ian Cook and Philip Crang's (1996) study of the spatially and temporally contextualized objectifications of social relations in contemporary London that allegedly comprise "a world on your plate," or in the "following" of foodstuffs like papaya (Cook 2004).

Material culture approaches have therefore provided a means for food studies across disciplines to engage with the materiality of food. Clearly, food does not lend itself easily to analysis in relation to some key themes in material culture which depend on the temporal durability of things, such as the accretion of both material and semiotic patina as things pass down generations, embedding and reproducing family relations. Nevertheless, the material of food, not least through its repeated location within rituals and habits holding together people's days and relationships, can be understood to objectify social relations and cultural meanings.

However, since the last years of the twentieth century, approaches that problematize the framing of materials within material culture approaches have increasingly been applied to understanding the materialities of food. For profoundly relational approaches like actor-network theory (ANT), material things do not only objectify, embedding and embodying social relations that preexist them. Rather, artifacts "construct, literally and metaphorically, social order ... They are not 'reflecting' it, as if the 'reflected' society existed somewhere else and was made of some other stuff. They are in large part the stuff out of which socialness is made" (Latour 2000: 113). ANT starts from a premise that repudiates the fundamental distinctions, not least between humans and nonhumans, the social and the natural, upon which divisions like that between materialism and idealism are built. Some of the now-classic studies through which ANT took form considered "actor-networks" including foodstuffs, such as

Michel Callon's (1986a) research on the scallops of St. Brieuc Bay or Bruno Latour's (1988) study of pasteurization. However, focus on foodstuffs was incidental, the materialities of the scallops or of milk sidelined in characterizing the heterogeneous networks of actors—both human and nonhuman, living and inanimate—comprising the networks being analyzed. ANT grew and spread from its origins in science and technology studies to have influence across the social sciences. Its direct application in relation to food has predominantly been through analyses of networks of production, as interventions into established approaches to agri-food production. Sarah Whatmore and Lorraine Thorne (1997) deploy ANT to understand the construction and maintenance of networks of fair trade coffee production, though the active role of coffee beans in the network is left mute. Similarly, David Goodman (2001) called for agri-food studies to engage with ANT and its relational understanding of materiality as a means of moving beyond commitments rooted in a materialism founded on a dualistic ontology.

So, while ANT has been central in the rise of relational understandings of materiality, its direct application to food has been limited. As late as 2007, Jane Bennett could justifiably argue that the agential capacities of food as *vital* matter remained fundamentally neglected. Drawing upon Latour but also broader currents of "post-humanist" theorization, she explores the relational agency of foodstuffs through the different affordances the vital materiality of foods offer to both situations of consumption and to the flesh and being of humans who ingest it (Bennett 2007). Emma Roe also attends to the relational materiality of food, working from literatures that are more concerned with the embodied and practical experiences of consumption, focusing on "things becoming food" through embodied, material practices (Roe 2006). Drawing on Marvin Harris (1985), Roe sets out to illuminate the question, "how do things like rancid mammary gland secretions, fungi and rock under particular circumstances become cheese, mushrooms and salt?" arguing that "things become food through how they are handled by humans, not by how they are described and named" (1985: 112).

Through attention specifically to the materiality of foods and their inherent vitality, relational materialist approaches draw attention to what is most distinctive about food as materials. First, that the stuff of food changes. Few material things exist as food prior to some degree of human engagement, through processing or cooking, and few foods stay food for long. As Roe argues, things become food; and as others have pointed out (Blake, in Cook et al. 2011; Watson and Meah, 2013), things un-become food through processes of material decay but also through the specifics of how food stuffs become enmeshed in the details of everyday practice that renders food as waste. Second, and more fundamentally, the materiality of food becomes the material of ourselves. Jessica and Allison Hayes-Conroy (in Cook et al. 2011) draw attention to the viscerality of our engagements with food, echoing Elspeth Probyn (2000).

Just what counts as the materiality of food therefore shifts with changing intellectual preoccupations and ways of thinking. Through material culture, relational materialism, and vitalism, food is revealed variously as objectification of social relations, carrier of meanings, a relational agent within networks, and a vital yet culturally contingent presence, co-constitutive with the practices and purposes that go on around it. Together, these different approaches, which can be partially gathered together around the concept of materialities, thoroughly repudiate any sense that the matter of food is mute, part of the passive material background for social action: they show the different ways in which the matter of food can be understood to matter.

See also body, eating, waste.

Matt Watson

MEDIA

A medium (plural media) is "any material through which something else may be transmitted" and media of communication are therefore "any means by which messages may be transmitted" (Hartley 2005: 142). Compared with John Hartley's definition, other definitions (e.g., media as the medium of communication between senders and receivers) place more emphasis on the "actors" in the communication process or on the actors' utilization of technologies. For example, Paul Hodkinson states, "Producers, along with the technologies they utilize and the content they distribute, are often collectively referred to as 'the media'" (2011: 2). In contemporary usage, the technologies that producers utilize are further classified into two categories: "old" media such as television, radio, films, newspapers, magazines, and "new" media such as the Internet and smart phones. Within food studies, the media are often treated with suspicion because of the power exercised by commercial interests in advertising and marketing food products and associated lifestyles.

In media and communications studies, definitions of the media are much debated, partly because of continuous developments in information and communication technologies (ICTs) and partly because of different theoretical and methodological approaches taken toward the media. In the twentieth century, the "media" usually referred to "mass media," which mostly represent a one-to-many communication model. Mobile phones and PCs with a predominantly one-to-one mode of communication were separated under the banner of telecommunication. But with the convergence of technologies (i.e., TV programs available on personal computers and smart phones), the distinction between "mass media" and telecommunication becomes less clear.

In this essay, the "media" include a broad range of content industries and technologies such as TV, cinema, radio, books, newspapers, the Internet, and so on. In some places, "food media" is used to refer to any of the media mentioned above with food-related content. It is beyond this essay's scope to provide an exhaustive review of all food media. Rather, this essay attempts to highlight the role of the media in the circulation—both as carrier and actor—of constructions and representations of food-related messages. It also discusses some wider impacts of these representations on our social life within which food is sometimes treated with suspicion.

Food Media and Culture

Food and media now seem to get along well with each other. This is partly because of the ubiquity of the media which has made it difficult to separate audiences from everyday mediated experiences (Devereux 2006). Our culinary experiences have also become heavily mediated. Television, for example, presents a very wide range of images of food. In particular, food and cookery programs have steadily increased in recent years, and their capacity to attract large audiences makes them a fixture of television schedules throughout the year (Dickinson 2005). Food writers and campaigners like Michael Pollan and Marion Nestle reach now mass audiences through their TV appearances and blogs as well as through their books and journal papers. Other food-related media such as cookbooks, cooking shows, food magazines, celebrity chef shows, food advertisements, and others continue to proliferate in public domains (Allan 2002: 146). The number of food forums on interactive media platforms such as the Internet has also increased rapidly. These online food forums and YouTube cooking footages attract a large number of "foodies" who now not only receive food messages, as they do on traditional media platforms, but also actively share their own experiences of food with others.

As is now well-established, food is a critical medium in the construction of social meanings and relations. The media also construct sociocultural meanings in particular ways, reproducing dominant (and other) social norms, beliefs, ideologies, discourses, and values in their representations, and influencing the audience who use media representation as a powerful source to understand meanings in the world around them (Devereux 2006: 15). When food is coupled with the media, it is not surprising to find that food media contribute significantly to the enrichment of audiences' social and cultural life. Early food media such as Elizabeth David's books seem to lay more emphasis on the subject of food itself (food recipes) than other social meanings refracted through the lens of food. In recent years, however, food media have increasingly expanded their focus outside of food, treating a wider range of sociocultural meanings (e.g., identity and lifestyle) and values (e.g., thrift and morality) as central subjects. The construction of self-expressive identities and lifestyles, including social constructions of gender, often appear in food media such as TV celebrity chef shows. For instance, femininity becomes an important theme running through the shows of celebrity chef Nigella Lawson. For Joanne Hollows (2003b), Lawson is more of a "domestic goddess" than a simple cook. Cooking for a new middle class, Lawson is "sensual/sexual" (Sanders 2009: 158). Viewers watch as a "pleasurable" experience in contrast to hard, time-consuming domestic chores. Another celebrity chef, Jamie Oliver, in his early TV appearances promoted not only "bare essential" recipes in Mediterranean cooking but also a new lad image with a slightly softer masculinity compared to Gordon Ramsay's hard-man image. More importantly, messages in Jamie Oliver's early shows linked food cooking by young men with a fun, casual, metropolitan and socializing lifestyle (Hollows 2003a). Jamie Oliver's *Naked Chef* shows not only educated audiences about how to cook but also used food as one element in an expressive display of lifestyle.

Messages about how we prepare, cook, and consume food and how this correlates with certain aspirational lifestyles are magnified through multiple media platforms. In many cases, popular media act as more than a means through which food-related messages are transmitted. Media can also be more broadly considered as part of popular culture, coexisting with culinary culture in contemporary cultural life. Food and media as interwoven cultural elements are captured in Rick Stein's recent food and travel programs *Tastes the Blues* on the BBC in which he pays homage to the blues music whose lyrics are ingrained with local food and dishes in Louisiana. Rick Stein, the chef/food writer/TV presenter, personifies the tight connection between food and media in contemporary popular culture.

Food Advertising

Perhaps food media shape our cultural norms and values even more directly via ever-present advertising which "endorses, glamorizes, and inevitably strengthens cultural values" (Pollay and Gallagher 1990, quoted in Emery and Tian 2010: 49). Advertising is ubiquitous as it appears on almost all forms of mass media—posters, billboards, Internet, TV, newspapers, magazines, movies, and so on. In a media-saturated age, advertising is most often encountered in the media. From a political-economic perspective, advertising is now an inseparable part of contemporary media. It acts as the bloodline of most media organizations. Media food advertising revenue now exceeds $30 billion per year and revenues are growing year by year (Brownell and Horgen 2003: 103).

It is in the content of advertising that we see the reproduction of social norms and values. As often argued in consumption literature, consumers want not only the physical product but its symbolic meanings, its "image" and the "statement" the product makes about the user. Symbolic meanings, ranging from social status to morality, are increasingly becoming selection criteria for consumers. The symbolic meanings have constituted an important aspect of modern advertising that draws on our deepest imaginings and desires, to sell us not only products that we need but also products that we want. Food advertising is no exception. Successful food advertising by Heinz in the late nineteenth and early twentieth centuries shows how gendered and colonial discourses were employed to construct symbolic meanings of "pure," "fresh," "white," and "civilized" (Domosh 2003). In more recent food advertisements reflecting moral values of food consumption, a prominent theme has been "natural," "green," and "sustainable" food products. New Zealand lamb, woodland chicken, and free-range, grass-grazing dairy cows have created imaginary spaces for consumers to fill in symbolic values such as sustainability and responsibility. Visual media (e.g., television) have become ideal platforms for recreating these imaginary signs on a daily basis, reinforcing our geographical imaginations. These imagined

geographies, signs and values usually have a premium attached to them, and it is consumers who are eventually paying for them. The $22 billion bottled water industry serves as a perfect example of advertisers turning natural free water into a commodity through the cultural meaning of water being natural, pure, and revitalizing (cf. Wilk 2006a). However, these cultural meanings and signs are contingent, very often generated by a series of structures such as political and social institutions that produce certain ideologies. For instance, discourses of sustainability, anti-industrial agriculture, and moral consumption were influenced by highly publicized food scares (e.g., BSE) in the last decades of the twentieth century in the United Kingdom and continental Europe, and by the subsequent reform in food safety regulation and management within government institutions and the food industry.

Commercial food promotion via mass media is thought to be one important factor that prevents the public uptake of healthier diets and patterns of eating (Dickinson 2005: 4). The more worrying fact is that a consistent body of research has demonstrated the negative impact of food and drink advertising on vulnerable groups such as children and young people. Maxine Lewis and Andrew Hill (1998) show that advertisements broadcast during children's television shows are dominated by foods of questionable nutritional value. Studies conducted worldwide suggest that food advertisements for children are often for unhealthy products—products high in fat and sugar such as sweets, sugary drinks, fast food, and sweetened breakfast cereals (Eagle et al. 2006; Dickinson 2005; Gamble and Cotugna 1999; Kaufman 1980). In the United States and United Kingdom, where the number of obese children has increased dramatically in recent years, research has established a link between the increase and the persuasive nature of food advertising (Strasburger and Wilson 2002). Other studies demonstrate the direct effect of food promotion on TV on children's food preference, knowledge, and behavior (e.g., Lewis and Hill 1998; Young 2003; Hastings et al. 2003). Research with new parents in China also found that infant formula advertising has direct or indirect influence on parental knowledge and behavior (Gong and Jackson 2012). Drawing on a wider context of health care system neoliberalization in China, this research argues that, in the absence of independent medical advice and affordable medical treatment, infant formula companies can make ill-founded health claims for their products and employ dubious promotional tactics. Under these circumstances, Chinese consumers exhibit considerable ambivalence about the advertising of infant formula, reflecting significant anxiety about its quality and safety.

The above concerns support Richard Hoggart's critique of advertising as "immoral or ugly": "a wicked misuse of other people," from half a century ago (Hoggart, quoted by Schudson 1981: 3). More generally, there has been much discussion about whether advertising provides useful information to customers or whether it manipulates consumers based on lies and persuasion. Some, including the founding father of modern public relations in the United States and the nephew of Freud, Edward Bernays, believed that manipulation of public opinion (via public relations) was necessary because most people "respond to their world instinctively, without thought" (Rampton and Stauber 2002: 42). The "duped" mass thesis has been challenged in later audience research as discussed in the next section. But for food advertising—particularly food advertising for children—research findings seem to emphasize the "sinister" side of the business. Over the years, academic interest in food advertising and health has been invoking debates among policy-makers and consumer interest groups. The Food Standards Agency and the Department of Health in the United Kingdom, for example, has commissioned a number of studies researching the consequences and promotional activities of food advertising (e.g., Dickinson 2005; Gunter et al. 2005; Matthews et al. 2009). Meanwhile, developments in media technologies (such as digitalization) have led to a rapid growth of TV channels available on a number of platforms (cf. Gunter et al. 2005; Hastings et al. 2003; Matthews et al. 2009). The increased volume of advertising, more subtle forms of advertising on commercial TV (e.g., program sponsorship, product placement, program-related merchandising), and advanced advertising techniques have all made media regulation of food advertising more challenging. How to better regulate advertising practices and to improve public health remain key issues that require joint efforts and responsibilities from media institutions, regulators, and the food industry.

Media Effect and Audiences

Debates surrounding the issue of food advertising and its negative impact on children's health are another area of concern about media "effects" that involve the relationship between audiences and food media in more general terms. Media effect and audience research has gone through a series of developments and revision since the mid-twentieth century. For members of the Frankfurt School, for example, the media are very powerful and media messages are directly absorbed into the hearts and minds of the masses. This perspective, sometimes known as the "hypodermic" model of media influence (Davis and Baran 1981: 25), has been challenged by many later studies ranging from empirical audience research in the United States influenced by social psychology to audience research influenced by British cultural studies (Hall 1980; Morley 1980). Several studies based on social psychology reviewed in the last section demonstrate different degrees of media influence on the audience. Research following the British cultural studies tradition also made a huge contribution to the understanding of audience reaction to media messages. This work demonstrated that instead of passively receiving media messages, audiences bring in their prior knowledge, experience, views, and social positions to their processing of media messages (Hall 1980). Studies have highlighted the domestic context of media consumption and the capacity of audiences and viewers to critically engage with mass media (e.g., Ang 1991, 1996; Morley 1992; Silverstone and Hirsch 1992). With regard to the influence of viewing of TV food programs (which also included nonadvertising content), Dickinson's (2005) study concluded that household members decoded television's food frames to provide explanations and justifications for their own or their family's eating, and television images of food were used as "a kind of resource on which members of the household may draw to help them make, and make sense of, food choices" (Dickinson 2005: 27).

Nick Piper's (2011) research also challenges the existence of a direct, linear relationship between media messages and audience reception. Focus groups and interviews with audiences in Rotherham and Tunbridge Wells in the North and South of England show that celebrity chef Jamie Oliver's TV series *Jamie's Ministry of Food* invoked different responses in each place including ambivalence, embarrassment, and anxiety. Much of the audience's feelings of embarrassment are related to the documentary's sensationalized presentation of family life amounting to a "pathologization" of the British working class (Hollows and Jones 2010: 308). Middle-class viewers' anxieties about class voyeurism arose from their awareness of the fact that pleasure can sometimes be generated from watching people transgress the norms of "good taste" on TV (Piper 2011). This shows again how food and media can work closely together to not only construct and reinforce people's cultural tastes, including the taste for "junk" food and popular media such as "reality TV" shows, but also how some audiences are able to critically engage with these constructions.

Other audiences' reactions to the series, rejecting its main objective of promoting "healthy eating," are organized through online activism. The development of media and communication technologies such as the Internet makes it possible for the public to voice concerns over "celebrity worship, the nanny state, corporate greed, media manipulation, regional stereotyping, cultural elitism and hypocrisy" (Jamiegohome. com 2008). This "back-talking" media platform complicates the process and direction of the transmission of food media messages. More importantly, the new platform challenges the gatekeeping role of the traditional mass media in constructing mainstream and sometimes elitist sociocultural values, norms, and ideologies. Defending British working-class food traditions (such as fish and chips), forum members challenge the imposition of middle-class food tastes. Jamie Oliver's approach to improving healthy eating is criticized by many.

For instance, expensive herbs required in his Italian recipes do not add much nutritional value (Hollows and Jones 2010: 312), but in his later shows he did include more easy-to-make, affordable, healthy food recipes. In some cases, then, popular media can play a key role in communicating health messages and making these messages accepted by the public. Jamie Oliver's food documentaries (notably *Jamie's School Dinners*) have had support from political parties and the government, but changes in dietary habit usually require more than top-down initiatives. Audience reception in households seems to be a crucial factor in effecting such changes. Policy actors, nutrition educationists and other interested parties need to be aware of how food media messages are received on the grassroots level and with what effect.

Media Representation of "Food Scares"

Related to the discussion of media effects is the assumption that the media influence public perceptions of health and risk in situations of "food scares" (Eldridge 1999). Such influence was documented in Jacquie Reilly's (1999) research which conducted focus groups in two phases (1992–3 and 1996) following the two peaks of media coverage of BSE. This research found that between the two peaks, when media coverage subsided, "respondents ... believed the disease had gone away, particularly since it had disappeared in media-coverage terms" (Reilly 1999: 135). As the evidence of the link between BSE and human-variant Creutzfeldt-Jakob Disease (CJD) surfaced in 1996, the public felt betrayed, contributing to a growing distrust of the authorities—government and experts included (Eldridge 1999; Reilly 1999; Pryer and Hewitt 2010). The cost of public mistrust is huge and the implications are profound. Even today in advanced industrial societies with relatively high food safety levels, public perceptions of food safety seem pessimistic: survey results found that almost half (48%) of EU citizens were concerned that food may damage their health (Eurobarometer 2010). Another example is public skepticism toward the safety of genetically modified (GM) food in Europe. In a report commissioned by the Parliament Office of Science and Technology (POST), the investigators concluded on a few factors underlying the "Great GM Food Debate." Among these factors, the erosion of public confidence in policy-making in food safety following the BSE incidents and the "campaign" journalism for a more transparent debate on GM food were found to have significantly influenced the GM food controversy (cf. Allan 2002: 170). Subsequent food policy and risk communication reforms have emphasized the importance of trust, openness, transparency, and dialogic and participatory methods (Smith et al. 2004; Davis 2010).

The role of the media in food risk communication is manifold. While some audiences in Reilly's (1999) research believed that the media acted as scaremongers in their coverage of BSE 1991–2, others believed that the media overall acted as a watchdog and revealed the secrecy and nontransparency of government health policy-making (Eldridge 1999: 126; Miller 1999: 1249). Others argue that "conspiracy theories" are easily exaggerated and consider BSE as a highly uncertain and controversial risk that inevitably undermined the accuracy of media coverage, especially in the early stages. As the "food scare" became politicized in its later stages, the media became the site for a battle between different interested parties including scientists, policy actors, the beef industry, and other interest groups (Allan 2002: 151; Eldridge 1999: 121). Competing definitional frames, explanations, and policies were vehemently debated in the media. Some even argue that the media as a whole became an interested party itself, actively participating in the health policy-making controversy (Miller 1999). With their own "logic" or specific interest, the media covered the story in a certain way. For example, research shows how the media sensationalize "food scares" as threats to public health to construct shocking headlines that arguably boost sales (Allan 2002: 149; Miller 1999: 1249). Moreover, new information, new angles, and controversy constitute important criteria of newsworthiness in journalistic work. The fact that "nothing was happening" in BSE between 1992 and 1995, which made the disease lose

its logical newsworthiness, explained the reasons why BSE did not receive sustained media coverage (Reilly and Miller 1997). Despite its potentially life-threatening nature which usually makes good headlines, BSE's newspaper coverage only peaked in 1991–2 and 1995–96 following two official statements respectively (Reilly and Miller 1997; Miller 1999). The first statement confirmed the way transmissible spongiform encephalopathies (TSEs) could jump the species barrier; the second statement was that BSE was the most likely cause of new, variant CJD.

Gong's (2011) research on media coverage of the global food price spike in 2007–08 also demonstrates similar media sensationalism whereby the food price spike came to be treated as a "crisis" by newspapers all over the world. Interpretations of the crisis were then further extended to a "humanitarian crisis," a "threat to civilization and culture," "the new face of hunger," a "silent Tsunami of hunger" and the threat of "mass starvation." In addition, media coverage of the food price spike was not sustained even through the spike was often described as a long-term condition that required long-term attention. Rather, the coverage was mostly prompted by high-profile activities of influential organizations and governments which show that event-ness and freshness were used as criteria in news construction by the media. For instance, news coverage peaked between April and July 2008 when a UN's World Food Programme publication referred to the food crisis as a "silent tsunami."

From these analyses, media coverage of "food scares," crises, risks, and controversies emerges as a complex process involving the influence of multiple actors with different and sometimes contradictory aims. To make things even more complex, different political systems provide the context for media's role in covering such events. These include the liberal democratic system in the United Kingdom which enabled a coordinating yet competing relationship between the media and policy-makers (Allan 2002), and the authoritarian system, which suppressed and contained media coverage in a recent "food scare" involving contaminated infant formula in China (Gong and Jackson 2012).

New Media and Food Activism

High-profile "food scares" such as BSE or the threat of an avian influenza pandemic affecting global food supplies have exacerbated public concerns and anxieties about food safety. At the same time, increasing numbers of grassroots movements organized by individuals and organizations have emerged, supporting more sustainable food production and consumption methods (e.g., Slow Food and Via Campesina). Some of the movements have gained high exposure via print and electronic media platforms. American writer Michael Pollan's (2009) book *Food Rules: An Eater's Manual* is one such publication, its ethical approach to food receiving great media attention. Across the Atlantic, other ethical food consumption initiatives such as Hugh Fearnley-Whittingstall's TV program about reducing waste in the fishing industry (*Fish Fight*) and Carlo Petrini's Slow Food movement have also been given high publicity by the mainstream media (Germov et al. 2011). Some of these movements, such as Slow Food, have also become increasingly media-savvy and sophisticated in their use of PR techniques, as they have developed their own "in-house publishing and media-liaison facilities" and "supportive journalistic networks" to ensure positive media discourses (Parkins and Craig 2006). The media seem to have become an integral part of the new discourse of ethical consumption, acting as cultural intermediaries for different parties and circulating their ideas and opinions in the public domain.

In recent years, there has been a proliferation of food activism on the Internet. Weblogs such as "Wasted Food" (http://www.wastedfood.com) maintained by American journalist and writer Jonathan Bloom represents such a trend. Burgeoning food activism on the Internet is associated with the "radical" and "alternative" nature of the medium but is also perhaps more closely related to the technological features of the medium. Multiple technological tools including e-mails, user groups, discussion forums, blogs, and social network sites (such as Facebook) have greatly enhanced the interactivity and swift communication between users. Alternative food network activists, for example, have

been using the Internet to explore online sales and distribution channels (Holloway 2002). E-mail has become a mundane communication method between consumers and producers. Likewise, the use of webcams from the "Adopting a Sheep: Cheese, Meat, and Manure" site allows consumers to monitor daily shepherding activities on their laptop or PC (Holloway 2002: 76).

In addition to assisting grassroots movements, the Internet also facilitates social marketing of public health authorities to change consumer behaviors for positive outcomes in public health campaigns. The National Health Service (NHS) in the United Kingdom has been using both TV advert and YouTube channels to promote its Change4Life and five-a-day campaigns. In the past, a "top-down" mode of communication usually dominated health communication, especially during situations of "food scares" where the discourses of food safety and security tend to be controlled by powerful actors such as policy-makers, food industry representatives and their public relations professionals, and the mainstream media. But thanks to the advances in media technologies such as the Internet, individual consumers and consumer groups, activists, NGOs, and charity organizations now can take part in the public debate by constructing, disseminating, and receiving their own messages. In the meantime, health authorities are also changing their model of communication by drawing on new media technologies that allow more public input and feedback.

New interactive media and traditional mass media are now working closely together. The example of organizing food supply from farmers in rural Suffolk to consumers in West London via the Internet demonstrates the medium's potential to overcome the locational disadvantages of remoteness in food distribution (Holloway 2002: 72), once consumers picked up this initiative from the mainstream media. In other cases, the Internet works together with the traditional mass media to create a bigger "synergy." Slow Food for instance, has a strong presence both on the Internet and in traditional media, claiming to have 100,000 members in 153 countries (Slow Food 2012). Both Michael Pollan's

Food Rules and Huge Fearnley-Whittingstall's *Fish Fight* have websites, which are being read worldwide, the latter even relying on the website to collect signatures for an online petition. These examples all demonstrate that the synergy created by multiple media platforms has the potential not only to convey messages to a broader audience but also to transcend national borders and form global networks.

It is important to note that the Internet, as with any other media, is embedded in existing social structures and relations. As Lewis Holloway (2002) demonstrates, alternative food networks such as myveggiepatch.com and "Adopting a Sheep" rely on romanticized images of the rural and emphasize the experience of hobby-farming for their consumers. In their research on newspaper coverage of Slow Food in Australia, John Germov and others (2011: 91) found that the coverage was predominantly positive and relied on three themes: conviviality (sharing the good life), slow food as socially and environmentally superior, and romanticization of the rural and the past. This shows that the sociocultural meanings that Internet-based alternative food networks draw on to appeal to ethical consumers are not a far cry from those used by the traditional mass media.

See also advertising, celebrity chefs, risk, trust.

Qian Gong

MEMORY

The Proustian moment, where the taste of a particular food sparks off a series of powerful personal memories, has become a common trope in contemporary food studies. For Italian food writer Marcella Hazan, it is the smell of sardines that always has this effect:

> There are some smells that have the power to summon intact a whole period of one's life. For me it is the odor of sardines roasting over a slow charcoal fire … and an image of my father's mother in never-changing long black dress and

black kerchief, bending over a wobbly grill set on bricks in our yard, waving at the embers with a fan of rooster-tail feathers. (quoted in Steingarten 1997: 254)

Here, as in so many other examples, food proves to be an ideal vehicle for evoking memory, being simultaneously tangible and symbolic, embodied and emotive.

Food memories can be both fondly reassuring and evocative of more vexed experiences, with family meals, for example, remembered both as a site of harmonious commensality and of heated conflict (see Katrak 1997; Counihan 2005; Hockey et al. 2007). Indeed, the relationship between food and memory is multiple and contested. Reviewing the anthropological literature on food and memory, Jon Holtzman (2006) identifies six key themes: embodied memories constructed through food; food as a locus for historically constructed identity (ethnic or nationalist); the role of food in various forms of "nostalgia"; dietary change as a socially charged marker of epochal shifts; gender and the agents of memory; and the contexts of remembering and forgetting through food. Holtzman finds this literature "rich and engaging" but criticizes it for being atheoretical and relying on popular constructions rather than on rigorous research (2006: 366; see also Holtzman 2009).

In search of firmer theoretical foundations for thinking about food and memory, food scholars have turned to recent work in oral history and narrative studies (Perks and Thomson 2006; Chamberlain and Thompson 1998). Work in this tradition examines the role of memory in shaping individual subjectivities, analyzing people's historical recollections in order to cast light on the social changes that have occurred within living memory. Such studies remind us how memories of the past are shaped by current concerns, approaching the past through the lens of the present (see Lowenthal 1985; Jackson 1999). Personal life histories are a particular form of narrative, often (re)told with a specific audience in mind and emplotted within wider narratives and discourses of the past. Oral historians also characteristically focus on the subjective qualities of how the story is told ("trusting the tale") rather than on whether particular memories are factually correct in their representation of past events. Oral testimony provides access to "the myths we live by" (Samuel and Thompson 1990), approaching myths not as demonstrably false but in the anthropological sense of stories that circulate in society, providing a moral commentary on the appropriate conduct of social life (cf. Cohen 1969).

Raphael Samuel and Paul Thompson also talk about the nature of collective memory, drawing on Maurice Halbwachs's (1992) ideas about *mémoires collectives* and the Durkheimian notion of the *conscience collective*. This is a contentious area that sometimes seems to imply the hypostatization of memory as the property of social groups rather than of individuals within groups. While memories are, in one sense, always experienced by individuals, there is also clearly a sense in which, for example, many British people share a common memory of the Second World War and of its impact on the nation's diet, whether or not they themselves had direct experience of food rationing. That these wartime memories continue to resonate many years after the event is demonstrated by the mobilization of such imagery in celebrity chef Jamie Oliver's TV series *Jamie's Ministry of Food* (broadcast in 2008).

Halbwachs's work also serves to remind us that our collective memories are forged as much through what we allow ourselves to forget as by what we choose to remember. David Sutton refers to the "editing out" of Turkish influences on Greek cuisine as a particularly revealing example of "hegemonic forgetting" (2001: 168), while Peter Jackson and others (2009b) demonstrate the role of selective remembering and forgetting in relation to the history of sugar in the United Kingdom. In this case, British sugar beet farmers are able to recall a heroic history of their role in protecting domestic consumers from the effects of wartime blockades (by substituting domestic sugar beet for imported cane sugar), while there is a much more disturbing amnesia concerning the history of slavery and empire associated with Britain's role in the sugarcane trade.

Memories of food can serve a significant role in the celebration of group identity as David Sutton demonstrates in his ethnography of the Greek island of Kalymnos: *Remembrance of Repasts* (2001). Invoking the idea of "prospective memory," Sutton shows how Kalymnians plan elaborate meals not just for their present enjoyment but also with the deliberate aim that they will be remembered later on, serving a community-building function both within the island and among the diaspora of Kalymnian migrants living elsewhere. Sutton argues that food's "memory power" derives from a process of synesthesia whereby food crosses over different sensory registers such as taste, smell, and hearing (2001: 17). There are many similar examples of the social embedding of memory in other times and places including Carole Counihan's (2004) work on family, food, and gender in twentieth-century Florence and Graças Brightwell's (2011) ethnographic work on Brazilians in London, where she argues that particular grocery shops and restaurants serve as a vehicle for an "economy of nostalgia" (*economia de saudade*), subtly combining commercial and cultural registers (money and meaning, business and belonging, retailing and relationships). Similarly, for historian Donna Gabaccia (1998), food has played a critical role in the making of Americans, providing avenues for ethnic assimilation and pathways for cultural pluralism. Food memories have even served as a kind of survival strategy for those whose lives have been threatened by starvation, as among the women of Terezin, who wrote down and shared recipes in the appalling conditions of a Second World War concentration camp (de Silva 1996).

Memory also has a commercial significance as food marketing frequently emphasizes bucolic images of the countryside, with pastoral allusions and idyllic representations of the rural conveniently obscuring the sheer hard work involved in much agricultural production. Such imagery conveniently blurs the distinction between personal memories of childhood and wider experiences of intergenerational change, merging biographical and chronological time. Memories of "nursery food," for example, often combine personal and collective memories, epitomized in Enid Blyton's apocryphal reference to "lashings of ginger beer," a phrase that never actually appeared in her *Famous Five* stories but that many people now fondly incorporate within their own memories of growing up in the 1940s and 1950s.

In the future, food scholars might engage more actively with the field of memory studies, where Pierre Nora has argued that "memory attaches itself to sites, whereas history attaches itself to events" (1989: 143) and where Paul Connerton (1989) has shown how societies remember through ritualized and embodied practices (cf. Seremetakis [1994] on perception and memory and their associated material culture). Finally, we should note that the food industry is not immune to the process of memorialization. This is evident not just in the proliferation of "heritage" foods and other kinds of invented tradition (such as Coronation Chicken, a dish that was created to memorialize the crowning of Queen Elizabeth II in 1953) but also in the tendency of major corporations to record their company histories, as the supermarket firm Tesco recently did in conjunction with the National Life Stories archive at the British Library. This provides oral historians, who are more used to recording the life stories of socially marginalized groups and individuals who have been "hidden from history," with some significant challenges (as discussed by Perks 2010). But it also presents some intriguing opportunities for mapping the interconnections between "public" (corporate, commercial) histories and "private" (individual, personal) memories (Russell 2008).

See also taste, time, tradition.

Peter Jackson

MORAL ECONOMY

The idea of a "moral economy" is often counterposed to the apparently rational operation of the political-economy. The contrast is part of a longer history that looks with suspicion on the commercialization and commodification of

social life and on consumption as a debased way of relating to the world. Tracing this history of ethics and value, Peter Leutchford (2005) suggests that the association of money and materialism with impoverished social relationships and hyperindividualism is a specifically Western idea, linked with various currents of thought from Aristotelian ethics to Marxian economics and Christian theology. Rather than seeing markets and morality as opposing terms, however—one concerned with the amoral pursuit of profit, the other with notions of caring and trust that are beyond price—this essay will argue that markets and morals are mutually constituted within the contemporary commercial cultures associated with the production, marketing, and consumption of food (cf. Jackson et al. 2000).

Morality is typically defined in terms of the good, right, or proper way to live, informed by one's religious beliefs or by some other socially approved code of conduct. While often used as a synonym for morals, "ethics" is sometimes restricted to Aristotelian notions of practical reasoning, while morality is reserved for systems of thinking based on notions of duty, obligation, and other principles of conduct as set out in Kantian philosophy. In relation to food, one might distinguish moral sentiments of trust and reciprocity, as they inform systems of individual or social actions for example, from ethical notions of fair trade or social justice as forms of reasoning that underpin such actions. In practice, however, the terms are often used interchangeably. Whether one is concerned with ethics or morals, the focus of debate is on claims about how to live the good life and tracing the wider implications of our individual actions and collective practices for other people and places.

Moral economy can be seen as part of a wider discourse about "cultural economy," referring to recent transformations in social life whereby "the economy is increasingly culturally inflected and … culture is more and more economically inflected" (Lash and Urry 1994: 64). In practice, however, "cultural economy" is usually associated with a narrow range of knowledge-based industries such as advertising or the "cultural industries" (cf. Amin and Thrift 2003).

While cultural economy refers to "the subtle imbrication of economic knowledge with other forms of cultural practice" (DuGay and Pryke 2002: 3), it does so frequently without any significant engagement with the moral dimensions of economic life (cf. Dixon 1999). Moral economy is, then, a subset of wider debates about cultural economy, where economic propositions are inseparable from moral ideas of propriety and value, trust and responsibility.

Moral Economy and Its Application to Contemporary Food Studies

The concept of moral economy has a long history, dating back to the foundational thinking of Adam Smith in the mid-eighteenth century. Best known for his *An Inquiry into the Nature and Causes of the Wealth of Nations* (1776) and often now regarded as a simple exponent of "free market" economics (as promulgated by the Adam Smith Institute in London, for example), Smith's arguments were, in fact, more subtle than this and should be interpreted in their historical context. At risk of oversimplification, Smith argued that enlightened self-interest, guided by the "invisible hand" of the market, might lead to a more just and equitable society than the prevailing world order that was organized in the interests of large corporations such as the East India Company, controlled by royal patronage and promoting unfair competition. This emphasis on fairness, equity, and social justice is developed further in Smith's *Theory of Moral Sentiments* (1759), where he argued that economic relations cannot be divorced from moral notions of "fellow-feeling," which we might today express through ideas of reciprocity and regard, trust and obligation.

More recent commentators on Smith's work such as Andrew Sayer (2000) have outlined a theory of moral economy, defined as the study of how economic activities are influenced by moral dispositions and norms, and how those norms may be compromised, overridden, or reinforced by economic pressures. In this view, markets and moralities are not mutually exclusive or opposing forces. Rather they involve reciprocal relations whereby markets depend

on and influence moral and ethical sentiments, while social norms, moral conventions, and other ethical considerations exert a powerful influence on economic behavior.

Recent thinking about moral economy also draws inspiration from Polanyi's *The Great Transformation* (1944/1957) in which he argued that the market economy and the modern nation-state developed in parallel, challenging those who argue that modern markets have become disembedded from the wider fabric of social life. Debates about the social embedding of economic life by authors such as Mark Granovetter (1985) and, in the context of food and farming, Jonathan Murdoch and others (2000), and Michael Winter (2003), owe much to Polanyi's pioneering work.

Polanyi's ideas were taken forward by the social historian E. P. Thompson (1971) in his study of the moral basis of preindustrial food riots and by the anthropologist James Scott (1976) in his study of Southeast Asian peasant society. Thompson saw food riots as a justifiable (moral) response by the peasantry to attempts to subject them to the logic of the marketplace as part of the wider disciplinary force of industrialization (cf. his earlier work [Thompson 1967] on the imposition of clock-time and the disciplinary strictures of factory work). Scott's work focuses on the process of subaltern resistance to colonial domination in Southeast Asia. In his analysis of the way peasants sought to ward off the fear of food shortages, Scott explores how an established system of patron-client relations, where wealthier peasants protected weaker ones, was broken down by the introduction of market forces, threatening the survival of the subsistence economy. Arguing that these circumstances increase the likelihood of outright rebellion, Scott focused on the "weapons of the weak," everyday forms of resistance used by the peasantry to subvert the power of the state and the market. Inspired by Scott and Thompson, some authors continue to restrict the idea of moral economy to a particular period of industrial development while others have sought to extend the idea to a range of (socialist and postsocialist) economies (see, for example, Mincyte 2011; Wilson 2012). In this essay, we also seek to establish a wider remit for the term, exploring the way ethical and moral sentiments permeate economic life.

Within the last ten years, work in agri-food studies has become increasingly interested in the moral and ethical aspects of contemporary food systems and especially how ethics shape the development of new and "alternative" forms of production-consumption networks (see, for example, Maye et al. 2007; Clarke et al. 2008). In many Western societies, these debates have been associated with the "quality turn" in food studies toward organic and/or more localized forms of production including the rise of farmers' markets, community-supported agriculture, and the Slow Food movement—developments that each contain their own ethical assumptions and social exclusions (Goodman 2003; DuPuis and Goodman 2005; Slocum 2007; Sassatelli and Davolio 2010).

While some have explored the ethical basis for asceticism and self-denial in relation to food (e.g., Lester 1995; Lawrence and Shapin 1998), excess consumption has more frequently been the subject of moral castigation, with ethical campaigns waged against meat-eating and alcohol consumption, in particular. So called "binge-drinking" has been a particular concern in the British media, compared unfavorably to the more modest and convivial forms of alcohol consumption perceived to exist elsewhere in Europe. These discourses sometimes reach the level of a full blown moral panic, especially when experienced by young women for whom more respectable behavior in public is deemed appropriate (cf. Skeggs 1997; Holloway et al. 2009).

Following a moral economy perspective, American sociologist Clare Hinrichs (2000) uses the concept of social embeddedness in her comparative exploration of the social relations of farmers' markets and community-supported agriculture (CSA). She shows how farmers' markets create conditions for closer social ties between producers and consumers while remaining fundamentally rooted in commodity relations, while CSA schemes represent an attempt to construct a new, ethically driven alternative to the conventional marketplace where producers and consumers share the risks and rewards of each season's agricultural harvest. Economic geographer Roger Lee (2000) applies

a similar argument in his analysis of small-scale horticultural nurseries in Britain, drawing attention to the social character of economic activity, including the "economic geographies of regard" that are founded on mutual interests and knowledge. Following Polanyi, James Kirwan (2004) has reviewed how the notion of embeddedness has been utilized within agri-food studies, drawing distinctions between strategies that create alterity (otherness), valorize local assets, or are simply a commercial appropriation. A debate has ensued between those who argue that ethically defined alternative food networks (AFNs) represent a radical and significant departure from conventional food systems and those who regard them as incremental or niche phenomena, rooted in the lifestyle preferences of relatively affluent social groups.

Typically, research in this vein has focused on AFNs rather than on "mainstream" food commodity chains. A key exception is the work of Lawrence Busch (2000) who employs the concept of moral economy in his analysis of the normative dimensions of grades and standards in agricultural production and food manufacture (see also Thompson 1996). Kevin Morgan and others (2006: 5) also use the concept in their study of place, power and provenance in contemporary food systems, arguing that a moral economy perspective could significantly enrich the agri-food literature. Kiri Le Heron and David Hayward (2002) have used a moral economy perspective to trace the articulation of moral values in the development and marketing of breakfast cereals, while Frank Trentmann (2007) uses the language of moral economy to provide a historical perspective on the ambivalent consumer politics of food in the modern world, contrasting advocates of fair trade with those who favor an open-market approach to fair trade.

The politics of fair trade have been debated at length, focusing on specific commodities like coffee, tea, and chocolate. While advocates argue that fair trade has offered producers a better deal than conventional trade, underpinned by a minimum price guarantee and a producer premium to be ploughed back into community initiatives, critics argue that the system impacts unfairly on those who are unable to join such schemes, distorting competition and adversely affecting the proper functioning of commodity markets. Researchers have focused on the ability of fair trade schemes such as Café Direct to cut out the "middle-man" and to deepen rather than lengthen commodity chains (Whatmore and Thorne 1997), while others have debated the ethics of caring for "distant strangers" rather than considering the needs of more proximate others (Jackson et al. 2009b). Critics also argue that fair trade may simply allow Western consumers to feel better about themselves, indulging in what Clive Barnett and others (2006) call a form of "moral selving" while not materially improving producers' lives. This may be particularly true when market prices are high and producers can get higher prices than the fair trade minimum on the open market. This can mean that lower quality goods are sold under the fair trade label, undermining any implicit relationship between fairness and quality. Finally, Barnett and colleagues (2005) have explored the way that fair trade positions consumers as individual actors, responsible for their own purchasing decisions, rather than addressing a more collective form of politics such as through municipal procurement policies.

Beyond the specific focus of fair trade and ethical consumption, the concept of moral economy has been applied to a wide range of current debates in food studies. We focus here on three such examples, examining the moral economy of shops and shopping, the politics of the international sugar trade, and the gendered politics of "feeding the family."

The Moral Economy of Shops and Shopping

The modern retail world may not look like very promising ground for locating a vibrant moral economy. In many accounts of contemporary retailing, a dismal picture emerges of alienated consumers whose sense of community has been thoroughly undermined by the relentless march of globalization. According to this view, the difference between places is being eroded by the steady imposition of a universal economic rationality, often characterized by reference to global brands as a process of McDonaldization

or Coca-Colonization (cf. Ritzer 1993). While we might expect the modern retail world to operate purely in terms of the cold logic of market economics, recent ethnographic work goes a long way in challenging this view, uncovering evidence of a vibrant moral community with a distinctively local sense of place.

In the United Kingdom, for example, the retail environment has been subject to a relentless process of retail consolidation whereby a handful of supermarket chains now dominate grocery purchasing, contributing to the demise of smaller independent stores (Blythman 2004). The Competition Commission has deliberated on the growing monopoly of the "big four" food retailers while a succession of government reports has focused on the threat that the continuous expansion of out-of-town shopping malls is posing to the social and economic vitality of town centers (Miller et al. 1998; Clarke et al. 2006). But the overwhelming evidence of recent ethnographic work on shops and shopping, in the United Kingdom and elsewhere, has been to emphasize the tenacity of ordinary consumers in carving out a space within the contemporary retail world through which to express the kind of moral sentiments that Adam Smith remarked upon: notions of respect and reciprocity, relations of trust and mutual obligation, feelings of loyalty and familial bonding.

In her book *Point of Purchase*, sociologist Sharon Zukin (2005) writes about shopping in the United States as both a tedious chore and a moral preoccupation. While her assertion that shopping "defines the spiritual territory of our lives" (2005: 2) may be an overstatement, she goes on to describe how shopping "teaches us how to live in a market society" (2005: 8). Her account of the history of shopping in the United States engages with "the big structures of the economy ... and the little structures of feeling and desire" (2005: 10), involving a balancing of freedom and routine, aesthetic pleasure and rational calculation, what you desire and what you know is right. She describes how shoppers wrestle with the "demons of desire" as they struggle to express their personal and familial values, concluding that shopping is not only or primarily about acquiring goods but a social encounter involving moral and aesthetic values (2005: 60–61). Zukin shows how shopping entails a serious social communion with people as well as a sensual communion with material things (2005: 251), ending with a vision of *what shopping should be*: an expression of our creative and ethical selves, giving pleasure, creating a public space and sharpening our sense of value (2005: 276–7)—a vision that Zukin finds currently easier to realize at her local farmers' market than at retail giants like Wal-Mart.

These ideas are pursued in greater ethnographic depth and detail in a series of studies in North London where anthropologist Daniel Miller has shown how consumers can express intense feelings of love and familial devotion through their routine shopping practices, where their purchasing decisions are driven by notions of quality and taste as well as by price and value, and where a purchase may be chosen with infinite care, based on an intimate knowledge of the recipient's personal preferences and desires. Mothers select food purchases and adjust the meals they cook to suit the tastes of different family members, putting other people's needs and desires ahead of their own. Shopping for food and other household goods is also often characterized by notions of deferred gratification, saving, and thrift, which Miller (1998b) likens to anthropological accounts of sacrifice in more traditional societies.

Miller's work also challenges the received wisdom that people feel greater attachment to their local corner shop and independent grocery stores than to large-scale shopping centers or supermarkets (cf. Everts and Jackson 2009). Many residents in his North London study were ambivalent about the local corner store, in terms of its pricing strategies and limited range of goods, for example, while over time they had become attached to even the most modern, large-scale, purpose-built shopping centers such as Brent Cross (Miller et al. 1998). Here in North London, older residents would "pop in" to the shopping center to buy a pint of milk or to "top up" on their weekly supermarket shop, using the mall as others would use their local high street or corner store. Indeed, particularly for older people, the mall offered a "domesticated" (safe, climate-controlled, pedestrianized) environment, which they preferred to their local high

street (frequently regarded as an unsafe, hostile, and dangerous place). It is easy to romanticize these sentiments, many of which are rooted in the specific history of the area, where notions of local familiarity and attachment are set against the fear of unplanned encounters with strangers (often defined in terms of ethnic or racial difference). But these encounters are shot through with ethical and moral considerations where fear and fascination, desire and dread, play off each other in often unanticipated ways.

Miller's work in North London challenges the idea that people's social investments and ethical relations can be "read off" from the built environment (Miller et al. 1998). Why, he asks, do local residents express such antipathy to "big box" retail stores such as Toys R Us when they feel no such aversion to a neighboring store of almost identical architectural design that's operating as a food co-op, selling locally grown fresh fruit and vegetables? This example reveals the limits of architectural determinism, showing how very similar environments can generate quite divergent views, depending on the nature of the social relations they encompass. In this case, parents felt intense ambivalence toward their children's avaricious pursuit of toys and other consumer goods, while their feelings toward the food cooperative were unambiguously positive. Their attitudes to the retail environment as a physical space, in this case at least, were outweighed by their moral and ethical sentiments toward different types of consumption and different kinds of commodity.

Miller's work also sheds light on another paradox of contemporary consumption: the prevalence of ethical consumption *as a discourse* compared with the general absence of ethical shopping *in practice*. In the course of his North London fieldwork, Miller found that consumers frequently expressed a preference for fair trade and similar goods, defined explicitly in terms of their "ethical" credentials, while such goods showed up relatively infrequently in their actual purchases. Rather than accusing consumers of hypocrisy by high-lighting the inconsistencies in their altruistic attitudes toward the environment (or "distant strangers") and their self-interested concern for the health and well-being of their nearest and dearest, Miller (2001: 124–5) shows how both sets of attitudes are informed by their own moralities. On the basis of his ethnographic work, Miller suggests that consumers rationalize their purchase of conventional (non–fair trade) goods on the basis of their "local" moral commitments to family and friends, where being thrifty is considered preferable to buying more expensive fair trade goods for the benefit of unknown strangers in far-off places. Miller suggests that there is a clear tension between the parochialism of morality versus the expression of a more global ethics and that familial morality is always likely to outweigh a more abstract ethic of care for distant strangers and disembodied Others. Miller concludes that it may be wiser to focus on "consumer ethics" (in general) rather than on "ethical consumption" (as a self-conscious practice engaged in by a minority of consumers).

The Moral Economy of the International Sugar Trade

A second example might seem an equally unlikely place in which to locate a vibrant moral economy, focusing on the contemporary sugar industry and its close historical associations with slavery. Research for the Food Stories project (Jackson et al. 2009b) shows that the history of sugar is characterized by a process of *selective remembering and forgetting* with significant differences between the beet and cane industries. Within the United Kingdom, sugar beet is recalled in terms of a "heroic" national history, where British farmers claim to have protected domestic consumers from the dangers of naval blockades during two world wars. By contrast, a process of amnesia seems to characterize the history of Britain's involvement in the sugar cane trade, conveniently obscuring sugar's implications with slavery and empire. It is often forgotten, for example, that sugar was one of the first products to be subject to a consumer boycott when in 1791 as many as 300,000 people refused to buy Caribbean sugar as an expression of their opposition to the slave trade.

While the process of selective remembering and forgetting articulates moral issues across time, many of the interviewees in the

Food Stories research project expressed ethical concerns through geographical notions of *connection and disconnection*, invoking a politics of scale, where what can be claimed or defended at one scale (the domestic or national, for example) may look quite different when examined at a different (international or global) scale. Accused by a clergyman of destroying the economy of the West Indies, for example, a beet producer in East Anglia replied that he was simply working within the rules established by the European Union while another farmer referred to his need to feed his wife and children, moving the ethical debate from international and regional scales down to the domestic level of individual families and households.

The moral economy of the sugar trade can also be described via notions of *visibility and invisibility*. This is apparent, for example, in discussions of the relative visibility of sugar and other foodstuffs. So, for example, even someone as heavily involved in the food business as cookery writer Jenny Linford claims that sugar is an "invisible" food: "It's taken for granted and we don't really think about … how it's produced, how we consume it, its presence in our household" (interviewed December 2005 for the Food Studies project). Likewise, in his magisterial history of sugar, Sidney Mintz argues that sugar's "astonishing versatility" as preservative, food, spice, décor, and medicine has contributed to its "near invulnerability to moral attack" (1985: 99). More recently, too, Gail Hollander (2003) has shown how U.S. producers have responded to their critics by trying to "renaturalize" sugar via narratives of place, freshness, and environmental sustainability. Compared to artificial sweeteners, they argue, sugar is a natural product whose dietary characteristics and nutritional value are beyond reproach.

The foregoing discussion has demonstrated the complex moral economy of the international trade in sugar where those involved in producing, manufacturing, and marketing sugar have to negotiate the product's historical links with slavery, the fraught politics of trade quotas, price subsidies, and import tariffs, and intense debates about the public health implications of a product that was described by one observer as "pure, white, and deadly" (Yudkin 1972).

"Feeding the Family" as a Moral Economy

In several recent studies of consumption, issues of moral economy are not a prominent part of people's everyday discourse of food. Many simply regard food as "fuel," described in functional terms as a way of maintaining the body. For others, food is more closely associated with concerns about personal weight and body image than with its moral economy, described through a vocabulary of control and restraint. Once the conversation turns to questions of "feeding the family," however, a moralized discourse soon emerges as noted in studies by Nickie Charles and Marion Kerr (1988), Anne Murcott (1983b, 2000) and, in the United States, by Marjorie DeVault (1991).

In a recent study of domestic provisioning in South Yorkshire, many female participants resorted to a language of obligation and duty, where routine housework including cooking and cleaning was described in terms of drudgery and responsibility (Meah and Jackson, 2013). As one woman remarked, "A good meal doesn't just happen"; it is the product of (in many cases economically unrecognized and socially invisible) human labor, mostly performed by women on behalf of other family members. There are, of course, exceptions to this general depiction of the drudgery of household labor. Another participant in this study enjoyed food shopping and loved cooking—taking responsibility for both these tasks and describing them in the moralized language of "keeping a good house," neither a duty nor an obligation but a source of pride. Another respondent spoke of her sense of obligation to her children: "I owe it to them … to show … an example … , because it's us that instils what good eating habits are." Many mothers felt guilty for not living up to their idealized image of "healthy eating," being forced by a variety of circumstances to compromise and fall back on "convenience" foods.

One forty-year-old mother spoke about her awareness of the price of food, and wanting to maximize the value derived from her food purchases. She spoke of the tension between economy and taste and the compromises involved in "being thrifty."

Similar arguments can be observed in David Evans's recent work on the moral economies of household waste, which seeks to challenge the popular claim that Britain is a "throwaway society" where consumers have a profligate disregard for the value of food (Evans 2012). While levels of domestic food waste in the United Kingdom are remarkable, claimed by some observes to be as much as a third of all food purchased (Stuart 2009), Evans's work shows that there are many reasons for this apparent wastefulness. Based on ethnographic work with households in South Manchester, Evans shows how waste is produced through the regular routines of domestic life and through the dynamic of people's everyday social relations where notions of "healthy eating" and thrift are juxtaposed with concerns about food safety and waste, where tensions are experienced between the desire to eat together as a family and the need to satisfy the varied tastes of different family members (including those described as "fussy eaters"). Evans's research shows little evidence of a carefree attitude to food. Instead, his work reveals how complex notions of freshness and convenience, novelty, and taste may lead to food being wasted, especially when combined with specific retail practices (such as increasing portion sizes and promotional deals such as buy-one-get-one-free).

Conclusion

As the previous case studies suggest, apparently rational decisions about the production, distribution, and consumption of food (usually described in terms of the operation of a disinterested political-economy) are susceptible to a range of ethical and moral concerns stemming from a range of political and emotional investments in food. A sharp distinction between morality and markets cannot be upheld in studies of commercial or domestic food provisioning (cf. Laura Shapiro's subtler distinction between the "emotional economy" of the kitchen and the "cash economy" of the commercial marketplace [2004: xxiii]). All these examples reinforce the need to think carefully about the complex ways in which the moral and political economies of food intersect.

See also choice, local-global, responsibility, trust.

Peter Jackson

N

Nutrition © ANGELA MEAH.

NUTRITION

Nutrition refers to the nourishment required by cells and organisms to support life. Nutritional science explores the metabolic and physiological responses of the body to diet, based on the recognition of six major classes of nutrients: carbohydrates, fats, minerals, protein, vitamins, and water. While often viewed as part of the medical or health sciences, John Yudkin and John McKenzie are firm in their assertion that "in the study of human nutrition, the social sciences are as important as the natural sciences" (1964: 9). Because of its associations with human health and well-being, however, the field is characterized by numerous debates and controversies as scientific measures (such as calorie intake or the body mass index) are invoked in the formulation of public policy as well as exploited for commercial gain in the private sector. Indeed, nutritional advice has for generations been dogged by normative (morally laden) judgments, leading some observers to make a distinction between "food" (which tastes good) and "nutrition" (food that's good for you) (see Belasco 2007: 197).

In the United States, such distinctions go back to the mid-nineteenth century and to what Harvey Levenstein calls the "new nutrition," which used scientific ideas developed in Germany in the 1840s and 1850s to recommend that people should select foods on the basis of their chemical composition rather than their taste, appearance, or other aesthetic considerations, telling people to eat "what was good for them" rather than "what they liked" (2003: 46). Soon, the expanding public high school system was training children to cook and giving them hygiene lessons, including advice on the virtues of "eating to live" rather than "living to eat" (2003: 79). With the birth of home economics, Levenstein claims, "Thousands of mainly middle-class female graduates of the nation's public school system had some knowledge of the basics of the New Nutrition" (2003: 79–80). These ideas prevailed until the 1920s when research on the vitamin and mineral content of food gave birth to a "newer nutrition" which, Levenstein suggests, was "made to order for the extravagant claims of food advertisers" (2003: 149).

According to Dana Simmons (2008), the Second World War created the conditions for nutrition to become a "science of social hygiene," shifting scientific debate from a clinical understanding of nutrition to a medical one concerning the etiology of malnutrition. Once the purview of colonial health researchers, dietary deficiency became an urgent medical issue on the European continent creating a vastly expanded "science of starvation." While the long-standing connection between inadequate nutrition and poor human health remains an urgent concern in many parts of the world, in the global North concern increasingly focuses on the consequences of "overnutrition" following the adoption of modern diets consisting of large quantities of processed food, high in sugar and added fats, together with low levels of consumption of fresh fruits and vegetables. Medical evidence suggests that such diets pose increasing risks of obesity and diet-related diseases such as hypertension, diabetes, and heart disease. Yet nutritional science is treated with skepticism by many food writers who associate it with a puritanical rejection of the pleasures of food. Julia Child referred derisively to "the nervous nutritional nellies" who treat food as medicine (quoted in Reardon 1994: 198), while Michael Pollan speaks dismissively of "a lot of what passes for nutritional science," describing the field as "a very young science … approximately where surgery was in the year 1650" (2009: xi–xvi). Food critic Jeffery Steingarten (1997: 168) talks about the "mass frenzy" and "paranoia" of the American dietary establishment, which he accuses of basic errors including the failure to distinguish between the consumption of saturated and unsaturated fats. Steingarten also challenges the public health consensus on salt, arguing that obesity and alcohol are more strongly associated with high blood pressure than salt consumption, though he admits that salt can exacerbate hypertension in those already afflicted with high blood pressure. Calling for a more balanced attitude among U.S. public health officials, Steingarten claims that salt is indispensable to good food and good cooking: "It sharpens and defines the inherent flavors of foods and magnifies their natural aromas. Salt unites the diverse tastes in a dish, marries the sauce with the meat, and turns the pallid sweetness of vegetables into something complex and savoury" (1997: 155). A similar skepticism is evident in Steingarten's essays "Salad the Silent Killer," "Pain without Gain," and "Murder, My Sweet." Whether or not one agrees with his analysis, it is clear that people's dietary decisions involve complex social and cultural judgments that cannot be reduced to simple nutritional measures.

Nutritional science's credentials have also been undermined by its associations with the multi-million dollar diet industry, described by Michael Pollan as the Nutritional Industrial Complex (2009: xv) and associated with a succession of fads and fashions, many of dubious value in terms of sustained weight loss and some posing serious health risks if followed obsessively. The history of nutritional science is also littered with controversies over the relative health benefits of particular products (such as butter and margarine) and debates over the perceived dangers of specific food innovations (such as the alleged carcinogenicity of artificial sweeteners like Aspartame). Matters are further complicated by weaknesses in the regulatory system in many countries including the United States, which restrict the use of the title "dietician" to those with specific professional qualifications while not offering similar legal protection to the label "nutritionist," which can be claimed by anyone.

Reflecting the contested nature of nutritional science, the modern food industry has long sought to finesse the distinction between healthy and convenient food, seeking to enable consumers to overcome the seemingly irreconcilable difference between foods that are healthy and/or fun, substantial and/or convenient, classy (in terms of their cultural capital), and/or available at a mass-market price (Belasco 2007: 209). The recent controversy over the alleged health benefits of probiotic yoghurts, incorporating beneficial bacteria that are said to improve human digestion, is just one example of how the food industry tries to straddle these contradictions, leading to increased public skepticism about such claims (*The Guardian* 2009), while the promotion of "low-fat," "lite," and "diet" alternatives to conventional products has been subject to widespread criticism, often substituting sugar for fat (or vice versa) in order to make up for the loss in flavor.

The science of nutrition is rooted in the distinction between different food types and in the belief that a healthy diet consists in the consumption of a varied diet, promoted in the United Kingdom via the "Eatwell plate" and in the United States by the "food guide pyramid," recently replaced by the "nutrition plate". While such advice seems sensible and well-intentioned, it fails to address some fundamental nutritional questions about why some diets seem healthier than others. By most nutritional standards, French people should have high levels of obesity and heart disease because of their above-average consumption of butter, cream, and eggs and other foods that are high in saturated fats and cholesterol, yet they appear to have much lower rates of coronary heart disease than most other Western nations. The so-called "French paradox" has no simple nutritional answer, prompting observes to look at different attitudes to food and other "lifestyle" factors (such as eating in company with family and friends, at longer sittings, and with less snacking between meals) rather than trying to identify a purely nutritional or statistical explanation (such as trying to calculate the alleged health benefits of drinking red wine or figuring out the effects of different methods of recording health and illness).

A final example of the importance of understanding the social and cultural context of nutritional issues is the recent use of the term "nutrition transition" (Popkin 2004) to refer to countries like Brazil and China, whose growing economic prosperity is leading increasing numbers of people to adopt a diet that is higher in meat and dairy products. Like other "transitions" (demographic, ecological, etc.), there is nothing inevitable about these changes, which reflect the aspirations of those with the means to access a protein-rich diet. These changes are held responsible for all kinds of negative consequences, from short-term spikes in agri-food prices to longer-term threats to global food security. But here, as elsewhere, what might seem like a simple dietary issue that can be expressed in purely nutritional terms requires a much more profound understanding encompassing its social, economic, cultural, and political dimensions.

See also eating, hunger and famine, science.

Peter Jackson

P

Packaging © ANGELA MEAH.

PACKAGING

Food packages are literally to be found everywhere, in supermarkets and convenience stores, in restaurants, in workplaces, and in the homes of consumers. As mundane and everyday as these cardboard boxes of flour and crackers, bottles of juice and water, plastic and paper wrappers of meat and cheese might seem, packaging is also important for the influence it exerts on the way food is produced, consumed, and perceived. Packages contain, preserve, and protect foodstuff during transport and storage, but they also supply information on and a symbolic dimension to the foodstuff they contain. They are active agents, providing the material and symbolic prerequisites for the contemporary food system. For example, the sociologist Franck Cochoy (2004) conceptualizes packages as socio-material devices playing an active role in shaping the practices of food production and consumption. And although not explicitly conceptualized in this manner, much of the broader research on food packaging also illustrates the active role of food packages in fostering the consolidation of the modern food industry and increasing the power of larger corporations.

Packages were a prerequisite for the development of the modern agri-food system, which started to develop in the eighteenth century when industrialization made people leave rural areas and move into the cities, thereby losing the ability to be self-sufficient in food (Beardsworth and Keil 1997). Instead of growing their own food, people had to buy the foodstuff they needed. Food markets and food shops became a common feature in cities, and this new way of producing, selling, and consuming food implied new demands in both transport and preservation. Aiding both preservation and long-distant transport, packaging played a central role in the development and organization of the commercial food system.

While introduced during the eighteenth century and becoming increasingly common in during the nineteenth century, the dispersion of packaging took a new leap in the mid-twentieth century due to the development of the self-service system. Paul du Gay (2004) has described the growth of self-service retailing in mid-twentieth-century Britain, showing that this process implied both a reorganization of shops and a transformation of how shopping was performed and understood. The self-service system meant that in-store displays of foodstuff were organized in a manner that enabled consumers to gather the merchandise themselves (du Gay 2004). Du Gay suggests that the practice of prepackaging was particularly important in this development as it allowed for increased individualization of merchandise and for more sophisticated marketing and branding practices.

The development of packaging as a marketing strategy has also been described by Cochoy (2004), who suggests that packaging and its development should be understood as a complex social process involving legal, regulatory, and commercial issues affecting both producers and consumers. According to Cochoy, the packaging innovation was a way for companies selling high-quality products to solve the problem of fraud against their products. By packaging their products and placing a brand name on them, it became harder for lower-quality products to be sold under their name. Through packaging, producers were able to signal differences to consumers that were otherwise hard for them to detect. Unfortunately, the increased use of packages made tasting food products impossible, but at the same time other characteristics could be named, underlined, or even invented. The content of a product could be described; best-before dates, warning tags, or other legislative information could be attached to the package; and symbolic aspects could be ascribed to the product through, for example, branding. In this sense, packaging fundamentally changed the relationship between producers and consumers. Packages let consumers know more about products than they would have been able to detect themselves. Also, packaging allowed not only for vendors but also producers and legislators to communicate with the consumer.

However, packaging not only aided in the distribution of food and informed consumers in a new manner. It also had an impact on what food people consumed and how they consumed it. During the 1950s, packaging and related preservation techniques offered consumers variety and made food less season-bound. It also paved the way for the development and selling of prepared foodstuff—an innovation that made a radically different way of cooking possible. As cooking was (and is) primarily considered a woman's responsibility, the introduction of packaged and prepared food was intimately interlinked with female practices and femininity. In her book *Dinner Roles: American Women and Culinary Culture*, Sherrie Inness (2001) explores how cooking literature published after the Second World War produced a certain (middle-class) femininity in relation to cooking. Packaging played a vital role in this production. Inness illustrates how this particular femininity was built around values such as creativity and efficiency, materialized through packaged food. Cookbooks assured women that high-tech appliances and packaged prepared food simplified cooking and thereby promised women the ability to spend less time in the kitchen and more time on personal interests and activities. Inness illustrates how the particular values of creativity and efficiency were key to making packaged and prepared foodstuff part of everyday cooking practices. Canned and prepared food had existed for many decades, but the 1950s cooking literature helped make them omnipresent (Inness 2001).

Hence, from an historical perspective, the work performed by packages in containing, preserving, protecting, informing, and selling foodstuff has been vital to the way food has been produced, sold, and consumed. Packaging played a vital part in the organization of the modern food system and in defining the relationship between its actors. What is more, packages have not only influenced the way food is produced, sold, and consumed but also how food was and is understood. According to Cochoy, packaging "teaches us to consider products under a new light; they deceive and inform us, they are symbolically seductive but they also reveal the hidden properties of products, they bind us to the egoist and material pleasure of consumption but they also uncover the political side of things" (Cochoy 2004: 223).

In the fields of food science and food technology, the focus is on the future rather than the history of packaging. In these fields, much effort has been placed on the development

of technologies and materials improving the quality and durability of packaged food. In recent years, the development of oxygen scavengers, flavor releasing/absorbing systems, time-temperature indicators, and antimicrobial containing films where foodstuff is packaged in particular atmospheres or particular materials in order to prolong durability or prevent the growth of bacteria (e.g., Ming et al. 1997; Ozdemir and Floroz 2004) have opened up new possibilities for the food industry. While many studies are dedicated to the development of these technologies, others have been devoted to evaluating the impact that different packaging techniques or materials might have on the food packaged (e.g., Law and Wong 2000; Blumenthal 1997) or how consumers react to and perceive food-packaging technologies (e.g., Siegrist et al. 2007). This research is orientated toward optimizing food quality in line with current production and retail practice. The focus is on the materiality of foodstuff per se and the temporalities of degradation and how it influences the organization of the food system. Discussions of technological innovations illustrate how packaging has an impact on the taste, color, durability, or mobility of foodstuff, and in the long run, the understanding of, for example, how food should taste, what it should look like, and how long it can be stored. And, although consumers are sometimes described as suspicious of technological innovations that contradict what they perceive as natural—for example, significantly prolonging the durability of foodstuff—historical analysis suggests that acceptance of new technologies is often only a matter of time (Hine 1995).

Knowledge of the relationship between packaging and consumers is also developed in research devoted to the ability of packaging to influence consumers' choice of foodstuff and consumption behavior (e.g., Thøgersen 1999; Scott et al. 2008; Do Vale et al. 2008). This branch of research is devoted to the ability of packages to communicate with consumers and influence their behavior. A study of Danish consumers and their choices of environmentally friendly packaging by John Thøgersen (1999) suggests that choice of packaging is reliant on consumers' development of norms. According

to Thøgersen, environmentally friendly packages become a means for consumers to act out
their beliefs and values. Another example is the
study by Maura Scott and others (2008) where
the impact of package size on self-regulation
was investigated. In this study, the focus is on
eating behavior rather than choice. Consumers believed that small packages help them
regulate their calorie intake. However, the study
suggests that eaters on a diet consume more
calories from small packages. In such studies,
packages are primarily conceptualized as vessels
of information/meaning to which consumers
respond in different ways. Packages are conceptualized as influencing consumers but only
as far as the choice situation goes—that is, the
choice of which packet to buy or how much to
consume. To get an understanding of the social
and cultural impact of packaging, one has to
move beyond studies of consumer choice and
instead turn to studies of packages in use.

Although mainly speaking of brands, Jennifer Chang Coupland (2005) illustrates how
packages work as commodifiers and how they
can be used as a means of manipulating the status of food as commodities. Removing a package
and storing foodstuff in a nonbranded container
functions as an important means of decommodification, while keeping the original branded
package is a way for consumers to maintain a
connection between the foodstuff and the market (see also Fournier 1998). Much as the use of
packaging technology could be used to manipulate the nature/culture divide, packaging and its
symbolic qualities can be used to maneuver the
status of food as commodity or noncommod-
ity. Another example is Richard Wilk's (2006a)
work on the practice of buying and drinking bottled water rather than tap water. Wilk's analysis
suggest that packaging per se can add value to
a product by playing on the insecurities of the
public and at the same time, by means of clever
market communication, to fill the product with
values significant to the product per se: in the
case of bottled water, naturalness and purity.
Wilk's argument resonates with a discussion by
Annemarie Mol (2009), who makes a more explicit suggestion that packages are active in the
performance of social categories (see Chatterjee 2007 for a similar argument regarding gender

construction and cosmetics packaging). Mol
contends that packages and their work have an
effect far beyond the choice situation. More specifically, she describes the ability of food packages to sell not only the foodstuff they contain
but also several other values (or goods as Mol
calls them). She takes a particular interest in the
package's ability to unite values or qualities often
perceived as contradictory such as healthy and
tasty or fair and delicious.

Food packaging has also been a key issue
in recent debates on sustainability and waste.
While packaging can reduce waste by prolonging the shelf-life of food, both in store and at
home, packaging is also a substantial source of
waste within the contemporary food system and
is therefore often described as unsustainable by
campaigning groups such as the UK's Waste
and Resources Action Programme (WRAP
2011; see also Stuart 2009). The EU Landfill
Directive was designed to reduce the amount
of food and other waste, encouraging recycling
and more sustainable forms of waste management. Wilk's (2006a) previously mentioned critique of the increased consumption of bottled
water in countries with clean tap water, available at low or no cost, provides an illustrative
example of the relationship between packaging
and waste. Bottled water has become a global
business, and Wilk argues that the successful
marketing and integration of bottled water in
consumers' everyday practices has led to a situation where a packaged product that provides
marginal or little benefit to consumers produces
an immense amount of waste. However, in some
cases packaging is also described as a way to increase sustainability. Going "green" is described
as an increasingly important aspect of package
design (Holdway et al. 2002). Using recycled
material, optimizing material usage, or designing packages in a manner saving space during
transport are examples of how food packaging
can be made more sustainable. Sustainability
efforts are often communicated via the packages themselves through various labels and/or
text. This way the consumer of, for example, an
eco-labeled and recyclable bottle of water is
made aware of the pitfalls of packaging while
at the same time he or she is offered a solution to the sustainability problem. Making

food packages more sustainable and making consumers aware of these efforts are appealing pursuits. But, as consumers are offered less resource-intensive food packaging and food practices, these "greening" efforts might prevent more reflexive and critical forms of consumption (cf. Fuentes 2011).

In summary, although food packages might seem mundane and unimportant, this brief review of previous research illustrates that they are far from passive artifacts. Rather, they should be perceived as active elements in the construction of social categories as well as central to the way retail and consumption practices are shaped and organized. Through their material, size, function, and look, packages make people do things in a particular way. Cochoy (2004) describes packages as encompassing symbolic appeals and seduction; they are part of the makings of routine and attachment, and they appeal to reflexive and calculative abilities as well as values and consumers' political commitments. All these dimensions prompt different actions by producers, retailers, and consumers.

See also aesthetics, brands, convenience, labeling, shopping, waste.

Maria Fuentes

PLEASURE

> The pleasures of the table—that lovely old fashioned phrase—depict food as an art form, as a delightful part of civilized life. In spite of food fads, fitness programmes, and health concerns, we must never lose sight of a beautifully conceived meal. (Julia Child, quoted in Reardon 1994: xvii)

This comment, by American television cook Julia Child, captures some of the tensions that surround pleasure when applied in the context of food. The idea that food can be a source of pleasure is often subsumed by a number of anxieties, ranging from the political and moral economies of production, food safety, provenance, quality, and food security, through to concerns about health and nutrition. Indeed, Paul Rozin (1999) reminds us, in relation to what and how we eat, that food is both a pleasure and a poison. This essay explores the "problem of pleasure" presented by food: how this has been managed historically and the subsequent impact on contemporary discourses concerning diet, health, nutrition, and the body, and the "revolution," largely attributed to the Slow Food movement, that has reconstituted culinary "pleasure" as something positive and desirable. Importantly, it also raises questions about to whom the pleasurable dimensions of food are accessible.

John Coveney (2006) provides a useful historical account of how pleasure has become problematized via the moralizing discourse in which the contemporary science of nutrition is embedded (cf. Crotty 1995). Drawing upon Foucault's work on *The History of Sexuality*, volumes 2 and 3 (1990 and 1992), Coveney traces the importance of moderation and self-mastery vis-à-vis pleasure back to the concern of dietetics in ancient Greece, when food "was a good deal more important than sexual activity" (Foucault 1992, cited in Coveney 2006: 32). For example, while the teachings of Epicurus advocate that pleasure is the greatest good, this was not understood in the modern sense of hedonistic excess, wanton luxury, or even "guilty pleasure," but, rather, that the way to attain pleasure was to live modestly and limit one's desires. By Roman times, the emphasis had shifted to the role which food played in the care of the self and how, through fasting and austerity, one's pleasure could be *enhanced*, a concept that is very different from contemporary understandings of moderation which invoke the limitation of pleasure (Coveney 2006: 36). In Christian times, Coveney notes, food and "appetite" had become linked with lust and the "pleasures of the flesh," with illness and disease considered to be manifestations of evil and sin. Pleasure was something to be eliminated altogether and the "civilizing of appetite" emerged as a concern within the Middle Ages (Mennell et al. 1992).

"Pleasure" became a pernicious concept within food nomenclature. While food historians Harvey Levenstein (2003) and Laura Shapiro (1986) have both documented the impact of food reform on the American diet in the late nineteenth and early twentieth centuries, resistance among food lovers has been accompanied by an emergent association of food with (ill-)health and the body, leading to what Rozin and others (1999: 164) describe as an "epidemic of food worrying," wherein food is conceptualized as a poison as much as it is a nutrient. The current "epidemic of obesity" and what Stephen Mennell and others refer to as a "fear of fatness" (1992: 49) have given rise to parallel concerns about slimming and the emergence of eating disorders, with the Internet now hosting a plethora of "pro-ana" websites and forums where "tips and tricks" for losing weight "safely" can be found. Given dominant discourses of restraint and dietary restriction, which are largely directed at female audiences, it is perhaps unsurprising that in a cross-country comparison of attitudes toward food undertaken by Rozin and others (1999), female students in the United States were most likely to indicate that if they could safely gain all their daily nutritional requirements, without hunger, from taking a pill, they would. Whether one is concerned about "supersized" or "superskinny" bodies, food and pleasure are also inextricably linked to issues concerning disgust and shame (Probyn 2000; Julier 2004). Indeed, Alice Julier notes the "deep-seated contradiction between disciplining the body and pampering the soul" (2004: 15).

How, then, have spaces been opened up for the relocation of pleasure in discussions about food in recent years—surely there *are* people who still enjoy their food? Speaking about identity, Elspeth Probyn (2000) notes the move toward experimentations with forms of pleasure that are not primarily sexual. Eating, she suggests, has reintroduced pleasure into the realm of the popular, where "pleasure" can be represented in an explosion of tastes. In drawing attention to the sensual nature of food, this has opened up a space in which the Freudian dimensions of food, sex, and eating have been exploited in literary culture. Here, for example,

we can locate Linda Jaivin's (1998) *Eat Me* and *The Sex Life of Food* by Bunny Crumpacker (2007). While British food writer and television cook Nigella Lawson has popularized the notion of "gastroporn" and is associated with having opened the door for others to regale audiences about the sensual dimensions of cooking and eating on British television and within food writing, Alice McLean (2004) highlights how "subversive" inclinations could be detected in British food writing as early as the 1950s through the work of Elizabeth David. Having spent six years eating and studying French, Greek, and Egyptian cuisine, David returned to Britain toward the end of the Second World War and reconstituted her gastronomic experiences in language, feeding "the hunger and imagination" of a ration-weary public with Mediterranean-inspired recipes that were "an articulation of embodied pleasure and her celebration of an aesthetic firmly grounded in the senses" (McLean 2004: 38–39). Meanwhile, food writer Joan Reardon (1994) highlights the role that M.F.K. Fisher, Julia Child, and Alice Waters have played in changing attitudes about food, dining, and pleasure in the United States. Indeed, in industrialized nations, cooking has been reconceptualized as something *pleasurable*: the sensory engagement with food's organoleptic properties is seen as an end in itself, be this concerned with its taste, smell, flavor, or texture.

Notwithstanding feminist critiques of the oppressive dimensions of "feeding the family," there is also an acknowledgement of the vicarious pleasure to be gained from the act of feeding others. This has variously been discussed by, for example, Anne Murcott (1983b, 2000), Alice Julier (2004), and Angela Meah and Matt Watson (2011). Moreover, in a UK report on the subject of "eating in" (SIRC 2006), cooking for friends is articulated as a form of "gift-giving." Here, commensality and the social dimension of pleasure associated with food and eating— the final phase of enjoyment that Alan Warde and Lydia Martens (2000) accuse sociologists of consumption of ignoring—is made visible. Whether eating "out" or sharing with others food we have cooked ourselves, "the shared affect associated with competent participation in a collectively constructed event gives some of the highest of social rewards" (Warde and Martens 2000: 210).

Perhaps one of the strongest forces for relocating pleasure in food has come with the rise of the Slow Food movement, emerging as an antidote to globalization and culinary homogenization (Chrzan 2004). While Slow Food might be regarded as contributing to an alternative politics of consumption via its attempt to "appropriate pleasure for political purposes" (Sassatelli and Davolio 2010: 208), at the local level it is understood as having provided the impetus for reminding consumers of the pleasures that can be associated with food. Indeed, Janet Chrzan notes that the "über-principle of Slow Food is the right to pleasure … adherents believe that true pleasure is to be found in the flavors, cuisines and practices of … good-tasting, sustainable local food" (2004: 120). Similarly, Wendell Berry suggests that part of the pleasure in eating is to be derived from an "accurate consciousness of the lives and world from which food comes from" (1992: 378). The premium attached to superior quality and locally produced food clearly indicates that access is not distributed equitably across social and cultural constituencies. Both logistics and adequate resources are, therefore, determinants of pleasure. Chrzan's commentary on the organization of Slow Food points toward an elite membership of local *convivia* in the United States, motivated less by the rhetoric of the Slow Food Manifesto than they are in bringing together food-lovers, learning about local food resources, and sharing "wonderful meals with congenial people" (2004: 123). This is echoed by Marie Gaytan (2004) and Sidney Mintz (2006), who point toward the largely white, Western, educated, and affluent constituency of Slow Food protagonists, leading Roberta Sassatelli and Federica Davolio to question whether Slow Food is subversive or elitist (2010: 208). A further point is illustrated via Gaytan's discussion of the imaginaries invoked among her participants, who demonstrate concern with "food tradition"—or the absence thereof—in the United States and a belief in a tradition of "rediscovery" of the culinary traditions associated with other cultures. This theme is also explored by Lisa Heldke (2003), who argues that "food adventurers" are

people who believe they have no culture of their own and therefore *appropriate* ("rediscover"?) the culinary practices of another. Again, these are typically middle-class and well-educated individuals.

The suggestion is, therefore, that whether it is through the ability to appreciate, access, and share superior quality sustainable food, the ability to recognize authentically "exotic" cuisine with the confidence to seek it out, or to "feel like a domestic goddess" through one's engagement with cooking, opportunities to separate discourses of pleasure from those emphasizing more negative dimensions of food and eating are perhaps only available to those with a particular level of social and cultural capital.

See also anxiety, appetite, emotion, sex, taste.

Angela Meah

PRACTICES

The term "practice" carries several meanings. In common usage, it refers to concrete doing (as opposed to abstract theorizing, for example) and to the repetitive doing of something to get better at it. Where researchers and intellectuals talk about practice, it is often to signal that they are alive to the lived experience of doing; to the fine grain of human existence, including that which escapes easy capture in words and other forms of representation. However, a number of thinkers have done plenty of abstract theorizing about practice, leading to potentially radical insights and claims. This essay first considers how food lends itself to analysis through the lens of practice in a general sense, before arguing that the utility of a practice approach to food only begins to be realized when it is fully appreciated that practice is more than simply what individuals do.

Food certainly lends itself to representation, as shown by the mass of print, broadcast, and digital media devoted to it. But the prevalence of food media is a consequence of the extent to which food is ingrained into the routines and conventions, pleasures and drudgery, of their audiences' daily lives. It is this taken for granted substrate of social existence that consideration of practice brings to light, and so food is a realm of the social which lends itself readily to exploration through a lens of practice, through a number of dimensions. For current purposes, we pick out three.

First, the bulk of human action around food is mundane and routinized. Keeping oneself or a household fed means treading a path amidst potentially bewildering complexity, requiring the coordination of ingredients, supplies, hardware, skills, energy, and time within the flow of everyday life, the space of the kitchen, and the requirements of self and others being fed. Acquiring food for most Western consumers entails navigating the aisles of supermarkets, which could overwhelm with the choices offered, choices that would have to be confronted in the light of matters of economy, taste (of self and others), pleasure, and risk. As with so many other fields of daily life, one can only navigate through all of this complexity by relying substantially on routine (Giddens 1984). This is most clear in the stereotypical weekly supermarket shop, where the harassed parent travels the same aisles in the same supermarket on the same path, adding much the same products to the trolley as last week and the week before. Even where food shopping is not so rigidly routinized, choices are typically made from a repertoire of foods that are narrow when compared to what is available. Past choices made by ourselves, or others (notably parents), become sedimented into routine. The possibility of taking the time to notice or choose something unusual or new is itself only made possible by the routinization of the bulk of food shopping.

Second, routine also underpins provisioning within the home, with some of the temporal aspects of cooking and eating clearly part of another theme recurrent in discussion of practice, that of convention. Popular discourses identify a process of deroutinization of eating patterns, symptomatic of ongoing fragmentation and speeding up of social time and dissolution of the family. While there is some evidence of change in how food practices are routinized, conventions of eating have been found to be surprisingly resilient in the face of social changes over recent decades (Warde et al. 2007). Time-use surveys reveal that

meal times remain as a broadly shared temporal rhythm within the day, with distinct profiles of temporal convergence in different national societies (Anderson 2011). For example, in France far more people eat at the same time as one another than in Finland (Shove 2009). Conventions of eating go far beyond the timing of eating, to gendered divisions of labor around food, table manners, tastes, and more. The fundamental location of food in the reproduction of daily lives and relationships is inseparable from its binding within diverse conventions and norms of right conduct, most of which are characteristics of mundane ways of doing, only becoming explicit where they are problematized by transgression. Michel de Certeau and colleagues (1998) excavate the convention-bound roles of food and drink in multiple ways. They do so clearly around bread and wine, arguing that for the families they worked with these were essential elements in the ordering of otherwise random goods from the shop into the organized entity of a family meal: "They have been chosen ... but it is in the kitchen that they become a succession unfolding according to a pre-existing canonical order" (1998: 85).

Third, as a realm of "doing," food is inseparable from themes of embodiment and tacit knowledge. Beyond the extent to which food is necessarily experienced corporeally, not only as multisensory external stimulus but in the process of incorporation, as internal, becoming body. A practice approach, while sensitive to embodiment in itself, has stronger associations with how the body is actively implicated in the flow of action, so much of which depends upon the capacities and competencies which seem to reside in the body beyond or beneath conscious reflexivity. Much of our doing around food depends upon such tacit skills. What seem the simplest, most fundamental actions, of cleaning or food preparation or eating, depend on competences that have become embodied. The effort it can require to take on these tacit skills becomes apparent when it is time to pass them on. For example, there can be few better ways of being made to realize one's own advanced skills at washing dishes than when ushering a child through the seemingly endless hours at the kitchen sink that it takes for them to become fully competent pot-washing practitioners.

These three themes show how approaches that take practice seriously can shed distinctive light on food and its location and complex roles in the reproduction of daily life and of the social. However, taking practice to refer to a particular sensitivity to the taken-for-granted foundations of human action only begins to deliver on the potential of a practice orientated approach. The reach of theories of practice goes well beyond the description of specific actions, to link individual performances—say of cooking or shopping—with the constitution and reproduction of social order.

One thing on which commentators on theories of practice agree is that there is no one theory of practice. Rather, there is a diffuse and in some ways fractured tradition with intellectual roots reaching back at least as far as Wittgenstein and Heidegger. For Schatzki (1996), whilst Wittgenstein did not write directly about "practices," his location of intelligibility and understanding in the flow of praxis, rather than in discrete human minds, provides the foundations for a theorization of practices for which "both social order and individuality ... result from practices" (Schatzki 1996: 13). Practices are not simply points of passage between human subjects and social structure. Instead, practices are at center stage, the location of the social (Reckwitz 2002), with implications for understanding agency and social order, stability, and change.

From these beginnings, visible only in retrospect, theories of practice took on more recognizable form from the 1970s. Diverse theorists including Taylor (1971), Bourdieu (1977, 1990), de Certeau (1984), and Giddens (1984) developed and deployed approaches in terms of practices. While conceiving of practices in different ways, each used the concept of practices as part of an approach that sought to understand the recursive, co-constitutive relations between human action and social structure. Giddens's theory of structuration most clearly locates practices within the recursive relations between human action and social structures. Systems of rules and meanings that structure human activity are themselves reproduced in the flow of that action. It is through practices that the "constitution of agents and structures are not two independently given sets of phenomena, a dualism, but represent a

duality" (1984: 25). It is practices themselves that provide the middle ground between individual action and social order. As Schatzki (1996: 13) has it, "both social order and individuality ... result from practices." Such a grand claim for the role and location of practices—as the site of the social (Reckwitz 2002; Schatzki 2002)—requires more explanation of what a practice is. For Reckwitz, a practice is

> a routinized type of behaviour which consists of several elements, interconnected to one other: forms of bodily activities, forms of mental activities, "things" and their use, a background knowledge in the form of understanding, know-how, states of emotion and motivational knowledge. (2002: 249)

This definition in itself could be read as consistent with understanding practice, as in common usage, as referring to what people do, while sensitive to the background or taken-for-granted character of doing. However, Reckwitz (2002: 250) goes on to explain that a practice exists as "a pattern which can be filled out by a multitude of single and often unique actions." So, a practice exists as an entity which has an existence which endures across individual moments of action (Shove et al. 2007). For example, the practice of baking is something we can meaningfully talk about. In representing it to ourselves or others, we can envisage the entities that are required to accomplish the practice—the materials and equipment, spaces, bodily activities, know-how, norms, rules, meanings, and purposes that are necessary to accomplish baking. While existing as an entity that is transcendent of individual incidences of doing, a practice must also exist as performances. It is through the accumulation of those incidences of doing that the "pattern" of the practice is repeatedly filled and so reproduced. It is only through the accretion of the moments in which people perform baking that the interdependencies between the elements comprising a practice-as-entity are sustained over time. It is through this duality of practice that practice theories provide a means of traversing between individual actions and what appear as the larger-scale structures of social order.

Radical implications flow from this philosophical position. First, it follows that practices, rather than either practitioners or their performances, are a viable focus for social analysis; indeed, they can be argued to be *the* focus. For Giddens:

> The basic domain of study of the social sciences, according to the theory of structuration, is neither the experience of the individual actor, nor the existence of any form of social totality, but social practices ordered across space and time. (1984: 2)

Second, and following directly from the first implication, a practice-theoretical approach decenters human individuals from analysis. Indeed, as Reckwitz (2002: 252) has it, people are the "carriers" of the practices whose patterns they fill through the performances with which they accomplish their daily lives. Rather than meanings, purposes, understandings, and know-how existing as attributes of the subject, they are "elements and qualities of a practice in which the single individual participates" (2002: 250).

This more theoretically programmatic understanding of practice has been applied to, or through, food by a range of writers. Michel de Certeau's influential exposition on *The Practice of Everyday Life* (1984) was substantially through discussion of food, particularly in the second volume of the work (De Certeau et al. 1998), subtitled *Living and Cooking*. Here, a practice approach is used both to explore the fine detail of private doing and the public realm of neighborhood. For Bourdieu, the fundamental character of food practices, not least the ways in which tastes, routines, and expectations around food are produced within the home from the earliest age, makes them significant in the processes of social reproduction and class distinction he explores (Bourdieu 1984).

More recently, in the wake of a resurgence of interest in practice theories in the twenty-first century, writers have engaged with food, and particularly social concerns around food, through the lens of practice. In relation to health, and particularly obesity, Delormier and others (2009) deploy Giddens's structuration theory to elucidate a framing of eating as social

practice. They do so to argue for the need to engage with social theory in order to move beyond the behavioralist models of action around food that dominate nutritional research and policy, to recognize the ways in which food consumption is structured through shared conventions and the distribution of resources. Reflecting the broader application of practice theories to matters of sustainability and everyday life (e.g. Røpke 2009), Bente Halkier (2009) explores how a practice approach can inform dealings with the environmental implications of food consumption, recognizing the profound interrelatedness of food practices with a range of attendant other practices, and the implications of routine and reflexivity in food practices, promoting "environmental performances" around food. Both Evans (2012) and Watson and Meah (2013) use a practice approach to explore how domestic food waste emerges from the micro-organization of everyday life.

It is at this fundamental level that theories of practice offer a very different view of the relations between subjects and their actions than that which is taken as conventional in dominant approaches to understanding behavior change in relation to food, not least in fields such as microeconomics or psychology, whether for objectives of individual health, national food security, or global sustainability. Practice approaches have been used to problematize and advance upon individualistic approaches to a range of other issues in relation to sustainability and health. A practice approach decenters individual choices to a narrative of the evolution of practice and with it the coevolution of the technologies, competencies, meanings, and temporalities that converge in a performance of the practice (Shove et al. 2012).

See also cooking, eating, shopping, work.

Matt Watson

PROVENANCE

Literally referring to place of origin (where things come from), "provenance" is derived from the French verb *provenir*. In everyday English usage, provenance is most often associated with artworks, antiques, and other cultural products. The word also refers to the way such products are authenticated as genuine through an understanding of their derivation. In a legal sense, provenance refers to the history of ownership and to the availability of appropriate documentation, providing a guarantee of legitimate ownership.

In relation to food and culinary culture, provenance refers to the geographical origins of a particular product (including ingredients and dishes) or a style of cooking (sometimes referred to as a cuisine). It is closely related to ideas of authenticity, evoking a relationship between food and place, and has similarities with ideas of heritage and tradition. Like these other words, provenance raises questions about the power of definition (including the authority to arbitrate between rival claims). In many cases, food producers have sought to lend the weight of legal authority to their provenance claims (cf. Coombe and Aylwin 2011). Within the European Union, for example, a welter of acronyms has developed within the overall legal framework of Protected Geographical Status, including Protected Designations of Origin (PDO), Protected Geographic Indication (PGI), and Traditional Speciality Guaranteed (TSG) (see Ilbery and Kneafsey 2000a). Similar labeling schemes exist in North America (Ilbery et al. 2005). These schemes are relatively recent devices, but they are related to concepts of brands and branding that have a much longer history, originally applied to the ownership of livestock (cattle and horses) and subsequently extended to a host of other products (Holt 2006a, 2006b; Pike 2011). Provenance claims are therefore a key component in how the relationship between power and place is played out along the food supply chain as Morgan and others (2006) outline in contexts as diverse as California, Tuscany, and Wales.

Protecting particular products using legal sanctions such as *Appellation d'Origine Contrôlée* are now so widespread that they are almost taken for granted. But they have distinctive histories. The AOC system, for example, was created in the early years of the twentieth century as an attempt by French wine producers to protect themselves against cheaper imports from Algeria and Spain (Stanziani 2004, 2005). Similar schemes now exist in other European countries. Questions of provenance are also central to the idea of *terroir*, where the value of a product is closely associated with the place from which it derives (cf. Trubek 2008). Though now imbued with almost mystical properties, provenance claims about terroir ultimately rest on the notion that the distinctive taste of particular products such as wine or cheese depends on local variations in climate and geology, sometimes also extending to specific methods of production, standards of husbandry, or the intimate connection between people and place (as in the connection between *pays, paysan,* and *paysage* in French). Indeed, it is no coincidence that questions of provenance are so prominent in relation to specific products like wine and cheese, reflecting the material connections between the vine and the soil or between the diet of sheep, goats, and cattle and the quality of the milk they produce. But, as the histories of Champagne and Camembert demonstrate, these distinctions are socially produced and politically contested, reflecting the desire to establish local or regional monopolies. In the case of Champagne, for example, producers in the Marne *département* in eastern France used AOC designation to decry "champagnes" from other places as bogus imitations, invoking the authenticating figure of Dom Pérignon, a monk who is sometimes credited with having invented the drink (Guy 1999). The story of Camembert's invention is equally contrived, in this case invoking the ingenuity of a local folk hero from Normandy, Marie Harel, as validation (Boisard 2003). Though subject to legal challenge from other regions and nations (Barham 2003; Gade 2004), the use of AOC and similar systems has enabled products like Champagne and Camembert to transcend their local origins and to become part of the national culinary heritage of France (Guy 2007; Trubek 2000). A similar process of "heritage valorization" has been at work in promoting tourism and rural development in France according to Bessière's (1996) work on *patrimoine culinaire*.

Recent work by Richard Le Heron's "Biological Economies" group in New Zealand has suggested that the concept of provenance has such wide appeal because of its ability to reach across the food supply chain, bridging the conventional divide between production and consumption. Le Heron argues that provenance is co-constituted by economic, institutional, and academic practitioners, all of whom have an interest in mobilizing the term, using provenance as a mark of distinction. Members of Le Heron's group talk about the way provenance is performed and enacted, exploring the way "provenance propositions" are advanced by different players in the agri-food system as a way of generating value (Le Heron 2011). This work also explores the extent to which provenance claims that have been successfully deployed in relation to one product (such as Hawkes Bay wine) can be extended to other products from the same region. In this case, provenance might serve as a vehicle in the process of brand-extension, with research focusing on the potential role of such provenance claims in local and regional economic development. The insistence in provenance claims on local difference or regional distinctiveness can also be associated with what Goodman (2003) describes as the "quality turn" in agri-food research, where the local is recast as a commodifiable form of difference. So, too, might claims about the geographical "embeddedness" of particular foods and distinctive production methods be described as an example of what Winter (2003) calls "defensive localism," protecting local interests against competition from elsewhere.

The idea of provenance can be criticized for implying a fixed and static relationship between food and place (where only the people in one specific place really know how to produce a particular dish, for example), denying the extent of culinary borrowing and the links between places. Geographers often employ the distinction between "roots" and "routes" to analyze these issues, exploring the lateral connections between places (routes) as well as the more vertical logic of people's historical attachment to a single place (roots) (cf. Crang and Jackson 2001). These ideas have been deployed in studies of "crossover foods" (Cook and Harrison 2003), where food associated with one particular social group or one specific place attempts to reach a

wider market without compromising its attachment to that place or those people. Notions of cultural and geographical hybridity can also be used to challenge traditional ideas about provenance, which sometimes imply a static relationship between people, product, and place (cf. Mitchell 1997).

Because ideas of provenance are so slippery when applied to food and culinary culture, they are readily exploited for commercial gain. This might involve deliberate deception or, more frequently, the invocation of a loose connection between food and place. The example of Oakham chicken comes to mind, where the British high-street retailer Marks and Spencer deployed a symbolic connection to place as part of a recent marketing strategy. Conceding that the choice of name was "essentially a marketing ploy," one of Marks and Spencer's product buyers admitted that "Oakham" was selected because of its "provenance-type imagery" rather than through any actual connection to the town of Oakham:

> It's more about an image than it is a place and provenance. I suppose it does sound British, there's a Britishness to it … and there's a provenance feel, a bit like Aberdeen Angus. Because that's effectively what we were looking for … the Aberdeen Angus of the poultry world. (quoted in Jackson et al. 2011: 64–65)

In this case, the strategy was a success, with sales increasing well ahead of the market and a similar policy has since been applied to a number of other products. In other cases, however, the strategy has provoked criticism. So, when Marks and Spencer was challenged about whether "Lochmuir Salmon" referred to a specific place in Scotland, they attempted to rebut the criticism by saying that the name had been chosen for its "Scottish resonance" on the same principles as "Oakham chicken" (*The Scotsman* 2006).

Food producers are increasingly employing these kinds of "imaginary geographies" in the way they story particular brands, raising difficult issues for consumers as they seek to juggle a number of competing marketing claims when buying food. These can range from questions of cost and convenience to various signifiers of quality (such as local or free-range), also including markers of ethical or environmental standards (such as fair trade or organic). Recent research in South Yorkshire (Meah and Watson, 2013) points toward the myriad of issues faced by consumers undertaking routine acts of household provisioning. The authors present an expanded view of "provenance" when explored from the ground up. Seen from the perspective of consumers, the "roots" or "routes" of production and exchange are subsumed under the wider ethics of care involved in feeding the family. Qualitative and ethnographic data from the study indicate how and why concerns about provenance—be these animal welfare, fair trade, environmental, localism—are enacted *and* resisted, enabling provenance to be conceptualized as a resource to be deployed in everyday food provisioning.

Finally, provenance can also be linked to questions of food safety through ideas of traceability and transparency in food supply chains. So, for example, in the 2008 "food scare" in China, when local supplies of infant formula were contaminated with melamine, foreign brands were accorded a privileged position in the marketplace, justifying a premium price, while local brands were regarded with suspicion (Gong and Jackson 2012). This case also demonstrates that the value attached to provenance is contingent, challenging the common assumption that "local" food is always considered preferable to "foreign" or imported food. In many cases, too, the link between provenance and traceability serves as an additional marketing message. In the case of Oakham chicken, for example (described above), the product label contains various kinds of information including the name of the specific farm on which each chicken was reared as well as a more generic endorsement from a "typical" farmer emphasizing the quality of the product (Jackson et al. 2011). As all these examples demonstrate, provenance claims are contingent and contested, with apparently simple notions of geographical origin subject to a range of interpretations at different points along the food supply chain.

See also artisan, authenticity, brands, exotic, local-global, quality, space and place, tradition.

Peter Jackson

Q

Quality © Angela Meah.

QUALITY

Despite its historical and contemporary importance, quality remains one of the fuzziest terms associated with food. The quality of food is both an empirical category that supposes the existence of qualities which can, in theory, be directly assessed by the consumer, and a normative one that ascribes a positive judgment to a product (Harvey et al. 2004). Like taste, quality relates both to the nature of a product and to its use. Indeed, quality has much in common with taste and in the work collected in Mark Harvey and colleagues' *Qualities of Food* (2004), the terms are often used synonymously. However, as Harvey and colleagues point out, quality is also associated with a range of other meanings of food that overflow those of taste.

Perhaps the most significant trend in the rise of quality as a key term in contemporary Western food systems has been the emergence of new conceptualizations of "quality" within "alternative" food networks. Many of the changes seen in Western food systems over the last thirty years, from the rise of the organics movement to a turn to local food and improved animal welfare, are bracketed together as part of a "quality turn" (Goodman 2003). Particularly associated with alternative food systems, the quality turn is often contrasted with the privileging of quantity in "industrial" production.

Standards of Quality

Establishing quality and conveying its presence is a key element in food systems. Within agricultural economics and food marketing, the quality attributes of food are conventionally separated into the "objective" characteristics of food "dealt with by engineers and food technologists" (Grunert 2005: 371) and "subjective" characteristics of food that are the realm of the consumer. In this perspective the successful development of food products involves matching the former with the latter and conveying the presence of quality to the consumer.

The standardization of quality and its communication takes the form of "quality marks." The origin of quality marks lies in the craft trades of medieval Europe. From the eleventh century, these were frequently organized into guilds which protected the economic interests of members, and which regulated and maintained the quality of products. For example, from 1300, silver and goldsmiths in England were compelled to take their work to the guild hall to be assayed and marked, "hall marks" that persist to the present day.

Quality measures such as hallmarks assume that the intrinsic qualities of products can be accurately assessed or measured by individuals or groups with the appropriate expertise or tools. Similarly, "quality assurance" in food has often focused on expert assessments of taste, and on the maintenance of consistent, standardized products. However, research on the "alternative food systems" that have emerged since the 1960s and particularly in the last two decades describes an increasing emphasis on the contextual emergence of quality. This work describes how quality is constructed and promoted rather than representing being intrinsic. Within the "quality turn," quality is understood less in terms of global standards and in terms of a focus on efficiency, efficacy, or price, but rather on the basis of environmental, nutritional, and/ or health qualities (Murdoch and Miele 1999). Definitions of quality within alternative food networks frequently oppose those of industrial food systems, insisting that quality exists only at the margins of globalized and industrialized food networks (Murdoch et al. 2000, although see Mansfield 2003).

Consequently, quality has become associated nonstandard markets and supply chains and with characteristics such as naturalness (Murdoch and Miele 1999); tradition, heritage, and craft skill (Bessière 1998; Paxson 2012); place and *terroir* (Ilbery and Kneafsey 2000a; Parrott et al. 2002); or welfare and sustainability—themes that are considered in other essays in this book.

The heterogeneous meanings of quality reflect the need for shared conventions of worth or value and shared forms of description that relate to these. These quality conventions work across scales, from that of the appearance or taste of a product to that of the production process. Drawing on the work of Luc Boltanski and

Laurent Thévenot (2006), Jonathan Murdoch and others (2000) use their work on organic cheese marking in Wales to draw diverse aspects of quality together into regimes of justification. They describe the multiple processes of "qualification" associated with different conventions of quality. The quality of small, local, organic cheese production emerges from its "domestic" qualities, linked to the places and scales of production; "personal" relationships between producers and local communities of consumers; its "public" performance which links specialty foods and the tourist market; and its civic or ecological characteristics, established as cheese-makers highlight sustainable, organic production processes.

Work by Nicholas Parrott and others (2002) emphasizes that the articulation of these quality conventions is itself spatially patterned. Focusing on geographical quality indicators, they argue that the importance of these indicators is underpinned by their place in "orders of worth," whereby the qualities of food are differentially assessed and valued within differing convention hierarchies in different places, particularly between northern and southern Europe. They suggest that in southern European countries, conventions of quality are associated with territorial, social, and cultural embeddedness. Consequently, the association of terroir and spatial designations with quality is taken as self-evident. In contrast, they argue that in the north "functional and aspatial" approaches dominate and that the association of local or ecological conventions with quality is established within the market-oriented context that dominates.

Unlike the distinction between objective and subjective qualities drawn above, this "economy of qualities" understands quality as emergent from an ongoing process of "qualification" and requalification, through interaction between consumers and other actors, food materials, and their spaces (cf. Callon et al. 2002; Lagrange and Valceschini 2007; Atkins 2011). It emphasizes the complex set of political, social, and material relations of production, trade, and consumption involved in establishing quality (Mansfield 2003). However, for these relations to be conveyed to other actors within food networks, systems such as hallmarking are required. Quality thus becomes objectified in labels and marks, which contribute to market valorization and which are institutionalized in the bodies responsible for these marks (Renard 2005).

Whose Quality?

The complexity of quality makes the process of qualification a key means of boundary-making and of determining the criteria of entry to particular food markets, and of creating distinctions in a saturated market of similar or identical food products (Renard 2005; Goodman 2008). In addition, the recognition that quality emerges from interactions and negotiations between diverse actors draws attention to the place of concerns such as power, space, race, and gender in the production of definitions of quality. It is common to describe the turn to quality as driven by heightened expectations of the consumer, an assertion based in sales evidence and research in agricultural economics and marketing (Grunert 2005), or by a response to a crisis of trust in industrial food production following a series of food scares (Murdoch et al. 2000; Renard 2005). International ISO 9000 quality standards place the emphasis on the role of demand in establishing product quality: "The totality of features and characteristics of a product or service that bear on its ability to satisfy stated or implied needs" (2004).

This definition of quality combines "objective" intrinsic features of a product with the subjective needs or requirements of consumers. Similarly, European regulations on geographical quality indicators emphasize rising European consumer demand for quality rather than quantity. Consequently, quality is often understood as a concept constructed at "the consumer level, which then works its way back through the commodity chain" (Mansfield 2003: 4). However, as Brian Ilbery and Moya Kneafsey describe, "The constantly negotiated character of the concept of quality itself means that there is potential for powerful actors within the food production–consumption chain to appropriate the term for their own products" (Ilbery and Kneafsey 2000b: 220).

This is seen in the expansion of the quality turn from its initial association with small producers to adoption as an important form of market distinction by large food companies. In turn, this has consequences for the elaboration of public and private standards against which the judgments of worth described above are performed.

The co-option of quality and of quality standards has been described across the regimes described above, including in relation to organic production (Guthman 2004b), in the welfare standards and provenance highlighted in "Lochmuir" salmon or "Oakham" chicken produced for Marks and Spencer in the United Kingdom (Jackson et al. 2007), and in the expansion of fair trade certification frameworks (Renard 2005). This adoption of quality and certification-led strategies by large retailers and manufacturers leads toward a proliferation of standards (and consequently their devaluation in the view of the consumer) but also to new forms of discipline in control as retailers introduce stricter controls on supply chains.

For example, Marie-Christine Renard (2005) describes the emergence of diverse practices through which the qualities of food are "qualified," standardized, and certified. She describes how certification comes to control market entry and acts as a source of power within food systems. Focusing on the case of fair trade, she describes how quality is established in ethical terms, based in civic values of justice and equity and in opposition to the dominant relations of the conventional food market. She describes how fair trade's norms and criteria for definition of quality have consequences for the organization of commodity chains in areas such as coffee production. In particular, Renard argues that the expansion of the fair trade network has displaced the producers in the global South who were at the heart of the initial development of the fair trade movement. As the

fair trade concept has become adopted more widely, it has increased in complexity, and certification has begun to operate internationally. Coordinating this international endeavor has prompted the centralization of the institution responsible. Renard shows that this regulatory reorganization, accompanied by changes in coffee commodity chains, has moved producers from the center of the fair trade movement and by requiring producers to bear the costs of certification, has decreased its appeal.

Conclusions

Quality has been at the heart of many of the recent changes in food systems examined in studies of food and society. These studies have successfully moved understandings of the basis of quality from the objective assessment of intrinsic characteristics to a dynamic, interactional, and relational process of qualification. Studying quality in this way draws attention to the power relations inherent in the development of the "quality turn." In addition, it highlights the adoption of quality within the "industrial" food systems against which alternatives define themselves, eroding distinctions previously drawn around characteristics such as taste (Lagrange and Valcheschini 2007). This is compounded by the success and expansion of organic, traditional, artisanal, or ethical production toward increasing industrialization. Consequently, future research will do well to attend to emerging ways in which quality differentiation occurs and in which products are qualified.

See also artisan, authenticity, local-global, safety, space and place, taste.

Richard Milne

R

Race © Angela Meah.

RACE AND ETHNICITY

"Race" is one of the most toxic words in the English language, associated throughout history with some of the most appalling instances of "man's inhumanity to man," from the Nazi Holocaust in the 1940s to apartheid South Africa (which persisted as an official state ideology until the country's first democratic elections in 1994). The language of race and racism is deeply contested within the social sciences though most scholars would agree that there is no serious scientific basis for dividing humankind into a series of distinct, separate, and hierarchically ordered "races," with genetic variation among humans now regarded as continuous rather than discrete. While the ontological status of race is still debated (cf. Saldanha 2006), it is now generally accepted that racialized divisions of humanity are socially constructed and that social science should devote itself to tracing historically and geographically specific forms of racialization (Miles 1989; Jackson and Penrose 1993).

Applying these ideas to the study of food, it is possible to trace the operation of ideologies of race and racism at every scale from the embodied level of individual food consumption to the larger scales involved in the construction of national diets and globalized inequalities in food consumption. We should also not need reminding that deeply racialized inequalities persist in even the most economically advanced countries. This was revealed in the 1960s when the Black Panther Party responded to the failure of city, state, and federal governments to address the needs of inner-city communities by introducing their own services to the people, including grocery giveaways and Free Breakfast Programs (Hilliard 2008). The persistence of racialized inequalities were revealed, once more, during the New Orleans floods in 2005 when, following the devastation wrought by Hurricane Katrina, thousands of people—including many impoverished African Americans—were exposed to extremes of food insecurity.

How, though, do these arguments apply to ethnicity, a term which often seems to have

escaped the vilification that has been applied to the closely related term "race"? Conventionally, "race" was taken to connote differences that are rooted in biology (such as genetic variations of skin color or facial features), while "ethnicity" referred to socially acquired differences (such as religion or language). But the distinction was often finely drawn, as, for example, when "ethnic" differences were treated as though they were ineluctable, rooted in notions of ancestry or tradition. Frequently, too, "ethnicity" has become implicated in shallow notions of multiculturalism, involving the celebration and commodification of identity and difference.

In food studies, distinctions of race and ethnicity are often caught up in notions of authenticity and exoticism, where members of a socially and politically dominant "mainstream" (who regard themselves as ethnically unmarked) seek to appropriate the material and symbolic goods of an ethnically identified minority. That markers of ethnic difference are often hierarchized is suggested by Lisa Heldke's work, which argues that, from a Northern European American perspective, certain foods are "ethnic" by nature and some are more "ethnic" than others: so "German food is ethnic, but Italian food is more ethnic, and Greek food more ethnic still. Foods from any part of Asia are yet more ethnic, and African foods are the most ethnic of all" (2003: 51). In the U.S. context, too, African American cultural critic bell hooks writes scathingly about the way that ethnicity is treated as a "spice" that can be used to enliven the dull dish of mainstream white culture (1992: 21), arguments that remind us of the need to interrogate constructions of "whiteness" as closely as more visible forms of ethnic and racialized difference have been interrogated (cf. Dyer 1997).

For all the tentativeness that we have learned to exercise around the language of ethnicity and race, there is also a more assertive quality to the discussion of racialized difference in the food studies literature that is motivated by the need to reclaim the systematically neglected contributions of subordinated groups to "mainstream" culinary culture. This is true, for example, of the revival of Soul Food among African Americans in the 1960s, where many ingredients of a "Southern diet" were shown to have African roots (Opie 2008). Controversially, however, a study such as *Ethnic and Regional Foodways in the United States* (Brown and Russell 1984) included contributions on Jewish Americans, Italian Americans, Russian Americans, Mexican Americans, Cajun Americans, Hindu Americans, and Florida Seminole Indians—but no discussion of the culinary culture of African Americans. Yet ingredients like black-eyed peas, fried chicken, and collard greens, as well as cornbread and yams, okra and squash, catfish and chitterlings are all now part of "the American diet" with distinctive regional origins that can be traced back through the history of the Atlantic slave trade. More attention might also be paid to how different ingredients reached the "New World," rendering their convoluted journeys more visible. The historical nature and contemporary significance of these entangled roots/routes is much disputed (Crosby 1972; Carney 2001). One such controversy surrounds whether Southern food poses a health risk to children because of its high salt, fat, and sugar content, or whether changing their diet risks "robbing a region of its culture" (*Christian Science Monitor* 2006).

Indeed, research by historian Katherine Parkin (2006) argues that, despite evidence of their distinctive consumption practices, African Americans were not seriously regarded as consumers by American advertisers throughout the twentieth century. Parkin reports a study of *The Negro Market*, undertaken by Raymond A. Bauer and Scott M. Cunningham in the 1970s, where they highlight that as early as 1930, African Americans were identified as having distinctive food preferences and that, in order to avoid ignoring their spending power, food advertisers were advised to demonstrate their concern for this population group by, for example, using African Americans in advertisements and considering their differential product usage and media preferences. Parkin concludes that "marketers did not listen to their own data in the 1930s and struggled to learn from these lessons throughout the rest of the century" (2006: 81).

There are fascinating debates about the positive cultural significance of food and cooking among African American households compared to their negative associations in some white households where kitchens came to be defined as a site of women's oppression. So, for example, bell hooks (1990) argues that, for her grandmother's generation, "homeplace" was a site of resistance to an oppressively racist society. This is not to deny, of course, that domestic space has also been a site of conflict and violence for many women. But the sense of home as a source of comfort and strength is a common feature of many African American women writers. Like hooks, Marvalene Hughes writes eloquently of the essence of black culture having been handed down through oral history, generation after generation in the African tradition, through the selection and preparation of "soul food." She continues, "The dominant figure in the cultural translation through food is the black woman. Her expressions of love, nurturance, creativity, sharing, patience, economic frustration, survival, and the very core of her African heritage, are embodied in her meal preparation" (1997: 272). Hughes also suggests that there are significant differences in attitudes to body image among white and black American women. For many black women, she suggests, "plumpness is a symbol of the wonderful job ... she is doing ... A big body to the Black woman represents health and prosperity ... but in [white mainstream] America thinness is beautiful" (1997: 273). An alternative reading of the relationship between African American women and food is provided by Doris Witt (2004). Based on her analysis of literary images from Aunt Jemima to the present, Witt argues that the conflation of black women and food has been a central structuring dynamic of twentieth-century U.S. psychic, cultural, sociopolitical, and economic life.

Finally, one might note the way that food has played a significant role in the adjustment of migrant groups to their changing transnational circumstances (as discussed by Gabaccia 1998; Forero and Smith 2011; and many others). Generations of migrants, refugees, and asylum-seekers have found solace in the taste of "home cooking" even as that food has become subtly adapted over time. Providing food, drink, and clothing to needy strangers has been a traditional way of showing hospitality to newcomers at least since Biblical times, a practice that still seems to be needed during periods of economic downturn even in relatively affluent Western economies like the United Kingdom (*BBC News* 2011). Food, then, is deeply racialized in its cultural meanings. As also with race and ethnicity, food is emotionally and ethically charged, constantly being reshaped by the shifting contours of the political and moral economy.

See also body, exotic, hunger and famine, security.

Peter Jackson and Angela Meah

RESPONSIBILITY

Conventional definitions suggest that to be responsible is to be morally accountable for one's actions. But morality and accountability are equally applicable at scales beyond the individual, as in current debates about corporate social responsibility within the food industry (see, for example, Adams 2005; Nestle 2002). Focusing on the distributed and relational qualities of responsibility opens up a series of wider questions about the geographies and temporalities of responsibility (Massey 2004), asking how our ethical and moral responsibilities are distributed across time and space as well as how they are negotiated in practice

In thinking about responsibility and food, we need to consider a variety of scales from national and international protocols about food safety, such as those associated with the *Codex Alimentarius*, to the domestic, personal, and embodied scales of caring for one's loved ones and the self. Other responsibilities are less immediate and more far-flung, including the lives of distant famers; the conditions in which animal products are farmed; and the environment, both now and in the future. Recent food safety "scares" have transcended these scales, including concerns about methyl-mercury in Japanese shellfish in the 1950s, BSE in UK cattle herds in the 1990s, the infant formula scandal in China in 2008, or the 2011 *E. coli* outbreak in Europe.

Each of these events has contributed to an increased awareness of the health risks associated with food safety, leading to an increased politicization of food production and regulation. Governments have legislated to encourage greater transparency and accountability, while retailers have attempted to "pass the buck" to producers (Havinga 2008), and producers (and the food media) have accused consumers of a lack of cooking knowledge and skill (see Jackson et al. 2010).

Issues of accountability, responsibility, and blame also emerge in relation to concerns about the current "obesity epidemic." This is reflected in increased litigation in the United States, where there have been (unsuccessful) attempts to highlight the food industry's culpability for the present crisis (see Adams 2005). It is in this domain that the tensions between personal and social responsibility are most clearly seen. While the passing of The Commonsense Consumption Act of 2003 by the U.S. Senate may reflect what Marion Nestle (2002) regards as an example of the power the industry, the Department of Health in England has been more directive in both highlighting the "major impact [of the food industry] on what people eat" and in emphasizing its "corporate social responsibility to promote healthy eating" (Department of Health 2004). Peter Jones and others (2006) have examined how major retailers in England have responded to the government's White Paper via their corporate social responsibility (CSR) agendas and in-store implementation, while Rachel Colls and Bethan Evans (2008) illustrate the "placing" of responsibility for children's healthy eating with parents and how this not only deflects responsibility from retailers to consumers but also ignores *children's* agency as embodied, responsible beings. Moreover, in conceptualizing responsibility as something contained within the individual, the authors suggest that supermarket CSR approaches in the United Kingdom fail to acknowledge the significance of a model of *collective* responsibility (cf. Gatens and Lloyd 1999), which emphasizes *relations of responsibilities* between different bodies, at different scales: personal, local, and global.

Drawing upon the work of feminist philosophers Moira Gatens and Genevieve Lloyd, Doreen Massey (2004) speaks of "geographies of responsibility," highlighting the way in which responsibility encompasses both time and space. Understood from this perspective, responsibility extends to the distant, as well as the local or personal—for events that took place in the past, as well as anticipated future outcomes, be these in relation to the self, local, or distant others, the environment, or nonhumans. That food consumption has significance beyond nutrition is reflected in a range of developments in recent years, many of which have emerged as "bottom up," as opposed to state-led, concerns. Food production and distribution are implicated in environmental and sustainability issues, in animal welfare, and in concerns about rural livelihoods—both nearby and in more distant contexts. These concerns have provided fertile ground for the emergence of "food citizenship" (Lockie 2009), a movement contributed to by individuals who are both aware of—and take responsibility for—the impact of their consumption decisions, particularly in terms of their ecological footprint. However, one does not have to belong to a social movement to be aware of the range of concerns consumers are now exposed to in everyday acts of food provisioning. As Angela Meah and Matt Watson (2013) point out, these not only include considerations regarding the health and well-being of one's self and immediate loved ones, but increasingly extend beyond the local to the global, to future generations and the conditions in which animals are reared, product labeling having become an important tool in producing "ethically competent consumers" (Miele and Evans 2010). With all this information to hand, one might imagine that consumers now have no excuse *not* to eat healthily, prepare food safely, and demonstrate a sense of responsibility for oneself as well as a range of distant and/or future others.

However, Clive Barnett and others (2005) argue against a model of responsibility that is based on individual human agency and presupposes that having knowledge of a range of outcomes obligates responsible action by individuals. They point out that "the politics of

consuming ethically might not be so straightforward as is sometimes supposed" (2005: 28). As Charlotte Weatherell and others observe, knowledge of or "interest" in a particular issue is not necessarily reflected in specific purchasing decisions since demand is traded-off against other more prosaic "expediency" factors (2003: 234), including resource and time constraints and the need to accommodate the tastes and preferences of various others. As Meah and Watson have highlighted, decisions *not* to consume as people perhaps feel morally obliged does not necessarily reflect a lack of responsibility toward producers, the environment, or nonhuman others. Rather, following Daniel Miller (1998b), we might interpret everyday provisioning decisions as demonstrations of responsibility, care, and love performed in the interests of one's immediate household, which cannot be subordinated to the needs of distant others. Meah and Watson illustrate the tensions, conflicts, and ambivalences between different dimensions of care and responsibility that consumers routinely negotiate, and how these are situated within the broader landscape of interactions, obligations, responsibilities, opportunities, and constraints afforded within everyday life.

As a morally loaded concept, exercising responsibility for food—whether in terms of food safety, nutrition, or the range of ethical dimensions to which consumers might feel obliged—should not be characterized as fixed, static, or located within the individual, but as mutable, relational, and contingent on context and scale.

See also governance, risk.

Angela Meah

RISK

It often seems that few things carry as much risk as the everyday act of eating. Over the last thirty years, food systems have seen the emergence of new hazards and the globalization of existing ones. Bovine Spongiform Encephalopathy (BSE), *Salmonella, E. coli O157*, pesticide residues, *Listeria*, genetically modified crops, *Campylobacter*, melamine, dioxins, Bisphenol A—the list of the actual or potential hazards negotiated in everyday consumption is seemingly endless.

This essay introduces the processes through which contemporary food risks are defined, assessed, managed, and encountered in the context of Ulrich Beck's (1992) seminal work on the risk society. The essay argues that the complexity of risk enables it to serve a range of functions in contemporary food systems, acting to coordinate approaches to food regulation and providing a stable means of understanding consumer behavior, related to the hazards associated with eating. However, it also suggests that a focus on risk reinforces the operation of power within food systems and does not necessarily reflect how consumers relate to food.

The Changing Nature of Risk

The framing of food in terms "risk" is comparatively recent, as is its association with consumption rather than production, with safety rather than quantity, and with a nexus of techniques of anticipation. As such, risk can be distinguished from the traditional hazards, threats, or catastrophes that have always accompanied food. For example, the specter of failed harvests has loomed over much of global agricultural history. Cato commented in the second century B.C. how, on poor-quality land "agriculture becomes a gamble in which the farmer hazards both his life and his fortune" (2007: 44). However, for Cato and contemporaries, although agronomy and good management could maximize a farmer's chances, the ultimate success of the "gamble" of agriculture relied on circumstances and agencies beyond human control that could not be anticipated.

Such determinism is representative of premodern worldviews (Beck 1992). However, in the seventeenth century a focus on gambling and the rules of chance formed the basis for the first systematic study and theorization of risk and probability by Pascal and Fermat. Their work laid the foundation for the calculation of devices such as marine insurance or long-term government bonds, which underpinned the economic expansion of Europe and enabled the emergence of ever-more refined methods of probabilistic analysis as "society became statistical" (Hacking 1990). In the eighteenth and nineteenth centuries, deterministic (or even fatalistic) worldviews were replaced with a probabilistic approach and a successful release from traditional constraints through technological and social innovation. Thus, in the last two centuries, Western food production and consumption have been freed from the tyranny of failed harvests through processes of substitution and appropriation.

Modernity's freedom from constraints has, however, become increasingly associated with risk, a term which is now primarily conceived of in terms of loss, rather than of success, and, Ulrich Beck argues, has changed in nature. Beck's influential risk society thesis (1992) contends that the nature, intensity, and prevalence of risk is the characteristic feature of contemporary Western society. For Beck, this relates to the frequency of specific hazardous events and to how discussions of "risk" emerge as "systematic ways of dealing with hazards and insecurities induced and introduced by modernization itself" (Beck 1992: 21).

Beck argues that the nature of hazards within what he terms "second modernity" is different from previous eras. Within the risk society, risks are catastrophic and reflexive; the greatest hazards we encounter are not those of natural disasters but are instead the product of human activity, particularly of scientific and technical development. Contemporary risks, Beck suggests, are unpredictable and latent within everyday life; they are not limited by time, space, or social class; they are complex in their causation and are not readily detectable without expert assistance—yet this assistance may be ambivalent. Consequently, Beck argues:

> The narrative of risk is a narrative of irony. This narrative deals with the involuntary satire, the optimistic futility, with which the highly developed institutions of modern society—science, state, business and military—attempt to anticipate what cannot be anticipated (2006: 329).

While adopting a realist approach to the nature of risks, Beck also points to the social construction of risk phenomena, arguing that the focus on risk is shaped by the greater ability of some groups to define situations as "risks." Alongside Beck's suggestion that it is the nature of risks themselves that has changed, a second body of work emphasizes the connections between the contemporary preoccupation with risk and changes in modern society. Drawing on the work of Mary Douglas (1966) and Helen Joffe (1999), "risk and culture" perspectives argue that the translation of "danger" into "risk" provides a basis for identity formation and for the reassertion of moral orders in the face of declining social cohesion. An obsession with risk provides a way of establishing unity in the face of disaster, of distributing blame and separating "us" from Others. A third set of "governmentality" perspectives develop on Foucault to describe how the production of scientific knowledge about risk enables new forms of social control.

Each of these perspectives on risk can readily be identified in discussion of food. In the following sections, this essay explores perspectives on risk, examining how the perception of changing risks has prompted the emergence of a cluster of techniques of risk governance.

Risk and Anticipation

The emergence of objectively new food risks and food "scares" is commonly associated with the changing scale, pace, and complexity of food systems and the introduction of new food technologies (Loeber et al. 2011). Beck's original treatise on the Risk Society was published shortly before the "food scares" of the 1980s and 1990s, which then seemed gruesomely to illustrate contemporary risks' "boomerang" (Beck 2006) quality. The case of BSE in particular demonstrated the risks introduced by modern methods of farming, regulation, and consumption. In the late 1980s, "mad cow disease" spread among British cattle herds, passed on through meat and bone meal feeds often containing cow carcasses. Between 1986, when a transmissible spongiform encephalopathy was first diagnosed in UK cows and 1996, the British government

repeatedly insisted that there was no risk of the disease being transmitted to humans. Yet, in March 1996, the health secretary acknowledged that BSE had indeed been communicated to humans.

BSE and scares over *Listeria, E. coli,* and *Salmonella,* Alar, growth hormones, and irradiation were associated with the intensification and rationalization of farming. As such, they exemplified the qualities of the risk society, including the quotidian exposure to hidden risks, the uncertain or unknown nature of these risks, and the frequently contradictory content of expert advice. They raised significant challenges to the assessment, management, and communication of food risks and spurred reform both in the United Kingdom and beyond.

The risk society thesis suggests the emergence of new forms of anticipatory governance that transform contingent and uncertain futures into manageable entities. Indeed, dealing with risks and the scientific and technical issues associated with food is a central concern of contemporary food systems. Prior to the mid-1980s, risk regulation regarded food and agricultural production systems as safe until scientifically proven otherwise. In the 1990s standard setting and enforcement by government was replaced by techniques of risk "governance," in which the state acted as auditor.

More recently, a greater range of interests have been incorporated into risk governance and the emphasis has shifted to trust-building strategies of transparency and accountability. This "third phase" (Smith et al. 2004) is reflected in the diverse reforms to food safety law in Europe and the United States since the late 1990s. The failure of food risk regulation in the case of BSE contributed to the establishment in 2000 of the semiautonomous Food Standards Agency. In the last decade, similar major reforms to food safety have taken place across Europe and North America, including the establishment of a central European Food Safety Authority (EFSA). In the United States, reforms introduced in the Food Safety Modernization Act of 2010 redefined the risk management roles of the U.S. Food and Drug Administration in the context of globalized food risks.

For Beck, the new risks of second modernity are invisible, inaccessible, and globally ubiquitous. Identifying, managing, and communicating these risks form the basis for the work of the new food safety agencies. The presence of *Listeria*, prions, melamine, or pesticide residues cannot be established without expert systems of scientific risk assessment that identify hazards and characterize their severity. Nor can they be managed without food safety regimes including Hazard and Critical Control Point Analysis (HACCP) or traceability, nor without risks being effectively communicated to the population. These three iterative and interacting elements—risk assessment, risk management, and risk communication—form the basis of risk analysis in contemporary food regulation and are codified in the international *Codex Alimentarius*. However, the definitions of risk within these expert systems are often not congruent with those of the public and the media, as explored in subsequent sections.

However, as Beck's work suggests, societal, economic, ethical, and environmental values must also be taken into account in the regulation of risk, and scientific assessments alone may not provide sufficient basis for their management. This is recognized in legislation such as the 2002 EU general food law regulation (178/2002), which institutes a "downstream" incorporation of values into the regulatory process based on mechanisms for public engagement and stakeholder consultation. However, sociological studies of risk assessment highlight that the "upstream" description and delineation of risks reflects the context in which they are produced (Wynne 1992; Winickoff et al. 2005).

Framing Risks

The identification of risks is not simply the recognition of a problem, but rather a process of framing (Stirling 2007; Winickoff et al. 2005; van Zwanenberg and Millstone 2005). As Beck (1992) argues, some groups are more able to define situations as risks than others. Risk assessments are embedded in socially derived "framing" assumptions. While this is recognized in the "iterative" nature of risk analysis frameworks,

divisions between risk assessment as scientific and risk management as the site where values are added occlude the role of value-based decisions within the former. Yet these decisions shape risk assessment by dictating the questions that are asked about how different types and sources of scientific uncertainty are incorporated, potentially leading to divergent answers to apparently straightforward questions (Stirling 2007). Moreover, risk framings implicitly empower some people as experts while others become marginalized, whether consumers or developing countries who do not have access to the "correct" vocabularies or tools to express or quantify concerns in terms of the dominant risk framing (Winickoff and Bushey 2010).

For example, David Winickoff and Douglas Bushey (2010) draw attention to the value choices regarding health, environment, and the action of regulatory power embedded in the definition and functioning of the *Codex* framework of risk analysis. In earlier work, Patrick van Zwanenberg and Erik Millstone (2005) powerfully describe the effect of framing in the case of BSE. Focusing on the work of the Southwood Working Party, commissioned by the Thatcher government to report on the risk of human transmission, they show that the working party's terms of reference framed the advice that emerged. The working party was told not to make recommendations that would lead to increased expenditure, to avoid alarming the public, and to consider the economic impact on the meat industry. Moreover, the group's membership included no experts on transmissible spongiform encephalopathies. The tacit political judgments that shaped the committee's work remained hidden, and its final report was for years presented by the Ministry of Agriculture, Fisheries and Food as constituting a *scientific* appraisal that the risk to humans of BSE was remote (van Zwanenberg and Millstone 2005).

The BSE case suggests that the framing assumptions of scientific deliberations about risk can influence regulatory questions in a number of ways, including which experts are deemed relevant and included; which questions are asked or avoided; which claims are scrutinized and which routinely accepted; which data are collected; which interpretations are accepted and which rejected; and which uncertainties are acknowledged and which discounted. Importantly, this research argues that it is impossible to remove framing assumptions entirely from the risk assessment process. Instead, Andy Stirling and colleagues have argued that risk assessment can be improved by making framings explicit and opening them up for discussion and debate (Stirling 2007).

Dealing with "Nonknowledge"

Opening up the framing assumptions of risk analysis also provides a means of dealing with the problems of "nonknowledge" associated with establishing the probabilities of ubiquitous, reflexive risks. Risk assessment, as practiced by bodies like EFSA, is particularly effective when risks can be known and quantified, and as such provides a potent basis for the formation of policy that anticipates calculable probabilities (Stirling 2007). However, as Beck's risk society thesis suggests, data about the likelihood of catastrophic events is rare and "rationality, that is, the experience of the past, encourages anticipation of the wrong kind of risk, the one we believe we can calculate and control, whereas the disaster arises from what we do not know and cannot calculate" (2006: 330).

Even in the case of everyday risks, scientific evidence is not always clear or univocal. As the UK Food Standards Agency candidly admits, "Experts can develop different ideas about some problems" (FSA 2001: 4.2). The question of risk is thus not only one of evidence but of its limits—what Donald Rumsfeld (in)famously described as the balance of known knowns, known unknowns, and unknown unknowns, or what we might more clearly delineate as risk, uncertainty, ambiguity, and ignorance (following Stirling 2007).

These four terms differ in the extent to which either the probabilities or outcomes incorporated into risk assessment are known. It is only when likely outcomes and the probability of their occurrence can both be known with some certainty that rigorous risk assessment is possible. At the other extreme, when neither probability nor likely outcome can be known, a state of ignorance exists and the techniques

of risk assessment are of little use. In between lie situations of uncertainty and ambiguity. In the latter, the probability of harm can be known, but the form of harm is unclear—as, for example, in debates about the ecological, food safety, or agronomic effects of genetically modified (GM) crops. Finally, in conditions of uncertainty, problematic outcomes are known, but there may be multiple, equally plausible judgments of their probability.

Again, the problems of food risk assessment can be illustrated through the case of BSE. As a novel disease, there was no way the emergence of BSE could be predicted. Nor could the likelihood that the disease would be transmitted to humans be established given the little that was known about the transmission of spongiform encaphalopathies between species, nor about the practices of animal slaughtering through which contamination may have occurred. Furthermore, the consequences of infection were unknown—in the 1990s, apocalyptic predictions about the future effects of Creutzfeldt-Jakob Disease (CJD) on the British population were relatively common (e.g., Rhodes 1997), yet the reality has been significant less calamitous. A state of ignorance existed with regards to both outcomes and their likelihood, making any assessment of risk problematic. Nevertheless, the BSE situation was exacerbated by the assumptions that "framed" the risk assessment process and by the ways in which the risks of beef consumption were communicated to the public.

The problems of dealing with conditions of ignorance and uncertainty were highlighted in UK debates about GM crops, which took place against the background of BSE. In the United States, agricultural biotechnology was framed by regulators as producing familiar products and consequently not a novel technological process, but as an extension of previous practices (Jasanoff 1995: 316). In contrast, opponents of GM food in the United Kingdom emphasized its disjuncture with earlier technologies. Consequently, while U.S. regulators drew on past experience as relevant, "the theme of nature's unpredictability echoed through official British policy" (Jasanoff 2005: 57). Together with wider EU regulation, this approach brought ecologically orientated expert perspectives together with a "normative posture which admitted more uncertainties and called for a precautionary approach to regulation" (Jasanoff 2005: 275). This approach typifies EU food regulation and was formalised in the 2000 Lisbon Treaty, which introduced the "precautionary principle," defined by Rene von Schomberg of the European Commission as follows:

> Where, following an assessment of available scientific information, there are reasonable grounds for concern for the possibility of adverse effects but scientific uncertainty persists, provisional risk management measures … may be adopted, pending further scientific information for a more comprehensive risk assessment, without having to wait until the reality and seriousness of those adverse effects become fully apparent (2006: 37).

The precautionary principle introduces strategies to deal with a lack of knowledge. However, it also opens up European food regulation to accusations of timidity and unfavorable contrasts with the value of "sound science." As Stirling (2007) argues, precaution also offers a way to be more measured and rational about uncertainty, ambiguity, and ignorance.

Risk Communication

The roots of specific efforts at "risk communication" lie in attempts by the nuclear and chemical industries to assuage public concern in the 1970s. These approaches were based on the notion that clear, understandable information was all that was needed to make people see the reality of risks. Similar strategies were adopted in the early years of the "food scares" of the 1980s and 1990s. However, these emerged within a context of increasing public disaffection and a loss of trust in Western governments. Widespread loss of confidence in the instruments of regulation rendered paternalistic statements such as the assertion of the safety of British beef less convincing.

The final leg of the tripartite Food Risk Analysis framework, risk communication, is described in the 2002 EU Food Law as "the interactive exchange of information and opinions throughout the risk analysis process." It aims to bring together a diverse range of actors, from consumers to NGOs, manufacturers, retailers, and various forms of scientific expertise. This exchange can be direct, as in the open consultations that now characterize European food regulation, or mediated, as in the large-scale government-sponsored surveys that attempt to capture the concerns of the population. For example, the Eurobarometer survey on food risk perception is supported by the European Food Safety Authority for the purpose of informing "timely, clear and effective communications regarding food safety" (EFSA 2010). Last conducted in 2005 and 2010, it draws on a representative sample from all twenty-seven EU member states.

The reform of risk communication has emphasized the importance of trust and has promoted dialogic and participatory methods and an increase in transparency as the means of establishing this trust (Smith et al. 2004). As described above, this is reflected in the statutory remit and institutional language of regulators such as the UK Food Standards Agency. Similarly, the European Food Safety Authority, established by European regulatory reform in 2003, is tasked with providing independent scientific advice on existing and emerging risks to risk managers across the EU's constituent nations. In the United States, the FDA has increasingly emphasized transparency as a result of President Obama's Memorandum on Transparency and Open Government (Obama 2009).

In the United Kingdom, the FSA's commitment to transparency extends from the processes of risk assessment through to those of risk management. The FSA's role is to provide risk assessments that are transparent, "unbiased and based on the best available scientific advice, provided by experts invited in their own right to give independent advice" (FSA 2001). However, as recent discussions at the FSA reflect, risk communication is increasingly not simply about providing information or assuaging public concern, but about reflecting the lacunae in the risk assessment process. In recent work on food allergies, advisors to the agency state, "It is important for scientists to be up-front and honest and to say why uncertainty exists, what is known and how opinions are obtained" (FSA 2011). This reflects the find-ings of research by Lynn Frewer and colleagues (1997) among others (see, for example, Stilgoe et al. 2006) that the honest admission of scien-tific uncertainty has a positive effect on the ef-ficiency of communication.

Risk and the Media

While risk communication has begun to move toward a dialogic engagement with the public, it has traditionally been dominated by a model that conceives the provision of information as the solution to "misperceptions" of risk by the public. As Jane Gregory and Steve Miller de-scribe, "Information does seem to be the central weapon mobilized, largely through the mass media, to diffuse the anxiety and opposition generated when citizens feel at risk" (1998: 168). The media thus represent a primary conduit for risk communication. However, this means that responsibility for disconnections between expert and lay perspectives on risk is frequently laid at the door of newspapers, TV, and, in-creasingly, the Internet.

For example, in the late 1990s, public con-cerns in the United Kingdom about GM food were frequently ascribed to media "scaremon-gering," which conjured risks that did not exist and played on public anxiety and uncertainty. The GM debate was a significant event in a long series of incidents in which the media have been deemed to have exaggerated or created fears about food risks, from the "Listeria hysteria" of the 1980s, through to the European E. coli scares of 2011. However, research on the tone of media reporting of risks and its effects on risk per-ception are less definitively condemnatory, as described in Sharon Friedman and colleagues' (1996) analysis of reporting surrounding the 1989 Alar food safety scare in the United States.

In the 1980s, the media in the United States reported that the chemical Alar, a ripening agent sprayed on apples, represented a cancer risk. Alar, produced by Uniroyal Chemical, had been approved for use for twenty years. How-ever, in the 1970s, studies suggested that Alar's active component, daminozide, and a derivative, dimethylhydrazine, were associated with cancer in mice. In 1984, the Environmental Protection Agency (EPA) reviewed the evidence, recom-mended lower acceptable levels of daminozide exposure, and requested further data. The EPA concluded in 1989 that while the risk fell within reasonable limits of one additional case per million, children were at greater risk, and that food use of daminozide should be stopped. However, at the same time, an environmental NGO, the National Resources Defense Coun-cil (NRDC), published a second analysis of the EPA data, which accused the EPA of being ir-responsible. The NRDC's report was covered in an exclusive *60 Minutes* program on CBS in February 1989, which opened with the lines: "The most potent cancer-causing agent in our food supply is a substance sprayed on apples to keep them on the trees longer and make them look better. That's the conclusion of a number of scientific experts, and who is most at risk? Children who may someday develop cancer." The report, also publicized by Meryl Streep, led to the withdrawal of apples from schools and supermarkets, and to one mother's call to the police to stop her daughter's school bus and remove the apple from her lunchbox (Gregory and Miller 1998). By June 1989, the controversy had died down. However, Alar had been with-drawn from sale and the apple industry had suffered major losses, a result that parallels the effect of BSE on the British beef industry or of dioxins in Belgium.

At the heart of the Alar controversy was the role of the media in creating what the agrochemical industry described as an "emo-tion-driven stampede" (in Gregory and Miller 1998: 170). The media were accused of being sensationalist and irresponsible. However, Friedman and others' (1996) analysis suggests that in fact, reporting was relatively balanced. The apple industry was the most cited source in a fifth of articles, compared with less than 7 percent for the NRDC. They conclude that, in general, it was not justified to blame the tone or content of media reporting for the Alar panic. However, they also point out that most reporting did not describe the scale of risk, nor give consumers anything to use as a yardstick against which to judge a one-in-a-million risk. Instead, as Sally Macintyre and colleagues (1998) describe in the case of BSE, the media provided an arena in which contests over the definition of risk take place. The media were more concerned with reporting the controversy over the definition of the risk than assessing what the risk actually was. Moreover, while reporting may not have been sensationalist in itself, the sheer volume of coverage that the controversy generated contributed to amplifying anxiety about apples. Consequently, Friedman and colleagues called for newspaper media to introduce a "complex" of risk coverage "that not only relate the news of the issue but also help explain the value judgments, the uncertainty, the potential impacts, the economic factors, the tradeoffs in costs and benefits and the science behind the news—the risk figures, exposure statistics and risk comparisons" (1996: 18).

The case of Alar provides an example of how media reporting emerges around food risk issues, in which sources of risk are invisible and the level of risk is unknown, and of this reporting's limitations. It also highlights the role of media reporting in driving governmental and corporate policy responses, as in the removal of Alar from the market. Finally, it suggests the importance of social context in establishing the salience and reception of risk issues. Alar became such a concern in part because apples play such a symbolically important role in American culture and in images of home cooking and healthy eating. The disjuncture between these images and stories of hidden chemical dangers accentuated risk concerns. Similarly, in Britain, concerns about the risks of BSE transmission to humans were accentuated not only by bungled efforts at assuaging public risk, but also by the centrality of beef to British culture (cf. Caplan 2000).

Reconstructing Risk

The focus on risk in contemporary society is reflected in new institutional arrangements of risk governance and the prevalence of risk reporting. The state of food risk governance fits closely with Beck's thesis about the reality, novelty, and distinctiveness of contemporary risks. In turn, it is associated with forms of information gathering such as surveys research, including the Eurobarometer, which take the ontology of risks as given and sets out to gather evidence about how they are understood by consumers. However, much sociological work suggests that "risk" has little salience in the context of everyday life, and describes the socially and culturally diverse ways in which consumers relate to food risks (Sellerberg 1991; Macintyre et al. 1998; Caplan 2000; Green et al. 2003; Shaw 2004).

Beck (1992) suggests that a defining feature of risk society is the way in which the uncertainty of expertise results in decision-making becoming increasingly individualized and "thrown back" onto the consumer. Consequently, knowing about and handling the risks associated with food has become "part of the ambivalent experience of modern everyday life" (Halkier 2004: 22).

Alison Shaw (2004) draws attention to the role of a range of factors in mediating consumers' experience of food risk, including the role of experience, the timescale on which risks operate, their severity, incidence, and salience, and the perceived effectiveness of personal risk management strategies and trust in sources of information and in regulatory systems. Following Beck, Shaw argues that a lack of trust in expertise leads lay people to make personalized, reflexive judgments of risk. She finds that attitudes to, and understandings of, food risk are embedded within the worldviews and situated knowledge of participants. Shaw suggests that understandings of risk draw on local and everyday knowledges and internally cohesive "alternative rationalities" that may not align with expert assessments of risk. Psychological work similarly describes how risk perceptions relate to people's previous dispositions toward risk and on the extent to which risks are seen as dreaded or unknown (McCluskey and Swinnen 2011).

Research by Judith Green and colleagues suggests that risks are subject to a range of quotidian management techniques, including heuristics, rules of thumb, or "strategies of confidence" rather than by negotiating competing expert risk assessments (Green et al. 2003; Sellerberg 1991). The case of date labeling in the

United Kingdom is instructive in this context. Survey research by the Food Standards Agency has repeatedly suggested that a significant percentage of consumers misunderstand the date labeling system, potentially putting themselves "at risk" from food-borne illnesses such as *Listeriosis* (FSA 2007). From a risk communication perspective, the problem lies with consumers' inability to grasp the meaning of labels and use them effectively. However, qualitative research suggests that consumers use labels in similar ways to other forms of risk information—that is, through interpreting them in specific local settings and in the context of situated social practices including the everyday rules of thumb used to establish whether food is "off" (Milne 2011).

In addition, the certainty implied by communication instruments such as date labels or press releases can itself contribute to consumer understandings of risk. As introduced earlier, research suggests that openness about uncertainty affects how consumers use risk information. The focus group work of Shaw (2004) or Green and others (2003) demonstrates that public understandings of risk are complex and multifactorial. Consequently, the latter argue that "an information strategy that is open about risk uncertainties may be, in the long term, more effective than one that attempts to simplify messages to reduce 'irrational' reactions" (Green et al. 2003: 526).

While Beck (1992) argues that contemporary risks transcend boundaries of gender, class, and ethnicity, Green and colleagues also point to the ways in which risks are differently perceived by different groups in society, with adolescents, family food providers, and older people each adopting radically different approaches to risks such as BSE. In particular, adolescents and older people were generally unconcerned about food risks, while those providing food for their children were more worried. However, despite the panoply of risks described above and the importance of food risk analysis frameworks to food safety governance, studies such as that by Green and others (2003) argue that risk is not always a salient concept for consumers. Green and colleagues found that for consumers across Europe, the riskiness of food was subsumed within other considerations, such as nutrition, health, or price. Risk thus "forms the tip of an 'iceberg' of related concepts" (Shaw 1999: 168) including trust, responsibility, and blame, and is used interchangeably with chance, danger, safety, or vulnerability. For Green (2009), this means that research that focuses on risk may preempt itself, finding risk where none existed before. Instead, she suggests that risk has become a "second order" object of enquiry, as research interest turns to understanding why and in which domains risk is salient and the implications of particular discursive evocations of "risk."

Conclusion

Given the invisible and pervasive character of the risks described by Beck (1992), it is perhaps unsurprising that some commentators have placed risk at the heart of diagnoses of an "age of anxiety" associated with food (Griffiths and Wallace 1998). However, the apparent lack of "risk consciousness" among consumers suggests that an important detachment exists between macrolevel institutional conceptualizations of the food supply and the nature of everyday consumption. While Beck's diagnosis of the risk society is convincing and has been enormously influential, it has been more difficult to demonstrate the existence of an anxiously reflexive uncertainty in research on consumer food choices (Green 2009). This reflects the conceptual slipperiness of "risk," whether as a real object of probabilistic assessment and public perception or as a constructed form of social distinction and medium for the politicization and disciplining of everyday life.

See also anxiety, governance, safety, science, trust.

Richard Milne

S

Skill © Angela Meah.

SAFETY

Eating is a fundamentally ambivalent experience, necessary for the maintenance of health but at the same time threatening exposure to illness and disease. Consequently, ensuring the safety of food supplies has been a perennial problem for human communities. It remains a pressing global concern: food-borne diarrheal diseases killed about 1.8 million people in 2005 (WHO 2007). In the United States, an estimated 128,000 people are hospitalized each year with a food-borne illness and 3,000 die (CDC 2011). This essay focuses on the mechanisms of food safety that have emerged as a defining feature of Western food systems and how they operate across a range of scales and spaces, from the global extension of regulatory regimes to the disciplining of domestic practices.

The Emergence of Food Safety as Object of Regulation

In newly industrialized nineteenth-century Europe, concerns about food safety focused primarily on adulteration. The food sold to the new urban population of the global North was frequently combined with chemicals to improve its color or flavor. Many of these were potentially harmful, as in the use of arsenic to dye red sweets. Revelations of the extent of adulteration prompted public outcry, most famously in the United Kingdom following Thomas Accum's (1830) *Deadly Adulteration and Slow Poisoning, or Disease and Death in the Pot and the Bottle*. Concerns about adulteration led to the introduction of the first food safety laws in the United Kingdom in the 1870s. In the United States, the first safety legislation was introduced in early twentieth century, prompted by the "meat scandal" that followed the poisoning of U.S. troops by "embalmed meat" during the Spanish-American War of 1898 and the publication of Upton Sinclair's *The Jungle* in 1906. *The Jungle* exposed the dubious practices of the large Chicago meatpacking plants in visceral terms: "This is no fairy story and no joke; the meat would be shoveled into carts, and the man who did the shoveling would not trouble to lift

out a rat even when he saw one—there were things that went into the sausage in comparison with which a poisoned rat was a tidbit" (Sinclair 1906/1965: 163).

Regulatory reforms were relatively effective in calming immediate concerns about food safety. In general, safety did not feature significantly again in the political, economic, or social life of food in the West until the 1970s (Cooter and Fulton 2001). One major exception was the long-running debate about whether milk should be routinely pasteurized to prevent the transmission of tuberculosis to humans. Indeed, pasteurization remains contested in both Europe and the United States, notably with reference to soft cheese production (see, for example, Enticott 2003; Atkins 2000). The pasteurization debate reflects two key discourses in the evolution of food safety through the twentieth century. The first is the relationship between concerns about deliberate adulteration or malpractice and those about the uncontrollable nature of contemporary risks, particularly chemical and microbiological hazards. Hence, past and present debates about pasteurization often contrast scientific definitions of bacteriological quality with the care and concern of producers and the economic and ethical goods these realize. The second focuses on the appropriate role of the state in assuring food safety. Throughout the first half of the twentieth century, successive British governments felt that food safety was best left to "market forces" (Phillips and French 1998). In the postwar years, governments remained reluctant to intervene in food safety beyond a "benevolent paternalism," which involved educating the public in food safety (Draper and Green 2002). However, in the late 1970s and 1980s, food safety became prominent in a political and media discourse which focused on the effects of large-scale food production, processing, and preparation.

The "Food Scare"

Concerns about food safety emerged in 1980s Britain in response to outbreaks of food-borne illness, leading to the identification of a new phenomenon: the "food scare." The term first appeared in the mid-1980s (Knowles et al. 2007) and typically referred to episodes of "acute collective anxiety" (Beardsworth 1990) sparked by reports of risks posed by invisible chemical hazards or food-borne pathogens. While food poisoning outbreaks had occurred previously, the food scares of the 1980s and 1990s were characterized by their association with heavy media coverage, which served to amplify the "deep-seated ambivalence of eating" (Beardsworth 1990: 11), transform food safety concerns into acute anxiety, and lead to changes in food purchasing and preparation behaviors.

The current wave of modern food scares in the United Kingdom can be traced back to the 1988 outbreak of *Salmonella*, which infected people around the country but most notably 120 members of the House of Lords, making it an unavoidable concern for the government. The broader safety of the food supply subsequently became the focus of widespread public disquiet, not least following junior health minister Edwina Currie's statement that the majority of the British egg supply was contaminated with *Salmonella* bacteria. The *Salmonella* scare was closely followed by the "Listeria hysteria," in which several outbreaks of listeriosis occurred and the bacteria were found to be widespread in cheeses, cooked meats, and pâtés. *Listeria* also caused scares in France, while *E. coli* poisoning emerged as a recurrent problem throughout Europe. Nor were the scares entirely microbiological—the contamination of Belgian beef with dioxins was one among a sequence of chemical-based safety concerns to emerge during the 1990s. In the United States, the safety of the food system was thrown into question by concerns about chemical additives, including sweeteners and preservatives, and outbreaks of *E. coli* and *Salmonella*.

Global Spaces of Safety

The series of food scares prompted widespread regulatory reforms, including the 1990 UK Food Safety Act, the establishment of the Food Standards Agency and the European Food Safety Authority, and the 1997 National Food Safety Initiative in the United States. In some cases, they contributed significantly to changes of government, as in the United Kingdom following BSE or Belgium following the dioxin scandal.

These efforts to control food safety involved the wider adoption of disciplinary regimes of surveillance and control associated with food standards and traceability mechanisms. They reflect the reality that food safety is no longer a national issue, as it arguably was when Upton Sinclair was writing. Food safety strategies that run from "farm to fork" now cut across traditionally separate regulatory domains and jurisdictions, constituting globally interconnected webs of safety and quality assurance. In this context, it is unsurprising to find Michael Taylor, the deputy commissioner for foods of the U.S. FDA, describing the interconnected nature of food safety in a speech in Beijing: "While we may differ in language, culture and economies, we are connected through the global marketplace, which makes it essential that we move forward on food safety together—regardless of where we call home" (Taylor 2011).

These remarks highlight the emphasis on "global food safety" contained within the 2011 U.S. Food Safety Modernization Act. They reveal how the governance of food safety within nation-states or trade blocs such as the European Union ripples through global supply networks. New requirements, such as the U.S. "Foreign Supplier Verification Program," suggest an internationalization of the regulatory gaze and the formation of new assemblages of global food safety. These consist of spatially extended networks of standards and associated architectures and facilities based on Hazard Analysis and Critical Control Point (HACCP) schemes and a range of good practice guidelines and traceability mechanisms.

HACCP methods were originally developed to ensure the safety of food for the U.S. space program, drawing on techniques from NASA's engineering management processes. In 1959, they were adopted by the Pillsbury food company following the contamination of ingredients with glass. HACCP procedures were subsequently developed within the *Codex Alimentarius* and harmonized in 1997. Regulatory requirements for HACCP were introduced within the U.S. meat and poultry food safety systems in 1996, and the Food Safety Modernization Act extended HACCP requirements through the U.S. food chain to all food businesses. Mandatory HACCP plans were introduced in the United Kingdom in 1990 and for food businesses across the European Union in 2004.

The key feature of HACCP is that it replaces the inspection of finished products with preventative measures formulated on the basis of a risk assessment. It is integrated into "good manufacturing practices" as a key part of food safety management and has several consequences for the ways food risks are approached and controlled. HACCP involves marshaling the behavior of both the human beings involved in food production and nonhuman chemical and biological entities, including foods themselves and the microorganisms that reside in them (Busch 2004). Moreover, HACCP mechanisms redefine the relationship between the food industry and the public regulators, placing retailers at the forefront of risk management. At the same time, HACCP mechanisms move the control of food safety away from production facilities, replacing these with a paper audit trail. It thus shifts attention to the role of microbes and away from questions of intentionality or organizational problems (Busch 2004), while the role of government food safety agencies becomes defined in terms of the inspection of HACCP plans, rather than of food products.

Global Chains, Local Links

Like HACCP's focus on critical control points, FDA Commissioner Taylor's speech, delivered in Beijing, reflects the definition of certain locales within extended food supply networks as potential sources of risk. Of these, China is perhaps the most significant and is responsible for an increasing proportion of Western food supplies. It is also a source of food safety anxiety for consumers, regulators, and food businesses in the United States and Europe. Describing Chinese food safety as "in the gutter," *The Economist* (2011) listed a series of recent crises, including the discovery of melamine in infant formula, the use of waste oil recuperated

from drains in cooking, and clenbuterol in pork. These scares underpin the FDA's efforts to extend its regulatory gaze. However, Chinese consumers' own anxieties about food safety are also driving domestic markets for imported "safer" products, such as formula milk (see Gong and Jackson 2012).

The implementation of global food safety regulation thus has global implications, as Susanne Freidberg (2004) illustrates in the case of traceability legislation. Drawing on the example of green bean production in Zambia and Burkina Faso, she describes the relationship between food safety practices in the global North for producers in the global South. A post-BSE focus on food safety, traceability, and due diligence required UK companies to demonstrate their care, including "that [they] only bought produce from growers who, in turn, provided evidence that irrigation water was clean, their worker hygiene facilities adequate, and their pesticide use correct" (2004: 174).

These requirements prompted a preference among supermarkets for larger, vertically integrated suppliers whose operations were more amenable to close control and audit via "rituals of verification." In turn, this drove the consolidation and rationalization of bean farming in countries exporting to the United Kingdom, while the differing food safety culture of French retailers enabled the persistence of small-scale production in francophone Burkina Faso.

Home Safe Home

"Food Safety practices should begin on the farm and be rigorously applied along the entire chain so that food products are safe for human consumption without the need for extraordinary measures. Consumers, however, are the critical endpoint along the food supply chain" (Verrill et al. 2012: 164). As this quotation from a group of FDA researchers shows, the global thread of food safety terminates in the domestic environment and the things that happen there. The home has become a key site at which food safety is threatened and ensured in contemporary Western societies. The food scares of the 1980s prompted consumers to reduce their purchasing of suspect products or to change their food preparation and storage behaviors (cf. Jackson and Everts 2010). However, they also reinforced the role of consumers in ensuring food safety. Preempting the language used by Linda Verrill and others (2012), the 1990 Richmond report into food safety in the United Kingdom described the domestic kitchen as "the last line of defense in the food chain" (Richmond 1990: 145).

Consumers are increasingly involved in food safety policy, and regulatory institutions, particularly in Europe, have attempted to develop new ways of regaining public trust. However, these regulatory reforms have also framed consumers as active agents in ensuring food safety (Halkier 2010). Consumers are held responsible for domestic management of food risks and conversely blamed for failures. Devices such as expiry-date labels and storage instructions aim to extend disciplined regimes of food safety into the home (Milne in press). As Bente Halkier (2010) describes, consumers are conceptualized as active choosers in relation to the management of food risks. As responsibility for food safety has become explicitly part of the consumer role, it becomes part of the performance of responsible citizenship through the protection and preservation of the security of the food supply through competency in food skills that enable the identification of good, safe food and its proper handling.

The culpability of consumers for food safety failures is established through their perceived lack of knowledge and skills for keeping food safe. This is reflected in research that focuses on consumers' food safety knowledges (e.g., Frewer et al. 2002; Wilcock et al. 2004; Verrill et al. 2012) and in campaigns that aim to improve food safety by improving this knowledge. However, there is little valid evidence that such campaigns have the desired effect (Milton and Mullan 2010).

Qualitative research on consumers' food safety behaviors suggests that they are complex, diverse, and embedded in the wider politics of food (Halkier 2010). Much of this work takes the form of describing how consumers draw on various cognitive and cultural resources in determining whether or not food is safe (e.g., Sellerberg 1991; Green et al. 2003; Shaw 2004). It provides a useful corrective to individualized

models that position consumer behavior in relation to information about dominant framings of food "risk." However, the difficulty of equating knowledge with action suggests the importance of understanding domestic food safety behaviors. For example, Angela Meah and Matt Watson's (2011) ethnographic work with multiple generations of the same families explores food safety behavior, critically examining the contention that contemporary consumers are "de-skilled" compared to previous generations. They argue that it is "simplistic and inappropriate" to assume that one generation excelled in cooking skills and that another is ignorant or lazy. Instead, they suggest that it is important to attend to the range of sources from which cooking knowledge is acquired and how it is articulated across different social and cultural contexts throughout the life-course. Such an approach provides an insight into how globally circulating discourses related to the safety of food are adopted and adapted in local contexts of consumption and within individual biographies and familial trajectories. However, further such work is needed to explore the relationships between the skills, materials, and knowledges associated with food safety.

Conclusions

This essay has considered the emergence over the last century of food safety as a major feature of food systems in the global North. It brings together discussion of HACCP with recent moves toward the globalization of food safety and its localization in the domestic environment. The essay suggests the value of whole-chain analyses of food safety that explore how global movements of food are accompanied by standards and codes that are ultimately realized and enacted in the home. Focusing on safety offers an opportunity to examine the work that goes into maintaining a constant "safe" state as food circulates.

See also anxiety, local-global, quality, risk, science.

Richard Milne

SCIENCE

Science occupies an important but contested place in contemporary food systems. The histories of science, food, and agriculture are closely entwined, from the nineteenth-century work of Liebig on nitrogen fertilizers and the basic components of food, to that of Mendel on genetic breeding techniques and Pasteur on food-borne disease and spoilage, to the identification of vitamins and the transformation of animal and plant reproduction. Science and technology have frequently acted as the site at which controversy and contestation has arisen between food producers, regulators, NGOs, and consumers, yet in other cases have been routinely incorporated and domesticated into the routines of everyday life. The role of science is apparent throughout contemporary food production and consumption—in increasing and managing production, in defining product safety and quality, and in determining what is good to eat. This essay focuses on the key role of science in agricultural production and in the rationalization of consumption, arguing that there is a need for work that connects these currently distinct worlds in order to understand the nature and distribution of knowledge production that shapes how and what food is eaten, where.

Science and the Problem of Food

Warren Belasco (2006) identifies the emergence in the late eighteenth century of three main narratives associated with the future of food, associated with the work of Thomas Malthus, the romantic socialist William Godwin, and the Marquis de Condorcet. These persist to the present day as the dominant lenses through which research and policy perceives relations between production, consumption, and population. Confronting the apparently looming crisis in food (and particularly meat) availability, each offered differing solutions: Malthus favoring population control; Godwin supporting voluntary asceticism; and Condorcet extolling the power of science. The latter's cornucopian vision based on innovation combined with good

governance has perhaps been the most influential, but Malthus's pessimism and Godwin's appeals to self-control remain prominent. As Belasco describes, Condorcet argued, "With proper encouragement of the agricultural 'arts' … a very small amount of ground will be able to produce a great quantity of supplies of greater utility and higher quality." And even if some upper limit were reached in the distant future, there were no theoretical obstacles to "manufacturing animal and vegetable substances artificially" (cited in Belasco 2006: 6).

For Condorcet, as for many subsequent writers, the hopes placed in science involve the potentially radical reimagination of food, most notably realized in the image of the "meal in a pill" (which recurs in science fiction) and in other equally synthetic substances. Nearly a century-and-a-half after Condorcet, Winston Churchill, writing on the state of the world "Fifty Years Hence," had a similar vision. For Churchill, meat harvested from microbes would be indistinguishable from its natural counterpart. Churchill described how "we shall escape the absurdity of growing a whole chicken in order to eat the breast or wing, by growing these parts separately under a suitable medium" (quoted in Belasco 2006: 37).

Churchill's and Condorcet's vision is reproduced again in contemporary discussions about in vitro meat. Patented in 1999, in-vitro meat—muscle tissue produced for human consumption using tissue engineering—is described by supporters as a potential solution to the environmental impact of meat agriculture and as a safer form of production (Stephens 2010). Its development highlights the persistence of concerns about meat production from Malthus to the present day and the continuing importance of food and agriculture in driving scientific development.

Scientific Agriculture

Inspired by visions of the transformation of the food supply, public support for research on food science persisted throughout much of the nineteenth and twentieth centuries. This included the funding of land-grant universities and experimental research stations in the

United States and of agricultural research stations in the United Kingdom and Europe. This primarily government-funded research resulted in the emergence of a new, scientific agriculture in the first half of the twentieth century, culminating in the development of new techniques for animal husbandry, such as artificial insemination, and of hybrid crops, chemical fertilizers, and pesticides. These led to significant increases in the production of both crops and meat, and to dramatic changes in the global agricultural landscape, in production practices, and in consumption habits, most notably in increased meat consumption in the global North.

However, by the late 1960s and 1970s the success and unintended consequences of scientific agriculture began to be questioned, most famously in Rachel Carson's *Silent Spring* (1962) and later in the work of Green Revolution critics such as Vandana Shiva (1991). Writing with force and eloquence, Carson highlighted the damaging environmental and health effects of agro-chemicals such as DDT, and concerns about pesticides persist as the most prominent consumer concern about food in Europe (EC 2006). In 1934, *Popular Science Monthly* had likened agricultural chemists to a "crack army" that "stands guard over the nation's food supply" (in Belasco 2006). By the 1970s though, consumers were far more ambivalent about chemistry, which was increasingly seen as threat rather than defense.

Since *Silent Spring*, concerns about the application of scientific research to food and the rationalization of agriculture have multiplied. In the 1980s, NGOs and campaigners highlighted concerns about irradiation, the use of Alar on apples, and about recombinant growth hormone for milk production. These debates seemed to illustrate Ulrich Beck's (1992) argument about reflexive modernization, in which science produces as well as solves societal problems. Further demonstration of the "boomerang" quality of the environmental and health risks created by science appeared to be provided by the controversial introduction of genetically modified (GM) crops, the most contested scientific development of recent years. In addition, agricultural biotechnology resurrects concerns about the social consequences of the Green

Revolution—its impact on small farmers and its role in opening up agricultural markets, and the food supply, to control by large-scale agroindustry (Shiva 1991).

Agricultural biotechnology has been no exception to the hopeful cornucopian visions that have always accompanied food science. Jack Kloppenburg (2004) quotes Kenneth Frey's hyperbolic 1984 presidential address to the American Society of Agronomy on the potential of biotechnology: "Let your imagination roam … The future for agronomy is not only bright, but it has no foreseeable bounds" (quoted in Kloppenburg 2004: 193). For agronomists, recombinant DNA technologies offered the promise of outdoing evolution and reproducing the gains achieved with the development of hybrid varieties. They foresaw a future in which biological and geographical restrictions on crop production would be loosened or removed so that "in 5 to 10 years, Saudi Arabia may look like the wheat fields of Kansas" (Mintz 1984, quoted in Kloppenburg 2004: 203). In contrast, critics of genetic modification envisaged a future in which governance trailed innovation, in which crops with corporate-owned genomes would create new environmental and social problems (Shiva 1991). Consequently, from the introduction of the first GM crops in the mid-1990s to 2008 protests over Monsanto's MON810 maize, agricultural biotechnology has been consistently controversial and at the heart of a reconfiguration of the relationship between science and society, particularly in Europe.

The majority of GM crops introduced to date are engineered for herbicide tolerance (such as Monsanto's "Roundup Ready" varieties), pest resistance, or both. Pest-resistant varieties frequently make use of a gene from the soil microorganism *Bacillus thuringiensis* (Bt) which codes for an insecticidal toxin. Geographer Nick Bingham (2008) describes the mobilizing promises that accompanied the introduction of the first Bt maize:

> Bt corn … was sold as the answer to the "ravages" (advertising material) of the European Corn Borer moth, whose larvae "devastated" (advertising material again) around 7 percent of the Midwestern U.S.

corn crop each year (including 20% of some fields). Farmers were told by promotional literatures that Bt corn would "simplify" their lives by "purifying the environment. (Bingham 2008: 114)

Following Sheila Jasanoff (2005), Bingham (2008) describes the introduction of Bt maize as part of a "socio-technical experiment" whose apparent immediate success in capturing 20 percent of the U.S. corn market bolstered an overall narrative of technological optimism around agricultural biotechnology. The economic and environmental promise of biotechnology was accompanied and supported by rhetorical efforts to link genetic modification to the narrative tropes described above. For example, Monsanto's adverts controversially claimed in 1998 that "worrying about starving future generations won't feed them. Food biotechnology will." The early promise of biotechnology positioned it as a "gene revolution" or "doubly green revolution" that would repeat the growth in productivity of the "green revolution" of the 1960s, a narrative that has reemerged in recent years (Brooks 2005). A 2009 Monsanto advert in the *New York Times* forged links with climate change, asking: "9 billion people to feed. A changing climate. Now What?" and answering that "the world's farmers will need to double food production by 2050. Biotechnology can help." With Condorcian optimism, biotechnology is presented as a technological fix to a looming Malthusian crisis.

However, the story of GM crops is somewhat more complicated. It can best be introduced through the example of a specific crop, maize. In 2007, it was estimated that 77 percent of U.S. maize was transgenic, featuring one or more herbicide-tolerant or pest-resistant traits (James 2007). Maize also represented 31 percent of the worldwide acreage of GM crops and was expanding the fastest. As Sarah Whatmore (2002b) describes in the case of soya, GM crops chart "hybrid geographies" as they move from prehistoric domestication to contemporary consumption. Since its domestication in Mexico more than 9,000 years ago, maize has become one of the mainstays of global agriculture, capable of growing in a range of latitudes and conditions. Kloppenburg (2004) argues that it was the early twentieth century development of high-yielding, but sterile, hybrid maize (corn) that allowed the "uncoupling" of seed as "seed" from seed as "grain" and provided the foundation for the capitalization of agriculture and the emergence of the U.S. seed industry. Maize products are now so widespread in the modern diet that Michael Pollan describes Americans as essentially "processed corn, walking" (2006: 23).

While GM crops have been relatively easily incorporated into the U.S. food system, in the United Kingdom and the rest of Europe their introduction has been less smooth. A de facto moratorium on the commercialization of GM crops ran from 1998 to 2003 across the European Union, and even since it was lifted, the authorization of new varieties has been hesitant and contested. This is exemplified by the 2008 case of Monsanto's MON810 maize, marketed as "Yieldguard" and authorized in the EU since 1998. MON810 was the second most approved variety worldwide and formed a large portion of the 18 percent of authorized GM varieties containing pest-resistant traits planted in 2006 (James 2007). In 2005, MON810 became the first GM variety to be planted in France, primarily for export to the Spanish animal feed market. For Clive James of the International Service for the Acquisition of Agri-biotech Applications, "the growing of even a token hectarage of Bt maize in France is an important and symbolic development" in light of the strength of opposition to GM crops (James 2007: 84). In the face of public opposition to the crops, the French government issued a nationwide ban on cultivating MON810 maize in January 2008, citing doubts as to its safety. Along with Austria, Hungary, and Germany, the French activated a "safeguard clause" in the European directive governing the release of GM varieties. This enabled member states to suspend planting approval when presented with new scientific evidence about its effects on the environment or human health. Yet in November 2008, the European Food Safety Authority (EFSA) concluded that the ban on MON810 maize was "scientifically unfounded" (GMO Compass 2008). Nevertheless, GM varieties remain few and far between in Europe.

The contested safety of MON810 echoed earlier debates around the toxicity of Bt pollen that highlight the problematic role of scientific expertise in establishing the safety or otherwise of scientific innovation. The early progressive narrative around Bt crops described by Bingham was challenged by the apparent discovery by John Losey and colleagues (1999) of the toxicity of Bt maize pollen to Monarch butterfly caterpillars. Losey and colleague's work appeared to provide critics with proof of the environmental risk of agricultural biotechnology, as well as an iconic image in the form of the Monarch, a symbol of U.S. "nature." In response, Monsanto adopted an argument traditionally deployed by environmental NGOs against regulatory and governmental analyses of claims of safety, suggesting that the research represented a mistaken extrapolation from laboratory science to field situations (Jasanoff 2005).

The introduction of agricultural biotechnology in Europe brought to the fore concerns around the sufficiency of scientific advice and the relationship between science, government, and industry. The cases of Bt pollen and MON810 illustrated the elusiveness and insufficiency of "sound science" to settle debates about the environmental and health effects of biotechnology. As such, they are indicative of the contours of the wider GM debate, where scientific and governmental assurances of safety have failed to acknowledge both the inherent uncertainty in such analyses and to open up the assumptions and values underpinning the development of the technology to wider debate (Wynne 2001). As such, they have broader implications for the introduction and governance of agricultural and food science.

Consuming Science and the Science of Consumption

Focusing on the case of GM crops reflects Anne Murcott's (1999) call for the sociology of food to attend to its scientific and technical aspects—for studies of consumption to remember production. However, problematically but perhaps inevitably, social scientific research is dominated by a focus on science as a component of food production that is challenging for consumers. Much research on food science, particularly in Europe, now focuses on the societal challenges raised by production technologies such as genetic modification, nanotechnology, or agro-chemicals. However, science has long been associated with the rationalization and structuring of consumption, from the domestic science and household management movement of the late nineteenth century to 1950s experiments in kitchen design and the rise of consumer science. Scientific discourses have not only been challenged but have contributed to and been incorporated within changing Western understandings of food. The emergence of food science has introduced new forms of expertise and new experts, who come to mediate relations between governments, consumers, and industry, and between consumers and food, often displacing traditional knowledges and practices. They are influential in redefining what constitutes food: as energy; as perished or edible; as an interacting complex of nutrients; or, as Hannah Landecker (2011) describes, as environmental "exposure." In turn, this defines what constitutes "good" food. Thus, within the nutrition movement of the early twentieth century, animal products were seen as the most efficient way to obtain the required calories and protein, a conclusion enthusiastically supported by the meat industry (Levenstein 1993).

The diffusion and acceptance of nutrition science—what Gyorgy Scrinis (2008) critiques as "nutritionism" or nutritional reductionism—is a central theme in contemporary food systems, whereby the study of consumption has become embedded in the quantitative rhetoric of nutrition science and calculations of calories, protein, and recommended daily allowances (Mudry 2009). Nutrition science folds together "scientific" questions with moral judgments of what is good to eat and provides an insight into the extension of scientific expertise within everyday life. Moreover, as Alan Beardsworth (1990) points out, nutritional science reveals the often changing and uncertain nature of scientific knowledge related to food and eating.

The birth of the "New Nutrition" (Levenstein 1993) took place in the 1870s and 1880s. It was pioneered by chemists, including Wilbur

Atwater, who trained and worked with German students of Justus Liebig, who had identified carbohydrate, fat, and protein as the constituent components of food as well as provided the scientific basis for the production of fertilizers. Early research on food consumption thus closely paralleled work on food production. Atwater led U.S. research into the composition of foods, exploring the relative quantities of the basic components in a range of foods. His work provided the basis for contemporary nutrition science, including the building of a "calorimeter" to assess the energy content of different foods and their metabolism by the body. Atwater's work was closely connected with solving the "social problem" of poor diet. He was active in establishing the science of nutrition as a tool of social policy and in producing the first "scientific" assessments of the recommended content of the diet. These were rapidly translated into definitions of good food, advice to "educate" the consumer, and by 1915 over thirty informational pamphlets on food and nutrition were widely distributed by the U.S. government (Nestle 2002).

With the work of Atwater and others, new forms of dietary discipline were introduced into consumption and the nutritional status of the population began to become the concern of the state. With the discovery of vitamins in the first decades of the twentieth century, nutrition also became a means of product differentiation, as fortified cereals, breads, and milk reached the market and public health advocates pointed out the depleted and deficient levels of vitamins in much processed food (Levenstein 1993).

For Scrinis (2008) and critics of the food industry including Michael Pollan (2009) and Marion Nestle (2002), the focus on "nutrients" in nutrition science has recently been co-opted by the food industry to market their products and to create confusion about healthy eating. Thus Nestle (2002) highlights the role of food industry lobbying in shaping government food recommendations in terms of molecules and nutrients such as sugar or saturated fats instead of the foods that contain them, such as meat. Scrinis extends this critique to challenge the scientific framing of foods in terms of nutrients at the expense of traditional, cultural,

sensual, and ecological qualities, highlighting its role in shaping the contemporary conceptualization of the body in terms of "the nutritionalized self" (2008:47). Similarly, Jessica Mudry's (2009) analysis of the quantitative rhetoric of U.S. nutrition advice argues that such an approach fails to capture the subjective, cultural, emotional, and qualitative nature of food and eating.

Much of this work focuses on the rhetorical or social "impact" of the scientific study of consumption. Taking her work into the laboratory itself, Hannah Landecker (2011) examines the reworking of nutritional thinking within contemporary food research, examining how nutritional "epigenetics" moves away from a focus on vitamin and mineral "building blocks." As she describes it, epigenetics—the study of inherited changes in gene expression, largely based on the statistical analysis of historical populations—focuses concerns on the relation between populations of genes (rather than people) and the environment. In this context, food is understood as an environmental exposure, "as a miasma of biologically active molecules in which genomes are immersed, determining and disturbing the physiology of metabolic regulation" (Landecker 2011: 169). Food policy that affects this environment, such as the addition of folic acid to bread, is connected with chemical changes in the expression of genes. This results in the problematization of metabolism rather than nutrients as the primary site for social efforts to reshape the body and for therapeutic intervention. This has implications for understandings of consumption, as food changes from individual choice to immersive miasma, metabolized by populations.

Conclusion

As Bruno Latour (1988) famously described in the case of Pasteurization, and as Michel Callon (1986a) showed in the farming of scallops in St. Brieuc Bay, the definition of problems and their solutions as "scientific" is not a result of the self-evident importance of knowledge but involves the *intéressement* and mobilization of a range of different actors. Despite Latour's and Callon's early focus, and despite the ubiquity of food science, there is comparatively little social science research that goes into the lab to explore its emergence or construction, or that examines the social strategies and means through which boundaries are established around new areas of food science. Given the importance of science to contemporary food systems, further critical work on food science is needed that connects consumption with production and examines how each is folded into the other.

See also innovation, nutrition, risk, safety, technologies.

Richard Milne

SECURITY

Security delineates a space free from care, worry, and anxiety. Security implies safety. Within a secure space subjects are free to move without impedance to their well-being. Security is freedom. Delineating a space of security, however, requires demarcating insecurity. A space of insecurity exists when the elements of security, freedom from care, worry, or anxiety are absent. Insecurity threatens security—the two terms are mutually construed. Spaces of security rely on an ideology of insecurity (Dikeç 2007) and the distribution of ideologically aesthetic objects (Rancière 2004): borders and boundaries that establish the secure from the insecure, devices that demarcate one from the other, and governance that controls what is allowed to cross in and out. Borders, however, are porous, space is leaky, and states of (in)security exist within these uneasy tensions. This essay explores how these ideas might be applied to the concept of "food security," including the way it has been mobilized through a biopolitics of fear and worry, governance and control—a biopolitics of anxiety.

Ideas about food security are organized around a variety of interrelated concepts such as access, health, or quality, concepts that come together to signal a broader concern with the well-being of a population. Defining food security, however, is more challenging. The current

World Health Organization (WHO) definition suggests that food security is achieved "when all people at all times have access to sufficient, safe, nutritious food to maintain a healthy and active life" (WHO 2012). The Food and Agriculture Organization (FAO), however, suggests that "food security" is a "flexible concept" that is defined through its usage within research and policy (FAO 2003: 25). The FAO go on to note the discursive shift that the concept has undergone since its introduction in the 1970s. For instance, the term started out as a way to articulate the (need for the) "availability of adequate food supplies," "steady expansion of its consumption," and "offset of fluctuation in production and prices" (2003: 26). By the early 1980s, the concept expanded to include access to basic food by "all people at all times," and by the 1990s this was again expanded to include "access of all people at all times to *enough food* for an *active healthy lifestyle*" (2003: 26, emphasis added). Unpacking these ideas and noting the way they change suggests an essentially Eurocentric shift to the framing of food security from one concerned about absolute poverty and starvation to one concerned with "lifestyle diseases," even though these may well represent a salient threat to world health (WHO/FAO 2003). In light of recent concerns about global climate change and its likely impact on the world's food supply, food security remains a subject of international policy debate. This debate focuses on a growing world population outstripping food supply, raising the specter of a return to Malthusian and neo-Malthusian principles of "population control." In any case, food security in these contexts implies a tangle of relations that revolve around notions of safety, access, quality, and rights within the food supply.

More recently, debates about food security have coalesced into neoliberal ideas of biosecurity and the governance of food as part of its globalized trade (Dunn 2007). For instance, recent "food scares" such as BSE in the United Kingdom or worldwide outbreaks of avian influenza (H5N1) have brought questions of food safety and security together with questions of economics, signaling a need (amongst some) to regulate more tightly and control the borders within which food travels (Hinchliffe and Bingham 2008). Borders themselves, however, are constituted at a variety of scales and within a variety of places and spaces that encompass food production, consumption, and everywhere in between. The conceptual shift in food security from one focused on ensuring an "inalienable right" to food to one concerned with the production, maintenance, and security of food borders is reinforced by the ideology of the "war on terror" and the supposed "threat" that terrorism might pose. Defending against these "threats" means that food security is now considered within the discursive logic of "homeland security" becoming part of a broader agenda for "national security" (see Chalk 2004), where it circulates with an unpredictable, uncertain, and modulated "affective intensity" (Milne et al. 2011) as part of a semiotic assemblage of nationalism, economy, and "emergency" (Massumi 2009). Because a security agenda focuses on governance and controlling mobility, linking food and its security to debates about national security ultimately leads to questions of biopolitics, biopower, and (food) sovereignty (McMichael 2005).

The transformation of "food security" from the "foundations of a decent life, a sound education and the achievement of the Millennium Development Goals" (Ban Ki-Moon 2009) to a component of a discursive "war on terror" suggests a shift away from an objective of aspiration within modern democratic society—an objective that implies a sense of inclusivity and global social, environmental, and economic justice—toward an ideology of exclusion. Within the space of this ideology, the interior is made "safe" through a ritualized performance of "security," while the exterior remains a zone of "insecurity" and threat. The organization of this space, however, is dependent on producing an object from which security is derived (Jackson and Everts 2010) and delineating a space from which security is required. This leads to a somewhat ironic juxtaposition where the production of "secure-space" requires fashioning an "insecure-space." Insecure space, however, is discursive because its formation depends on the possibility of a threat materializing. Insecure-space becomes a space of uncertainty and unknowing, while secure-space is one of anxiety of the unknown.

This is an ideological construct that separates secure from insecure, "us" from "them," but the construct is put into practice materially, socially, and discursively through such devices as borders, fences, or scanners, as well as through policy, governance, and policing. The result is that food security has become a thing to defend.

See also anxiety, governance, space and place.

Ben Coles

SEX

The conflation of food and sex has increasingly figured as a dynamic within contemporary food media. Exploring this hyphenation within popular culture, Elspeth Probyn indicates that there is a sense that "sex on its own is no longer terribly interesting" (2000: 72) and, consequently, food writing and food programs have developed as a form of pornography whereby cooking has become foreplay and eating is fucking (Crumpacker 2006: 54). While there may be some truth in the boundaries of mainstream sex being pushed in different directions, this essay contends that the "sexing up" of food has emerged because it is *food*, rather than sex, which is no longer terribly interesting on its own.

Coupling "Appetites"

While it might be imagined that the sexualisation of food and cooking is a feature of modernity—British food writer Nigella Lawson suggesting that "gastroporn" is the last allowable excess in "our puritanical age" (1999: 154)—television chefs and cookery writers are in fact, consciously or otherwise, reviving traditions which are centuries old. Indeed, Chinese philosopher Mencius (fourth century B.C.) is reported to have said, "*shi se xing ye*" (appetite for food and sex is nature) (Farquhar 2002: 1). This "comradeship" between food and sex, as Judith Farquhar (2002: 28) puts it, results from the innateness of appetite, an intermingling of alimentary and sexual regimens which connect and disconnect at the point of the body (Deleuze and Guattari 1988). That these regimens should be intermingled is unsurprising when we consider Freud's theories of sexuality and his approach to hunger, which he uses as a metaphor for the libido, likening the release of sexual tension with the sating of hunger. Indeed, for Freudians, the first stage of psychosexual development among infants, the oral stage, is inextricably linked to eating and food.

Cooking as "Foreplay"; Eating as "Fucking"

While few—until recently—may have thought about the erotic dimension of a Christmas or Thanksgiving turkey being opened up, the empty cavity being lovingly stuffed, by hand, with a sumptuous mixture that will ooze moistness when cooked, or the sensuous feel of a silky ball of chapatti dough as it is kneaded and caressed, the relationship between the sensuality of food and sex is not a discovery of contemporary "gastro-pornographers" in North America, Australia, and Europe. The recognition of cooking as "foreplay" is something that can be dated back to pre-Christian times, before appetites became something in need of "civilizing" (Mennell et al. 1992). In Roman literature, for example, Apuleius in *The Golden Ass* describes how Lucius watches Fortis as she prepares dinner and is aroused by her activities. The eroticism of the description, the power of the seduction, lies in the movement of Fortis's body as she handles the food and stirs the pots, how she glances at him as she puts the spoon to her lips and tastes the dish, visual tropes that have become familiar to modern consumers as both male and female cooks have indulged in "real food orgasm" on our television screens (Probyn 2000: 4). The sensuality of food—its sight, sounds, tastes, and capacity to sate—has also been reflected in a range of cinematic representations, some more risqué than others. Consider the young disciple of Julia Child in the American film *Julie and Julia* (2009) as she replaces sex with cooking, much to her husband's frustration, attempting to cook her way through Child's *Mastering the Art of French Cooking* in a year; or the true

story of paralyzed Jean-Dominique Bauby, in *Le Scaphandre et le Papillon* (*The Diving Bell and the Butterfly*; 2007), who imagines himself seated at a table laden with delicacies, eating together with one of his carers, using their fingers to feed each other, oyster juices dripping from their chins; or in the Mexican film *Como Agua para Chocolate* (*Like Water for Chocolate*; 1992), where Tita, the female protagonist, is described as creating dishes so potent with emotion and passion that they have a profound impact on all who consume them (Parasecoli 2008). When asked what the secret of her dishes is, she says that they are cooked "with love." More explicitly, food features as part of the principal characters' sex games in the 1986 film *9½ Weeks*, while *The Hunger* (1983) highlights how vampire appetites can only be sated by the literal consumption and incorporation of another, feeding like an infant unable to control its appetite.

There is a veritable feast of images of food and sex within popular culture, and yet academic writing in this area is characterized by relative famine, the marked exception being Elspeth Probyn (2000), writing in Australia, who seeks to use the materiality of eating, sex, and bodies to draw out an alternative way of articulating an ethics of existence. Reminding us of the failed sexual revolution that was supposed to liberate women in the bedroom, Probyn highlights how the kitchen is now being sold as the new site of sensual liberation for women, with food replacing the "props" of the bedroom. Indeed, she cites Linda Jaivin's (1998) best-selling novel, *Eat Me*, the opening chapter of which describes a graphic scene in a supermarket where a woman is seen pleasuring herself with soft-fruits before taking on the (male) store detective with an English cucumber. The detective submits to the whip-bearing female protagonist following taunts of "eat me, you coffee stain. You slice of mouldy cheese. You slab of five-day-old horsemeat" (1998: 5). Probyn argues that Jaivin's hyphenation of sex and food through this orgy of fruit and vegetables fundamentally queers hetero-sex (2000: 72–73). Moreover, Probyn points out that replacing scantily clad young women with a plate full of expensive and delicious-looking food on the bonnet of a car is more likely to end in a sale:

"Forget sex sells," she insists, "these days food sells" (2000: 65).

Infusing Food with Sexiness

But there is nothing inherently "sexy" about the industrialized food, which became increasingly ubiquitous in the global North following the Second World War. The sensual engagement with food in its "natural" form has been replaced by packet-opening, rehydrating, defrosting, and microwaving. And far from constituting "foreplay," even when done from "scratch," everyday family cooking in advanced industrialized nations—much like conventional ("vanilla") sex—can become rather dull and routine, a duty or obligation to be performed largely by women. Indeed, Sherrie Inness notes that during the Second World War, American women were encouraged to perceive the serving of a family meal as a "quintessential icon of being a woman and a mother" (2001: 136), which is not a particularly sexy image. While food adventurers have, literally, sought to "spice-up" "boring" Western diets by turning to more "exotic" culinary cultures (Heldke 2003), it is little wonder that in an age constituted by public anxieties concerning nutrition, obesity, and diet-related illness, new approaches have been required to encourage a shift away from processed and unhealthy foods, which require more "assembling" than cooking and which put the fun and pleasure back into food, whether for children or for adults. This may explain the revival of sexual imaginary within popular images of food preparation.

As Probyn observes, television cooks and celebrity chefs have played a key role in "sexing up" food and cooking, and food writing and cookery programs have emerged as acceptable forms of "gastro-pornography." Exuding testosterone, professional "chunks" (chef-hunks)—to use John Newton's terminology (quoted in Probyn 2000: 66)—have helped reconstitute the kitchen as a space in which men can demonstrate skill, competence, and competiveness without compromising their masculinity. Meanwhile, those male chefs who are presented in domestic kitchens, particularly younger men like Jamie Oliver, are not averse to cheeky innuendo. A number of British cooks and food writers have encouraged viewers to believe that they are broadcast from the intimacy of their own kitchens. Nigella Lawson—in particular—has blurred the boundaries between bedroom and kitchen in domestic spaces in evoking sexual metaphors during her cooking programs, "spanking" pomegranates, for example, while relying heavily on sexual innuendo and the sounds of sexual intimacy to convey "food orgasm." Probyn notes that cooks are not necessarily required to be sexy themselves—even the unlikely duo of Clarissa Dickson Wright and Jennifer Patterson emerged as gay icons in the United Kingdom and Australia through the glimpses of female homo-sociality they provided via their banter and own brand of innuendo. In defiance of official advice about healthy eating, Nigella Lawson and the *Two Fat Ladies* (Dickson Wright and Patterson) gave consumers—and women in particular—permission to cook and eat food *and* enjoy it (cf. Hollows 2003b).

In spite of the explosion of interest in food programs and food writing, however, cooking experimentation is reported as remaining a largely vicarious indulgence: something that people engage with as voyeurs, preferring to read about or watch (Short 2006) but—as with conventional pornography—unlikely to be lived out in practice (Parasecoli 2008: 3). Parasecoli has questioned whether the appeal lies principally with the celebrity chefs/cooks who provide glamour and insights into high-end foods that are largely inaccessible to mass audiences. Smoldering and simmering as they tease their creations onto plates, television cooks embody the intermingling of sex and food, revitalizing the character of both in our sensory imaginations. Going down on a creaming cock made of large tulle cones with apple-ginger custard and Tokay caramel (Probyn 2000: 65) certainly sounds more exciting than eating a cream cake, just as a mélange of limbs basted in a jus of emotions sounds so much more appealing than vanilla sex.

See also body, eating, gender, pleasure.

Angela Meah

SHOPPING

In recent years, shopping has become the most common way for people in Western societies to acquire food. Instead of growing their own vegetables, meats, or grains, or baking their own bread, people visit their local supermarkets, delis, corner shops, or food markets to acquire foodstuffs, increasingly also shopping online. Like most of the stuff people rely on to sustain themselves and their everyday practices, foodstuffs are distributed through a commercial system and acquired through shopping. But, as common and ordinary as food shopping might seem, it is a highly complex and culturally embedded practice. Shopping for food should not be understood only as the functional act of buying goods in order to bring food to the table. As suggested by Pasi Falk and Colin Campbell (1997: 5), "People do things at shopping sites that cannot be reduced to the instrumental act of buying." Although speaking of shopping in general, Falk and Campbell's statement is applicable to food shopping as well. As a subset of household provisioning, food shopping involves not only acquiring foodstuff but also looking and desiring goods without necessarily buying anything. It involves aesthetic issues of display, comparative shopping, and practices like "window shopping."

Like other food practices such as growing vegetables or cooking, food shopping is a learned skill (Jackson and Holbrook 1995). It involves not only know-how and competence, like estimating the quality of goods or economic calculation, but also how to interact with the material setting of a shop, sales people, and other consumers. Like other forms of consumption, food shopping is a social act. Where and how people shop for groceries and other foodstuff is intertwined with and reproduces different social and cultural categories. Research from various disciplines has demonstrated that shopping for food is part of not only the enactment of, for example, family, ethnic, and gendered identities, but also the commercial landscape and the marketplace itself. This essay will address a few of these enactments by reviewing a selection of research on the topic of food shopping. However, shopping is a vast research area and

the selection of work addressed here should therefore be treated as suggestive rather than conclusive.

Shopping is often derided as a vacuous, materialistic, and self-indulgent practice. It is not seen as serious or productive. For a long time, this view also had consequences for how shopping was treated within the social sciences. Although it was closer to the center of attention of disciplines like marketing, shopping was more or less neglected in other fields before the mid-1990s. However, since then the view of shopping has changed radically in most social science fields and is now treated as a serious sociocultural issue. Many studies in various disciplines describe shopping as a significant expression of relationships, including love and the enactment of family (e.g., Fischer and Arnould 1990; Miller 1998b; Falk and Campbell 1997; Chochoy 2008; Everts and Jackson 2009). For example, Daniel Miller's (1998b) "theory of shopping" is based on a collaborative ethnography, arguing that household food shopping practices in London are driven by love of family members. While other theories of shopping often depict it as an expression of personal identity, Miller suggests that shopping as an activity is not necessarily directed toward the person doing the shopping. Instead, Miller suggests, shopping should be seen as a way to maintain and express relationships between "the shopper" and someone else. Miller builds his argument on the fact that his (predominantly female) informants' descriptions of shopping are stories of devotional love. The informants describe their shopping efforts as directed toward and shaped by the well-being and nurturing of their children and partners rather than themselves. Miller also connects these expressions of love with theories of sacrifice. He suggests a parallel between the shopping behavior of the informants and acts of sacrifice, as it has been described in the anthropological literature. Miller argues that shopping is an act of maternal sacrifice, whereby value is produced through expenditure on others. Miller's informants often talked about shopping as a way to save money, to be thrifty, and to invest in their families. In their shopping stories, informants described how the labor they invested in shopping was turned into value, distributed among family members. For these participants at least, shopping was framed as an act of investment rather than expenditure.

Miller's work illustrates the significance of food shopping in maintaining relationships and the enactment of "family." It has been highly influential and much appreciated, but it has also been subject to critique. While some authors point out the apparent lack of reference to related work in marketing theory and consumer research (Woodruffe-Burton et al. 2002), others have criticized Miller's representation of women, and especially single women, deeming it an "overly conservative view of household formation" (Reimer and Leslie 2004: 192). Regardless of how one feels about Miller's representation of women, shopping has repeatedly been described as "women's work" (Fischer and Arnould 1990; Thompson et al. 1990). Historical work on the development of department stores and supermarkets suggests a particularly strong connection between women and shopping (e.g., Abelson 1989, 2000; Glennie and Thrift 1996; Fredriksson 1997). Department stores and grocery shops were developed and organized to cater to white, middle-class, female consumers. In *Building a Housewife's Paradise: Gender, Politics and American Grocery Stores*, for example, Tracey Deutsch (2010) describes the development of the American grocery store as embedded in gender relations, social politics, and political economy. Deutsch ascribes the practices and preference of women an important role in the development and success of this retail sector. According to Deutsch, the development of the retail sector must be understood as framed by gender and social politics. In relation to groceries, she argues:

> The formal rules of governance (for example, collection of the sales taxes) intersect with less formal power relations of social life (for example, grocers' conversations with customers). Sometimes ethereal ideas about how women ought to behave took on material, economic, and structural importance in the spaces of stores and in the policies they imposed. (Deutsch 2010: 3)

Since grocery stores, like department stores, developed in relation to ideas of a female consumer

within the food retailing industry, shopping practices were reshaped by twentieth-century ideas of women and femininity, including the way women were expected to behave but also how they behaved—that is, how they provided for their families. Deutsch ascribes some of the success of the grocery store to the particular sociality it provides. While earlier food shopping practices built on a sociality of interaction with vendors (e.g., haggling), the modern grocery store provided a different and more anonymous sociality, less reliant on personal relationships and more discriminating in terms of the control of vendors (Deutsch 2010). In these places, middle-class women could experience a sense of freedom unattainable in other public places. The relationship between female consumers, femininity, and shopping emphasized in many analyses of the history of retailing and shopping is present in contemporary work on shopping as well. Contemporary shopping is also described as predominantly feminine and, like other food practices such as cooking or eating (e.g., Meah and Watson 2011), shopping for food is still described as co-constitutive of gender (Fischer and Arnould 1990; Miller 1998b).

Besides gender, food shopping has also been described as involved in enactments of ethnicity. Buying and eating specific kinds of food or a specific cuisine can be one way to enact ethnicity (e.g., Petridou 2001). In addition, as research in geography and consumer culture has shown, where and how people shop for food can also be a part of the enactment of ethnic identities. In the coauthored volume *Shopping, Place and Identity*, Miller and others (1998) investigate the relationship between shopping and the expression of gender and ethnic identities. Although not specifically writing about food shopping, the authors suggest that shoppers use the commercial environment of malls and shops as a medium for adhering to or diverting from objectified ideas of ethnicity. Shopping in a particular shop or mall, while avoiding others, is an example of this process. Hence, shopping practices can be a way of materially and spatially anchoring ethnic and gendered identities.

The findings and themes addressed in *Shopping, Place and Identity* resonate with other studies of shopping. Lisa Peñaloza (1994), for example, addresses the relationship between shopping and ethnicity in a study of how Mexican immigrants become acculturated to American commercial culture through shopping behavior. Peñaloza's ethnographic study suggests that shopping offers different means for acculturation but also for resistance and as a basis of segregation. For example, she describes how provisioning or shopping for food offered immigrants an opportunity to avoid limitations experienced in other areas due to difficulties with a new language. In the area where Peñaloza conducted her study, Mexican stores, merchandise, advertisements, and other offers in Spanish were common along with Spanish-speaking staff. But her informants also described the difficulties they experienced while shopping such as familiarizing themselves with the new currency. Being able to eat the food they ate in Mexico provided consumers with a taste of home. Many informants stuck to the same food shopping practices they carried out in their home country. But there were also differences. For example, Peñaloza reports how informants rejected consumption patterns associated with the United States, such as packaged, prepared, and frozen foods. Being able to keep their food habits through the accommodating ways of shopkeepers and marketers helped "validate the presence of Mexican immigrants and legitimized Mexican culture in the United States" (Peñaloza 1994: 43).

Besides illustrating how food shopping can be constitutive of relationships, including family and identity categories such as gender and ethnicity, previous research also illustrates how the performance of relationships and identity through food shopping is intertwined with and co-constitutive of the market. Shopping for food can thus be understood in terms of how market places are enacted (Everts and Jackson 2009; Cochoy 2008).

One example of the material enactment of markets is Franck Chochoy's (2008) sociological study of shoppers' use of shopping carts. Inspired by actor-network theory, Cochoy uses the shopping cart as a point of departure for developing a theory of how materiality influences the way shoppers perform calculations. Like Miller and others, Cochoy describes shopping as a social act and suggests that the

calculations of shopping are linked to a particular form of sociality produced around the shopping cart. The shopping cart works as a material anchor around which friends, partners, or parents shopping with children "cluster" and interact while avoiding social interaction with other shoppers. This particular sociality is an important aspect of the different forms of "calculation" that Cochoy suggests shoppers perform. Besides traditional *calculation*—that is, rational choices based on quantified measures (such as how much an item cost in relation to others or how much the total sum of shopped items might be)—shopping carts facilitate what Cochoy calls *qualculation*—that is, choices based on the estimation of the qualitative aspects of goods. The shopping cart also affords *calqulations*—that is, interactive deliberations where cluster members trace or copy the choices of other members. Cochoy derive the concept "calqulation" from the French verb "calquer" translating as to trace or copy. Calqulating means anticipating, measuring, testing, influencing, and correcting the discrepancies between one's position and that of one's partner, and the other way around. It should be seen as a term designating "the building of a shared project, but also the activation of a collective rationality, which functions less as a distributed cognition or as an average rationality than as a 'doubled' or 'adjusting' rationality" (Cochoy 2008: 30). Cochoy's study suggests that shopping practices and the materiality they involve are both constituted by and constitutive of relationships between family members. It suggests that the economic calculations and rationality traditionally ascribed to shopping or choice situations are framed by other estimations and negotiations. Suggesting the term "calqulation" also underlines the benefits of approaching shopping as a practice—that is, something that is performed rather than as an end result. And, in these shopping performances, social categories such as family are anchored.

Also addressing the relationship between the sociality of shopping and the performance of market places, Everts and Jackson (2009) examine how shoppers' understandings of grocery stores and supermarkets have an impact on the enactment of shopping places. The authors argue that, while these places are often described in relation to historical progression (i.e., grocery stores being premodern and supermarkets modern), the distinction should actually be understood as a result of different forms of contemporary sociality. Everts and Jackson argue that grocery stores are enacted through shopping practices whereby shopkeepers shop with their customers while supermarkets are enacted through minimum interaction between shoppers and staff. Shopping for food then becomes a way not only to get food on the table and maintain family relations but also to play a part in the enactment of the marketplace itself.

To summarize, food shopping—like other shopping practices—has been shown to interlink with the enactment of social categories such as family, gender, and ethnicity. Food shopping is a sociocultural practice and should therefore be understood as such. In order to understand how people shop for food and what consequences their shopping practices have, the social and cultural context of food shopping should be acknowledged. However, taking the sociocultural context into account is not enough. As previous research demonstrates, food shopping is also a material and spatial practice. Taking the material and spatial aspects of shopping into account and analyzing how these aspects interplay with sociocultural factors is necessary for understanding how food shopping works and its implications for contemporary social life.

See also consumption, gender, markets, practices.

Maria Fuentes

SKILL

A skill, writes sociologist Richard Sennett (2008: 37–38), is something that is developed through trained practice and is embedded in routine. It is something that is often characterized by lengthy periods of apprenticeship, discipline, and training, processes that are perhaps not readily associated with the domestic, and even less so with domestic cooking. Nonetheless, "ordinary" food preparation has been conceptualized as a site that brings together tacit and embodied knowledge in the form of skilled practice that is rehearsed and performed, drawing upon memory and habit (cf. Sutton 2006). This essay will explore how "skill" has been celebrated and valued during different historical periods and how, with the increasing mechanization and industrialization of the agri-food sector, what constitutes "skill" has shifted and with what effect. The essay also explores the public and private dimensions of the performance of skill and, relatedly, who can therefore be said to demonstrate it and in what contexts. Seen from this perspective, "skill" is not a value-free concept but confers power and—in different contexts—reinforces social constructions of both race and gender.

Skill in Context

Embedding, Sennett suggests, is a process essential to all skills since it involves the conversion of information and practices into *tacit* knowledge (2008: 50), a process that, not untypically, might have taken several years to acquire prior to the introduction of routinized mechanization (Braverman 1974). Indeed, the emergence of classical science led to printers, weavers, and smithies, for example, being identified as *craftsmen*, a term that applied to men and contributed to the gendering of skill (Sennett 2008: 23). Importantly, there is evidence of a public and private dimension to skill. Indeed, the public activity of weaving enabled Athenian women to be identified as skilled craftworkers, while private activities, which hold no public standing (such as cooking), did not.

One might assume that craft-skills hold particular cachet compared to those activities that are not embedded via processes of organized training and repetition. But, as Sennett points out, if the artisan or skilled craftsman was celebrated in the time of Homer, there is evidence of the value of skill and craftsmanship diminishing over time. For example, he notes how Aristophanes "treats the potters Kittos and Bacchios as stupid buffoons due to the work that they do" (2008: 23). Not surprisingly, the onset of rapid mechanization following the Industrial Revolution threatened the work of artisan craftsmen (2008: 39) and Harry Braverman (1974: 430) has reminded us of the relative nature of "skill." For example, 100 years ago, when few people knew how to drive, driving was considered to be a skill, while the ability to manage a team of horses was not. The opposite would now be true. Braverman suggests that it is our relationship with machinery that has resulted in the reconstitution of different types of "skilled" and "unskilled" activities, the machine facilitating the creation of the term "semi-skilled" in the 1930s by the US Bureau of the Census. Craftsmen, Braverman notes, continued to be classed as skilled and laborers were unskilled, while those who operated machinery were regarded as semi-skilled, regardless of the limited period of training that might be required to master their responsibilities (1974: 428). This "illusory upgrading" of certain skills, writes Braverman, led to the rapid growth in clerical and sales occupations and was concomitant with a decline in traditional craft industries (1974: 435). He observes, "For the worker, the concept of skill is traditionally bound up with craft mastery—that is to say, the combination of knowledge of materials and processes with the practiced manual dexterities required to carry out a specific branch of production. The breakup of skills and the reconstruction of production as a collective social process have destroyed the traditional concept of skill … [leaving] to workers a woefully inadequate concept of skill: a specific dexterity, a limited and repetitive operation" (1974: 443–4), which ultimately equates with "deskilling."

Power, Ideology, and Skill

Clearly, the reconstitution of skill is linked with the capitalist mode of production, something that has not escaped the attention of Marxist and socialist feminists. In the United Kingdom, for example, sociologist Cynthia Cockburn (1981, 1985, 1997) has written extensively on the relationship between gender and technology, noting that in threatening the livelihoods of skilled men, men have responded to technologization by demarcating and defending areas of competence (1985: 33) while women have tended to be sequestered into those roles with limited physical mobility and that are also regarded—by men—as boring, repetitive, and lacking creativity. For Cockburn, the "purposeful differentiation between skilled and unskilled workers" played an active role in the construction of gender (1981: 49). She cites Anne Phillips and Barbara Taylor (1980) in pointing out that "far from being an objective fact, skill is often an ideological category imposed on certain types of work by virtue of the sex and power of the workers who perform it" (Cockburn 1981: 49). Indeed, since mechanization has led to the association of skill with specific dexterities, modernity has also witnessed the increased valorization of "nimble-fingered" workers, often women. While the nimble-fingered third world female worker is renowned for her suitability to contemporary industrial discipline, being patient, dexterous, and submissive (Mills 2005: 117), women were no less important to the postwar economic expansion of the textile industry in Northern England. However, as Peter Jackson (1991, 1992) notes of one mill in Bradford, a workforce comprised largely of Eastern European women was gradually replaced by Pakistani men. Jackson observes:

> Jobs that were formerly ascribed to women because of their "nimble fingers" now became associated with the manual dexterity of immigrant men. The work was still categorized as "unskilled," however, as ideologies of racial inferiority replaced patriarchal assumptions about the nature of "women's work," with similar effects on the level at which it was remunerated. (1991: 208)

As argued by Phillips and Taylor (1980), neither women nor immigrant male workers had much power in these contexts.

Technology, Perceptual Skills, and Cooking

Although general in its application, the preceding discussion of skill provides a useful context for understanding perceptions of cooking in places like the United Kingdom where there has been an alleged decline of cooking skills in recent years (see Short 2006; Meah and Watson 2011). Rather than rehearse well-worn discussions concerning the impact of industrialized food production and emergence of "convenience" foods, here we briefly explore the role of technology in transforming, or reconstituting, skill before examining who is deemed to perform cooking skill, and in what contexts.

While French sociologist Luce Giard (1998) has suggested that the introduction of electrical innovation in the kitchen transformed the cook into an unskilled "pusher-of-buttons," others have highlighted that in the context of contemporary cooking, "skill" involves more than simply understanding ingredients. Indeed, baking has been described as a "science" since it relies on precise measurement and knowledge of ingredients. Frances Short (2006) goes further in pointing out that baking a cake is more than just a mechanical action; it involves skills of judgment and understanding:

> A cook opens the oven door, examines her cake (perceptual skills), and then closes the oven door for further cooking or removes the cake from the oven. It is not our manual ability but our cognitive (perceptual skills), that inform us whether the cake is cooked and determine the mechanical action that follows. (2006: 8)

Likewise, in reporting on the introduction of thermostat-controlled cookers and, later, microwave ovens—assumed to have taken all the stress out of cooking on solid fuel stoves or open fires—Elizabeth Silva observes that the recipe books produced for women users of these technologies "demand assessment from the cook and in many cases knowledge of some arithmetic to define proportions of time in accordance to weight, thickness, and intensity of application of heat" (2000: 618). Thus, as Cockburn (1981) notes, the relative importance of the intellectual and physical dimensions of skill can be seen to shift over time and in response to changing technologies at the household level, as well as changes in the way that food is produced, packaged, and distributed.

But *when* is cooking regarded as a skill, and *who* is perceived as possessing culinary skill?

Cooking and Art: The Culinary Skills Hierarchy

Looking at the genre of French food writing, Luce Giard (1998) notes a distinction between books produced by male and female authors. While the former describe the cuisine of great moments and great chefs, the latter focus on traditional, homely, quotidian cooking, on the art of making use of leftovers, and on cooking on a shoestring budget (1998: 217). Citing Carol Field's (1997) work, Vicki Swinbank also writes on the skills of wartime Italian women who, in spite of scarcity, managed to "coax intense flavors from the most humble ingredients ... [divining] ways to keep pears, lemons and melons fresh through winter" (2002: 467). She notes that while these grandmothers' recipes have been drawn upon and adapted by male haute cuisine chefs, there has been little acknowledgement of their humble origins. Indeed, a gendered culinary hierarchy was reinforced by French chef Paul Bocuse, who asserted, "I intend to repeat my conviction here that women are certainly good cooks for so-called traditional cooking ... Such cooking is, in my opinion, not at all inventive, which I deplore" (cited in Giard 1998: 217).

Seen from this perspective, skill, inventiveness, and creativity are all necessary components in elevating everyday cooking into something an "art." For Meredith Abarca (2006), reporting her research with working-class Mexican and Mexican American women, bridging the gap between the everyday and "art" is not as impossible as may be supposed by the male custodians of the professional culinary arts. Drawing upon the observations of her participants, she posits the idea of "homemade culinary art," a challenge to those, such as philosopher Jean-Francois Revel, who distinguish between "popular" and "erudite" cuisine. The former, Revel claims, is represented by traditional and regional foods. But in order to be metamorphosed from edible raw materials to "culinary arts," they must enter the domain of erudite cuisine. Popular cuisine, he observes, is "based on age-old skills, transmitted unconsciously by way of imitation and habit, of applying methods of cooking patiently tested and associated with certain cooking utensils and recipes prescribed by long tradition … grounded in peasant traditions." By contrast, "erudite cuisine is achieved only through training and education; it is based [on] invention, renewal [and] experimentation … [it] is what 'fathers' do in professional kitchens; 'mothers' in the home kitchens do 'popular' cuisine" (cited in Abarca 2006: 84). Returning to the understanding of skill outlined above, Revel's assertions, on the one hand, acknowledge the place of tacit knowledge, while, on the other hand, displacing this within the culinary hierarchy in favor of formalized training.

What these discussions reveal is the slipperiness of the concept of skill and its meaning and relevance to those using the term. As Phillips and Taylor observe, far from being objective in its relevance and applicability, "skill" does, indeed, appear to be an ideological category, and one that is used to both create and reinforce social constructions of gender (and relatedly, power), not least in the way that different types of work are valued and remunerated.

See also artisan, cooking, gender, innovation, work.

Angela Meah

SPACE AND PLACE

Place, space, and food are interrelated. The material, social, and discursive relations that reproduce place are imbedded into the very stuff of food. Furthermore, because each place is unavoidably interconnected with other places, these too are embedded into the very stuff of food, making food an assemblage of place. Space, too, is implicated in these relationships. Places are joined together through space, and, as foodstuffs move from place to place, they move through space. And, just as food comes from multiple places, food can come from multiple spaces. These spaces are held in tension

between multiple places, and spaces too become part of a food's geography.

While place and space may be central concepts in human geography, their meaning remains elusive and contested. Geographer Robert Sack (1997) and other humanist scholars of place (such as Relph 1976; Tuan 1974, 1977; Buttimer and Seamon 1980) sought to understand the relationship between humans and the world we inhabit. By positioning place and place-making as the fundamental ways in which (we) humans engage with and understand the world around us, these authors deploy "place" to differentiate the inhabited and the lived from the unknown, suggesting that place-making transforms space into the known (Tuan 1977). This positions place between us and the wider world, mediating our experience of reality and allowing us, through place, to make sense of the world. Place becomes an extension of the body, and vice versa. For Sack (2003), in particular, this means that place and place-making are moral projects, an idea that is pressing if we consider more fully the relationship between food, place, and eating. Place is also an everyday word that stands for an everyday idea, but in this sense, place provides the foundation for everyday experience. This "locates" place as neither object nor subject, but rather the site "upon which subjectivity is founded" and the "frame in which objectivity, subjectivity and intersubjectivity are located" (Malpas 1999: 40). Because of this somewhat peculiar relationship, place is not fixed. Rather, it is an emergent process of assemblage as social, material, and discursive relations come into being through the interdependence and interrelation of other geographical processes, such as the social, cultural, economic, ecological, and biophysical.

Geographer Doreen Massey (1993, 2005) describes place as a coordinate located in time and space. She refers to a relational or "progressive" sense of place that can be conceptualized in terms of place's unique connections with other places. Rather than focusing inwards and backwards on the boundaries of place as a frame between object and subject as humanists might do (cf. Relph 1976; Malpas 1999), Massey proposes a conception of place(s) as a local materialization of broader "global" interaction(s) and processes. This leads to a relational view of space, where the "global" is reproduced locally by and within place (cf. Cresswell 2004).

Place and food are undeniably interrelated. The materiality of a foodstuff is constituted from the biophysical properties of place—energy from the sun, minerals, moisture, and so on. These properties are ingested into the body when we eat. In some instances, when foods have a particularly attractive biophysicality, these properties are celebrated, and the food comes with a label of geographical designation. Food, however, is more than its materiality, and place is more than its biophysical properties. One requirement beyond simply being ingestible for an object to become food is that it nourishes the body. This often involves more than the delivery of biophysicality and the provision of biological subsistence. Food plays a social role and has cultural meaning, all of which are also embedded into place. Massey (1991) and Sack (1997) remind us, however, that places are always connected to other places, and the relations that combine to form one place may be implicated in the formation of others, meaning that while a foodstuff may physically come from one place, it is more likely that it comes from many places all at once. The social, discursive, and material relations that comprise each place through which food passes are imprinted into food, and this constellation of places ultimately lead to a food's *geography*. Eating food is to embody these geographies, and—because place-making is a moral project making us complicit in its creation—it is little wonder that the place of food matters so much to matters of food.

A Moral Economy of the Placeless Foodscape

Place matters to food. That is to say, where food comes from and how it is made is important. As agri-food systems have become more "global" through the intensification and industrialization of production, imaginations of place have been increasingly evoked within the collection of initiatives, movements, systems, networks, and other forms of food provisioning that are

typically labeled as "alternative." Through various material-semiotic assemblages, such as the labeling and display that make overt references to a food's "geography," and the specialized locales of retail and consumption, such as farmers' markets, fair trade/organic/farm shops, that reinforce these geographies, "alternative foods" and the geographical processes that underlie them are articulated through a variety of socio-spatial metaphors and scalar constructs that imply a sense of morality and ethics bound up with their consumption (cf. Goodman et al. 2010b). "Local food systems," "slow food movements," "community-supported agriculture," "alternative food networks," producer/consumer (re)connection or shortened supply chains (to name a few) are all organized around ideological positions of social and ecological justice. More broadly, they are organized around rhetorical positions of alterity and opposition to dominant forms of food provisioning, enacted through discourses of place and scale, activating moral dualities of right and wrong.

One of the dominant recent tropes within food research—as well as discourses around food "in practice"—is the idea that much of contemporary food comes from a placeless foodscape, a "landscape" comprised of undifferentiated and interchangeable commodities, where food seems to come from anywhere and nowhere at all. This sense of a geographical "nonplace" (Augé 1994) is juxtaposed with notions of placed and otherwise "alternative" foods. As geographical theories of place have been "brought into conversation" with food's oppositional and alternative politics and practices (Harris 2010; Feagan 2007) and utilized to examine the organizing principles of alternative food, the placeless foodscape is largely disregarded within these debates. It is set up as the center of power to be challenged through an "alternative" food system, but once positioned, it is analyzed through a reductive form of Marxist materialism, summarily dismissed within food debates as a sterile space of corporate capitalism.

Within so-called alternative food movements, "alternative foods" are positioned as the "right" foods, produced and consumed in the "right" ways. These foods are meant to satisfy our individual and increasingly collective cravings for healthy, ethical, and environmentally sound consumption as well as fitting into broader notions of taste, goodness, and quality. The right modes of production are those that not only take into consideration social, ecological, and, increasingly, animal justice, safety, and tradition, but also effectively manage the ways in which these aspects often compete with each other. The right ways to consume are those that reproduce seemingly "core" social values, such as family, kinship, and fellowship, while acknowledging the broader social implications that consumption might have. Ultimately, however, and what makes these foods "right" is that the right foods seem to come from the right kind of places that map onto our imaginations about what food places ought to be like. The "wrong" kinds of food are portrayed as unhealthy, unethical, and/or unjust to people, animals, or the environment. They are produced in such ways that seemingly ignore social and ecological welfare by putting profit before justice; their consumption cuts against the values of family, kinship, and fellowship. They seemingly have no embedded meanings and their social relations are bound up in the relationships of objects and the commodity fetish. Most importantly, however, these types of foods do not seem to have a geography at all. They come from the placeless nongeographies of industrialized capitalism and agri-business that are organized transnationally, comprise the agri-industrial food complex, and result in a "placeless foodscape." The result of these moral geographies of food is that place is privileged and cast as a site of embedded meanings and social relations, which, when speaking of food, are perceived as good things. Placelessness, on the other hand, is utilized to denote an arena of production and consumption where meaning and social relations are "thin" and "desiccated," derived from the calculus of commodities and commoditization (cf. Relph 1976). Questioning the existence of a "placeless" foodscape, this essay focuses attention on the sphere of transnational, industrialized food production, which has too readily been dismissed as unworthy of further critical examination. Its particular focus is on the ways in which consumers engage with

the geographies of food by enacting their own narratives of place and scale.

The relationships between right and wrong, place and placelessness, are underpinned by geographical concepts of place and scale, as well as imaginations and visions about these concepts. Critiques of "alternative" foods have focused on the juxtaposition of the so-called alternative with its supposed other—mainstream or conventional—and on the resultant alternative/conventional duality (Whatmore et al. 2003; Kirwan 2004). Although "alternative" is still used as a part of the nomenclature of food studies, commentators have questioned its analytical utility and have instead concentrated on the ways in which "the specific ordering and spatiality of particular projects can effectively challenge centers of power in the food supply" (Holloway et al. 2007: 15). In the process of eroding one binary, however, others are reproduced. The idea of challenging "centers of power" implies a scalar arrangement—specifically, that centers are organized at a large scale and that they derive their power from this organization. Furthermore, it assumes that projects of respatialization, such as rescaling and replacing, can and should be utilized to oppose these centers of power within the food system. One result is that oppositional food projects may well seek to reorganize the politics of food production, but in doing so may also shift the politics of consumption, suggesting that notions of food justice are situational and dependent on where in the food system they are located and toward whom they are orientated.

Place, Scale, and Provenance

Another entry point into this discussion about place and food is the notion of provenance. As a geographical instrument, provenance encapsulates understandings about where food comes from, how food is made, and where food might have been as it travels from where it is made to where it gets eaten. It encompasses food's spatial, social, and cultural dimensions (Morgan et al. 2006: 4) by placing food into some type of geographical narrative that connects one place to another. The spatial extent of these narratives depends on positioning within the food system and the degree to which agents that comprise the "world of food"—growers, retailers, importers, exporters, and/or end-consumers—embed meanings into food, its production, and its consumption. Implicit provenance claims are made as consumers choose to buy particular products from particular places. These are the same geographies that David Harvey (1990) asks us to consider as part of our geographical imaginations and therefore make explicit, so that we might better understand the impacts of our consumption choices on other places. The choices that underlie implicit claims, however, are often routine, nonreflexive, and subject to a variety of other negotiations that inform consumer identity (Warde 2005). Provenance for end-consumers, however, can be made explicit as well. Devices such as product origin labels and packaging provide consumers with an entry point into the often-opaque geographies that comprise the contemporary agri-food system. They give consumers information about where a particular food was made and relate that information to perceived understandings about quality and safety. These perceptions, however, are mediated through consumer knowledges about those very same origins and products are evaluated, at least in part, on preconceived notions about how food from those places ought to be, whether or not there is a material basis for that evaluation (Lusk et al. 2006). Recent legal controversies in the European Union/United Kingdom over origin labeling indicate that clear and straightforward food labeling comprises a core value for end-consumers and is crucial to maintaining a safe and resilient food system (Verbeke 2005). Increasingly, "merely" knowing a product's origin is not enough. Information about who made it, how it was made, and whether or not it conforms to a number of different types of standards is becoming increasingly important.

Provenance, however, is more than a label of origin. Where a food comes from is also mediated by retailers. This could be as simple as a particular supermarket or as complicated as shopping at a range of different places. This type of provenance is located within a range of socially and culturally embedded practices that include but are not limited to consumption. Likewise, ideas about provenance are important to both

conventional agri-industrial foods, where it acts as a unifying concept within supply-chain management and to the various schemes, networks, and initiatives that comprise what have come to be known as "alternative" foods. Some of the underlying ideas of provenance—such as "knowing" where food comes from, how it was made, and who the farmer/producer is, perhaps identifying with both places of production and consumption through processes of "reconnection" or otherwise understanding a food's geographies—are, however, often associated with the ideas surrounding alternative foods, movements, or initiatives. From this perspective, information about provenance is used to evoke place, and place narratives are evoked within a discourse of the otherwise "placeless" foodscape of conventional agri-industrial food. Discursively, provenance provides a framework through which to verify, trace, unveil, or otherwise "follow" the paths that bring food to the table and in the process act as a mechanism to ensure that the foods we eat satisfy our various material, social, cultural, and/or ethical criteria.

At its center, provenance is a geographical construct that links ideas about place and place-making to the ways in which objects move through time and space. This makes provenance an instrument of scale that can be simultaneously enacted globally, locally, regionally, nationally, and so on; make connections between different scales; and be deployed to inscribe particular foods within particular geographies or indeed food more broadly within particular kinds of geographies. These kinds of geographies are encapsulated by the types of images that surround alternative foods. In light of recent "food scares" and a seeming (and growing) mistrust of an industrialized agri-food system that, by virtue of its size and complexity, might appear opaque, a turn to provenance on the part of consumers might be viewed as a way to return to a type of eating, and a type of food provision, that is more easily understood, more tangible, more manageable, and, through the frameworks of place and place-making, more real or at least more real-feeling (Sack 1992, 2003). So while notions of provenance suggest that *where* things come from is important, the *where* is nuanced and subject to wider cultural and social negotiations, and is subject to often banal as well as extraordinary geographical arrangements of place.

Linking ethics to place and place-making through objects like food also exposes an imaginary dimension to consumption that is otherwise organized around effecting particular material-based ethical agendas. In what he calls a "geographical problematic," Sack (2003) contends that places are constructed by people based on how they *think* reality *ought* to be; Sack is quick to note that "ought" implies a morality to place-making, meaning that though places can be neither right nor wrong, they can appear to satisfy (or not) some imaginative criteria about what makes them seem right or wrong; a geographical imagination becomes one component to making the right place. As places are remade to reflect the anxieties and ethics broadcast "up" the commodity chain by consumers, they are fashioned around imaginary notions of the right kind of place that satisfy consumer ethics and anxieties. These consumer imaginations are informed through a variety of discursive devices: labels, packaging, other material semiotics, as well as through wider narratives about what consumption and by extension production ought to be. These perspectives suggest that, through provenance, ethics and affects are performed through material practice but produced as geographical imaginations about place are mobilized. The relationship between imagination and morality in place is linked to material understandings of provenance. While materially "unveiling" the commodity fetish, declarations of provenance also work to produce a "double commodity fetish" whereby the material geographies that link one place to another are displaced (cf. Cook and Crang 1996).

Feelings and senses about where food comes from lead not only to places where food is grown but also to a milieux of different places where food and foodstuffs might be found. These places assemble to inform consumer understandings and imaginations about food, its production, consumption, and, ultimately, its geographies. From the perspective of end-consumers, provenance is a socially and culturally constructed concept that folds well-worn imaginary tropes of landscape and rurality together with distinctly modern, often urban and classed, forms of provisioning that produce imaginary geographies of both the consumption and production of food and how they ought to be. Neither provenance nor the various imaginative geographies that are generated around it are tied solely to end-consumers. Rather, like justice and ethics, provenance is situational and dependent on location, and it is fashioned by "consumers" all along the supply chain to signal imagined relations between material production and consumption more broadly—consumption after all is informed by more than the materialities of the objects to be consumed.

As a result, provenance is tied to ideas about traceability, a concept that itself is deployed by a variety of actors within the supply chain. As ideas, it could be argued, traceability and provenance arose as antidotes to risk and anxiety. While material traceability in the food system has a legal function (e.g., should something go wrong, someone can be held to account), its deployment is bound to the potential and the unknown. This relates to two intertwined ideas about commodities: production and consumption. On the one hand, and borrowing from a particularly geographical perspective on the commodity fetish, provenance and traceability become ways to ensure a kind of ethical perspective on food. The other perspective, borrowing from sociology and Charles Perrow (1999) in particular, is that modern systems, like the contemporary agri-food system, are extremely big and complex, which both makes understanding them in their entirety nearly impossible and their periodic failure extremely likely. Provenance and the idea of traceability provides one way in which these systems can be materialized or otherwise comprehended and one way in which these systems can be rationalized and managed. Devices like provenance and traceability become ways for all consumers to make sense of food systems and ultimately a tool to direct management responses and strategies when something goes wrong. A turn to provenance suggests a reclamation of food from a placeless foodscape on the part of consumers and an unveiling of the material, social, and discursive relations that separate production from consumption. Provenance, however, is itself discursively enacted as a means through which localities are (re)connected (e.g., "local" consumers [re]connected with global "producers"), so long as they fit into consumers' wider geographical framing of how food ought to be. In the process, material geographies are bypassed and a commodity fetish is reproduced.

Place and (Safe) Space

Regardless of its configuration (e.g., alternative, conventional, "placed" or "placeless"), one of the distinguishing facets of the modern agri-food system—because of its complexity, or indeed despite it—is the need for it to be regulated. The regulation of food, however, involves a spatial logic that is linked to place, place-making, and resultant geographical imaginaries. Histories of food regulation are about establishing where and how food is made available to consumers. Until the early twentieth century, along with other forms of fraud, food contamination and adulteration presented significant health as well as social and economic risks to the consuming public. This resulted in the need on the part of government to control and regulate what goes into food from the perspective of health and safety as well as the ways in which foods are measured and labeled—the latter is a way to establish provenance so that consumers in effect get what they pay for. Markets and particularly market halls were specifically established as centralized locales where state regulations could be enforced (Schmiechen and Carls 1999) and the authority of the state reproduced through such measures as penalties, fines, and taxation. These histories of food governance and regulation are more broadly tied to the expansion of state power (Bobrow-Strain 2008), and they signal a need on the part of the state to formalize the spaces of the economy by demarcating acceptable practices and devices for trade.

Contemporary food regulation reflects a decentralization of governance as it has shifted from the authority of the state to the supposedly democratic space of the market. This neoliberal approach to governance transfers regulatory control and enforcement to private actors and institutions, resulting in an economy that relies

on trading standards and conventions rather than the rule of law. This results in a kind of borderless space where goods and services flow freely, even across national and international boundaries, so long as they meet pre-established standards, as well as having access to certification. Food also circulates within this type of neoliberal "regulation space"; however, for food, as well as other goods, their entry into this space is policed by particular procedures and practices constituted by particular places.

One such practice is encapsulated in the concept of Hazard Analysis and Critical Control Points (HACCP). Developed by NASA as a way to govern the construction of complex machinery, HACCP governance has since been utilized to mitigate the risk of system failure. At its core are processes that identify particular moments and locales within a system where and when tolerances might be exceeded, contamination allowed, or otherwise where and when things might "go wrong," causing a system to break down. The idea behind HACCP is that, if these "critical" points are located and if auditing and other assurance procedures are in place to ensure that these points remain stable, the rest of the system is less likely to fail. The focus on "critical points" frees up resources so that only particular instances are monitored. These critical control points then act as gateways into the system at large. When it comes to food production, critical points are located in key areas where foods might somehow go wrong. These points encompass locales like biosecurity barriers (doors or windows), points where foods are cleaned or cooked (to remove contaminants), refrigeration, packaging, or anywhere else where the food's stability might become compromised. Inside HACCP-led safety regimes, food is free to circulate because effectively the system is designed to preclude failure except at the critical points where risk is managed through robust procedures. HACCP is an organizing principle of identifying and mitigating failure rather than a prescribed set of procedures. Within the world of food, there are few legal requirements for HACCP, other than that HACCP plans must be in place. Ideas of HACCP and similar governance schemes rely on a neoliberal spatial logic that establishes tightly controlled, closely regulated borders (such as at critical points) that exclude entry into systems, but that are topologically "flat," frictionless networks once these borders are crossed (Gilbert 2005). This spatial logic can be mapped onto a kind of Cartesian space that is held in tension between specific places (e.g., critical points that regulate entrance and access), between which objects are able to move freely. Configuring governance space this way takes on geopolitical and economic significance as individual state borders are less relevant to the maintenance of governance space than individual actors located at specific points.

Extending the spatial logic of a "governance space"—controlled by specific points, locales, and ultimately individual practices in individual places—leads back to dualistic notions of geographical imaginaries and imaginative geographies. Because they are based on a notion of possible future system failure, HACCP plans and other governance schemes organized around similar ideological positions rely on paradoxical understandings and spatializations of risk. Drawing from Perrow (1999), they assume that systems will remain intact should tolerances be maintained but cannot account for when tolerances are unknown. In other words, systems fail because the correct tolerances were not understood. This systems approach to governance space leads to the creation of a "safe-space" within which, should nothing untoward happen, objects and subjects remain safe. However, it is not possible to understand the constitution of safety until notions of safety are transgressed. HACCP space, governance space, or indeed "safe-space" becomes a zone of inclusion and exclusion where critical points, locales, and places are—to paraphrase Donald Rumsfeld—regulating "known knowns" and "known unknowns" but leaving "unknown unknowns" to possible futures.

Conclusions

This essay has argued that notions of space and place are central to food studies rather than being confined to a specialist geographical vocabulary. Whether through provenance claims or geographies of regulation, commodity chains or consumer imaginaries, space and place play a key role in the production and consumption of food, taking on social, economic, political, and ultimately moral significance. This essay has also considered some of the interrelations between place, space, and food. Using concepts such as "placeless foodscapes" and "provenance," it has examined the different ways in which place and food relate and are related. Tied into its discussion are notions of geographical imaginations and imaginative geographies—the ways in which some consumers envision the places of food—and the ways in which they might relate to food's production and consumption. The essay then stepped back to consider the different kinds of spaces that are mobilized through food and the ways in which different kinds of places are implicated in these forms of spatial reproduction. Building from this discussion of place, food, and geographical imaginations are ideas surrounding the ways in which places are ingested into the body, being literally embodied, when food is eaten. Indeed one of this essay's main arguments is that because places are embodied when food is ingested, it is necessary to think about how places are configured, reproduced, and assembled into geographies, which are then ingested. Place matters because food matters.

See also foodscapes, governance, moral economy, provenance.

Ben Coles

SUSTAINABILITY

The global food system devours resources, and excretes its pollution and waste, on a scale to compete with any other field of human activity. It is also profoundly vulnerable to the processes of resource depletion and environmental change that underpin concerns over sustainability. Food therefore provides a lens on the fundamental bind of sustainability: how to provide the necessary goods for present human lives without damaging the bases for future human lives.

In itself, "sustainability" is a very simple concept. If something is sustainable, it has the capacity to persist. Sustainability only becomes politically urgent or contested when it refers to a given thing or field of activity—and in relation to a specified or implicit period of time. In focusing on food, some space is immediately staked out in the contested conceptual terrain of sustainability. In common use, sustainability is often taken to refer to human responsibilities for "natural" entities and processes. However, over thousands of millennia and several episodes of mass extinction, life has shown itself to be remarkably resilient. It will surely bounce back from the present period of large-scale anthropogenic species extinction, regardless of how well humanity comes out of it. Consequently, "environmental sustainability" is really about social sustainability, in the sense that it is about maintaining the ecosystem services on which human lives depend. The open meaning of the word sustainability has enabled its appropriation for so many purposes that it circulates as a generally well-meaning but vague notion. That it is at the core of any means of meeting the profound challenge of feeding a likely population of nine billion from 2050 shows that sustainability is both political and urgent.

The relation between sustainability and food can be looked at from two directions. From one direction, considering food and sustainability means looking at the environmental impact of the food system. Taking a whole systems approach, agriculture and food production account for a large proportion of anthropogenic greenhouse gas emissions. Estimates vary for just what proportion of such emissions food accounts but top out at around one-third, more than double the emissions of transport worldwide (Pretty et al. 2010). Conversion of land to agriculture, and the industrialization and intensification of agriculture, contribute substantially to reductions in biodiversity, soil quality, and fresh water availability. Given the centrality of food to human life, culture, and economies, it is unsurprising that it accounts for a large proportion of the damage being done to the environment through human activity—but that makes food all the more central a focus for concern about sustainability.

From the other direction, the issue becomes the vulnerability of the food system to resource depletion and environmental change. The flip side of the environmental consequences of the food system is its environmental dependencies. While its massive contribution to greenhouse gases is substantially thanks to the potent emissions from livestock's digestive systems, it is also indicative of the food system's enormous dependence on fossil fuels. From inputs of hydrocarbon fertilizers to the diesel in supermarket trucks, food systems are vulnerable to the imminence of peak oil—the point at which global oil supplies begin to diminish. Climate change, to which the food system contributes, promises unknown challenges to future food production, as weather systems respond unpredictably to warming global temperatures. The steady degradation of the world's cultivated soils and the depletion of accessible fresh water add to the bleak picture (Foresight 2011).

Of course, this global picture masks huge variations in both causes and consequences. It goes almost without saying that consumption by the relatively rich of the world is implicated in an uneven share of the environmental harm resulting from the agri-food system, while the relatively poor suffer disproportionately from the consequences. While this is partly due to the inequalities in calorific intake, it also reflects the patterns of culturally embedded diets and patterns of eating. Livestock production has been estimated to account for almost one-fifth of anthropogenic greenhouse gas emissions (FAO 2006b)—more than half of all the emissions resulting from food production. Yet animal products provide less than one-fifth of average calorie intake worldwide (FAO 2010). The changing location of meat in the routines, norms, and meanings of eating (Beardsworth and Keil 1991; Fiddes 1991) is therefore of central importance to the sustainability of food systems. The twentieth-century convergence of industrialized food production and rising affluence in countries like those of Western Europe and North America saw the progressive normalization of eating meat as part of daily meals, including through the role of meat in the emergence and growth of fast food. Between 1960 and 2000, meat production more than trebled

(Speedy 2003), while the world population doubled, reflecting the growing role of meat in diets, with the distribution of growth globally showing that eating more meat tends to be a corollary of having more money (Popkin 2007). This trend continues today with increasing affluence in countries like China and Brazil being accompanied by increasing consumption of meat and dairy, with serious consequences for the sustainability of a food system capable of feeding nine billion (Godfray et al. 2010). Meanwhile, fruit and vegetables grown in heated greenhouses, or flown across continents, compete with meat and dairy on measures of environmental impact. Increasing expectations of the availability of fresh foods therefore have similar implications to rising consumption of meat.

The example of meat consumption shows how dynamics at the heart of global-scale challenges to sustainability link to the patterns and routines of shopping, cooking, and eating.

The accounting of sustainability through increasingly economistic framings, exemplified by the rise of the carbon economy, typically sidelines the grounding of environmental impacts and consequences in differences in ways of living. As demographer Joel Cohen (1995) points out, the earth can support many more vegetarians than it can meat-eaters. The details of diet and the cultural embeddedness of particular patterns of growing and eating therefore have profound consequences for future human well-being. Shifting food systems onto a sustainable footing will require changes and interventions throughout those systems, from agri-industrial production to the meanings and norms that shape consumption in the home.

See also security, waste.

Matt Watson

T

Taste © ANGELA MEAH.

TASTE

Taste is constructed, commodified, cultivated, and contested in contemporary food systems, a quality of both consumers and products. This essay focuses on the emergence of standards of taste and their association with particular approaches to the study of food and society. Humans are faced with what Paul Rozin (1976), famously described as the "omnivore's dilemma." Able to eat just about anything, the biggest question is what to eat; a question that is resolved differently in the varying cuisines within and between nations and social groups (cf. Fischler [1980] on the related idea of the omnivore's paradox). At the heart of this variation is the question of "taste": not only in a narrow sense of the perception of food qualities in the mouth and nose (although this plays a central role), but also in the cultural elaboration and disputation of food habits, customs, and practices. This essay explores how standards of taste about food are formed and circulate. It argues that recent developments that focus on the embodied activity of taste-making provide a productive avenue for future work that reintroduces the experience of eating, drinking, and tasting to discussions of taste.

What is Taste?

Contemporary concepts of taste combine the physiological and the aesthetic. Across languages, words for aesthetic judgments are inextricable from the experience of eating and the complex relations between subjects, objects, and practices of taste. However, taste's original meaning is closer to that of touch, and it was only from the fourteenth century that it acquired its aesthetic connotations (Williams 1976).

In his classic *Physiology of Taste* (1826), the French gourmet Jean-Anthelme Brillat-Savarin described taste as having three forms: that of the organ of flavor appreciation, a sensation that is excited by sapid bodies, and the capacity of these bodies to impress the taste organs and arouse the sensation of taste. He argued that taste serves two functional roles in maintaining our bodies, inviting us "by pleasure to repair the continual losses brought about by life" and

allowing us to choose "from among the diverse substances that nature presents, those that nourish us best" (1826: n.p.).

The contemporary physiology of taste distinguishes four basic taste sensations that are experienced by all mammals—bitter, sour, salty, and sweet—usually supplemented by a fifth, umami, and more recently by a sixth, that of fat. The experience of taste occurs when taste receptors detect the chemicals associated with each taste, including salt cat-ions, sugars, and organic compounds that produce bitterness. These basic taste sensations are detected by taste buds, small clusters of cells found on the tongue that are continually renewed. However, despite the popular focus on "taste buds," most of what is commonly referred to as taste (but what might more accurately be described as flavor) occurs in the nose, as chewing releases odorants that are detected in the nasal cavity. The ability to taste varies. For example, women have more taste buds than men and are more likely to be "super-tasters," while in general perceiving greater sweetness and bitterness (Bartoshuk and Duffy 2005). In the 1930s, it was accidentally found that around a quarter of people are taste-blind to the bitter chemical phenylthiocarbamide. Since then, it has been suggested that some preference for sweetness is linked to genetic variation in the ability to taste PROP (6-n-Propylthiouracil), which tastes bitter to some but not others.

Taste and Distinction

Despite the functionalism laid out by Brillat-Savarin (1826), the physiological experience of taste goes only part way to explaining why some things are consumed and not others, and provides no insight into how tastes are used to classify both things and people. As Stephen Mennell suggests, "Taste in food, as in other domains of culture, implies discrimination, standards of good and bad, the acceptance of some things and the rejection of others" (1985: 20). Debates about taste relate to the production and validation of claims about the worth or beauty of things. However, the nature of these standards and their relationship with objective knowledges and subjective experiences of taste have been the subject of significant philosophical debate. This peaked during the seventeenth century, at around the same time as taste became closely associated with aesthetic judgment (Williams 1976). In *Of the Standard of Taste* (1757/2005), David Hume argued for the existence of a uniform sense of artistic judgment in human nature and explained differences in taste judgments according to the natures of individuals and of different "ages and nations" (1757/2005: 205). Thirty years later, Immanuel Kant's *Critique of Judgement* (1790/2008) provided the most detailed and influential account of taste prior to the late-twentieth century. Kant, like Hume, was concerned with the irresoluble "antinomy" that lies at the heart of taste: the relationship between individual experiences, which are unique and subjective, and universal standards of what is good and beautiful.

For Kant, the subjective experience of taste was inextricable from individual pleasure and desire, yet claimed to relate to universal rules that were valid for all. The problem, then, is that judgments of taste have to retain their connection to inner subjective experience, such as the pleasure derived from a particular food, while existing in connection with shared cognitive structures—judgments of taste are made with a "universal voice." Thus, while it is possible to provide taste judgments that distinguish, for example, whether something is sweet or bitter, it is impossible to provide a universally valid verdict on whether any particular sweetness or bitterness is pleasant. Instead, Kant argues that a disinterested standard of beauty exists, independent of subjective experience or individual desires. This "aesthetic judgment capable of making a rightful claim upon the assent of all men" (Kant 1790/2008: 44) is what determines standards of taste.

The relationship between the freedom and idiosyncrasy of individual taste and the existence or not of independent standards of taste remains the central question in defining taste. However, over the last century, sociological approaches have described how Kant's antinomy is negotiated in everyday life through social formations or figurations that provisionally overcome these oppositions and that explore the nature of "pure" taste (Gronow 1997; Bourdieu

1984; Simmel 1971). In particular, these challenge the "denial of the social" within discussion of taste and explore the relations between standards of taste and social distributions of power and resources.

Cultures of Taste

Tastes in food vary between and within countries and societies, and exploring their distribution has formed a major strand of work across the social sciences. For Claude Lévi-Strauss (1963), the examination of the configuration and distribution of tastes formed part of his wider program of structural anthropology. As he puts it in elaborating his concept of gustemes, "Like language … the cuisine of a society may be analysed into constituent elements, which in this case we might call 'gustemes,' and which may be organized according to certain structures of opposition and correlation" (1963: 86). He then used these oppositions and correlations to draw distinctions between the cuisines of France and the United Kingdom. Lévi-Strauss characterizes each cuisine along axes of endogenous/exogenous, according to the extent to which they use national or exotic ingredients; central/peripheral, by whether they are concentrated on staple foods or accompaniments; and as marked/not marked, according to whether they are savory or bland. Lévi-Strauss's (1963) work represents the first significant attempt to conduct a comparative analysis of food tastes, although the binary categories through which the analysis was constructed ultimately led to the reiteration of a somewhat caricatured account of bland, parochial British tastes compared to the sophisticated cosmopolitanism of French taste. Subsequent work extends Lévi-Strauss's discussion by exploring the codes and structures that govern taste, notably Mary Douglas's (1971) work on "deciphering" the meal.

However, the major strand in contemporary sociological discussion of taste explores the role of taste in expressing and reproducing social distinctions. Mennell (1985) situates discussion of evolving tastes in the United Kingdom and France in relation to broader processes of social development. He describes the progressive refinement of the practices of eating in

Europe, culminating in the emergence of haute cuisine in France in the nineteenth century, which drove relentless innovation in dishes and flavors by chefs such as Antoine Carême and Auguste Escoffier. Mennell argues that, in part, the complex system of taste that prevailed in France reflected the declining political power and revenues of the nobility, prompting new displays of superiority, including the ability to discuss and argue about taste (Mennell 1985; Gronow 1997). Yi-Fu Tuan (1993) compares this European aesthetic of food preparation and eating with that of China. In China, Tuan suggests that an emphasis on the "pleasures of the palate" drives the consumption of a wide variety of foods and is accompanied by a proliferation of terms describing taste and texture. He highlights the exacting standards of preparation and provenance that emerge from the Chinese "love of food," citing the example of Confucius, who "did not eat meat which was not cut properly, nor what was served without its proper sauce" (Tuan 1993, reprinted in Korsmeyer 2005: 231), and the connoisseur who transported casks of fresh Huich'uan spring water by sea for his tea. Tuan's examples not only show the relationship between the experience of the taste of food and its role in the expression of "high culture" in both Europe and China, but also the differing ways in which these are articulated.

The most influential description of taste in terms of distinction is that of Pierre Bourdieu, who built on earlier work by Thorsten Veblen and Georg Simmel to argue that "taste is the basis of all that one has—people and things—and all that one is for others, whereby one classifies oneself and is classified by others" (1984: 56). Pierre Bourdieu's discussion of taste considers how it is made through and in turn indicates social categories, especially class. In particular, he argues, against Kant, that the prevailing standard of "good taste" within a society is that of the elite class and that, consequently, individual aesthetic judgments of taste "consciously and deliberately or not … fulfil a social function of legitimating social differences" (1984: 7). Our tastes—including the food we eat, how we eat, and how much we eat—express and embody our place in the social order,

revealing information about us to others as well as constructing our sense of identity.

Bourdieu's study is based on large surveys of French households conducted in the 1960s and early 1970s, which describe differences in the food habits of classes in 1960s French society. In short, Bourdieu suggests that the upper classes use their taste in food to differentiate themselves from the lower classes. What counts as "good taste" is distinguished by its distance from "necessity." The middle classes then seek to emulate the tastes of the upper class, leading to a further development of elite tastes in an ongoing "arms race" of ever greater refinement. As Bourdieu suggests: "Taste … functions as a sort of social orientation, a 'sense of one's place,'" guiding the occupants of a given place in social space towards the social positions adjusted to their properties, and towards the practices or goods which befit the occupants of that position" (1984: 466). He describes how social structures are internalized, embodied, and re-enacted in the performance of social practices. In doing so, he moves discussion of taste away from the cognitive, conscious making of distinctions and focuses on taste as formed by habitus, a system of embodied dispositions that shape people's wants and desires and that reflect and reproduce the distribution of economic, cultural, and social resources among social classes. He develops on similar previous discussions by Veblen and others to connect questions of taste, class, and the body, pointing to the body as

> the most indisputable materialization of class taste, which it manifests in several ways. It does this first in the seemingly most natural features of the body, the dimension … and shapes … of its visible forms, which express in countless ways a whole relation to the body, i.e. a way of treating it, caring for it, feeding it, maintaining it, which reveals the deepest dispositions of the habitus. (1984: 190)

The foods chosen, cooking styles, and the relationship between food, the body, and manners are all, for Bourdieu, used to reproduce societal distinctions. For example, the newly wealthy are found to eat larger quantities of expensive but heavy or rich foods, often prepared in elaborate or exotic ways for special occasions. In contrast, professionals tended to eat more "refined," light, or delicate foods that were often quick to prepare, reflecting the likelihood that women in these households were working outside the home. He suggested the latter group were likely to value formality and good manners at meals rather than the quality of the food and often served simple, well-presented foods on special occasions. This group also perceived French society in general as eating too much. These judgments contrast with what Bourdieu identified as the tendency of the working classes to emphasize "convivial indulgence" and meals that take a long time to prepare, reflecting classed conceptions of gender roles in cooking.

In the United Kingdom, Alan Warde's (1997) analysis of twenty-five years of the Food Expenditure Survey also showed class differences in taste, with the middle classes (social groups I and II) more likely to purchase foods with perceived health benefits (e.g., fresh fruit and vegetables, wholemeal bread, skimmed milk, and yoghurt). In contrast, the working classes were more likely to consume more sweet, fatty, or satisfying foods (e.g., white bread, sugar, cooked meats, and burgers). Outside continental Europe, Richard Wilk (2006b) describes how "high colonial" tastes in Belize were tightly structured along hierarchical lines with the elite consuming locally produced food prepared according to metropolitan norms and the working class consuming readily available local food, while the middle classes consumed accessible "foreign" food in order to distinguish themselves from the class below.

The distinctions between the classes displayed in the selection, presentation, and conceptualization of food emerge, for Bourdieu, from the uneven distribution and restraints of economic and cultural capital. The latter represents the learned knowledges and competencies that are derived from lifelong immersion in a particular habitus. Importantly, although such capital can be objectified, as in an etiquette guide, or institutionalized, as in an etiquette course, it is also embodied, and therefore less fungible and easily transformed than economic capital. Thus the nouveaux riches, although wealthy, have not acquired knowledge of the

"correct mode of comportment," which derives from social origin and childhood education or enculturation in "good taste." For the elite, the etiquette and manners associated with good taste are self-evident and natural. For others, their insecurity and overly tight adherence to rules serves to reinforce how they are perceived by others.

Bourdieu and Contemporary Taste

While hugely influential, Bourdieu's discussion of taste has been criticized on a number of accounts. Bourdieu set out to describe the stable features of society, at a time when he perceived sociology as obsessed with change and mutation. Perhaps inevitably therefore, his work is static and deeply rooted in the world of 1960s France that it describes. It is unable to account for either the historical emergence of its configuration of tastes or for rapid changes in taste without these involving the introduction of new social hierarchies. In addition, Bourdieu's analysis of taste as a strategic tool in the oppositional relationships between social classes is potentially less relevant in contemporary, pluralistic societies for three reasons. The first is that contemporary food markets are based on what Mennell (1985) describes as "diminishing contrasts" and "increasing variety"—a homogenization of cuisine that is captured and critiqued in works such as George Ritzer's (1993, 1998) McDonaldization thesis. In this context, there is less room for the expression of distinctive tastes, accompanied by an explosion in the diversity of tastes. In contrast, others contend that society is becoming increasingly individualized. Ulrich Beck's (1992) risk society thesis and related work on reflexive modernization (Beck et al. 1994) both emphasize the extent to which consumers are alone, together. Thus, one could argue that in a diverse landscape of food options, the expression of taste becomes the expression of individual, rather than class, identities.

Finally, it may be that the traditional influence of high culture on tastes, epitomized by haute cuisine, is in decline, and that openness to diversity is replacing exclusivity as a means of distinction (cf. Peterson and Kern 1996). Josée

Johnston and Shyon Baumann (2007) examine this thesis in the context of gourmet food magazines, exploring the apparently egalitarian ethic that valorizes exotic and "authentic" food, in which *Gourmet* magazine features recommendations for burgers. Johnston and Baumann describe how value is attached to

> seemingly "simple" foods that come from highly specific places off the middle-class tourist path, [which] are produced by hard-working rural people with non-commercial motivations, [which] have ties to specific personalities and culinary artists (especially in wealthy settings), [which] have a rich history, and [which] are consumed in casual, "simple" settings. (2007: 187)

However, Johnston and Baumann (2007) argue that despite the emergence of omnivorous tastes, Bourdieu's description of exclusivity remains important. Their work shows how a perspective on a specific world of taste, that of gourmet food magazines, illustrates the emergence of new hierarchies. They describe how the emergence of omnivorous tastes involves new forms of distinction performed through the valuing of authenticity and exoticism as legitimizing features of "good" food. Consequently, potentially egalitarian and democratizing criteria in fact work to validate a relatively narrow range of foods that require individuals to have considerable cultural and/or economic capital. Despite the appearance of democratized, omnivorous tastes, the importance of elite gatekeepers remains, although their form may have changed.

Taste, Expertise, and Exclusivity

Following Bourdieu, good taste is understood as that of the ruling class, is defined and maintained by the social elite and emerges from a particular habitus that makes it appear "second nature." However, even within the elite, certain individuals have long been seen as having an extraordinary ability to taste; a skill that, as Kant (1790/2005) points out, is etymologically and historically associated with conceptions

of wisdom. For example, the Roman courtier Petronius was described by Tacitus in the *Annals* as an "arbiter of taste" (*elegantiae arbiter*), without whose approval the emperor Nero "thought nothing smart or elegant" (2003: 390), but whose position ultimately led to his betrayal and suicide. In the eighteenth century, Hume described the existence of "men [sic] of delicate taste" who "even during the most polished ages [are] so rare a character" (1757/2005: 206). Similarly, Brillat-Savarin (1826) lauds the gustatory sensitivity of the "connoisseurs [who] can distinguish the flavor of the thigh on which the partridge sleeps from the other," holding them up as a demonstration of the "supremacy of Man [sic]" over animals. In the early nineteenth century, "gastronomes" such as Brillat-Savarin himself or Alexandre Grimod became influential as the prestige previously associated with aristocratic patrons declined following the French Revolution (Mennell 1985). These individuals were central in defining elite "canons of correct taste," often associated with discrimination, delicacy, and choice, although they were also, Mennell argues, influential in circulating this taste to a wider audience through their extensive writings.

Codes or guidelines of taste remain evident in relation to products such as wine and cheese, forming "semi-objective" aesthetic standards that provide a resource for evaluations of the inherent and relative worth of things, and are shared within and between groups of people (Gronow 2004). In specialized domains, these remain associated with the biological capacities of particular individuals. Indeed, certain expert tasters—including wine critic Robert Parker, coffee cupper Gennaro Pelliccia, and restaurant critic Egon Ronay—protect this biological capital through insurance policies, often for several million dollars. However, the broad trends of taste homogenization and/or diversification described above also imply a changing role for elite taste experts. Beyond a few specialized, esoteric areas, it is no longer possible to regard taste as

> ineffable, indivisible, [and] unquestionable, embodied by persons who somehow inherited impeccable judgement and whose judgements were therefore not open to dissection into component parts

which might be scrutinised forensically and held up to challenge. (Harvey et al. 2004: 2)

Traditional standards of taste have been replaced by new bodies and new forms of expertise that perform taste judgments in new ways and with reference to different conventions of value. Socially shared and binding forms of taste judgment continue to exist; the "aesthetic codes that determine the inner value and worth of things to people" (Gronow 2004: 45), but are defined in context and shift as they circulate between actors in food networks. Because they are shared, they can be used in advertising and product marketing to provide taste aspirations that echo class-defining characteristics of taste. However, they are also open to change and evolution.

The democratization of standards of taste as universally accessible judgments associated with particular social worlds provides a productive avenue for the development of research into food tastes. Jukka Gronow suggests that aesthetic standards emerge from group participation in specific social worlds and ultimately act as the boundaries of, and characteristic quality of, a social world clustered around a core object, experience, or event (Gronow 2004). However, not all participants of social worlds are equally engaged. Thus, while there are some who are actively and deeply involved in the worlds of wine tasting and the production and reproduction of wine quality, there are immeasurably more people who are simply "tourists" in that world, and yet more who are disengaged and dispassionate strangers (Gronow 2004). The relationship between these insiders and tourists reimagines the distribution of "good taste" previously associated with class. Hence, those who are heavily engaged in social worlds are socialized in the associated knowledges and behaviors, while those who are tourists may be lacking in these.

Gronow's (2004) use of social worlds theory offers a potential means of engaging with a fragmented "ecology" of taste standards and, he argues, of understanding the contrast between the relative lack of variety in everyday food consumption and the panoply of exotic and specialized foods within popular culture. He suggests that the visibility and apparent accessibility of the

social worlds of food enables consumers to "visit" them. Taking the approach further, he identifies two sets of social worlds that cluster around particular approaches to food and standards of taste (what Mol [2009] describes as "yummy" and "healthy"), which differ from the hierarchical systems described by Bourdieu. The first of these is associated with culinary taste, cooking skill, and etiquette. It incorporates a range of core concerns, from haute cuisine and wine tasting to vegetarianism to provenance and the Slow Food movement. Gronow contrasts this with a second set of worlds associated with health and fitness, which he terms "dietary" as opposed to "taste" worlds. As with the former, however, insiders in social worlds such as that of Weight Watchers find that they fill their time and provide a source of meaning and identity, while tourists may dip into their regimes in passing.

The adoption of a social worlds perspective on taste provides a means of understanding how, in fragmented "postmodern" societies, standards of taste are established and the goodness of a food determined. It also points to the importance of continuity between expert and lay tastes in establishing the value of expertise in food markets. Without the accessibility of social worlds to consumers and their less refined sensory abilities, the value of taste expertise diminishes.

Taste as Corporeal Activity and Social Practice

For a long time, aesthetic thinking in philosophy drew a parallel between physiological and aesthetic taste (Gronow 1997). Yet, following Kant, aesthetics became separated from bodily experience and from the "near" senses of taste and smell. Although the work introduced above explores the circumstances under which these standards emerge, the Kantian devaluation of sensory experience persists in approaches to taste as a social phenomenon. These approaches obscure the importance of food itself and its relationship with the body, the practice of "applied taste" that excited Brillat-Savarin.

For Bourdieu, the body represents the locus at which class differences in taste are displayed, but has little involvement in this process.

Reintroducing the body and the materialities of food requires an approach that attends to tasting as a "collective technique" and explores the assemblages of intersubjectivity through which standards of taste emerge and function (Hennion 2007a, 2007b; Mol 2009; Shapin 2012). In the work of Antoine Hennion and Genevieve Teil (Hennion 2007b, 2007a; Teil and Hennion 2004), this approach is used to explore taste as emergent from "attachments" between tasting bodies and tasted objects, rather than as an existing quality of each. Teil and Hennion (2004) concentrate on the activities of "amateurs," particularly in the areas of music and wine tasting. The term is not only intended to imply a contrast with "professional" tasters but also to capture the Latin etymology of the term in love or passion. As Hennion suggests, taste here is considered the product of the "act of tasting, the gestures that allow it … the know-how that accompanies it … in the tiny ongoing adjustments that lay it out and favour its felicity and reproducibility" (2007a: 101).

In conceptualizing tasting as activity, as something one has to "do," Hennion introduces contingent assemblages of interacting components. This irreducible heterogeneity includes communities of cognizant subjects who provide the framework and foil for the expression of individual tastes; devices, instruments, and conditions of tasting, including the time and space in which tasting occurs and the associated tools and rules; the body that processes and experiences taste and becomes aware of itself in the process (what Latour [2004a] describes as learning to be affected); and finally the material object of taste, whose differences and effects emerge from the tasting. Within collectives or communities of amateurs, individual taste takes on a reflexive nature and involves an engagement with the emerging characteristics of objects and a constant comparison and contrast with the tastes of others. Rather than being a question of social distinction, taste is itself social, produced through association or attachment and a constant working on oneself, to develop one's sensibilities. For Hennion (2007b), these elements of taste constitute the basic framework of the "spaces of taste" and their differing articulation provides for comparison between differing

forms of attachment. For example, Elspeth Probyn (2012) draws on Hennion to develop a materialized discussion of taste that explores the emergence of localized food communities in the context of globalization. Concentrating on oysters, Probyn seeks to use the affective act of tasting and eating to highlight the economic and emotional ties that bind communities of fishermen, academics, restaurateurs, and school children together.

The appearance of communities of amateurs who form a public targeted around a core object can potentially be understood as replacing the social elite described by Bourdieu. In their operation, these communities echo the social worlds of taste described by Grunow. This approach also provides a means of bringing to the fore the heterogeneous products, devices, instruments, discourses, rules, and bodies associated with "tasting" in these worlds. To date, this work has focused primarily on the taste worlds of amateurs or enthusiasts, and the extent to which Teil and Hennion's description of taste-making is applicable in general has yet to be explored. However, Hennion's description of taste and of the ways in which the "space of taste" is filled with tools, devices, frames, and collectives is similar in many ways to descriptions of social practices. Indeed, Sylvia Gherardi (2009) directly develops this work to describe taste as central to practices: taste represents "a preference for the way we do things together"; is based on a subjective attachment to the object of practice; is acquired and taught as one becomes a "practitioner"; and, following Teil and Hennion (2004), is an activity performed within a practice. Taste thus becomes integrated into practice, rather than separated as in Bourdieu's work.

In the course of this essay, we have moved from a conceptualization of standards of taste derived from a Kantian ideal, through the social determination of taste within class structures or social worlds to consider its emergence through the articulations between reflexive bodies and food matters within social practices of tasting. This approach offers potential for research that explores how, where, and in relation to which instruments, devices, and places the practices of taste-making are performed and their role in establishing embodied forms of normativity (cf. Mol 2009; Shapin 2012). However, it also suggests the ongoing importance of Bourdieu's work on taste and of considering the continuing role of distributions of economic, cultural, and biological resources in the experience of taste. Such research would explore how the subjectivity and apparent arbitrariness of taste is negotiated and managed, to explore how, when there is famously "no accounting for taste," taste can be accounted for.

See also choice, class, eating, exotic, gourmet, pleasure.

Richard Milne

TECHNOLOGIES

Technologies can be thought of as the practical application of skills and knowledge, including scientific knowledge, to human activity. More commonly, technologies are regarded as particular instruments or artifacts that are operated in some way by humans to perform certain functions, such as a spoon to stir the soup or a robotic arm packaging baked snacks. The question of "nonhuman" technologies (for instance, the use of tools by primates) further complicates attempts at definition. As Warren Belasco (2006) confirms in his history of the future of food, consumers have always been ambivalent toward technological innovations in relation to food; some of the reasons for this will be explored in this essay.

Taking issue with the multiple meanings of technology, Stephen Kline (1985) has sought to clarify four uses of the term: technology as *artifact* or *hardware*; technology as the *sociotechnical systems of manufacture*; technology as *know-how* or *methodology*; and technology as *sociotechnical systems of use*. In referring to sociotechnical systems of manufacture and of use, he proposes that technology can be understood as the interaction of people, resources, machines, and institutions geared toward the production of a particular technological artifact (such as a type of novel

food packaging) or the interactions that occur in the application of a technological artifact. Kline considered the notion of purposeful innovation in sociotechnical systems to be a defining characteristic of humankind. Such systems are not predetermined, and in their seminal work on the "social construction of technology" (termed the SCOT approach), Trevor Pinch and Wiebe Bijker argued that technological artifacts emerge as a result of group interactions. Through interactions, one particular vision of a technology succeeds at the expense of alternative variants, which are lost to history (Pinch and Bijker 1984).

When considering food, a broad understanding of technologies (incorporating artifacts, methodologies, and sociotechnical systems) leads in many directions, including manufacturing processes, domestic ovens for cooking, materials for food preservation, shopping lists, livestock rearing practices, haulage transportation, nutrition labels, the "supermarket shop," and patent rights over seeds. The length of the list emphasizes the fact that food is unavoidably connected to technology in all its forms. However, while the availability of food has been greatly enhanced by the application of technologies, not all these applications have produced the outcomes intended, or have been free from controversy.

Among those technologies mentioned above, the role of haulage trucks in the reconfiguration of the U.S. food system has been thoroughly detailed by Shane Hamilton (2008). In this historical monograph, Hamilton demonstrates that technological infrastructure, guided by political and social processes, plays a crucial role in steering the trajectory of contemporary food production and retail. In this way, generally applied technologies can have a pivotal role in changing everyday food practices and their political-economic organization. Famously, at the global scale, the expansion of merchant shipping and rail networks in the late nineteenth century coincided with the rise of colonial forms of food commodity production and transportation (Hobsbawm 1987). A comparable revolution has occurred with the implementation of increasingly sophisticated logistics and supply chain technologies, principally organized by transnational retailers and with implications for the entire agri-food system (Wrigley et al. 2005; Busch 2007).

Within the household, technological devices have, to varying degrees, altered the work of domestic food preparation in many countries. However, longstanding human technologies such as knives have undergone many cycles of change and product differentiation based upon materials, styling, cost, and culture. In the United Kingdom, Angela Meah and Peter Jackson (2013) have considered the gendered utilization of technology in the kitchen, with men more readily adopting technological artifacts associated with the world of professional chefs and women more often utilizing "standard" technologies in routine food preparation, including their hands. Considerations of more novel domestic food technologies used in the home have been undertaken by Rodrigo Ribeiro and Harry Collins (2007), who explore the partial synthesis of tacit knowledge within the automated bread-maker, and Mónica Truninger (2011), who details how people become users of the Bimby multifood processor through practical social events led by trained demonstrators.

The incorporation and utilization of household food technologies can be contrasted with the high-profile controversies associated with genetically modified (GM) foods. The application of genetic modification techniques to produce crops and livestock has attracted considerable academic attention, with numerous accounts exploring the development and application of agricultural biotechnologies in capitalist agriculture (e.g., Goodman et al. 1987; Busch et al. 1991; Goodman and Redclift 1991; Kloppenburg 2004) and the trade and policy implications of these technologies and associated intellectual property regimes (e.g., Bernauer 2003; Jasanoff 2005; Sell 2009; Tansey and Rojette 2008). As Fred Buttel (2005) has argued, many of the more recent arguments made against the use of genetically engineered plants in agriculture in the global North have addressed environmental concerns and risks to health, rather than the ownership and use of genetic material. These concerns have been particularly manifest in public and policy attitudes toward GM foods in Europe.

Since the mid-1990s discussions of food, technologies, and public and political uncertainty have become more prominent owing to a series of food safety events. In this context, Gene Rowe and Lynn Frewer (2000) and Alan Irwin (2001) offer influential analyses of approaches to public participation in science and technology policy-making, with the BSE controversy recognized as being critical to public skepticism. Questions over the implications of scientific and technological developments in the food sector often demonstrate a close alignment between scientific knowledge and technological application.

Public perceptions of new food technologies have been considered by Fanny Rollin and others (2011), who discuss consumer attitudes towards five novel food technologies: nanotechnology, genetic modification, nutrigenomics, food irradiation, and animal cloning. In focusing on these diverse technologies, the authors highlight a range of public concerns. Genetic modification is identified as the most well-known, with variations in public attitudes across Europe (though generally not favorable) and the United States (more favorable), and there some evidence that Chinese consumers are willing to pay a premium for such products. Animal cloning meets resistance in Europe, with a strong call for clear labeling of relevant products. Food irradiation is also viewed negatively, though the authors suggest that access to information about this technology changes consumer attitudes. Nanotechnology is less well-known, with consumers across North America and Europe being ambivalent. Mixed attitudes toward nutrigenomics were reported, with some studies suggesting a willingness to undergo genetic testing and others identifying a confluence between nutrigenomics and genetic modification in the views of consumers.

The five technologies discussed above all share the characteristic of relative novelty, certainly in comparison to longstanding food technologies such as preservation through salting and selective plant breeding. Critical voices have termed the products derived from such novel technologies "technofoods," suggesting that they do little to address underlying problems with the agri-food system (Nestle 2002). This compound term draws attention to contemporary anxieties about the centrality of technology to food and life. As Lowe and others (2008) have suggested, the complex, technology-driven food system has attracted opposition on ethical and environmental grounds. Support for farmers' markets, community-supported agriculture, and local supply chains all suggests that, for some consumers, there exists a desire to bypass this complex system and reduce the role of technological developments. One aim of reducing the role of technology in food is to pursue authenticity and tradition in order for food to be imbued with more desirable qualities. From a rather different position, one skeptical observer vouches for the "realness" of a Birds Eye Traditional Chicken ready meal, a product made possible by Clarence Birdseye's quick-freeze technology (Self 2011). As Belasco (2007) observes, much effort has been expended by the food industry to resolve the implicit tensions between technology and tradition.

In this respect, the role of *machine*-facture— as distinct from *manu*-facture—in food production is a recurring area of contention. From a Marxist perspective, machine-facture has enabled capitalists to increase labor productivity through the use of machinery, while deskilling and alienating workers (Braverman 1974; Mohun 1991). For others, the modern factory can be considered a place of experimentation, central to the reconfiguration of identity and democracy (Miller and O'Leary 1994; Miller and Rose 1995). Certainly, accounts of the labor process in highly mechanized food manufacturing have detailed a (retailer-driven) nexus of improved working conditions and exacting product standards and deadlines. In relation to the French meat-processing and confectionary sectors, distinctive arrangements are said to have supported relatively good wages, offset by the continuous pressure to increase work intensity (Caroli et al. 2009), while in the UK context it has been argued that food hygiene is often prioritized above health and safety (Lloyd and James 2008). These assertions evoke the literary and investigative endeavors of Upton Sinclair (1906/1965), in particular his concern to highlight poor working conditions in the considerably more dangerous (and less mechanized)

abattoirs of the early twentieth century United States.

Considering technologies and food also brings into focus speculations about the future. Belasco (2008) suggests that the future growth of meat-based diets will deepen existing problems produced by mainstream, grain-intensive livestock and dairy production systems. Here technology is not implicated directly as a cause for concern, as with public mistrust toward new food technologies. Instead, it could be argued that a sociotechnical-systems approach to technologies needs to be taken in order to acknowledge how ongoing ways of producing and eating food are mediated by technology. The challenges of food security have renewed debate over the importance of technologies, in particular the science and technology-focused "greener revolution" proposed by the UK government's chief scientist Sir John Beddington (2010). Of course, such revolutions in the past have been criticized—not least for damaging environmental and social conditions in the global South— and praised—for raising yields and reducing crop damage. These arguments are likely to become more intense as new technologies emerge and socioecological conditions are placed under greater strain.

Current considerations of the role of technology in future food production are being expressed in the language of "sustainable intensification." For Charles Godfray and others (2010) this means avoiding simplistic formulations that lend themselves to seeking quick-fix technical solutions to easily identifiable problems. In supporting such an approach, they suggest,

> Technologies must be directed at the needs of those communities, which are often different from those of more developed country farmers. To increase the likelihood that new technology works for, and is adopted by, the poorest nations, they need to be involved in the framing, prioritization, risk assessment, and regulation of innovations. This will often require the creation of innovative institutional and governance mechanisms that account for socio-cultural context (for example, the importance of

women in developing-country food production). New technologies offer major promise, but there are risks of lost trust if their potential benefits are exaggerated in public debate. Efforts to increase sustainable production limits that benefit the poorest nations will need to be based around new alliances of businesses, civil society organizations, and governments. (Godfray et al. 2010: 816)

These arguments capture the importance of ensuring that technology is practically appropriate for the local context, as the application of inappropriate agricultural and food technologies can exacerbate issues of food poverty and inequality (Millstone et al. 2009).

It now seems impossible to conceive of food without technologies, whether understood as the sociotechnical systems of retailer-orientated supply chains or as artifacts used to prepare and eat a meal. It is also difficult to imagine that contestation over the form and application of technologies will ever cease. New technologies will materialize and become recognized means of changing food practices, while others will fail to be realized.

See also innovation, kitchens, risk, safety, science, trust.

Richard Lee

TIME

Food, as matter and as meaning, is made in and through time. Food production is shaped by the turning and tilting of the earth in relation to the sun, itself the foundation of human experience of time in the cycles of days, seasons, and years. Meanwhile the daily rhythms of hunger and satiety, and the practices of provisioning and eating that are constituted around them, provide much of the underpinning of the shared structuring of time, to the extent that it can be argued that time is made in and through food.

It is possible to open with these two apparently contradictory propositions—that food is made in and through time, and that time is made in and through food—because time is not one thing. It is fundamental to so many aspects of being human and of social existence that it defies definition other than in its own terms. Attempts to impose intellectual order on thinking about time in social theory have generally deployed a dualism that distinguishes, variously, clock-time, machine-time, chronological-time, or linear-time from rhythmic, organic, biographical, or cyclical time. This dualism finds its parallels in characterization of collective social orientations toward time, such as distinguishing societies ordered around modern historical understandings of time from those ordered around traditional cyclical understandings (Adam 2006). One side of these various dualisms have a common root, referring to an essentially Newtonian understanding of time. For Newton, time could be conceived in absolute terms, as linear and amenable to standardized measurement. This is time as constituted by clock mechanisms. On the other side are looser understandings of time as constituted by human experience, whether through direct experience of temporal rhythms—of days and seasons, growth and decay, birth and death—which can be figured as prior to the social, or also as constituted through the rhythms of social life. For Émile Durkheim (1912/2001), it is in the rhythm of social life that the category of time is constituted (Nowotny 1992). That is, time as it has presence in society derives from the patterning of collective social activities. Any of these different understandings of time can be found in food and the practices that are constituted around it. Together, they illuminate the shifting role of food in relation to time within broader shifts in social temporal orientation and organization.

Food and Shifting Temporal Orientations

Food is clearly bound up with those basic temporal rhythms that characterize organic time. While the world's wealthy can enjoy consuming fresh unseasonal produce thanks to globalized supply chains, food production remains bound to the cycle of the seasons and consumption still follows seasonal variations. In Japan, according to Daniels (2009: 172–3), "The arrival of seasonal foods such as water melons, mountain vegetables or mandarins, often gifts, caused real excitement and resulted in lively discussions about particular smells and tastes." Specific foods and uses of food are bound up in seasonal festivals, such as the traditional meals in Northern Europe marking Christmas, the timing of which is aligned with pre-Christian festivals to mark the winter solstice, or the rituals of fasting, and foods representing rebirth, in festivals that celebrate the spring.

Shifting to the scale of days, eating generally provides a temporal structure—for example with breakfast to mark the beginning of the day, the working day divided around a midday meal, and an evening meal marking the end of the day. Daily routines of eating have been collective within households and communities, providing a rhythm not only of eating but also of other activities throughout the day, as well as providing the temporal basis for bringing people together in the same place and time to share food. These social routines, constituted in part by their relation both to the spinning of the planet and to the speed of human metabolism, are building blocks of an organic experience of social time.

However, food is not only an anchor to organic time. It is also subject to linear time, and it can be located as part of the historical dynamics that have apparently rewrought societal orientations to time. Specialization of space for food production and divisions of labor such that substantial proportions of populations do not have to be preoccupied with gathering or growing food are necessary conditions for the development of any level of complex social organization and social hierarchy. Marshall Sahlins (1972) argued that hunter-gathering provided the basis for "the original affluent society," with needs and wants satisfied in less time than is typically spent working in economically advanced countries in the late twentieth century. However, the economic system Sahlins explains is one with little or no processes of accumulation, which is necessary for the development of more complex societies. Industrialization could not have come about without the ongoing reorganization of food production in time and space such that steadily less time per capita is spent on the

production of food. In short, the temporal rationalization of food production is fundamental to modernity.

As part of these same historical processes, the organic rhythms of eating can be incorporated into the strictures of clock-time. Eviatar Zerubavel (1981) locates the institutionalization of when and for how long to eat within the strict scheduling that was characteristic of medieval Benedictine monasteries. The *horarium* scheduled monastic activity across seasons and down to hours. In so doing, it institutionalized a specific understanding of time—as something that can be measured and counted. Through this, the monasteries "constituted the original model for all modern Western schedules" (1981: 31). Indeed, the possibility of understanding time in this way, as a resource that can be allocated to specified activities, is fundamental to E. P. Thompson's (1967) classic account of the shifting relations between time, society, and economy in modern industrial societies. It is only through this move that time can be commodified, such that time can be spent, saved, and sold—and given monetary value. Through the progressive discipline of the clock, both labor and household routines became increasingly aligned to the temporal logic of the factory, with breaks for eating during the working day strictly scheduled and meals at home timed according to the working day as defined by the factory. The shifting relations between "family time" and "industrial time" were closely examined by Tamara Hareven (1982), arguing that family time, while rewrought by the demands of industrialization in late nineteenth to early twentieth century America, was resilient, and an active presence in the modern factory. The uneasy fit between established rhythms of eating with the drive to efficiency characteristic of industrial production has been demonstrated by the continuous history of industrial disputes and government regulation around tea breaks and lunch times, with the imposition of Taylorist principles designed to regulate and discipline the workforce.

In the first half of the twentieth century, this modernist economy of time spread into the details of food work in the home. Progressively, logics of efficiency and rationalization were deployed into domestic kitchens, through discourses of domestic economy, through education, technologies and their marketing, and through the reshaping of domestic space in ways intended to enhance time efficiency (Hochschild 1997). These measures principally aimed to increase the efficiency with which food could be put on the table and ancillary activities of clearing and cleaning accomplished. As such, it served to re-embed ideals of regular and shared mealtimes within a household, coinciding with historically distinctive ideals of family life and domestic divisions of labor.

However, the same logics of reducing the temporal demands of domestic food provisioning have traveled elsewhere since the mid-twentieth century. Convenience foods and fast foods represent the extension of historical processes through which time and labor have been redistributed, increasingly reducing the demands for time (and skill and effort) in the processes of final food processing and cooking. Once again, this change in the temporal organization of food provisioning reflects broader narratives of social change and relations to time and economy. Convenience and fast foods do not only reduce a consumer's total time commitment to providing food for themselves or others; they also make the activities of providing food more flexible in the coordination of a day's activities. In this way, such foods function along with a range of innovations in both domestic technologies and systems of provision that enable the provision of food within a household to become increasingly flexible. Elizabeth Shove and Dale Southerton (2000) trace the history of the domestic freezer in these terms. Initially developed and sold as a means for providing an alternative to bottling to preserve surplus produce, freezers increasingly became used to enable cooking to be temporally separate from eating, by freezing cooked dishes for future use. Broader systems of provision became reshaped around the possibilities afforded by home freezers, especially once they could be coupled with a microwave oven. Supermarkets—themselves fundamentally implicated in shifting time commitments around food provisioning over recent decades—developed frozen foods aisles, which in turn are dependent on the development of the means of producing and transporting frozen foods. Increasingly, frozen food aisles, and people's freezers, were filled with ready meals. Across each of these phases of freezer history, technology enabled the shifting of time commitment to food provisioning. The freezer is but one element in the increasing flexibility of time commitment around food. Southerton (2009) tells of the temporal coordination of different practices that made the Monday evening meal stew for Mrs Friend, a 1930s housewife who used the leftovers from Sunday dinner along with the heat for long, slow cooking provided by the fire kept going to enable all the laundry to be done on washday (Monday) to produce a stew. It is difficult to think of such a closely knit and extended process of coordination in the domestic provision of meals for a household today. Indeed, the increasing temporal flexibility of what needs to go on around eating that is characterized by fast and convenience foods has resulted from, and enables, a broader sense of the fracturing and flexibility of collective rhythms that is taken to characterize late modernity.

Many contemporary anxieties around food circulate around its shifting relation to time, such as fears about the breakdown of shared mealtimes and, with that breakdown, the erosion of family life; or the effects of on-the-go snacking on health; or the easy availability of fast foods on obesity. Many concerns about the late-modern relation between food and time crystallize in the Slow Food movement, for which the social role of fast food and convenience foods is symptomatic of a lack of commitment to food in terms of time as well as of money and effort, in both production and consumption, that amounts to a devaluing of a fundamental human good.

Polytemporality and the Resilience of the Rhythms of Food

Food and its shifting relations to time can therefore be located within large-scale historical shifts. The temporal organization of food production, processing, cooking, and eating from field to fork has been rewrought in ways demanded and enabled by broader processes of economic and social change, and has always been part of the distinctive patterns of temporal organization that have characterized different periods. However, while grand historical narratives of change can be compelling, particularly when it comes to something like food, they of course have limited reach. The changes described by these narratives have reality, but the complex temporalities of food and their inseparability from the fundamentals of human being and from broader patterns of temporal organization mean that there is only so much room for change. Indeed, close attention to what people do around food, whether through close-grained ethnographic study or through analysis of international time-use diaries and secondary data, shows the remarkable extent to which the temporal organization of food in daily life is resilient. In-depth qualitative research on food practices uncovers the extent to which providing food for a household continues to demand much in the way of temporal coordination (DeVault 1991; Kaufmann 2010; Meah and Watson 2011). These demands are fulfilled through a substantial degree of routinization, from shopping through to meal timing and extending to a limited, if flexible, repertoire of meals. International and historical analysis of time-use diaries show that, while time spent in preparing food and in eating it together with other people has diminished, change is incremental with differences between some countries far greater than change over a few decades within a country. For example, Warde and others (2007) found that in 2000, the average time spent eating in the home in the United Kingdom was fifty-four minutes per day. While this was twenty-five minutes less than in 1975, the difference is less than with homes in France in 1998, where over one-and-a-half hours was spent eating in the home on average. Analysis of the collective rhythm of eating through the day shows continuing patterns of coordination that are distinctive between countries. Cecilia Díaz-Méndez and colleagues (2010) show distinctive differences between Spain, where a large proportion of the population are eating simultaneously at around 2:00 P.M. and 9:00

P.M., compared to much smaller proportions of people eating simultaneously in the United Kingdom.

These continuous patterns in the temporal organization of food in daily life reflect how time and food relate so completely. Food and eating have their own inescapable temporal characteristics. First, taking food simply as fuel and nutrition, we are bound to the speeds and capacities of our own bodies, our metabolism, energy storage capabilities, and hunger responses. While variations in how eating is organized across nations shows that there is substantial cultural contingency in the detail, wherever it is possible the norm is to eat several times every day. Even if science fiction fantasies of pills to meet all our nutritional needs were realized (Belasco 2006), there would still be an organically based rhythm to our ingestion of pills. Second, food also has its own temporal characteristics, there being little which originates as and remains food over long periods. Generally, matter has to go through processes, physically, semiotically, and practically, to *become* food, whether through cultivation of crops, manufacturing process, cooking, or incorporation into a culturally meaningful "eating event." Matter constituted as food tends then to have a limited life where it can remain as food. Indeed, matter presented as food that does not degrade on a timescale at most of years tends to have trouble fitting into the cultural category of food, as highlighted by online videos and exhibits exploring the "immortal" characteristics of McDonald's burgers, with claims of apparently unchanging "bionic burgers" up to eighteen years old (Foley 2007). Finally, food is, of course, far more than matter and nutrition. The innumerable social goods that are performed and experienced in and around food mean that food must take time. Consequently, food continues to be the basis of some of the most fundamental social events through which our sense of time is constituted.

See also convenience, materialities, memory, technologies, tradition.

Matt Watson

TRADITION

The recent proliferation of what David Sutton (2001: 126) calls "nostalgia cookbooks" is an indication of an increasing fascination with "traditional" methods of food production and cooking knowledge, skills, and practice in the United States and beyond. This essay begins by exploring a wider literature that debunks the idea that tradition is timeless and fixed, with an implied continuity with the past (Hobsbawm and Ranger 1983), before focusing on the term's convergence in aspects of food production and consumption and why—in the context of nutritional industrialization, more unstructured eating, "fast food," wider gaps between farmers and consumers, and perceptions of an impoverished culinary legacy (Bessière 1998)—recourse to tradition has become increasingly salient.

According to Eric Hobsbawm and Terence Ranger, tradition is a retrospective, invented phenomenon that is most likely to occur when "a rapid transformation of society weakens or destroys the social patterns for which "old" traditions had been designed" (1983: 4). Others have highlighted the role of memory and nostalgia in "distorting" the past (e.g., Hewison 1987) and how present circumstances inform the way the past is publicly remembered, described by Patrick Wright (2009) as "cultivated" and wrapped up in "ideological mists" that go beyond tradition. On a more private level, Stevi Jackson (1999: 24) explains how "the present significantly shapes the past in that we are constantly reconstructing our memories, and our understanding of who and what we are, through the stories we tell to ourselves and others." Also emphasizing the role of the present in informing representations of the past, David Lowenthal (1985) notes that memories continually change to conform with present needs. Moreover, he observes, "The need to use and reuse memorial knowledge, and to forget as well as to recall, force us to select, distil, distort and transform the past, accommodating things remembered to the needs of the present" (1985: 194).

Although none of these authors was speaking specifically in relation to food, their arguments are undoubtedly applicable in the context of current popular and policy discourses concerning a return to "traditional" values regarding what we eat, how it is produced, where it is purchased, how it is stored, how it is prepared, who it is shared with and on what occasions, and how it is disposed of. The alleged "impoverished state of domestic cooking" (Short 2006) has become the focus of much discussion in the United Kingdom, where food producers have invoked discourses regarding deskilling among consumers, along with an acknowledgement of their increasing distance from primary foodstuffs in their raw state because of the mediating role of the retail industry and lack of direct contact with agriculture (Jackson et al. 2010: 182). In tandem with this have been reported concerns about the "decline of the family meal" (Murcott 1997) and its alleged contribution to the decline in family life. While these scripts of the past clearly reflect a valorization of the "traditional" to meet the needs of a culinarily "impoverished" present, Angela Meah and Matt Watson (2011) contest the extent to which older generations of British consumers were, indeed, "saints in the kitchen." Reporting on the United States at the turn of the twentieth century, Laura Shapiro documents the emergence of the domestic science movement, which saw "traditional" approaches to cooking being displaced by science and technology, the latter having gained "the aura of divinity" (1986: 4). Likewise, Cecilia Novero reports how, in Germany, the interwar project of modernization led to a displacement of traditional cuisine since this "art" was "no longer appropriate to … the needs of the modern world" (2000: 170). Indeed, Shapiro writes that exponents of a modernized, scientific approach to cooking specifically eschewed "tradition," including the intrafamilial, intergenerational transfer of cooking knowledge since "as they saw it, domestic science would recast women's lives in terms of the future and haul the sentimental, ignorant ways of mother's kitchen into the scientific age" (Shapiro 1986: 9).

In the "postmodern" period, characterized by the increasingly transnational and "creolized" character of food, traditional "national" dishes (for example, bread-and-butter pudding or tripe, in England) have increasingly appeared on restaurant menus in what Allison James refers to as "acts of defiance" in the face of the trend toward more global food cultures (2005: 381), also witnessed in the revival of so-called "peasant" dishes elsewhere in Europe. For example, Vicki Swinbank (2002) reports the appropriation of grand/mothers' recipes by haute cuisine chefs. Likewise, Jacinthe Bessière discusses how traditional food and cuisine have become important to tourism in rural France. Here, the transfigured modern diet has awakened a newly found gastronomical curiosity, which urban dwellers seek to satisfy, and take solace in, while holidaying in the countryside (1998: 24), enabling them to feel greater proximity to both the "traditional" and the "natural."

In her discussion of traditional food and cuisine as tourist attractions in rural France, Bessière explores the Latin etymology of the concept of tradition and the verb *tradere*, meaning "to transmit" or "to deliver" (1998: 26). Drawing on Danièle Hervieu-Léger's (1996) definition of tradition as "the combination of representations, concepts, theoretical and practical know-how, behavior, attitudes, etc. that a group or a society accepts to ensure the continuity between past and present," Bessière suggests that the traditional practices that contribute to a sense of "heritage" are simultaneously part of the present, while at the same time holding promises for the future (1996: 26). Heritage, she says, can therefore be viewed more as a social construction than something fossilized and unchanging that is "handed down."

In this context, Sutton's (2001) work *Remembrances of Repasts*, based on work undertaken on the Greek island of Kalymnos, is particularly insightful. Discussing "traditional" Kalymnian cooking practices and how these are conferred via informal "apprenticeships" based upon observation and experiential learning, Sutton parallels cooking with smithying. Both sets of skills are based upon "stocks of knowledge" (2001: 126), drawn upon contingently rather than being followed to the letter, allowing room for innovation, adjustment, and personal signature. Here, as in other Mediterranean societies, recipes are passed down orally between family members, and Sutton suggests that it is through the process of writing recipes down that tradition gets fixed. Drawing upon Carol Field's (1997) work with Italian *nonnas* (grandmothers), Sutton also

highlights how traditional cooking practices are not impervious to change: these women, like their daughters and granddaughters, have adapted their practices to modern demands, employing, for example, "shortcuts" to facilitate speed in preparing and cooking food. Writing in the United Kingdom, Meah and Jackson (2013) report ethnographic work with a Pakistani woman in her mid-fifties who has embraced the availability of ready-made *chapattis* and pastry, ending hours of laborious food preparation for her extended family. This woman was unapologetic in her use of cooking tools that enable her to conduct meal preparation more efficiently: "I can't be bothered … I find it easier and it's time-saving as well … This is the easy way out. Thank God for these gadgets."

Notions of tradition are also invoked in marketing even the most technologically sophisticated food products—engineered through genetic modification, cloning, or nanotechnology—where a sense of nostalgia for long-established food products ("*Ah Bisto!*") impels manufacturers to strive for the familiar taste and appearance of "traditional" products. These foods should, in Belasco's words, "look and taste like the foods that *someone's* grandma made, if not in reality then at least in Golden Age sitcoms, the glossy pages of *Saveur* [gourmet magazine], or on the Food Channel" (2008: 118).

Tradition, then, is not a timeless or fixed concept. While recourse to traditional patterns of cooking and eating may be invoked as a nostalgic antidote to the "postmodern menu" (James 2005) and the alleged deskilling of present and future generations of "cooks," it is clear that the menus and practices of bygone eras cannot simply supplant the developments that have evolved in present-day food production and consumption. As Bessière observes, the relationship between past and present, between the traditional and the innovative or modern, is fluid, dialectical, and dynamic. Returning to the role of memory and notions of relationality, the past is refracted through the lens of the present and is equally constitutive of both the present and the future.

See also artisan, authenticity, cooking.

Angela Meah

TRUST

Trust is an essential component of social order. To trust is to act in concordance with another in anticipation of future action and as such is critical to the performance of social and economic relations. Without it, "society itself would disintegrate" (Simmel 1907/2004: 177). Food and trust are historically inextricable, linked in the performance of sociality and commensality. Eating with others, or eating food prepared by others, involves placing trust that the food has not been poisoned or otherwise adulterated. It involves operating in the absence of complete knowledge about food preparation or provenance. Trusting in food avoids the anxious "vague sense of dread" (Luhmann 1979: 4) associated with a lack of trust.

This essay introduces theoretical perspectives on trust and associated terms, and the study of trust in food, particularly focusing on work that adopts a relational perspective on trust, consumption, and institutionalization. It then considers the public and private pursuit of trust before raising questions that problematize the definition and geographies of trust. The essay asks whether analyses of trust have global relevance or whether it is a Western and specifically European concern, emergent from a spatially and temporally specific configuration of food pathologies, practices, and publics.

Trust is individual and relational, rational, and emotional. Prior to the Enlightenment, the prevailing form of trust in European societies was faith in God, accompanied by that expressed in interpersonal relationships between patients and doctors or between traders and merchants, or the personal trust placed by soldiers in their commanders (Zachman and Østby 2011). Since then, political and social theorists from Thomas Hobbes and David Hume to Niklas Luhmann and Anthony Giddens have been concerned with describing the nature of trust and characterizing the necessary conditions for its emergence.

Questions of trust and distrust are a defining feature of contemporary Western food systems, associated with wider distrust in the institutions of the state and the market and with the extension of food supply chains. For some consumers, trusting involves reconnecting with food production, as evidenced in the emergence of "alternative" food networks. For others, trusting in food regulation and retailers frees them from the need to know. Trust in food varies between countries, between food products and over time (Kjaernes et al. 2007). It has been most widely studied in Europe and particularly in the United Kingdom. The nadir of British trust in food can be dated to March 20, 1996, when the health minister Stephen Dorrell announced that a link had been established between the cattle disease BSE and a new human variant of Creutzfeldt-Jakob Disease. For consumers in the United Kingdom and elsewhere, it became difficult to trust British food or the ability of the government and its scientific advisors to keep it safe. The case of BSE is often used to illustrate the role of the safety crises of the 1980s and 1990s, and the cumulative effects of scaremongering media coverage, in promulgating distrust in the food supply in Europe (e.g., Knowles et al. 2007). However, the relationship is not so simple. There appears to be no clear relationship between national levels of trust in food or the various bodies associated with its production and regulation and the number of food scandals that occur in a country or the amount of information circulating in the media, and responses to food crises vary enormously (Kjaernes et al. 2007).

Theorizing Trust

A prominent tradition in Anglo-Saxon theorizations of trust builds on the work of David Hume, Adam Smith and later utilitarian perspectives such as that of Herbert Spencer that describe the role of trust in enabling market exchanges and maximizing self-interest. Trust depends on ongoing relationships between individuals, and these in turn constitute social forms of trust. As Hume described, "Constancy in friendships, attachments and familiarities is commendable, and is requisite to support trust and good correspondence in society" (1751, quoted in Hardin 2006: 20).

In this work, a person or organization is deemed to be trustworthy if it is their interests to be so—if the trustee's interests are "encapsulated" in those of the trusted, whether in terms of direct gain or the maintenance of reputation (Hardin 2006). Trust in institutions within society is based on rational evaluation by citizens, with good performance leading to trust and bad performance to skepticism. This emphasis on rational choice in the placing of trust has proved particularly influential in approaches to trust and food risk that focus on information or on attitudes to institutions. However, it is accompanied by a lineage of work that analyses the cultural nature of trust and emphasizes the role of shared norms and expectations, predictable acts of cooperation, and the constitution of trust within everyday practices.

Classical sociological studies of trust emphasize the relationship between types of trust and prevailing social relations. For example, Ferdinand Tönnies drew an influential distinction between social forms in terms of premodern relations of *gemeinschaft*—governed by common beliefs and values, in which trust is based on habit and familiarity—and modern forms of association (*gesellschaft*), in which individual self-interest is to the fore and in which trust relations are built through instrumental rationality and familiarity using surrogates such as professional reputation (Salvatore and Sassatelli 2004). The distinction is illustrated by Axel Leijonhufvud's example of Bodo (1995, in Hardin 2006), a man living in tenth-century St. Germain, then a hamlet outside Paris. Thanks to the extensive archives kept by the local church, the life of Bodo is well documented. Leijonhufvud shows that everything consumed by Bodo was produced by around fifty people, all of whom would have been known by him and most of which were produced by himself and his family. In this community, trust was based on routine, personal relations. Leijonhufvud contrasts this with an imaginary Monsieur Baudot, a contemporary resident of St. Germain, now placed deep within the sprawl of the city, whose consumption is entwined in global networks of trade, regulation, and governance. For Baudot, a citizen of modern France, trust is a different matter to Bodo's close personal relations and is assured through instruments that are designed

to reduce the contingency and complexity of modern life.

A similar divide is drawn in analyses of food systems between the nature of trust in premodern societies, in which the classification of foods as safe and edible was established through religious taboos, rituals, and ultralocal provisioning, and disembedded modern societies, in which the identification of trustworthy foods has shifted to the nation-state, food businesses, and scientific expertise (Zachman and Østby 2011). However, it can be argued that surrogates such as reputation, which enable the emergence of generalized trust, are themselves the product of past interactions, rooted in habit and community, and that the distinction between gemeinschaft and gesellschaft is less clear-cut. Moreover, the order in which these regimes succeed each other is not inevitably that of a progression toward disembedding. Thus, in contemporary food systems, embedded and local "regimes of trust" (Sassatelli and Scott 2001) may sit alongside those that are disembedded and institutionalized, and may either preexist or react to them.

A key feature of much work on trust has been its discussion of the relationship between what is known and unknown. Georg Simmel's definition of trust (or confidence) was as "the hypothesis of future conduct, which is sure enough to become the basis of practical action [involving] … a mediate condition between knowing and not knowing another person" (1906: 450) and their intentions or actions. Although Simmel emphasizes the relationship between trust and knowledge, he also suggests that the precise nature of the balance between knowledge and nonknowledge that requires the placing of trust is determined by the "historical epoch, the ranges of interests, and the individuals" (1906: 450). Simmel's concept of trust is grounded in specific social conditions that determine the form and quantity of knowledge required to act. However, it is also dependent on the natures of the individuals involved, and as such remains both individual and social.

Giddens (1991) similarly emphasizes the importance of knowledge in trust, suggesting that trust in expertise and professional knowledge enables modernity to become disembedded yet also allows people to operate in circumstances of partial knowledge to minimize the risks to which they are exposed. Trust is thus inextricably linked to the risk theorizations of Giddens and of Ulrich Beck (1992), as individualized "reflexive consumers" act under uncertainty in increasingly complex systems and within uneven distributions of power and resources. Consequently, for Giddens (1991), trust provides "emotional innoculation" against the "existential anxieties" of reflexive modernity, while Piotr Sztompka (1999) describes the need for an "enlarged pool of trust" to cope with the risk society.

Niklas Luhmann builds on Simmel to argue that trust is a means of reducing social complexity to manageable levels by "blending ... knowledge and ignorance" (1979: 26). Trust provides generalizations that allow shortcuts when decisions are made that are knowingly based on incomplete knowledge. Similarly, David Lewis and Andrew Weigert argue that without trust, "the monstrous complexity posed by contingent futures would again return to paralyze action" (1985 in Mollering 2001: 410). Luhmann argues that trust is based on systems and posits that these have internal control mechanisms that prevent them from failing. For example, in the case of science, mechanisms of publication and peer review by appropriately qualified individuals enable knowledge to be trusted without direct witnessing to its circumstances of production. Similarly, in the case of food, regimes of traceability, labeling, and certification come to stand in for direct access to production. In Luhmann's terms, these mechanisms represent the institutionalization of distrust, which ultimately secures the trustworthiness of the system.

Concern with trust in food is often equated with a perceived "crisis of consumer confidence" in food. For many writers on trust, including Simmel, confidence and trust are synonymous, and they are treated as such in this essay. However, it is worth bearing in mind that Luhmann and others distinguish between the active, voluntary nature of trust and general confidence in the proper workings of the system based on shared expectations. In turn, this opens the way

for a creeping loss of confidence in the system that does not necessarily equate with distrust (Luhmann 1988). In addition, it points to the role of trust in operating at the limits of society where "systemically defined role expectations are no longer viable" (Seligman 1997, in Salvatore and Sassatelli 2004: 27). This allows the distinctions between forms of trust in different social orders (as described earlier) to be nuanced to highlight the place of trust at the borders of premodern society and its role in operating where institutionalized confidence cannot.

As Guido Mollering (2001) points out, Simmel's understanding of trust combined an emphasis on partial knowledge (introduced above) with a notion of a "mystical faith of man in man" (cited in Mollering 2001: 417). However, others build on Simmel to emphasize the interconnections between the reflexive and emotional aspects of trust. Lewis and Weigert argue that "trust in everyday life is a mix of feeling and rational thinking" (1985 in Mollering 2001: 410), while Mollering focuses on the leap of faith associated with the granting of trust. This emphasizes not only the unknowns but also the unknowables that must be surmounted in order to act. Similarly, Barbalet (1998) situates an emotive confidence in oneself, prior to trust in others or confidence in the occurrence of future events, as creating a willingness to act. The social experience of the emotive and reflexive elements of trust have yet to be examined in any detail in social studies of food beyond studies of marketing (e.g. Locander and Hermann 1979). As described elsewhere, recent work on food and emotion, and food and anxiety, suggests the value of attending to the complex connections between emotional states, social conditions, and routinized behaviors (Jackson and Everts 2010). Future work might usefully consider confidence as a counterpart to anxiety, as an affective state that enables action and that is framed and shaped through engagement in particular social practices.

Trust in Food

In response to a perceived crisis in consumer confidence in food, policy-makers and food experts have often approached increasing trust as a question of providing further information, a technocratic solution often described as the "knowledge-deficit model." This is based on an understanding of the role of trust as part of individual consumers' cognitive processes associated with decision-making about risks. Trust, in this model, is an individual disposition that drives behavior. In turn, when public perceptions of food risk differ from those of experts, the former are considered subjective or irrational, with a lack of information seen as leading to a deficit of trust. In deficit approaches, a lack of trust can be remedied by the provision of more or better information. However, such information provision has rarely proven effective, and distinctions between subjective perceptions and objective risks have been challenged, with both shown as drawing on a range of social, cultural, and psychological resources. Within this approach, trust is central to the perception and management of risk, particularly in assessing the trustworthiness of those communicating risk information.

Changing understandings of public perceptions of risk have led to efforts at "public engagement," two-way deliberative processes that draw consumers into regulatory decision-making. These emphasize that the placing of trust is a product of the provision of information and the trustworthiness of its source. Both engagement and deficit models continue to focus on information and on science and expertise. As such, they retain a focus on the cognitive elements of trust and cleave to a conceptualization of trust as an individual disposition that influences behavior (Kjaernes et al. 2007). However, it is not clear that increased information results in increased trust rather than elevated anxiety about the things that remain unknown. Indeed, Unni Kjaernes and others (2007) argue that a focus on the provision of information becomes tautological, as trustworthy information produces trust yet must already be trusted in order to do so. As such, they suggest that cognitive models cannot provide the basis for institutional trust or explain why some people are trusted and not others, and that cognitive models overemphasize the role of science and expertise in

the placing of trust. Instead, they argue for a relational approach that reintroduces the role of markets and regulatory arrangements.

As described earlier, the relationship between levels of trust in food and the occurrence of "food scares" is unclear. In fact, Kjaernes and colleagues' study of Denmark, Germany, Great Britain, Italy, Norway, and Portugal finds high levels of trust in expertise and in the safety of food and little pervasive mistrust in food authorities. Their research, conducted in 2002, suggests that people are optimistic about the safety of food and that it may be misleading to focus research on trust/distrust in food on questions of safety instead of price and quality, which are a source of greater worry. They show systematic differences in the levels of trust and distrust accorded to different institutions and the variation in these levels between countries. Levels of trust in food are high in the United Kingdom, Denmark, and Norway but lower in Italy and Portugal and socio-demographic differences in trust are inconsistent.

To explain these findings, Kjaernes and others (2007) build on the theorizations introduced above to explore the association of trust with social relations and institutionalized patterns of consumption. In particular, they draw on both cultural and institutional models of trust to focus on how trust enables, and emerges within, everyday social practices that include flexible but predictable routines of purchasing, preparing, and eating food. Kjaernes and colleagues highlight the emergence of trust within interactions between actors involved in food networks, which differ between countries and food items and the processes of institutionalization associated with trust and distrust. Drawing on theories of social practice, they describe institutionalization as the development of normalized avenues through which consumption occurs. The institutional arrangements that emerge from these normalized acts of consumption can take the form of organizations, from the household to public bodies, that interact in formalized ways with other institutions, as through contractual or regulatory agreements. In particular, relations between state regulatory bodies, market organizations such as supermarkets, and forms of consumption vary from one country to the next. Kjaernes thus describes how trust in food thus comes to incorporate "the concrete organization and performance of food institutions" (2006: 911) but in a manner that goes beyond the rational-choice theorizations of trust introduced earlier. In particular, they are able to show that both low levels of trust in food in Italy and Portugal and high levels in Norway are related to levels of trust and skepticism toward food institutions and cultural differences in attitudes and practices related to food.

Establishing Trust

Unni Kjaernes and Arne Dulsrud (1998), following Giddens's (1991) partitioning of trust, identify three social contexts in which trust and distrust emerge in relation to food (cf. Hansen et al. 2003). These highlight the complex relationships between the individual, interpersonal, institutional, and cultural aspects of trusting. In the first (individual) setting, trust is a relation with a single product or object, such as a chicken. This object can be dealt with in isolation, either by handling it with care or disposing of it. However, if one is beset with a series of these individual decisions, such decisions can become psychologically and socially overwhelming. One recourse is that highlighted by Ann-Mari Sellerberg (1991), who describes the heuristic "strategies of confidence" used by consumers to establish the safety of their food. Similarly, Green and others (2003) draw on focus groups conducted in a number of European countries to show the "rules of thumb" that are used by consumers. Secondly, Kjaernes and Dulsrud identify "relational" trust, which emerges through the experience of interactions between people and which is typified by the personal encounters prioritized within the space of the farmers' market or the purchasing of food direct from the farm. However, the most significant context, which they describe as "structural," is "system" trust, in which trust that food is safe is placed in government institutions or food producers. According to Berit Nygård and Oddveig Storstad (1998), it is this form of trust that is most prominent in discussions of food safety involving trust expressed in

terms of the reliability of the food sector. Distrust may result in exit from these systems, as in the formation of markets for alternative forms of food production or in the voicing of protest (cf. Hirschman 1970).

The perceived crisis in trust in food has prompted a range of responses from those involved in food production, regulation, and retailing across the various contexts of trust. However, these are far from uniform and draw on differing "regimes" (cf. Sassatelli and Scott 2001) that enact trustworthiness in varying ways within the public and private spaces of agri-food systems and at a range of geographical scales. This reflects the extension of questions of trustworthiness beyond matters of information or knowledge about institutional behavior to incorporate shared, transparent norms and expectations of behavior and competence. For example, Kjaernes and others (2007) compare the contrasting cultural and institutional dynamics that correspond with high levels of trust in food in the United Kingdom and Norway. While the former features an open-market, wholesale reform of a centralized regulatory system and globalized provisioning, the latter is characterized by producer-dominated regulation, standardization, and protectionism.

The example of the United Kingdom highlights the preeminent importance of reestablishing public trust in food among European policy concerns and the relationship between institutional and cultural conceptualizations of trust. A perceived collapse in public trust prompted reform of food regulation across Europe, and, as in North America, has also spurred the emergence of new social movements associated with food. A host of new regulatory bodies has been established to restore public trust in the regulation of the food supply, including the UK Food Standards Agency (FSA), the Belgian Federal Agency for the Safety of the Food Chain (AFSCA), the Norwegian Food Safety Authority, and the Agence Française de Sécurité Sanitaire des Aliments (AFSSA) in France. At European level, a new European Food Safety Authority (EFSA) was established in 2003.

In the United Kingdom, institutional changes seem to have been successful in reestablishing public trust in the food supply. In a study published a decade after Stephen Dorrell made his announcement to the House of Commons, Corinne Wales and others (2006) describe how Britain had "recuperated" to have one of the highest levels of trust in its food supply in Europe. However, the success of these institutional reforms has been implemented within the norms and expectations associated with the institutions of food governance and provisioning in the United Kingdom. Furthermore, the pursuit of trustworthiness is not solely the aim of public institutions, nor is it solely a question of consumption.

A declining trust in food has been attributed to long-term changes in the relationship between consumers and suppliers whereby the former have become distanced from the circumstances of production (Blay-Palmer 2008). The manufacturing of trust has become an everyday activity of food retailers in both the industrialized and alternative food sectors. The emergence of local networks that promote personal interaction with consumers represents one way through which suppliers have attempted to reestablish trust in food. For Alison Blay-Palmer, "Trust comes from asking the person selling you the meat where it comes from, how it was raised and killed. This knowledge reassures consumers … they are able to mitigate their fear" (2008: 126). However, not all efforts at reconnection involve the personal touch. The "quality turn" is supported by a raft of certification process and symbols of quality and authenticity that aim to establish trusting relations between consumers and distant producers and loyalty on the part of the former.

While questions of trust and reconnection can clearly be seen in the emergence of alternative food networks focused on personal interaction or quality, gaining or regaining consumer trust is also the "paramount concern" of supermarkets (Mintel 2009, quoted in Richards et al. 2011). From the consumer's viewpoint, a lack of confidence in the state may be compensated for by a greater willingness to trust in the governance of food by private bodies, particularly large supermarket retailers. This replacing of systemic trust in turn requires the establishment of trusting relations between actors in

networks of food supply. Thus, as Jane Dixon describes it, "To operate trustworthy supply chains, supermarkets must use their finely honed relationships with producers and consumers to control the qualities of what is produced and what is consumed" (Dixon 2007: 39).

As Andy Bond, then-CEO of Asda-Walmart argued in a 2009 speech, "The most valuable thing customers can give you is their loyalty" (2010: 126). The importance of trust, and the work that goes into trust-building, emphasizes the vulnerability of retailers, as trust lost is difficult to regain. The fragility of trust leads Jane Dixon to suggest that trust contains "the seeds of its own destruction" (2007: 39). As Dixon describes, supermarket activities associated with "buying" consumer loyalty involve "forging associations with valued institutions, practices, people, and portfolios of products and services" (2007: 48). Elsewhere, Dixon and Catherine Banwell describe the purposeful reembedding of trust in corporate foods as part of "the battle between technical rationality and reflexive consumers" (2004: 123). They describe it as a process of co-opting credible third parties, including the employment of experts by food firms, the sponsoring of scientific endeavors, and partnerships with the public sector. Carol Richards and others (2011) argue that trust is a "strategic variable" for food marketers, which can be identified, commoditized, and sold alongside other qualities of food. They identify several mechanisms of "trust manufacturing" adopted by supermarkets in response to the challenges presented by the various alternative food movements. These include efforts to enhance their reputation by association, direct quality claims associated with forms of certification that parallel those of the alternative food movement, and discursive claims-making through the symbolic representation of tradition and authenticity.

Establishing the basis for trusting relations between consumers and retailers involves the establishment of mechanisms of trust and distrust that mediate between retailers and their geographically distributed supply networks. Focusing on the consequences of a lack of consumer trust for relations between actors in supply networks, Adam Lindgreen and Martin Hingley

(2003) explore the response of UK supermarket Tesco to the outbreak of foot and mouth disease (FMD) in 2001. On the basis of six interviews with supermarket managers and suppliers, they examine the steps taken by Tesco and suppliers to reestablish consumer confidence in meat production. They suggest that the formation of new guidelines for the management of the supply chain and new partnerships with meat suppliers enabled Tesco to produce information that was previously unavailable.

The broad aim of the new food institutions and systems of certification is to moderate power and information imbalances in the food system. Following Luhmann, new food institutions and systems enable trust by institutionalizing distrust (Kjaernes 2006). This is primarily pursued through an emphasis on transparency and openness, as in the case of the UK Food Standards Agency, or as in Bond's comment, "Consumers have lost trust in big business. The only way to regain trust, and therefore loyalty, is to demonstrate genuine openness and transparency and to involve consumers in decisions that shape how the business is run" (2010: 123)

As Bond suggests, this move to transparency involves a recognition of consumer agency within food systems, allowing consumers to know how standards are set and to engage in their setting, opening a space for skepticism and debate within regulation. For example, the Phillips report (Phillips et al. 2001) which examined the failings of UK food regulation in the case of BSE stressed that trust could only be generated by transparency and openness about uncertainty in the scientific investigation of risk and the deliberations of advisory committee. As the report concludes, this call for transparency involves a reciprocal placing of trust in the public on the part of government.

As in the case of public institutions, the private manufacturing of trust involves the performance of transparency and the auditing of supply chains, which, it is assumed "not only demonstrates accountability, but also builds trust between those 'checking up' and those being checked-up on" (Freidberg 2007: 328). However, the value of such auditing and transparency has been questioned in arenas such as supermarket supply chains in which the

"checkers" have less tacit knowledge than those on whom such transparency focuses, but more power. Freidberg's focus on transparency and the "imperial knowledges" through which supermarkets assure the quality of food through distributed supply chains introduces the consequences of European consumer trust and distrust for non-European suppliers, including those in the global South, and those who target EU markets, as in the Hungarian paprika producers discussed by Zsuzsa Gille (2009). In addition, it points to the role of power in determining what is seen and what is hidden by transparency itself. Thus, for example, the efforts of retailers to materialize the metaphor of transparency in supermarkets with glass walls or carrot-sorting plants with webcams (Bond 2010) or the opening of FSA board meetings to the public may merely create new spaces of secrecy within food supply and regulation. Indeed, as Onora O'Neill (2002) argues, it may be that transparency in fact prevents the possibility of trust by removing conditions of non-knowledge. As such, the values that underpin the pursuit of trust should perhaps be those of honesty rather than openness, and secrecy, particularly in regulation, should be acknowledged as sometimes both necessary and desirable. In turn, research that explores the boundaries of secrecy, openness, and transparency and their materialization within the food system could contribute significantly to understandings of trust in food.

The Geography of Trust

There is a geography of trust, whereby citizens of some countries are generally more trusting while others appear less so. However, there is also a spatial patterning of evidence associated with trust that is underscored by Susanne Freidberg's (2007) discussion of the imperial knowledges associated with transparency and audit. The majority of studies focus on Europe, particularly those that focus on the institutionalization of distrust, and to a lesser extent Australia and the United States in the case of alternative food movements and supermarket power. However, the value of work that extends discussion of trust outside Western Europe and North America is suggested by Melissa Caldwell's (2004) analysis of the work undertaken by McDonald's to cultivate trust in their restaurants in Moscow. Her work highlights the role of trust-building in processes of domestication and localization. While often accepted as "modern" in some ex-Soviet states including Estonia (Rausing 1998), Western goods in Moscow immediately after the fall of the Berlin Wall were often seen as inherently dirtier, suspect and less trustworthy than equivalent Russian goods. Thus, Caroline Humphrey (in Rausing 1998) describes how her middle-class Muscovite hosts preferred "our fatherland butter" over competing U.S. brands or considered Western salami to be contaminated or tainted with unhealthy chemicals.

Caldwell describes how McDonald's positioned itself in relation to the Russian concept of *nash* ("ours"), a term that captures intimacy, familiarity, and sociality and is part of a wider discourse regarding the value of domestic production. The firm attempted to establish its position as a responsible member of the community by facilitating connections among consumers, including establishing a collectors' group for McDonald's children's toys, and by emphasizing the local provenance of food. The success of the strategy ultimately led to marketing that positioned the company within the trusted community of Muscovites as *Nash Makdonald's* ("our McDonald's"). While this might be analyzed as the cynical manipulation of consumers by a powerful multinational, Caldwell instead draws attention to the power of Muscovites in controlling the granting of trust by setting standards to which McDonald's was obliged to adapt.

On one level, the paucity of research on trust outside Europe echoes the overall emphasis in studies of food and society on the global North. However, it also emphasizes the geographies of how crises in trust in the food system have been perceived, responded to, and studied. The overwhelming Eurocentricity of studies of trust in food raises interesting questions for further research to explore whether the problematization of trust in food represents a temporally and spatially situated moment in the history of food, and, if so, why. In particular, comparative work that extends the findings of Kjaernes and others (2007) beyond Europe could make a valuable contribution to research on food systems while Caldwell's discussion of Moscow suggests the need for studies that explore the "trust work" undertaken by different actors in food systems elsewhere in the world.

See also anxiety, brands, emotion, governance, risk, safety, science.

Richard Milne

V

Values © Angela Meah.

VALUES

"Value" is a deeply ambivalent word, referring simultaneously to the price of goods (their market value) and to the things we value or hold dear that are often considered beyond price. Indeed, Marx made the key distinction between the practical or use-value of goods and their exchange-value in the marketplace. Further complexity is added when aesthetic values are conflated with ethical or moral values, and when attempts are made to calculate the economic value (through cost-benefit analyses and similar techniques) of environmental and other nonmonetary "services" (O'Neill et al. 2008).

Noting the gamut of implications and contradictions raised by this one word, anthropologist Daniel Miller seeks to transcend the implicit duality of value and values, asking, "Where does value come from and how does it manage to transcend what seems like a common sense duality between these two forces of the disembedded market ... and contextualised exchange?" (2000: 78). He goes on to argue that the exchange of goods is a process that creates value, not just one that establishes monetary equivalence between the goods being exchanged. Value, Miller argues, is not something that exchanged goods are reduced to but something created in the very act of exchange. Applying these ideas to the social significance of material culture (though not specifically food), Miller argues against the tendency to derogate the meaning of things as of "merely sentimental value," using a wealth of ethnographic evidence to demonstrate the ability of material goods to provide emotional comfort and to promote a sense of well-being and collective belonging (cf. Miller 2008). Asserting the importance of the context in which transactions occur, Miller argues that in some circumstances value elides any simple distinction between the pure forms of market exchange and gifting, as commercial transactions are capable of creating "value" in the full and ambiguous colloquial sense of the term (2000: 82).

These more subtle analyses of value, values, and valuing have seen a revival in the understanding of values that, only a few years ago,

Steven Hitlin and Jane Piliavin (2004) described as a "dormant" concept in sociological research. The dormancy of the concept may have been attributable to the reductionist tendency (in policy and other circles) to see values as an explanatory concept, shaping attitudes and behavior, rather than as phenomena that themselves need to be explained.

In food studies, the tensions between different notions of value and values have been fully exploited both academically and in the marketplace. Particular commodities are described as being "good value," often in an attempt to distinguish them from goods that are merely cheap and hence of lesser worth. Supermarkets frequently distinguish their "value" lines from more expensive "premium" brands, while consumers often employ a distinction between price and value, where perceived quality may be taken to justify a higher price, therefore representing better value.

Studies of fair trade and ethical consumption also frequently employ the language of value(s), arguing that producers should be given a greater share of the market value of goods, reducing the amount that goes to traders and other "middle men." The logic of fair trade makes an appeal to consumers' ethical values, expressed through the language of the market in seeking to redistribute the commercial value derived from particular goods at different points along the supply chain. This is sometimes expressed in terms of the value attached to *deepening* the relationships between producers and consumers within particular commodity networks, resisting the market logic of *extending* (or lengthening) them over ever-greater distances (cf. Whatmore and Thorne 1997).

The popular distinction between ethical values and the commercial value or price of goods has been exploited in a variety of social movements that seek to promote nonmonetary values such as improved animal welfare, better terms and conditions for agricultural workers, or more socially and environmentally sustainable modes of production. That such developments can lead to an increase in the price of goods (an "ethical premium") further illustrates the permeable boundary between value and values.

One recent initiative that seeks to exploit this opportunity is the development of so-called values-based supply chains (or "value chains" for short). Value-based supply chains seek to distinguish themselves from conventional supply chains (which prioritize the creation of "added value") by being based on collaborative principles and high levels of trust among the strategic partners who commit themselves to long-term trading relationships. The partners also seek to maximize their mutual welfare (in terms of fair profit margins and equitable wages, for example) and to differentiate their products in terms of quality and functionality and/or in terms of their environmental and social attributes (Pullman and Dillard 2010). According to the former CEO of one major company that has made the journey from conventional supply chain to "value chain," the U.S. food service distributor Sysco Corporation changed its mantra from "fast, convenient, and cheap" to providing food with "romance, memory, and trust" (Wallace Center 2011). There are many similar examples within the contemporary food industry where companies are seeking to exploit the potential of what Kevin Morgan and others (2006) call the "new moral economy" of food.

A final example of the way in which social, environmental, and other values have been employed to challenge the conventional agri-food system is the rise of the Slow Food movement. Established by Carlo Petrini in 1986 as a response to the opening of a McDonald's fast food restaurant in Rome, the Slow Food movement now has over 100,000 members worldwide with chapters in over 100 countries that organize *convivia*, where people meet to enjoy good food, to attend wine tastings, and to participate in local farmers' markets. The movement is dedicated to the preservation of traditional and regional foods, supporting local businesses, and promoting sustainable modes of production. The mission of Slow Food International is described as

the promotion of "good, clean and fair food for all" (Slow Food 2011), but commentators have reached very different conclusions about how far the movement is realizing its ethical goals in practice. Heather Paxson is very positive in her assessment of the ethical potential of "Slow Food in a fat society." She argues that eating is morally evaluated in the United States primarily in terms of the need for self-control, exercised in relation to personal health and body image. By contrast, she suggests that the dietary ethos of Slow Food is notable for its comparative disregard of bodily aesthetics and its secondary attention to nutrition. She commends its "less narcissistic" culinary ethics for emphasizing our responsibilities to human and animal others, to cultural heritage, and to the environment (Paxson 2005). Noting the "heightened aesthetic appreciation" involved in the Slow Food movement, Mara Miele and Jonathan Murdoch conclude that these aesthetic dimensions "hold some relative autonomy from economic and social criteria" (2002: 325), while others have highlighted more contradictory tendencies within the movement. Observing that the local is often a site of inequality and hegemonic domination, for example, Melanie DuPuis and David Goodman claim that while the Slow Food movement is led by left-leaning Carlo Petrini, much of the funding for its Terra Madre conference came from the neoliberal state and from the right-wing National Alliance (2005: 363). Food, it seems, is no exception to the tensions that exist between use-values and exchange-values in other domains, and among our economic, social, and political values.

See also commodities, moral economy.

Peter Jackson

W

Waste © ANGELA MEAH.

WASTE

Waste is matter that has crossed a contingent cultural line that separates it from stuff that is worth keeping or using. The stark statistics representing just how much matter could be used as food crosses that line, to become waste, are staggering in themselves. When viewed against the backdrop of climate change, peak oil, and global food security, the scale of food waste becomes almost bewildering. Why does so much matter that could have been food cross the line to become waste? Answers are to be found throughout food systems, for in food as most everywhere else there is little that can count as either production or consumption that does not entail wasting.

Waste in general has only a recent history of sustained exploration as something other than a technical issue requiring efficient management. From sporadic earlier engagements (Thompson 1979; Rathje and Murphy 1992; Gandy 1994), work on the cultural locations of waste and wasting began to burgeon with the turn of the twenty-first century (Strasser 2000; Hawkins and Muecke 2003; Scanlan 2005; O'Brien 2007). Research on waste has increasingly moved away from a focus on what happens to materials that have already been categorized as waste, to understand the processes through which materials end up being so categorized. This has been pursued substantially through engagement with work on consumer culture, particularly with debates around material culture and around everyday practice (Hawkins 2006; Gregson et al. 2007; Bulkeley and Gregson 2009). Strands of this work have moved more thoroughly into relational materialist perspectives, through which the *matter* that is wasted is an agent in the situations where it becomes waste (Hawkins 2009; Gregson et al. 2010).

Food waste as an issue has an even shorter and sparser history of social scientific engagement to date. Indeed, academic interest has generally trailed behind the recent ascendancy of food waste as a political issue, which has occurred as the twin concerns of climate change and food security cast more urgent light on the scale of food waste. Estimates of total food waste throughout the global food system range from 30 percent to 50 percent (Godfray et al. 2010; Foresight 2011). Measurement of food waste at the global scale is, of course, inaccurate with inherent challenges in working out just what matter could have become food and in accounting for food which has not passed into any waste stream that can be counted (for example, if a crop is ploughed back into the soil). Indeed, the very definition of food waste is unfixed and contested. All definitions will encompass wholesome food intended for human consumption which is lost from the food system, the most obvious forms of food waste. However, for some definitions, food waste also encompasses food that could be eaten by humans but is instead fed to animals, reflecting the low efficiency of animal products as a means of producing food. Finally, some argue that "over-nutrition"—the gap between food energy consumed and the food energy needed, manifested in growing rates of obesity—should also be considered as food waste (Parfitt and Barthel 2011). These broader definitions are contentious, reaching into culturally embedded patterns of food consumption and highlighting the deeply political character of food waste and its links to broader issues of profound inequality around food. For the rest of this essay, food waste is taken to represent food that is intended for human consumption.

Food waste not only occurs in countries that are rich enough to be profligate with this most fundamental resource. Unsurprisingly, rich countries waste more, with whole-system per capita food waste in Europe and North America estimated at 280–300 kilograms per year, compared to waste in sub-Saharan Africa and South and Southeast Asia of 120–170 kilograms per year (Gustavsson et al. 2011). The main sources of this waste in the food chain vary in different parts of the world. Immediate postharvest losses are highest in poorer countries due to relatively limited storage and transportation infrastructures, while in rich countries, where food infrastructures are more effective, a much higher proportion of food waste comes from consumers (Godfray et al. 2010). It is estimated that per capita, consumers in Europe and North America typically waste more than ten times the amount of food compared to consumers in sub-Saharan Africa or South and Southeast Asia (Gustavsson et al. 2011).

Food waste associated with consumption practices is not restricted to what ends up in the household waste bin. A substantial proportion of fresh food waste in industrialized countries' food systems results from the interactions of supermarkets with consumer buying habits. According to Tristram Stuart (2009), much fresh produce never leaves the farm because it does not reach the quality standards—covering shape, size, and weight as well as taste and nutritional attributes—of supermarket buyers. This is clearly a situation that can only exist in circumstances of overproduction and low relative cost of food. It is an indication of how the convergence of industrial agriculture, supermarkets, and the very low relative cost of food has enabled changes in norms and expectations around food, here with deleterious consequences for sustainability and food security. More broadly, the very low price of food relative to income in wealthy countries can be supposed to relate to the high levels of domestic food waste in those countries. Whilst contemporary critiques of behavior changing initiatives persuasively argue the limits of changing practice through such blunt instruments as price signals (Seyfang 2006), it seems unlikely that the 18 percent reductions in levels of domestic food waste in the United Kingdom between 2006–7 and 2010 (Quested and Parry 2011) are unconnected to the roughly 20 percent rise in food prices that occurred between those years.

Even in rich countries, consumer food waste accounts for at most 40 percent of total food waste. However, it is on consumer food wasting that most of the small amount of social scientific attention to food waste has focused. There are good reasons for this, beyond domestic food waste being more publicly visible than other sources and more amenable to social scientific inquiry. If domestic food waste could be cut, it could in principle result in lower overall demand and therefore proportionally less food waste right back up through the food system. David Evans has opened up household food

waste in the United Kingdom through close ethnographic scrutiny of domestic practices (Evans 2011, 2012). Based on work in areas of Manchester in the United Kingdom, Evans goes beyond the stark statistics of food waste, contesting the inferences of profligacy that follow from them, to unpick the complex social relations from which food waste emerges. Matt Watson and Angela Meah (2013) also show how the tensions that arise as anxieties of food safety on the one hand, and food waste on the other, are negotiated into domestic practices enable the excavation of the processes through which matter which could be food becomes matter which is waste. Understanding these microscale processes and practices is significant because the total food thrown away by UK households each year—around eight million tons (Quested and Parry 2011)—results from the innumerable moments in millions of kitchens in which something passes a line that differentiates "food" from "waste."

In particular, the ways in which research participants are reported to negotiate date labels (Milne et al. 2011; Watson and Meah 2013) provides a ready empirical opportunity for exploring the relations from which food waste emerges. Date labels have been implicated in engendering food waste by disempowering consumers from making their own judgments about the deterioration of food. This research has showed how, in general, date labels would be just one input into a decision about whether food was still food or had become waste, a decision that would play out differently depending on a whole range of converging relations and concerns. The deliberation that can go into deciding to consign food to the bin is indicative of a general resistance to wasting food. This resistance, however, was rarely articulated by participants in relation to concerns about greenhouse gas emissions or global food security. Rather, resistance to wasting emerges as expressions of thrift (Evans 2012), a concern for resource responsibility and conservation closer to home, enacting a combination of concerns—from pragmatic conservation of household time and money to a culturally embedded sense of responsibility to the food itself—that are situated within the nexus of practices and routines through which food provisioning is accomplished within a household. This ongoing accomplishment demands coordination of complex flows and relations between foods, products, technologies, skills, meanings, values, and purposes within the spatial and temporal conditions of people's daily lives. Domestic food waste thus emerges as the fallout from the organization of everyday life.

Some level of food waste is inevitable. Indeed, waste is arguably present wherever there is consumption, resonating with the inseparability of the etymology of "consumption" from that of "waste." According to Raymond Williams, "consume" was long a negative term: "it meant to destroy, to use up, to waste, to exhaust" (1976: 78), only taking on a more neutral meaning from the mid-eighteenth century. While consumption now carries the full range of moral weightings, including its location as a virtue for citizens of neoliberal economies, consumption remains inseparable from the production of waste. Waste is an inescapable consequence of material production and the fact that mostly the matter that can be food degrades rapidly over time makes waste all the more probable for food production.

However, rates of wasting that may reach 50 percent of total production are clearly a long way from whatever level of wasting might be considered optimal. As diets shift with rising affluence in countries like Brazil, India, and China, the overall level of food waste seems likely to increase, especially if more radical understandings of food waste, encompassing livestock feed and overnutrition, are adopted (Parfitt and Barthel 2011). This makes finding ways of reducing food waste throughout food systems all the more urgent. The UK's Global Food and Farming Futures Project (Foresight 2011) suggests that halving global food waste by 2050 is a realistic target, which it estimates could reduce total food requirement in 2050 by an amount roughly equivalent to one-quarter of production in 2011. Whether it occurs within industrial food production or by being scraped into a domestic compost bin, food waste is a challenging issue to deal with, but amongst possible actions to ameliorate the pressing problems around food in the twenty-first century, it is a relatively easy target.

See also consumption, labeling, materialities, security, sustainability.

Matt Watson

WORK

In much of the recent food studies literature an emphasis on identity, meaning, and consumption has led to a comparative neglect of the sheer hard work involved in growing, making, selling, and preparing food. While there are some excellent accounts of farm work and household provisioning (e.g., Newby 1977; DeVault 1991), there is much less research on the labor process involved in food processing and manufacture and remarkably little about the work that takes place in professional kitchens, restaurants, and food service. This is all the more surprising as the food and drink industry is a major part of most Western economies, employing people in a range of sectors including farming and fishing, food manufacture and retailing, restaurant and café work. In the United Kingdom, for example, the food and drink industry accounts for 7 percent of GDP and employs around 3.7 million people, while food and drink is the United Kingdom's largest single manufacturing sector (Cabinet Office Strategy Unit 2008: 8). In the United States, the food and drink industry employs 12.8 million people and half of all adults are reported to have worked in a restaurant at some time in their adult lives (National Restaurant Association 2011).

Food work is often laborious, badly paid and sometimes downright dangerous. The tragic death of twenty-one Chinese cockle-pickers in 2004, cut off by the incoming tide in Morecambe Bay, drew public attention to the exploitative and hazardous conditions of many agricultural workers in the United Kingdom (*The Economist* 2004). Such poorly regulated employment niches, controlled by agricultural gang-masters, are an example of what Piore (1979) calls a "secondary labor market" comprising low-wage, temporary, or seasonal jobs, often involving dangerous and physically demanding work. The geographical distribution of insecure agricultural work also helps explains what Scott and Brindley (2012) call the "new geographies of migrant settlement" in the United Kingdom, with large numbers of Eastern European workers (Poles, Slovakians, and Lithuanians) located in market towns and rural places like King's Lynn, Peterborough, and Fenland—areas that are not traditionally associated with high concentrations of ethnic minorities.

As Raymond Williams (1976) reminds us, in common usage "work" is often reduced to the labor involved in regular paid employment. The reduction of "work" to formal paid employment gave rise to the feminist critique of women's unpaid labor in the home (Dalla Costa and James 1972; Oakley 1974), with "labor" retaining its strong associations with pain and toil as well as having strong class connotations. Williams also suggests that the idea of working for one's livelihood came into being with the invention of agriculture (1976: 335). Later, strong links developed between the time involved in paid work and notions of leisure and other forms of respite from factory-based work, described by E. P. Thompson (1967) in terms of the coevolution of clock-time and industrial work-discipline. These distinctions have been blurred with the recent celebrity-endorsed rise of home cooking as a leisure pursuit (Hollows 2003a), an activity that takes time and effort but that may not be considered "work" in the sense of onerous paid employment or the demands of routine domestic provisioning.

The sociology of work has tended to focus on industrial employment rather than on the work of farming or food manufacture. The labor conditions of meat-packers and agricultural workers have, of course, been explored in American literature, notably in Upton Sinclair's *The Jungle* (1906), which examined the appalling conditions in Chicago's slaughter houses and meat processing plants, and by John Steinbeck in *Of Mice and Men* (1937), which traced the plight of migrant workers in the Salinas Valley in California during the Great Depression (see also Mitchell 1996). The labor process is also central to Friedland's pioneering work on the U.S. lettuce industry (Friedland et al. 1981)

and to the later work it inspired such as Freidberg's (2004) study of the production of French beans in Zambia and Burkina Faso. Studies of food manufacturing, such as Lien's (1997) ethnography of "Viking Foods" in Norway, have also tended to focus on the processes of product innovation and marketing rather than on the mundane and repetitive tasks of production-line workers. Likewise, studies of restaurants have tended to focus on the creative work of the professional chef rather than on the less visible, mundane, and repetitive work of other kitchen staff (cf. Ferguson and Zukin 1998). There are, of course, some notable exceptions such as Fine's (1996) study of the culture of restaurant work and Crang's (1994) ethnography of "Smokey Joe's", which focuses on the public role of waiting staff in terms of performance and display rather than on more mundane aspects of their working lives. Journalistic accounts can also be revealing such as Jeffrey Steingarten's (1997) essay "The Waiting Game," where he enrolled at the New York Professional Service School in order to learn the tricks of the trade, including how to increase tips through conversational and selling skills, how to handle difficult customers, and how to create a good final impression. The idea of managing the emotional work of encounters with customers was central to Arlie Hochschild's (1983) study of "emotional labor," which focused on flight attendants but which is also relevant to other routine face-to-face service jobs such as restaurant work. Hochschild's ideas have since been extended to take greater account of the embodied aspects of interactive service work via the notion of "aesthetic labor" (Witz et al. 2003).

Sociologists have commented extensively on the highly gendered division of domestic labor but rather less on the class and ethnic division of labor at work in the restaurant trade (though see Zukin's [1995] essay on artists and immigrants in New York City restaurants). There has also been a gulf between the intense interest of food writers in the proficiency of the professional expert chef—named, personified, and lionized—and the almost total neglect of the embodied experience of the many other people involved in making and serving food—typically unnamed, impersonal, and frequently exploited.

Social hierarchies at work are often sustained through the recognition of skill and expertise. This applies, for example, to the distinction between chefs and cooks, the former having been formally trained and professionally credentialized, the latter assumed to be untutored and having only "native" skill. Skill itself is a highly contested concept with greater economic value attached to mental rather than manual skills. So, too, in the case of craft work, the skills of the artisan may be culturally revered but only modestly rewarded (cf. Sennett 2008). Heather Paxson dwells on these distinctions at length in her comparison of artisanal and industrialized forms of cheese-making, the former involving hands-on knowledge and sensuous understanding, the latter being a highly automated and standardized procedure. According to Paxson (2011), craft practice involves know-how and intuition rather than formal academic knowledge. It is acquired through habit and involves tactile, bodily encounter ("developing a feel for the curd"), working with the active ingredients rather than trying to subdue or control them.

There have also been important arguments about the deskilling of work within contemporary capitalism, where a standardized division of labor throughout the manufacturing sector has replaced a diversity of manual skills and mental aptitudes (Braverman 1974; Burawoy 1979). Perhaps as a result of such deskilling, food work also features prominently in accounts of workplace crime, often seen as a form of resistance to managerial control where "donkey jobs" (such as supermarket work) are subject to rule-bending, speeding up or slowing down, collusion, sabotage, and associated fiddles (cf. Mars 1982). Work should clearly feature strongly on the food studies agenda with an emphasis on the interplay of culture and economy, markets and morality, value and values.

See also artisan, class, gender, skill, time.

Peter Jackson

Further Reading

The interdisciplinary field of "food studies" is growing so fast that it is getting increasingly hard to keep up with everything being published. This short guide provides some suggestions for how to navigate this burgeoning field, highlighting some introductory accounts, some important edited collections, encyclopedias, and readers, some classic studies, and some key contributions from different disciplinary perspectives.

As an introduction to the field it is hard to beat Warren Belasco's *Food: The Key Concepts* (Berg 2008), which is wide ranging and entertainingly written. There are many edited collections and readers on food among the best of which are Carole Counihan and Penny Van Esterik's *Food and Culture* (Routledge 1997); James Watson and Melissa Caldwell's *The Cultural Politics of Eating* (Blackwell 2005); and Carolyn Korsmeyer's *The Taste Culture Reader* (Berg 2005). Though compendious in scope, there are some excellent encyclopedias and multivolume histories of food that are well worth dipping into. See, for example, Andrew Smith's *The Oxford Encyclopaedia of Food and Drink in America* (Oxford University Press 2004) and Fabio Parasecoli and Peter Scholliers's *A Cultural History of Food* (Berg 2012), which moves from antiquity to the modern age in six multiauthored volumes. With 2,650 entries, Alan Davidson's *Oxford Companion to Food* (Oxford University Press 1999) also demands respect and admiration.

There are some important historical studies of food with which all food scholars should be familiar. They include John Burnett's *Plenty and Want: A Social History of Food in England from 1815 to the Present Day* (Routledge, third edition, 1989); Stephen Mennell's *All Manners of Food: Eating and Taste in England and France from the Middle Ages to the Present* (University of Illinois Press, second edition, 2006); Margaret Visser's *Much Depends of Dinner* (Grove Press 1986); and Harvey Levenstein's two-volume culinary history of America: *Revolution at the Table: The Transformation of the American Diet* (Oxford University Press 1998) and *Paradox of Plenty: A Social History of Eating in Modern America* (Oxford University Press 1993).

On the relationship between food and globalization, see Alessandro Bonnano, Lawrence Busch, William Friedland, Lourdes Gouveia and Enzo Mingione's *From Columbus to ConAgra* (University of Kansas Press 1994); Philip McMichael's *The Global Restructuring of Agro-Food Systems* (Cornell University Press 1994); and David Goodman and Michael Watts's *Globalizing Food: Agrarian Questions and Global Restructuring* (1997). There is also the useful review essay "Food and Globalization" by Lynne Phillips in the *Annual Review of Anthropology* (2006, Vol. 35).

There are numerous single-discipline introductions to food studies of which the following is a very brief selection. In anthropology, see Carole Counihan's *The Anthropology of Food and Body* (Routledge 1999); Johan Pottier's *Anthropology of Food* (Polity 1999); and Sidney Mintz and Christine DuBois's review of the anthropology of food and eating in the *Annual Review of Anthropology* (2002, Vol. 31), which includes an excellent discussion of food insecurity, eating and ritual, and eating and identity. In human geography, see David Bell and Gill Valentine's *Consuming Geographies: We Are Where We Eat* (Routledge 1997) and the three review essays on "Geographies of Food" by Ian Cook in the journal *Progress in Human Geography*, aptly titled "Following" (2006, Vol. 30), "Mixing" (2008, Vol. 32), and "Afters" (2010, Vol. 34). In sociology, see Stephen Mennell, Anne Murcott, and Anneke Van Otterloo's *The Sociology of Food* (Sage 1992); Alan Warde's *Consumption, Food and Taste* (Sage 1997); and Alan Beardsworth and Teresa Keil's Sociology On the Menu (Routledge 1997). In philosophy, see Carolyn Korsmeyer's *Making Sense of Food* (Cornell University Press 1991); Lisa Heldke's *Exotic Appetites Sociology on the menu* (Routledge 2003); and the edited compilation by Deane Curtin and Lisa Heldke, *Cooking, Eating, Thinking* (Indiana University Press 1992). Feminist studies of food are voluminous, but a good starting point is Elspeth Probyn's *Carnal Appetites: Food Sex Identities* (Routledge 2000). For cultural studies of food, see Bob Ashley, Joanne Hollows, Steve Jones and Ben Taylor's *Food and Cultural Studies* (Routledge 2004), and for media and communication studies, see Janet Cramer, Carlnita Greene and Lynn Walter's *Food as Communication/Communication as Food* (Peter Lang 2011).

There are many fascinating studies of single-food commodities, including Mark Kurlansky's studies of *Cod* (Knopf 1997) and *Salt* (Walker & Co. 2002); Sidney Mintz's classic study of sugar, *Sweetness and Power* (Penguin 1986); Mark Pendergrast's history of *Coca-Cola* (Basic Books 2000); Andrew Smith's study of *The Tomato in America* (University of South Carolina Press 1994); and Melanie Du Puis's study of milk, *Nature's Perfect Food* (New York University Press 2002). There is also an excellent website of educational resources on food and other commodities, which takes its inspiration from Arjun Appadurai's injunction to "follow the thing": http://www.followthethings.com

Besides these academic studies, there are many polemical arguments and debates about the politics of food, often highly critical of agri-business and the power of the supermarkets. For a selection of these (where the argument is encapsulated in the subtitle), see Eric Schlosser's *Fast Food Nation: The Dark Side of the All-American Meal* (Houghton-Mifflin 2001); Felicity Lawrence's *Not On the Label: What Really Goes Into the Food on Your Plate* (Penguin 2004) and *Eat Your Heart Out: Why the Food Business is Bad for the Planet and Your Health* (Penguin 2008); Joanna Blythman's *Bad Food Britain: How a Nation Ruined Its Appetite* (Fourth Estate 2010); Tim Lang and Michael Heasman's *Food Wars: The Battle for Mouths, Minds and Markets* (Earthscan 2004); and Tristram Stuart's *Waste: Uncovering the Global Food Scandal* (Penguin 2009). For a mix of academic research and stirring polemic, see Michael Pollan's many books, starting with *The Omnivore's Dilemma: A Natural History of Four Meals* (Penguin 2006); Raj Patel's *Stuffed and Starved: Markets, Power and the Hidden Battle for the World Food System* (Portobello 2008); and Erik Millstone and Tim Lang's *The Atlas of Food: Who Eats What, Where and Why* (Earthscan, second edition, 2008). Marion Nestle's blog is also full of stimulating material on contemporary food politics: http://www.foodpolitics.com/.

Finally, to keep up-to-date, the field is well-served by a wide range of academic journals such as *Food, Culture and Society* (the journal of the Association for the Study of Food and Society) together with a host of more specialist titles such as *Appetite, Agriculture and Human Values*, the *Journal of Rural Studies*, and *Sociologia Ruralis*. Bon appétit!

References

Aaker, D. A. (1991), *Managing Brand Equity*, New York: Free Press.

Aaker, D. A. (1996), *Building Strong Brands*, New York: Free Press.

Aarseth, H. (2007), "From Modernized Masculinity to Degendered Lifestyle Projects: Changes in Men's Narratives on Domestic Participation 1990–2005," *Men and Masculinities*, 11: 424–40.

Abarca, M. E. (2004), "Authentic or Not, It's Original," *Food and Foodways*, 12: 1–25.

Abarca, M. E. (2006), *Voices in the Kitchen: Views of Food and the World from Working-Class Mexican and Mexican American Women*, College Station Texas: Texas A&M University Press.

Abelson, E. (1998), *When Ladies Go A-Thieving: Middle-Class Shoplifters in the Victorian Department Store*, New York: Oxford University Press.

Abelson, E. (2000), "Shoplifting Ladies," in J. Scanlon (ed.), *The Gender and Consumer Culture Reader*, New York: New York University Press, 309–29.

Accum, T. (1830), *Deadly Adulteration and Slow Poisoning; or Disease and Death in the Pot and the Bottle*, Edinburgh: Adam Black.

Adam, B. (2006), "Time," *Theory, Culture and Society*, 23: 119–38.

Adams, C. J. (1990), *The Sexual Politics of Meat: A Feminist-Vegetarian Critical Theory*, New York: Continuum.

Adams, C. J. (2003), *The Pornography of Meat*, New York: Continuum International.

Adams, J., Hennessy-Priest, K., Ingimarsdottir, S., Sheeshka, J., Ostbye, T., and White, M. (2009), "Changes in Food Advertisements During 'Prime-Time' Television from 1991 to 2006 in the UK and Canada," *British Journal of Nutrition*, 102: 584–93.

Adams, R. (2005), "Fast Food, Obesity and Tort Reform: An Examination of Industry Responsibility for Public Health," *Business and Society Review*, 110: 297–320.

Adema, P. (2000), "Vicarious Consumption: Food, Television and the Ambiguity of Modernity," *Journal of American and Comparative Cultures*, 23: 113–23.

Adema, P. (2006), "Festive Foodscapes: Iconizing Food and the Shaping of Identity and Place," PhD thesis, University of Texas.

Adler, T. A. (1981), "Making Pancakes on Sunday: The Male Cook in Family Tradition," *Western Folklore*, 40: 45–54.

Adorno, T. W. (1958), "The Essay as Form," *New German Critique*, 32 (1984): 151–71.

Adorno, T. W., and Horkheimer, M. (1944/2002), *Dialectic of Enlightenment*, Palo Alto, CA: Stanford University Press.

Akrich, M. (1992), "The De-Scription of Technical Objects," in W. Bijker and J. Law (eds.), *Shaping Technology, Building Society: Studies in Sociotechnical Change*, Cambridge, MA: MIT Press, 205–24.

Alcalde, M. C. (2009), "Between Incas and Indians," *Journal of Consumer Culture*, 9: 31–54.

Alexeyeff, K. (2004), "Love Food: Exchange and Sustenance in the Cook Islands Diaspora," *The Australian Journal of Anthropology*, 15: 68–79.

Allaire, G., and Wolf, S. (2004), "Cognitive Representations and Institutional Hybridity in Agrofood Innovation," *Science, Technology and Human Values*, 29: 431–58.

Allan, G., Crow, G., and Hawker, S. (2011), *Stepfamilies*, Basingstoke: Palgrave Macmillan.

Allan, S. (2002), *Media, Risk and Science*, Buckingham, Philadelphia: Open University Press.

Amin, A., and Thrift, N. (eds.) (2003), *The Cultural Economy Reader*, Oxford: Blackwell.

Anderson, B. (2011), "Practice Hunting," Paper presented at ESRC Sustainable Practices Research Group Workshop, Lancaster University.

Anderson, B., and Harrison, P. (2006), "Questioning Affect and Emotion," *Area*, 38: 333–5.

Ang, I. (1991), *Desperately Seeking the Audience*, London: Routledge.

Appadurai, A. (1981), "Gastro-politics in Hindu South Asia," *American Ethnologist, Symbolism and Cognition*, 8(3): 494–511.

Appadurai, A. (ed.) (1986a), *The Social Life of Things: Commodities in Cultural Perspective*, Cambridge: Cambridge University Press.

Appadurai, A. (1986b), "On Culinary Authenticity," *Anthropology Today*, 2: 24–25.

Appadurai, A. (1988), "How to Make a National Cuisine: Cookbooks in Contemporary India," *Contemporary Studies in Society and History*, 30: 3–24.

Appadurai, A. (1996), *Modernity at Large: Cultural Dimensions of Globalization*, Minneapolis: University of Minnesota Press.

Arvidsson, A. (2005), "Brands: A Critical Perspective," *Journal of Consumer Culture*, 5: 235–58.

Arvidsson, A. (2006), *Brands: Meaning and Value in Media Culture*, London: Routledge.

Atkins, P. J. (2000), "The Pasteurization of England: The Science, Culture and Health Implications of Milk Processing, 1900–1950," in D. Smith and J. Phillips (eds.), *Food, Science and Regulation in the 20th Century*, London: Routledge, 37–51.

Atkins, P. J. (2010), *Liquid Materialities: A History of Milk, Science and Law*, Farnham, Surrey: Ashgate.

Atkins, P. J. (2011), "The Material Histories of Food Quality and Composition," *Endeavour*, 35: 74–9.

Atkins, P. J. (in press), "Social History of the Science of Food Analysis and the Control of Adulteration," in A. Murcott, W. Belasco, and P. Jackson (eds.), *The Handbook of Food Research*, Oxford: Berg.

Atkins, P. J., and Bowler, I. (2001), *Food in Society: Economy, Culture, Society*, London: Arnold.

Auden, W. H. (1947), *The Age of Anxiety: A Baroque Eclogue*, New York: Random House.

Augé, M. (1994), *Non-Place: Introduction to an Anthropology of Supermodernity*, London: Verso.

Avakian, A. V. (ed.) (1997), *Through the Kitchen Window: Women Explore the Intimate Meanings of Food and Cooking*, Boston: Beacon.

Avakian, A. V., and Haber, B. (eds.) (2005), *From Betty Crocker to Feminist Food Studies: Critical Perspectives on Women and Food*, Amherst, Boston: University of Massachusetts Press.

Ban, Ki-Moon (2009), "Food, Nutritional Security, Foundation of a Decent Life," Speech to the UN General Assembly. Available at http://www.un.org/News/Press/docs/2009/sgsm12496.doc.htm (accessed December 3, 2011).

Barbalet, J. (1998), *Emotion, Social Theory and Social Structure: A Macrosociological Approach*, Cambridge: Cambridge University Press.

Barbalet, J. (2002), *Emotions and Sociology*, London: Wiley-Blackwell.

Barham, E. (2003), "Translating Terroir: The Global Challenge of French AOC labeling," *Journal of Rural Studies*, 19: 127–38.

Barling, D., Lang, T., and Caraher, M. (2002), "Joined-up Food Policy? The Trials of Governance, Public Policy and the Food System," *Social Policy and Administration*, 36: 556–74.

Barndt, D. (2002), *Tangled Routes: Women, Work, and Globalization on the Tomato Trail*, Lanham, MD: Rowman and Littlefield.

Barnett, C., Cloke, P., Clarke, N., and Malpass, A. (2005), "Consuming Ethics: Articulating the Subjects and Spaces of Ethical Consumption," *Antipode*, 37: 23–45.

Barolini, H. (1997), "Appetite Lost, Appetite Found," in A. V. Avakian (ed.), *Through the Kitchen Window: Women Explore the Intimate Meanings of Food and Cooking*, Boston: Beacon Press, 228–37.

Bartoshuk, L., and Duffy, V. B. (2005), "Chemical Senses," in C. Korsmeyer (ed.), *The Taste Culture Reader: Experiencing Food and Drink*, Oxford: Berg, 25–33.

Batada, A., and Borzekowski, D. (2008), "Snap, Crackle-What?: Recognition of Cereal Advertisements and Understanding of Commercials' Persuasive Intent among Urban,

Minority Children in the US," *Journal of Children and Media*, 2: 19–36.

Baudrillard, J. (1970), *The Consumer Society: Myths and Structures*, London: Sage.

Baudrillard, J. (1983), *Simulations*, New York: Semiotext(e).

Bauman, Z. (2006), *Liquid Fear*, Cambridge: Polity Press.

Baxter, J. (2002), "Patterns of Change and Stability in the Gender Division of Household Labour in Australia 1986–1997," *Journal of Sociology*, 38: 399–424.

BBC (2009), "'Organic' Has No Health Benefits' (July 29). Available at http://news.bbc.co.uk/1/hi/health/8174482.stm (accessed January 14, 2013).

BBC (2011a), "'Benefit Delays Forces People to Use Food Banks', Charity Says" (November 11). Available at http://www.bbc.co.uk/news/uk-15683902 (accessed January 14, 2013).

BBC (2011b), "Kraft Cuts 200 Jobs at Bournville, Chirk and Marlbrook." Available at http://www.bbc.co.uk/news/uk-england-16047813 (accessed February 24, 2012).

Beardsworth, A. D. (1990), "Trans-science and Moral Panics: Understanding Food Scares," *British Food Journal*, 92: 11–16.

Beardsworth, A., and Keil, T. (1991), "Vegetarianism, Veganism, and Meat Avoidance: Recent Trends and Findings," *British Food Journal*, 93: 19–24.

Beardsworth, A., and Keil, T. (1997), *Sociology on the Menu: An Invitation to the Study of Food and Society*, London: Routledge.

Beck, M. (1993), "Only Food," in R. Scapp and B. Seitz (eds.), *Eating Culture*, New York: State University of New York Press, 89–91.

Beck, U. (1992), *Risk Society: Towards a New Modernity*, London: Sage.

Beck, U. (2006), "Living in the World Risk Society," *Economy and Society*, 35: 329–345.

Beck, U., Giddens, A., and Lash, S. (1994), *Reflexive Modernization: Politics, Tradition and Aesthetics in the Modern Social Order*, Palo Alto, CA: Stanford University Press.

Beddington, J. (2010), "Food Security: Contributions from Science to a New and Greener Revolution," *Philosophical Transactions of the Royal Society B*, 365: 61–71.

Beeton, I. (1861), *The Book of Household Management*, reprinted 1880, New York: Farrar.

Belasco, W. J. (1989), *Appetite for Change: How the Counterculture Took on the Food Industry*, New York: Pantheon Books.

Belasco, W. J. (2006), *Meals to Come: A History of the Future of Food*, Los Angeles: University of California Press.

Belasco, W. J. (2007), *Appetite for Change: How the Counterculture took on the Food Industry*, 2nd ed. Ithaca, NY: Cornell University Press.

Belasco, W. J. (2008), *Food: The Key Concepts*, Oxford: Berg.

Belk, R. W., Güliz, G., and Sören, A. (1997), "Consumer Desire in Three Cultures: Results from Projective Research," in B. Merrie and D. J. MacInnis (eds.), *Advances in Consumer Research*, Provo, UT: Association for Consumer Research, 24–28.

Bell, D., and Hollows, J. (2007), "Mobile Homes," *Space and Culture*, 10: 22–39.

Benjamin, W. (1936), "The Work of Art in the Age of Mechanical Reproduction," reprinted in H. Arendt (ed.) (1969), *Illuminations*, New York: Schocken Books, 217–51.

Bennet, K. (2006), "Kitchen Drama: Performances, Patriarchy and Power Dynamics in a Dorset Farmhouse Kitchen," *Gender, Place and Culture*, 13: 153–60.

Bennett, J. (2007), "Edible Matter," *New Left Review*, 45 (May–June): 133–45.

Bennett, J. (2009), *Vibrant Matter: A Political Ecology of Things*, Durham, NC: Duke University Press.

Bennett, T., Savage, M., Silva, E., Warde, A., Gayo-Cal, M., and Wright, D. (2009), *Culture, Class, Distinction*, London: Routledge.

Berg, M., and Akrich, M. (2004), "Introduction—Bodies on Trial: Performances in Medicine and Biology," *Body and Society*, 10: 1–12.

Berg, M., and Mol, A. (1998), *Differences in Medicine: Unraveling Practices, Techniques and Bodies*, Durham, NC: Duke University Press.

Bernauer, T. (2003), *Genes, Trade and Development: The Seeds of Conflict in Food Biotechnology*, Princeton, NJ: Princeton University Press.

Berndt, C., and Boeckler, M. (2009), "Geographies of Circulation and Exchange: Constructions of Markets," *Progress in Human Geography*, 33: 535–51.

Berry, W. (1992), "The Pleasures of Eating," in D. W. Curtin and L. M. Heldke (eds.), *Cooking, Eating, Thinking: Transformative Philosophies of Food*, Bloomington, Indianapolis: Indiana University Press, 374–9.

Bessière, J. (1996), *Patrimoine culinaire et tourisme rural*, Tourisme en Espace Rural, Paris: Collège Des Etudes.

Bessière, J. (1998), "Local Development and Heritage: Traditional Food and Cuisine as

Tourist Attractions in Rural Area," *Sociologia Ruralis*, 38: 21–34.

Best, J., and Horiuchi, G. T. (1985), "The Razor Blade in the Apple: the Social Construction of Urban Legends," *Social Problems*, 32: 488–99.

Bestor, T. C. (2004), *Tsukiji: The Fish Market at the Center of the World*, Berkeley, Los Angeles: University of California Press.

Bianchi, S., Milkie, S., Sayer, L., and Robinson, J. (2000), "Is Anyone Doing the Housework?: Trends in the Gender Division of Household Labor," *Social Forces*, 79: 191–228.

Bildtgård, T. (2009), "Mental Foodscapes: Where Swedes Would Go to Eat Well (and Places They Would Avoid)," *Food, Culture and Society*, 12: 498–523.

Bingham, N. (2008), "Slowing Things Down: Lessons from the GM Controversy," *Geoforum*, 39: 111–22.

Blair, T. (2002), "Tony Blair's Speech on Scientific Research to the Royal Society." Available at http://www.isaaa.org/kc/Publications/htm/articles/Position/speechfull.htm (accessed January 12, 2012).

Blay-Palmer, A. (2008), *Food Fears: From Industrial to Sustainable Food Systems*, Aldershot: Ashgate.

Blay-Palmer, A., and Donald, B. (2006), "A Tale of Three Tomatoes: The New Food Economy in Toronto, Canada," *Economic Geography*, 82: 383–99.

Blumenthal, M. M. (1997), "How Food Packaging Affects Food Flavour," *Food Technology*, 51: 71–74.

Blunt, A. (2005), *Domicile and Diaspora: Anglo-Indian Women and the Spatial Politics of Home*, Oxford: Blackwell.

Blunt, A., and Dowling, R. (2006), *Home*, London: Routledge.

Blythman, J. (2004), *Shopped: The Shocking Power of British Supermarkets*, London: Fourth Estate.

Blythman, J. (2006), *Bad Food Britain*, London: Fourth Estate.

Bobrow-Strain, A. (2008), "White Bread Bio-Politics: Purity, Health, and the Triumph of Industrial Baking," *Cultural Geographies*, 15: 19–40.

Boisard, P. (2003), *Camembert: A National Myth*, Berkeley: University of California Press.

Boltanski, L., and Thévenot, L. (2006), *On Justification: Economies of Worth*, Princeton, NJ: Princeton University Press.

Bond, A. (2010), "Empowering the New Consumer," *International Commerce Review*, 8: 122–6.

Bondi, L. (2005), "Making Connections and Thinking through Emotions: Between Geography and Psychotherapy," *Transactions of the Institute of British Geographers*, 30: 433–48.

Bordo, S. (1990), "Reading the Slender Body," in M. Jacobus, E. F. Keller, and S. Shuttleworth (eds.), *Body/Politics: Women and the Discourses of Science*, New York: Routledge, Chapman and Hall, 83–112.

Bordo, S. (1992), "Anorexia Nervosa: Psychopathology as the Crystallization of Culture," in D. W. Curtin and L. S. Heldke (eds.), *Cooking, Eating, Thinking: Transformative Philosophies of Food*, Bloomington, Indianapolis: Indiana University Press, 28–55.

Bordo, S. (1993), *Unbearable Weight: Feminism, Western Culture and the Body*, Berkeley: University of California Press.

Botsman, R., and Rogers, R. (2010), *What's Mine is Yours: How Collaborative Consumption is Changing the Way We Live*, London: Collins.

Bourdieu, P. (1977), *Outline of a Theory of Practice*, Cambridge: Cambridge University Press.

Bourdieu, P. (1984), *Distinction: A Social Critique of the Judgment of Taste*, London: Routledge and Kegan Paul.

Bourdieu, P. (1990), *The Logic of Practice*, Cambridge: Polity Press.

Bourke, J. (2003), "Fear and Anxiety: Writing about Emotion in Modern History," *History Workshop Journal*, 55: 111–33.

Braverman, H. (1974), *Labor and Monopoly Capital: The Degradation of Work in the Twentieth Century*, New York: Monthly Review Press.

Brembeck, H. (2011), "Preventing Anxiety: A Qualitative Study of Food and Pregnancy," *Critical Public Health*, 21: 497–508.

Brembeck, H., Mörck, M., and Ekström, K. E. (eds.) (2007), *Little Monsters: (De)coupling Assemblages of Consumption*, Berlin: LIT Verlag.

Brennan, T. (2004), *The Transmission of Affect*, Ithaca, NY: Cornell University Press.

Breslau, D. (2000), "Sociology after Humanism: A Lesson from Contemporary Science Studies," *Sociological Theory*, 18: 289–307.

Brewer, J., and Trentmann, F. (eds.) (2006), *Consuming Cultures, Global Perspectives*, Oxford: Berg.

Brightwell, G. (2011), "A Taste of Home? Food, Identity and Belonging among Brazilians in London," PhD diss., Royal Holloway, University of London.

Brillat-Savarin, J. A. (1826), *The Physiology of Taste*. Available at http://www.gutenberg.org/cache/epub/5434/pg5434.html (accessed December 3, 2011).

British Library (2012), "Food Stories." Available at http://www.bl.uk/learning/histcitizen/foodstories (accessed December 20, 2012).

Brooks, S. (2005), "Biotechnology and the Politics of Truth: From the Green Revolution to an Evergreen Revolution," *Sociologia Ruralis*, 45: 360–79.

Brown, J. L., and Miller, D. (2002), "'Couples' Gender Role Preferences and Management of Family Food Preferences," *Journal of Nutrition Education and Behaviour*, 34: 215–23.

Brown, L. K., and Russell, K. (eds.) (1984), *Ethnic and Regional Foodways in the United States*, Knoxville: University of Tennessee Press.

Brownell, K. D., and Horgen, K. B. (2003), *Food Fight: the Inside Story of the Food Industry, America's Obesity Crisis*, New York: McGraw-Hill.

Buckingham, D. (2009), "The Appliance of Science: The Role of Evidence in the Making of Regulatory Policy on Children and Food Advertising in the UK," *International Journal of Cultural Policy*, 15: 201–15.

Bugge, A., and Almås, R. (2006), "Domestic Dinner: Representation and Practices of a Proper Meal Among Young Suburban Mothers," *Journal of Consumer Culture*, 6: 203–28.

Bulkeley, H., and Gregson, N. (2009), "Crossing the Threshold: Municipal Waste Policy and Household Waste Generation," *Environment and Planning A*, 41: 929–45.

Burawoy, M. (1979), *Manufacturing Consent*, Chicago: University of Chicago Press.

Burke, D. (1998), "The 'Yuk' Factor," in S. Griffiths and J. Wallace (eds.), *Consuming Passions*, Manchester: Mandolin, 48–57.

Burnett, J. (1989), *Plenty and Want: A Social History of Food in England from 1815 to the Present Day*, London: Routledge.

Burns, J. (1983), "A Synoptic View of the Food Industry," in J. Burns, J. McInereny, and A. Sinbank (eds.), *The Food Industry: Economics and Policies*, London: Butterworth-Heinemann, 1–17.

Busch, L. (2000), "The Moral Economy of Grades and Standards," *Journal of Rural Studies*, 16: 273–83.

Busch, L. (2004), "Grades and Standards in the Social Construction of Safe Food," in M. Lien and B. Nerlich (eds.), *The Politics of Food*, Oxford: Berg, 163–78.

Busch, L. (2007), "Performing the Economy, Performing Science: From Neo-Classical to Supply Chain Models in the Agri-Food Sector," *Economy and Society*, 36: 437–66.

Busch, L. (2010), "Individual Choice and Social Values: Choice in the Agrifood Sector," Paper presented at the XVII World Congress of the International Sociological Association, Gothenburg, Sweden.

Busch, L., Burkhardt, J., and Lacey, W. B. (1991), *Plants, Power, and Profit: Social, Economic and Ethical Consequences of the New Biotechnologies*, Oxford: Blackwell.

Buttel, F. H. (2005), "The Environmental and Post-Environmental Politics of Genetically Modified Crops and Food," *Environmental Politics*, 14: 309–23.

Buttimer, A., and Seamon, D. (eds.) (1980), *The Human Experience of Space and Place*, London: Croom Helm.

Byrne, A., Whitehead, M., and Breen, S. (2003), "The Naked Truth of Celebrity Endorsement," *British Food Journal*, 105: 288–96.

Cairns, K., Johnston, J., and Baumann, S. (2010), "Caring about Food: Doing Gender in the Foodie Kitchen," *Gender and Society*, 24: 591–615.

Caldwell, M. (2004), "Domesticating the French Fry: McDonald's and Consumerism in Moscow," *Journal of Consumer Culture*, 4: 5–26.

Çaliskan, K., and Callon, M. (2010), "Economization, Part 2: A Research Programme for the Study of Markets," *Economy and Society*, 39: 1–32.

Callon, M. (1986a), "Some Elements of a Sociology of Translation: Domestication of the Scallops and the Fishermen of Saint Brieuc Bay," in J. Law (ed.), *Power, Action and Belief: A New Sociology of Knowledge?*, London: Routledge and Kegan Paul, 196–233.

Callon, M. (1986b), "The Sociology of an Actor-Network: The Case of the Electric Vehicle," in M. Callon, J. Law, and A. Rip (eds.), *Mapping the Dynamics of Science and Technology: Sociology of Science in the Real World*, Basingstoke: Macmillan, 19–34.

Callon, M., Méadel, C., and Rabeharisoa, V. (2002), "The Economy of Qualities," *Economy and Society*, 31: 194–217.

Cameron, J. (1998), "The Practice of Politics: Transforming Subjectivities in the Domestic Domain and the Public Sphere," *Australian Geographer*, 29: 293–307.

Campbell, C. (1989), *The Romantic Ethic and the Spirit of Modern Consumerism*, Oxford: Blackwell.

Campbell, C. (2004), "I Shop therefore I Know I Am: The Metaphysical Basis of Modern Consumerism," in K. M. Ekström and H. Brembeck (eds.), *Elusive Consumption*, Oxford: Berg, 27–44.

Campbell, H. (2000), "The Glass Phallus: Pub(lic) Masculinity and Drinking in Rural New Zealand," *Rural Sociology*, 65: 562–81.

Campbell, H. (2005), "The Rise and Rise of EurepGAP: European (Re)invention of Colonial Food Relations?," *International Journal of Sociology of Food and Agriculture*, 13: 1–19.

Caplan, P. (2000), "Eating British Beef with Confidence: A Consideration of Consumers Responses to BSE in Britain," in P. Caplan (ed.), *Risk Revisited*, London: Pluto Press, 184–203.

Caraher, M., Lang, T., and Dixon, P. (2000), "The Influence of TV and Celebrity Chefs on Public Attitudes and Behavior among the British Public," *Journal for the Study of Food and Society*, 4: 27–46.

Carney, J. A. (2001), *Black Rice: The African Origins of Rice Cultivation in the Americas*, Cambridge, MA: Harvard University Press

Carolan, M. (2006), "Social Change and the Adoption and Adaptation of Knowledge Claims: Whose Truth do you Trust in Regard to Sustainable Agriculture?," *Agriculture and Human Values*, 23: 325–39.

Caroli, E., Gautie, J., and Lamanthe, A. (2009), "The French Food-Processing Model: High Relative Wages and High Work Intensity," *International Labour Review*, 148: 375–94.

Carrier, J. (1990), *Gifts and Commodities: Exchange and Western Capitalism since 1700*, London: Routledge.

Carrigan, M. H., and Randall, C. L. (2003), "Self-Medication in Social Phobia: A Review of the Alcohol Literature," *Addictive Behaviors*, 28: 269–84.

Carrigan, M., Szmigin, I., and Leek, S. (2006), "Managing Routine Food Choices in UK Families: The Role of Convenience Consumption," *Appetite*, 47: 372–83.

Carson, R. (1962), *Silent Spring*, Boston: Houghton Mifflin.

Cato, M. P. (2007), "Roman Farm Management: The Treatises of Cato and Varro," Project Gutenberg Ebook. Available at http://www.gutenberg.org/files/12140/12140-8.txt (accessed December 3, 2011).

Centers for Disease Control (CDC) (2011), "Center for Disease Control Estimates of Foodborne Illness in the United States: 2011 Estimates," CDC Factsheet. Available at http://www.cdc.gov/foodborneburden/2011-foodborne-estimates.html (accessed April 12, 2012).

Chakrabarty, D. (2008), *Provincializing Europe: Postcolonial Thought and Historical Difference*, Princeton, NJ: Princeton University Press.

Chalk, P. (2004), *Hitting America's Soft Underbelly: The Potential Threat of Deliberate Biological Attacks against the U.S. Agricultural and Food Industry*, Santa Monica, CA: RAND Corporation.

Chamberlain, M., and Thompson, M. (eds.) (1998), *Narrative and Genre*, London: Routledge.

Charles, N. (1995), "Food and Family Ideology," in S. Jackson and S. Moores (eds.), *The Politics of Domestic Consumption*, London: Prentice Hall/Harvester Wheatsheaf, 100–15.

Charles, N., and Kerr, M. (1988), *Women, Food and Families*, Manchester: Manchester University Press.

Chatterjee, I. (2007), "Packaging of Identity and Identifiable Packages: A Study of Women–Commodity Negotiation through Product Packaging," *Gender, Place and Culture*, 14: 293–316.

Cheng, H., Kotler, P., and Lee, N. R. (2011), *Social Marketing for Public Health: Global Trends and Success Stories*, Sudbury, Mississauga, London: Jones and Bartlett Publishers.

Chernin, K. (1986), *The Hungry Self: Women, Eating and Identity*, London: Virago Press.

Chi, H.-C., and Jackson, P. (2011), "Thai Food in Taiwan: Tracing the Contours of Transnational Taste," *New Formations*, 74: 65–81.

Christian Science Monitor (2006), "Southern Discomfort Food" (February 6). Available at http://www.csmonitor.com/2006/0206/p20s01-lifo.html (accessed January 14, 2013).

Christie, M. E. (2006), "Kitchenspace: Gendered Territory in Central Mexico," *Gender, Place and Culture*, 13: 653–61.

Chrzan, J. (2004), "Slow Food: What, Why and to Where?," *Food, Culture and Society*, 7: 117–32.

Clarke, I., Hallsworth, A., Jackson, P., De Kervenoael, R., Perez del Aguila, R., and Kirkup, M. (2006), "Retail Restructuring and Consumer Choice 1: Long-Term Local Changes in Consumer Behaviour: Portsmouth, 1980–2002," *Environment and Planning A*, 38: 25–46.

Clarke, N., Cloke, P., Barnett, C., and Malpass, A. (2008), "The Spaces and Ethics of Organic Food," *Journal of Rural Studies*, 24: 291–30.

Classen, C. (1993), *Worlds of Sense: Exploring the Senses in History and across Cultures*, London: Routledge.

Clough, P., and Halley, J. (2008), *The Affective Turn: Theorizing the Social*, Durham, NC: Duke University Press.

Cobb, R. (1970), *The Police and the People: French Popular Protest, 1789–1820*, Oxford: Clarendon Press.

Cochoy, F. (2004), "Is the Modern Consumer a Buridan's Donkey? Product Packaging and Consumer Choice," in K. M. Ekström and H. Brembeck (eds.), *Elusive Consumption*, Oxford: Berg, 205–27.

Cochoy, F. (2008), "Calculation, Qualculation, Calqulation: Shopping Cart Arithmetic, Equipped Cognition and the Clustered Consumer," *Marketing Theory*, 8: 15–44.

Cockburn, C. (1981), "The Material of Male Power," *Feminist Review*, 9: 41–58.

Cockburn, C. (1985), *Machinery of Dominance: Women, Men and Technical Know-How*, London: Pluto Press.

Cockburn, C. (1997), "Domestic Technologies: Cinderella and the Engineers," *Women's Studies International Forum*, 20: 361–71.

Cockburn, C., and Ormrod, J. (1993), *Gender and Technology in the Making*, London: Sage.

Cohen, J. E. (1995), *How Many People can the Earth Support?*, London: WW Norton & Company.

Cohen, L. (2003), *A Consumers' Republic: The Politics of Mass Consumption in Postwar America*, New York: Knopf Doubleday.

Cohen, P. S. (1969), "Theories of Myth," *Man*, 4: 337–53.

Cohen, S. (1972), *Folk Devils and Moral Panics*, London: MacGibbon & Kee.

Coleman-Jensen, A., Nord, M., Andrews, M., and Carlson, S. (2011), *Household Food Security in the United States in 2010* (ERR-125), Washington DC: US Department of Agriculture, Economic Research Services.

Coles, B. F., and Crang, P. (2010), "Placing Alternative Consumption: Commodity Fetishism in Borough Fine Foods Market, London," in T. Lewis and E. Potter (eds.), *Ethical Consumption: A Critical Introduction*, London: Routledge, 87–102.

Colls, R., and Evans, B. (2008), "Embodying Responsibility: Children's Health and Supermarket Initiatives," *Environment and Planning A*, 40: 615–31.

Connerton, P. (1989), *How Societies Remember*, Cambridge: Cambridge University Press.

Connolly, W. E. (2002), *Neuropolitics: Thinking, Culture, Speed*, Minneapolis: University of Minnesota Press.

Conran, T. (1977), *The Kitchen Book*, London: Mitchell Beazley.

Constance, D. H., and Bonnan, A. (2000), "Regulating the Global Fisheries: The World Wildlife Fund, Unilever, and the Marine Stewardship Council," *Agriculture and Human Values*, 17: 125–39.

Cook, G. (2004), "'The Scientists Think and the Public Feels': Expert Perceptions of the Discourse of GM Food," *Discourse and Society*, 15(4): 433–49.

Cook, G., Pieri, E., and Robbins, P. T. (2004), "The Scientists Think and the Public Feels: Expert Perceptions of the Discourse of GM Food," *Discourse and Society*, 15: 433–49.

Cook, I. (1995), "Constructing the Exotic: The Case of Tropical Fruit," in J. Allen and C. Hamnett (eds.), *A Shrinking World?*, Oxford: Oxford University Press, 137–42.

Cook, I. et al. (2004), "Follow the Thing: Papaya," *Antipode*, 36: 642–64.

Cook, I., and Crang, P. (1996), "The World on a Plate," *Journal of Material Culture*, 1: 131–53.

Cook, I., Crang, P., Thorpe, M., and Crouch, D. (2000), "Regions to be Cheerful: Culinary Authenticity and Its Geographies," in I. Cook, D. Crouch, S. Naylor, and J. Ryan (eds.), *Cultural Turns/Geographical Turns*, Harlow: Pearson Education, 107–39.

Cook, I., and Harrison, M. (2003), "Cross-Over Food: Re-Materialising Postcolonial Geographies," *Transactions of the Institute of British Geographers*, 28: 296–317.

Cook, I., Hobson, K., Hallett, L., Guthman, J., Murphy, A., et al. (2011), "Geographies of Food: Afters," *Progress in Human Geography*, 35: 104–20.

Coombe, R. J., and Aylwin, N. (2011), "Bordering Diversity and Desire: Using Intellectual Property to Mark Place-Based Products," *Environment and Planning A*, 43: 2027–42.

Counihan, C. (1999), *The Anthropology of Food and Body: Gender, Meaning, and Power*, New York, London: Routledge.

Counihan, C. (2004), *Around the Tuscan Table: Food, Family and Gender in Twentieth Century Florence*, London: Routledge.

Counihan, C. (2005), "The Border as Barrier and Bridge: Food, Gender and Ethnicity in the San Luis Valley of Colorado," in A. V. Avakian and B. Haber (eds.), *From Betty Crocker to Feminist Food Studies: Critical Perspectives on Women and Food*, Amherst, Boston: University of Massachusetts Press, 200–17.

Coupland, J. C. (2005), "Invisible Brands: An Ethnography of Households and the Brands in Their Kitchen Pantries," *Journal of Consumer Research*, 32: 106–18.

Cova, B., and Dalli, D. (2009), "Working Consumers: The Next Step in Marketing Theory?," *Marketing Theory*, 9: 315–39.

Coveney, J. (2006), *Food, Morals and Meaning: The Pleasure and Anxiety of Eating*, 2nd ed., London: Routledge.

Cowan, R. S. (1983), *More Work for Mother: The Ironies of Household Technology from the Open Hearth to the Microwave*, New York: Basic Books.

Coxon, T. (1983), "Men in the Kitchen: Notes on a Cookery Class," in A. Murcott (ed.), *The Sociology of Food and Eating: Essays in the Sociological Significance of Food*, Aldershot: Gower, 172–7.

Crang, M., and Thift, N. (eds.) (2000), *Thinking Space*, London: Routledge.

Crang, P. (1994), "It's Showtime: On the Workplace Geographies of Display in a Restaurant in Southeast England," *Environment and Planning D: Society and Space*, 12: 675–704.

Crang, P., Dwyer, C., and Jackson, P. (2003), "Transnationalism and the Spaces of Commodity Culture," *Progress in Human Geography*, 27(4): 438–56.

Crang, P., and Jackson, P. (2001), "Geographies of Consumption," in D. Morley and K. Robins (eds.), *British Cultural Studies*, Oxford: Oxford University Press, 327–42.

Cresswell, T. (2004), *Place: A Short Introduction*, Oxford: Blackwell.

Cronon, W. (1991), *Nature's Metropolis: Chicago and the Great West*, New York: Norton.

Crosby, A. W. (1972), *The Columbia Exchange: Biological and Cultural Consequences of 1492*, Westport, CT: Greenwood.

Cross, G. (2002), "Valves of Desire: A Historian's Perspective on Parents, Children and Marketing," *Journal of Consumer Research*, 29: 441–7.

Crotty, P. (1995), *Good Nutrition? Fact and Fashion in Dietary Advice*, St Leonards: Allen and Unwin.

Crumpacker, B. (2006), *The Sex Life of Food: When Body and Soul Meet to Eat*, New York: St. Martin's Press.

Cummins, S., and MacIntyre, S. (2002), "'Food Deserts': Evidence and Assumption in Health Policy", *British Medical Journal*, 325: 436.

Cummins, S., and Macintyre, S. (2002), "A Systematic Study of an Urban Foodscape: The Price and Availability of Food in Greater Glasgow," *Urban Studies*, 39: 2115–30.

Curtin, D., and Heldke, L. (eds.) (1992), *Cooking, Eating, Thinking: Transformative Philosophies of Food*, Bloomington: Indiana University Press.

Czarniawska, B., and Löfgren, O. (2012), *Managing Overflow in Affluent Societies*, New York: Routledge.

D'Adamo, P., and Whitney, C. (1998), *Eat Right for Your Type*, London: Century.

Daily Telegraph (2011a), "Plans for 'Mega Dairy' Scrapped Amid Fears for the Environment" (February 16). Available at http://www.telegraph.co.uk/earth/earthnews/8328927/Plans-for-mega-dairy-scrapped-amid-fears-for-the-environment.html (accessed January 14, 2013).

Daily Telegraph (2011b), "UN Declares First Famine in Africa for Three Decades as US Withholds Aid" (July 20). Available at http://www.telegraph.co.uk/news/worldnews/africaandindianocean/somalia/8648296/UN-declares-first-famine-in-Africa-for-three-decades-as-US-withholds-aid.html (accessed January 14, 2013).

Dalla Costa, M., and James, S. (1972), *The Power of Women and the Subversion of Community*, Bristol: Falling Wall Press.

Daniels, I. (2009), "Seasonal and Commercial Rhythms of Domestic Consumption: A Japanese Case Study," in E. Shove, F. Trentmann, and R. Wilk (eds.), *Time, Consumption, and Everyday Life: Practice, Materiality and Culture*, Oxford: Berg, 171–88.

Darwin, C., Ekman, P., and Prodger, P. (1872/1998), *The Expression of the Emotions in Man and Animals*, 3rd ed., London: Harper Collins.

David, E. (1950), *A Book of Mediterranean Food*, London: John Lehmann.

Davis, D. K., and Baran, S. J (1981), *Mass Communication and Everyday Life: A Perspective on Theory and Effects*, Independence, KY: Wadsworth Publication.

Davis, S. (2010), "Changes to Food Risk Management and Communication," in P. Bennett, P. K. Calman, S. Curtis, and D. Fischbacher-Smith (eds.), *Risk Communication and Public Health*, Oxford: Oxford University Press, 1–16.

De Botton, A. (2001), *The Consolations of Philosophy*, London: Penguin Books.

De Botton, A. (2002), *The Art of Travel*, London: Penguin Books.

De Botton, A. (2005), *Status Anxiety*, London: Penguin Books.

De Certeau, M. (1984), *The Practice of Everyday Life*, Minneapolis: University of Minnesota Press.

De Certeau, M., Giard, L., and Mayol, P. (1998), *The Practice of Everyday Life, Volume 2: Living and Cooking*, Minneapolis: University of Minnesota Press.

De la Pradelle, M. (1995), "Market Exchange and the Social Construction of a Public Space," *French Cultural Studies*, 6: 359–71.

De la Pradelle, M. (2006), *Market Day in Provence*, Chicago: University of Chicago Press.

Deleuze, G., and Guattari, F. (1988), *A Thousand Plateaus*, London: Athlone Press.

Delormier, T., Frohlich, K. L., and Potvin, L. (2009), "Food and Eating as Social Practice–Understanding Eating Patterns as Social Phenomena and Implications for Public Health," *Sociology of Health and Illness*, 31: 215–28.

Department of Health (2004), *Choosing Health: Making Healthier Choices Easier*, London: Stationery Office.

Department of Health (2010), *Healthy Lives, Healthy People: Our Strategy for Public Health in England*, London: Stationery Office.

De Silva, C. (ed.) (1996), *In Memory's Kitchen: A Legacy from the Women of Terezín*, New York: Jason Aronson.

Desjardins, E. (2010), "Place and Food: A Relational Analysis of Personal Food Environments, Meanings of Place and Diet Quality," PhD diss., Wilfrid Laurier University, Waterloo, Ontario.

Deutsch, J. (2005), "'Please Pass the Chicken Tits': Rethinking Men and Cooking at an Urban Firehouse," *Food and Foodways*, 13: 91–114.

Deutsch, T. (2010), *Building a Housewife's Paradise: Gender, Politics, and American Grocery Stores in the Twentieth Century*, Chapel Hill: University of North Carolina Press.

DeVault, M. L. (1991), *Feeding the Family: The Social Organization of Caring as Gendered Work*, Chicago: University of Chicago Press.

Devereux, E. (2006), *Understanding the Media*, London: Sage.

Diaconu, M. (2006), "Reflections on an Aesthetics of Touch, Smell and Taste," *Contemporary Aesthetics*. Available at http://www.contempaesthetics.org/newvolume/pages/article.php?articleID=385 (accessed October 15, 2011).

Díaz-Méndez, C., García-Espejo, I., Callejo, J., Southerton, D., and Warde, A. (2010), "A Comparative Analysis of Food Consumption in United Kingdom and Spain," Paper presented at the XVII World Congress of Sociology, Gothenburg, Sweden.

Dickinson, R. (2005), *Food on British Television: Multiple Messages, Multiple Meanings*, Leicester: University of Leicester Publications.

Dickinson, R. (in press), "Food and the Media: Production, Representation and Consumption," in A. Murcott, W. Belasco, and P. Jackson (eds.), *The Handbook of Food Research*, Oxford: Berg.

Dickinson & Morris (2012), Home page. Available at http://www.porkpie.co.uk (accessed May 23, 2012).

Dikeç, M. (2007), "Revolting Geographies: Urban Unrest in France," *Geography Compass*, 1: 1190–206.

Dimitri, C., and Oberholtzer, L. (2010), "Marketing U.S. Organic Foods: Recent Trends from Farms to Consumers," *USDA Economic Information Bulletin*, 58: 1–27.

Dixon, J. (1999), "A Cultural Economy Model for Studying Food Systems," *Agriculture and Human Values*, 16: 151–60.

Dixon, J. (2007), "Supermarkets as New Food Authorities," in D. Burch and G. Lawrence (eds.), *Supermarkets and Agri-Food Supply Chains: Transformations in the Production and Consumption of Foods*, Cheltenham: Edward Elgar Publishing, 29–50.

Dixon, J., and Banwell, C. (2004), "Re-Embedding
    Trust: Unravelling the Construction of Modern
    Diets," *Critical Public Health*, 14: 117–31.

Dolan, C., and Humphrey, J. (2001), "Governance
    and Trade in Fresh Vegetables: The Impact of
    UK Supermarkets on the African Horticulture
    Industry," *Journal of Development Studies*,
    37: 147–76.

Dolphijn, R. (2004), *Foodscapes: Towards a
    Deleuzian Ethics of Consumption*, Delft: Eburon
    Publishers.

Domosh, M. (2003), "Pickles and Purity: Discourses
    of Food, Empire and Work in Turn-of-
    Century USA," *Social and Cultural Geography*,
    4: 7–26.

Donovan, M. G. (2008), "Informal Cities and the
    Contestation of Public Space: The Case of
    Bogotá's Street Vendors, 1988–2003," *Urban
    Studies*, 45: 28–51.

Dorling, D. (2009), "The Age of Anxiety: Living in
    Fear for our Children's Mental Health," *Journal
    of Public Mental Health*, 8: 4–10.

Douglas, M. (1966/2002), *Purity and Danger: An
    Analysis of Concepts of Pollution and Taboo*,
    London: Routledge & Kegan Paul.

Douglas, M. (1971), "Deciphering a Meal," reprinted
    in M. Douglas (1975), *Implicit Meanings: Essays
    in Anthropology*, London: Routledge & Kegan
    Paul, 249–75.

Douglas, M. (1975), *Implicit Meanings: Essays
    in Anthropology*, London: Routledge &
    Kegan Paul.

Douglas, M. (2003), *Risk and Blame: Mary Douglas
    Collected Works*, vol. 12, London, New York:
    Routledge.

Do Vale, R. C., Pieters, R., and Zeelenberg, M.
    (2008), "Flying under the Radar: Perverse
    Package Size Effects on Consumption Self-
    Regulation," *Journal of Consumer Research*,
    35: 380–90.

Draper, A., and Green, J. (2002), "Food Safety and
    Consumers: Constructions of Choice and Risk,"
    Social Policy and Administration, 36: 610–25.

Drèze, J., and Sen, A. (1991), *The Political Economy of
    Hunger*, Oxford: Oxford University Press.

Duckham, A. N., and Masefield, G. B. (1970),
    Farming Systems of the World, London:
    Chatto & Windus.

Du Gay, P. (2004), "Self-Service: Retail, Shopping
    and Personhood," *Consumption, Markets and
    Culture*, 7: 149–163.

Du Gay, P., and Pryke, M. (eds.) (2002), *Cultural
    Economy*, London: Sage.

Dunant, S., and Porter, R. (eds.) (1996), *The Age of
    Anxiety*, London: Virago.

Dunn, E. (2007), "*Escherichia coli*, Corporate
    Discipline and the Failure of the Sewer State,"
    Space and Polity, 11: 35–53.

DuPuis, E. M. (2002), *Nature's Perfect Food: How
    Milk became America's Drink*, New York: New
    York University Press.

DuPuis, E. M., and Goodman, D. (2005), "Should
    We Go Home to Eat? Towards a Reflexive
    Politics of Localism," *Journal of Rural Studies*,
    21: 359–71.

Durkheim, E. (1912/2001), *The Elementary
    Forms of Religious Life*, Oxford: Oxford
    University Press.

Dworkin, S. L., and Wachs, F. L. (2009), *Body Panic:
    Gender, Health and the Selling of Fitness*, New
    York: New York University Press.

Dyer, R. (1997), *White: Essays on Race and Culture*,
    London: Routledge.

Eagle, L., Bulmer, S., De Bruin, A., and Kitchen,
    P. (2006), "Advertising and Children: Issues
    and Policy Options," *Journal of Promotion
    Management*, 11: 175–94.

Earle, M. D. (1997), "Innovation in the Food
    Industry," *Trends in Food Science and
    Technology*, 8: 166–75.

Eberstadt, M. (2009), "Is Food the New Sex?," *Policy
    Review*, February–March: 25–40.

The Economist (2004), "The Parable of the Cockle
    Pickers" (February 12). Available at http://
    www.economist.com/node/2426566 (accessed
    January 14, 2013).

The Economist (2011), "Food Safety in China: In the
    Gutter." Available at http://www.economist.
    com/node/21534812 (accessed February 21, 2012).

Eden, S. (2011), "Food Labels as Boundary Objects:
    How Consumers Make Sense of Organic and
    Functional Foods," *Public Understanding of
    Science*, 20: 179–94.

Eden, S., Bear, C., and Walker, G. (2008),
    "Understanding and (Dis)trusting Food
    Assurance Schemes: Consumer Confidence
    and the 'Knowledge Fix,'" *Journal of Rural
    Studies*, 24: 1–14.

EFSA (2010), "New Research Results on EU
    Consumers' Perceptions of Food-Related
    Risks," European Food Safety Authority
    press release. Available at http://www.efsa

europa.eu/en/press/news/corporate101117.htm (accessed December 14, 2012).

Einsiedel, E. (2002), "GM Food Labeling: The Interplay of Information, Social Values, and Institutional Trust," *Science Communication*, 24: 209–21.

Eldridge, J. (1999), "Risk Society and the Media: Now You See It, Now You Don't," in G. Philo (ed.), *Message Received: Glasgow Media Group Research 1993–1998*, Essex, New York: Longman, 106–27.

Elias, N. (2000), *The Civilizing Process: Sociogenetic and Psychogenetic Investigations*, revised ed., Oxford: Blackwell.

Emanuel, R. (2000), *Ideas in Psychoanalysis: Anxiety*, Cambridge: Icon Books.

Emery, C., and Tian, K. R. (2010), "China Compared with the US: Cultural Differences and the Impacts of Advertising Appeals," *International Journal of China Marketing*, 1: 45–59.

Engels, F. (1845/1969), *The Condition of the Working Class in England in 1844*, London: Panther.

Enticott, G. (2003), "Lay Immunology, Local Foods and Rural Identity: Defending Unpasteurised Milk in England," *Sociologia Ruralis*, 43: 257–70.

Eurobarometer (2010), *Special Eurobarometer 354: Food Related Risks*, Brussels: European Commission.

Evans, D. (2011), "Blaming the Consumer—Once Again: The Social and Material Contexts of Everyday Food Waste Practices in some English Households," *Critical Public Health*, 21: 429–40.

Evans, D. (2012), "Beyond the Throwaway Society: Ordinary Domestic Practice and a Sociology of Household Food Waste," *Sociology*, 46: 41–56.

Everts, J., and Jackson, P. (2009), "Modernisation and the Practices of Contemporary Food Shopping," *Environment and Planning D: Society and Space*, 27: 917–35.

Ewan, S., and Ewan, E. (1982), *Channels of Desire*, New York: McGraw-Hill.

Falk, P., and Campbell, C. (1997), *The Shopping Experience*, London: Sage.

FAO (2003), *Trade Reforms and Food Security: Conceptualizing the Linkages*, Rome: Food and Agricultural Organization.

FAO (2006a), *Food Security: Policy Brief*, Rome: Food and Agriculture Organization.

FAO (2006b), *Livestock's Long Shadow*, Rome: Food and Agriculture Organization.

FAO (2008), *The State of Food Insecurity in the World*, Rome: Food and Agriculture Organization.

FAO (2010), *Statistical Yearbook 2010*, Rome: Food and Agriculture Organization.

Farb, P., and Armelagos, G. (1980), *Consuming Passions: The Anthropology of Eating*, Boston: Houghton Mifflin.

Farquhar, J. (2002), *Appetites: Food and Sex in Post-socialist China*, Durham, NC: Duke University Press.

Farris, P., Reibstein, D., Bendle, N., and Pfeifer, P. (2010), "Metrics that Matter—To Marketing Managers," *Journal of Research and Management*, 6: 18–23.

Feagan, R. (2007), "The Place of Food: Mapping Out the 'Local' in Local Food Systems," *Progress in Human Geography*, 31: 23–42.

Featherstone, M. (1982), "The Body in Consumer Culture," *Theory, Culture and Society*, 1: 18–33.

Featherstone, M. (1991), *Consumer Culture and Postmodernism*, London: Sage.

Featherstone, M. (2000), *Body Modification*, London: Sage.

Featherstone, M., Hepworth, M., and Turner, B. S. (1991/2001), *The Body: Social Process and Cultural Theory*, London: Sage.

Ferguson, P. (2004), *Accounting for Taste: The Triumph of French Cuisine*, Chicago: University of Chicago Press.

Ferguson, P., and Zukin, S. (1998), "The Careers of Chefs," in R. Scapp and B. Seitz (eds.), *Eating Culture*, Albany, NY: State University of New York Press, 92–111.

Ferrero, S. (2002), "Comida sin par: Consumption of Mexican food in Los Angeles: 'Foodscapes' in a Transnational Consumer Society," in W. Belasco and P. Scranton (eds.), *Food Nations: Selling Taste in Consumer Societies*, New York: Routledge, 194–219.

Fiddes, N. (1991), *Meat: A Natural Symbol*, London: Routledge.

Field, C. (1997), *In Nonna's Kitchen: Recipes and Traditions from Italy's Grandmothers*, New York: Harper Collins.

Fine, G. (1996), *Kitchens: The Culture of Restaurant Work*, Berkeley: University of California Press.

Fine, G. A., and Turner, P. A. (2001), *Whispers on the Color Line: Rumor and Race in America*, Berkeley: University of California Press.

Finello, C. (2010), "Food Styling: Balancing Ethics and Aesthetics," *The Artful Palate*. Available at http://myportfolio.usc.edu/finello/2010/02/food_styling_striking_a_balance_between_a_realistic_photograph_and_selling_the_dish.html (accessed October 15, 2011).

Finkelstein, J. (1993), "Dining Out: The Hyperreality of Appetite," in R. Scapp and B. Seitz (eds.), *Eating Culture*, New York: State University of New York Press, 201–215.

Fischer, E., and Arnold, S. J. (1990), "More than a Labour of Love: Gender Roles and Christmas Gift Shopping," *Journal of Consumer Research*, 17: 333–45.

Fischler, C. (1980), "Food Habits, Social Change and the Nature/Culture Dilemma," *Social Science Information*, 19: 937–53.

Fischler, C. (1988), "Food, Self and Identity," *Social Science Information*, 27: 275–92.

Fisher, M. F. K. (1949), *An Alphabet for Gourmets*, New York: Farrar, Straus and Giroux.

Fligstein, N., and Dauter, L. (2007), "The Sociology of Markets," *Annual Review of Sociology*, 33: 105–28.

Floyd, J. (2004), "Coming Out of the Kitchen: Texts, Contexts and Debates," *Cultural Geographies*, 11: 61–73.

Foley, L. (2007), "The World's First Bionic Burger" [video]. Available at: http://www.youtube.com/watch?v=mYyDXH1amic (accessed December 12, 2012).

Food Sovereignty (2011), "Food Sovereignty: a Right for All." Available at http://www.foodsovereignty.org/Portals/0/documenti%20sito/About%20us/Food%20Sovereignty-%20A%20Right%20For%20All%20Political%20Statement%20.pdf (accessed November 30, 2011).

Forero, O., and Smith, G. (2011), "The Reproduction of 'Cultural Taste' amongst the Ukrainian Diaspora in Bradford England," *Sociological Review*, 58: 78–96.

Foresight (2007), *Tackling Obesities: Future Choices*, London: Government Office for Science.

Foresight (2011), *The Future of Food and Farming: Challenges and Choices for Global Sustainability*, London: Government Office for Science.

Foucault, M. (1990), *The History of Sexuality: Volume Three, The Care of the Self*, Harmondsworth: Penguin.

Foucault, M. (1992), *The History of Sexuality: Volume Two, The Use of Pleasure*, Harmondsworth: Penguin.

Fournier, S. (1998), "Consumers and their Brands: Developing Relationship Theory in Consumer Research," *Journal of Consumer Research*, 24: 343–53.

Fox, R., and Smith, G. (2011), "Sinner Ladies and the Gospel of Good Taste: Geographies of Food, Class and Care," *Health and Place*, 17: 403–12.

Frake, C. O. (1964), "How to Ask for a Drink in Subanun," *American Anthropologist*, 66: 127–32.

Fredriksson, C. (1997), "The Making of a Swedish Department Store Culture," in P. Falk and C. Campbell (eds.), *The Shopping Experience*, London: Sage, 111–35.

Freeman, J. (2004), *The Making of the Modern Kitchen*, Oxford: Berg.

Freidberg, S. (2003), "Editorial: Not All Sweetness and Light: New Cultural Geographies of Food," *Social and Cultural Geography*, 4: 3–6.

Freidberg, S. (2004), *French Beans and Food Scares: Culture and Commerce in an Anxious Age*, Oxford: Oxford University Press.

Freidberg, S. (2007), "Supermarkets and Imperial Knowledge," *Cultural Geographies*, 14(3): 321–42.

Freidberg, S. (2009), *Fresh: A Perishable History*, Cambridge, MA: Harvard University Press.

Freidberg, S. (2010), "Ambiguous Appetites," *Food, Culture and Society*, 13: 477–91.

Freud, S. (1930), *Civilization and its Discontents*, London: Hogarth Press.

Freud, S. (1936), *The Problem of Anxiety*, New York: Psychoanalytic Quarterly & W.W. Norton.

Frewer, L. J., Howard, C., and Shepherd, R. (1997), "The Influence of Initial Attitudes on Responses to Communication about Genetic Engineering in Food Production," *Agriculture and Human Values*, 15: 15–30.

Frewer, L. J., Miles, S., Brennan, M., Kuznesof, S., Ness, M., and Ritson, C. (2002), "Public Preferences for Informed Choice under Conditions of Risk Uncertainty," *Public Understanding of Science*, 11: 363–72.

Friedan, B. (1963), *The Feminine Mystique*, London: Victor Gollancz.

Friedland, W. H., Barton, A. E., and Thomas, R. J. (1981), *Manufacturing Green Gold: Capital, Labour, and Technology in the Lettuce Industry*, New York: Cambridge University Press.

Friedman, S. M., Villamil, K., Suriano, R. A., and Egolf, B. P. (1996), "Alar and Apples: Newspapers, Risk and Media Responsibility," *Public Understanding of Science*, 5: 1–20.

Friedman, T. L. (2005), *The World Is Flat: A Brief History of the Twenty-First Century*, New York: Farrar, Straus and Giroux.

Friedmann, H. (2007), "Scaling Up: Bringing Public Institutions and Food Service Corporations into the Project for a Local, Sustainable Food System in Ontario," *Agriculture and Human Values*, 24: 389–98.

Frohlich, X. (2011), "Imaginer des Consommateurs, Constituer les Sujets: L'Étiquetage Nutritionnel aux États-Unis, 1945–1995," *Science de la Société*, 80: 11–27.

Fromartz, S. (2006), *Organic Inc.: Natural Foods and How They Grew*, Boston: Houghton Mifflin Harcourt.

FSA (2001), "The Food Standards Agency's Approach to Risk." Available at http://www.food.gov.uk/multimedia/pdfs/riskapproach.pdf (accessed March 19, 2012).

FSA (2007), "Consumer Attitudes to Food Survey." Available at http://webarchive.nationalarchives.gov.uk/20120206100416/http://food.gov.uk/news/newsarchive/2007/feb/cas2006 (accessed March 19, 2012).

FSA (2011), "Key Messages from a Panel Debate on the Difficulty of Communicating Advice to the Public where the Science is Uncertain or Knowledge is Developing." Available at http://www.food.gov.uk/multimedia/pdfs/keymessagesciencefoodallergy.pdf (accessed March 19, 2012).

Fuchs, D., Kalfaglanni, A., and Havinga, T. (2011), "Actors in Private Food Governance: The Legitimacy of Retail Standards and Multistakeholder Initiatives with Civil Society Participation," *Agriculture and Human Values*, 28: 353–67.

Fuentes, C. (2011), "Green Retailing: A Socio-Material Analysis," *Institutionen för Service Management*, Lund: Lund University.

Furst, T., Connors, M., Bisogni, C. A., Sobal, J., and Winter Falk, L. (1996), "Food Choice: A Conceptual Model of Process," *Appetite*, 26: 247–66.

Future Foundation (2006), "Takeaway and Convenience Food Predicted to be Worth £12.3bn in 2015" Press release (March 20). Available at http://www.futurefoundation.net/press_release/show/19 (accessed 14 January 2013).

Gabaccia, D. (1998), *We Are What We Eat: Ethnic Food and the Making of Americans*, Cambridge, MA: Harvard University Press.

Gade, D. W. (2004), "Tradition, Territory and Terroir in French Viticulture: Cassis, France and Appellation Contrôlée," *Annals of the Association of American Geographers*, 94: 848–67.

Galbraith, J. K. (1958), *The Affluent Society*, New York: Houghton Mifflin Company.

Gamble, M., and Cotugna, N. (1999), "A Quarter Century of TV Food Advertising Targeted at Children," *American Journal of Health Behavior*, 23: 261–67.

Gandy, M. (1994), *Recycling and the Politics of Urban Waste*, London: Earthscan.

Gatens, M., and Lloyd, G. (1999), *Collective Imaginings: Spinoza, Past and Present*, London: Routledge.

Gavron, H. (1966), *The Captive Wife*, Harmondsworth: Penguin.

Gaytan, M. S. (2004), "Globalising Resistance: Slow Food and New Local Imaginaries," *Food Culture and Society*, 7: 97–116.

Geertz, C. (1979), "Suq: The Bazaar Economy in Sefrou," in C. Geertz, H. Geertz, and L. Rosen (eds.), *Meaning and Order in Moroccan Society: Three Essays in Cultural Analysis*, Cambridge: Cambridge University Press, 123–225.

Gelder, K., and Jacobs, J. (1995), "Uncanny Australia," *Cultural Geographies*, 2: 171–83.

Germov, J., Williams, L., and Freij, M. (2011), "Portrayal of the Slow Food Movement in the Australian Print media: Conviviality, Localism and Romanticism," *Journal of Sociology*, 47: 89–106.

Gherardi, S. (2009), "Practice? It's a Matter of Taste!" *Management Learning*, 40: 535–50.

Giant Food (2011), "Nature's Promise." Available at http://www.giantfood.com/our_stores/offerings/brands/index.htm?brnd=NATURE_PROMISE (accessed October 26, 2011).

Giard, L. (1998), "Doing Cooking," in M. De Certeau, L. Giard, and P. Mayoll (eds.), *The Practice of Everyday Life Volume 2: Living and Cooking*, Minneapolis: University of Minnesota Press, 149–247.

Giddens, A. (1984), *The Constitution of Society*, Cambridge: Polity Press.

Giddens, A. (1991), *Modernity and Self-Identity: Self and Society in the Late Modern Age*, Cambridge: Polity Press.

Giddens, A. (1992), *The Transformation of Intimacy*, Cambridge: Polity Press.

Giddens, A. (2006), *Sociology*, 5th ed., Cambridge: Polity Press.

Gilbert, E. (2005), "The Inevitability of Integration? Neoliberal Discourse and the Proposals for a New North American Economic Space after September 11," *Annals of the Association of American Geographers*, 95: 202–22.

Gilbert, R. I., and Mielke, J. H. (1985), *The Analysis of Prehistoric Diets*, Orlando: Academic Press.

Gille, Z. (2009), "The Tale of the Toxic Paprika: The Hungarian Taste of Euro-Globalization," in M. Caldwell (ed.), *Food and Everyday Life in the Postsocialist World*, Bloomington: Indiana University Press, 57–77.

Gillespie, M. (1995), *Television, Ethnicity and Cultural Change*, London: Routledge.

Gilmore, J. H., and Pine, J. B. (2007), *Authenticity: What Consumers Really Want*, Boston: Harvard Business School Press.

Gleick, P. H. (1993), "Water and Conflict: Fresh Water Resources and International Security," *International Security*, 18(1): 79–112.

Glennie, P., and Thrift, N. (1996), "Consumption, Shopping and Gender," in N. Wrigley and M. Lowe (eds.), *Retailing, Consumption and Capital: Towards the New Retail Geography*, Harlow: Longman, 221–37.

GMO Compass (2008), "EFSA: 'Ban on Cultivating MON810 Maize in France is Unfounded.'" Available at http://www.gmo-compass.org/eng/news/390.efsa_ban_cultivating_mon810_maize_france_is_unfounded.html (accessed April 21, 2012).

Godfray, H. C. J., Beddington, J. R., Crute, I. R., Haddad, L., Lawrence, D., et al. (2010), "Food Security: The Challenge of Feeding 9 Billion People," *Science*, 327: 812–18.

Gong, Q. (2011), "The Anxiety that Never Was? The Roles of the Newswires in Constructing Food Crises", Presentation to the Association of American Geographers' annual meeting, Seattle, Washington.

Gong, Q., and Jackson, P. (2012), "Consuming Anxiety? Parental Practices after the 2008 Infant Formula Scandal in China," *Food, Culture and Society*, 15: 557–78.

Gong, Q., and Jackson, P. (in press), "Mediating Science and Nature: Representing and Consuming Infant Formula Advertising in China," *European Journal of Cultural Studies*.

Goodman, D. (2001), "Ontology Matters: The Relational Materiality of Nature and Agro-Food Studies," *Sociologia Ruralis*, 41: 182–200.

Goodman, D. (2003), "The Quality Turn and Alternative Food Practices: Reflections and Agenda," *Journal of Rural Studies*, 19: 1–7.

Goodman, D. (2004), "Rural Europe Redux?: Reflections on Alternative Agro-food Networks and Paradigm Change," *Sociologia Ruralis*, 44: 3–16.

Goodman, D., and Redclift, M. (1991), *Refashioning Nature: Food, Ecology and Culture*, London: Routledge.

Goodman, D., Sorj, B., and Wilkinson, J. (1987), *From Farming to Biotechnology: A Theory of Agro-industrial Development*, Oxford: Blackwell.

Goodman, D., and Watts, M. J. (eds.) (1997), *Globalising Food: Agrarian Questions and Global Restructuring*, London: Routledge.

Goodman, M. (2008), "Towards Visceral Entanglements: Knowing and Growing the Economic Geographies of Food," in R. Lee, A. Leyshon, L. McDowell, and P. Sunley (eds.), *A Compendium of Economic Geography*, London: Sage, 242–57.

Goodman, M., Goodman, D., and Redclift, M. (eds.) (2010), *Consuming Space: Placing Consumption in Perspective*, Farnham: Ashgate.

Goodman, M., Maye, D., and Holloway, L. (2010), "Ethical Foodscapes?: Premises, Promises, and Possibilities," *Environment and Planning A*, 42: 1782–96.

Goody, J. (1982), *Cooking, Cuisine and Class: A Study in Comparative Sociology*, Cambridge: Cambridge University Press.

Gorman-Murray, A. (2008), "Masculinity and the Home: A Critical Review of a Conceptual Framework," *Australian Geographer*, 39: 367–79.

Grabher, G., Ibert, O., and Flohr, S. (2008), "The Neglected King: The Customer in the New Knowledge Ecology of Innovation," *Economic Geography*, 84: 253–80.

Gram, M. (2007), "Whiteness and Western Values in Global Advertisements: An Explorative Study," *Journal of Marketing Communications*, 13: 291–309.

Grandclement, C. (2009), "Wheeling One's Groceries around the Store: The Invention of the Shopping Cart, 1936–1953," in W. Belasco and R. Horowitz (eds.), *Food Chains: From Farmyard to Shopping Cart*, Philadelphia:

University of Pennsylvania Press,
233–51.

Granovetter, M. (1985), "Economic Action
and Social Structure: The Problem of
Embeddedness," *American Journal of Sociology*,
91: 481–510.

Green, J. (2009), "Is it Time for the Sociology of
Health to Abandon 'Risk?'," *Health, Risk and
Society*, 11: 493–508.

Green, J., Draper, A., and Dowler, E. (2003), "Short
Cuts to Safety: Risk and 'Rules of Thumb' in
Accounts of Food Choice," *Health, Risk and
Society*, 5: 33–52.

Greenaway, A., Larner, W., and Le Heron, R.
(2002), "Reconstituting Motherhood:
Milk Powder Marketing in Sri Lanka,"
*Environment and Planning D: Society and
Space*, 20: 719–36.

Greer, G. (1970), *The Female Eunuch*, London:
Granada.

Gregory, J., and Miller, S. (1998), *Science in Public:
Communication, Culture, and Credibility*,
Cambridge, MA: Perseus Publishing.

Gregson, N., Metcalfe, A., and Crewe, L. (2007),
"Identity, Mobility and the Throwaway
Society," *Environment and Planning D: Society
and Space*, 25: 682–700.

Gregson, N., Watkins, H., and Calestani, M. (2010),
"Inextinguishable Fibres: Demolition and the
Vital Materialisms of Asbestos," *Environment
and Planning A*, 42: 1065–83.

Griffiths, S., and Wallace, J. (eds.) (1998),
Consuming Passions: Food in the Age of Anxiety,
Manchester: Manchester University Press.

Grigg, D. (2002), "The Worlds of Tea and Coffee:
Patterns of Consumption," *GeoJournal*,
57: 283–94.

Gronow, J. (1997), *The Sociology of Taste*, London:
Routledge.

Gronow, J. (2004), "Standards of Taste and Varieties
of Goodness: The (Un)predictability of
Modern Consumption," in M. Harvey, A.
McMeekin, and A. Warde (eds), *Qualities of
Food*, Manchester: Manchester University
Press, 38–60.

Grosz, E. (1998), "Bodies-Cities," in H. Nash and
S. Pile (eds.), *Places Through the Body*, London:
Routledge, 41–51.

Grosz, E. (2008), *Chaos, Territory, Art: Deleuze
and the Framing of the Earth (The Wellek
Library Lectures)*, New York: Columbia
University Press.

Grunert, K. G. (2005), "Food Quality and Safety:
Consumer Perception and Demand," *European
Review of Agricultural Economics*, 32: 369–91.

Grunert, K. G., Jensen, B. B., Sonne, A.-M., Brunsø,
K., Byrne, D. V., et al. (2008), "User-Oriented
Innovation in the Food Sector: Relevant
Streams of Research and an Agenda for Future
Work," *Trends in Food Science and Technology*,
19: 590–602.

Grunert, K. G., and Wills, J. M. (2007), "A Review
of European Research on Consumer Response
to Nutrition Information on Food Labels,"
Journal of Public Health, 15: 385–99.

The Guardian (2008), "Crop Switch Wordens
Global Food Price Crisis" (April 5).
Available at http://www.guardian.co.uk/
environment/2008/apr/05/food.biofuels
(accessed January 14, 2013).

The Guardian (2009), "Are Probiotics Really
That Good for Your Health?" (July 25).
Available at http://www.guardian.co.uk/
theguardian/2009/jul/25/probiotic-health-
benefits (accessed January 14, 2013).

Guerrero, L., Guardia, M. D., Xicola, J., Verbeke,
W., Vanhonacker, F., et al. (2009), "Consumer-
Driven Definition of Traditional Food
Products and Innovation in Traditional Foods,
A Qualitative Cross-cultural Study," *Appetite*,
52: 345–54.

Gunter, B., Blades, M., and Oates, C. (2005),
*Advertising to Children on TV: Content, Impact
and Regulation*, Mahwah, NJ: Lawrence
Erlbaum Associates.

Gunter, B., Hansen, A., and Touri, M. (2010),
*Alcohol Advertising and Young People's
Drinking: Representation, Reception and
Regulation*, Basingstoke: Palgrave Macmillan.

Gussow, J. D. (1978), *The Feeding Web: Issues in
Nutritional Ecology*, Palo Alto, CA: Bull
Publishing.

Gustavsson, J., Cederberg, C., Sonesson, U.,
Otterdijk, R. V., and Meybeck, A. (2011),
*Food Losses and Food Waste: Extent, Causes
and Prevention*, Rome: Food and Agriculture
Organization.

Guthman, J. (2003), "Fast Food/Organic Food:
Reflexive Tastes and the Making of 'Yuppie
Chow'," *Social and Cultural Geography*
4: 45–58.

Guthman, J. (2004a), "Back to the Land: The
Paradox of Organic Food Standards,"
Environment and Planning A, 36: 511–28.

Guthman, J. (2004b), *Agrarian Dreams: The Paradox of Organic Farming in California*, Berkeley: University of California Press.

Guthman, J. (2007), "The Polanyian Way? Voluntary Food Labels as Neoliberal Governance," *Antipode*, 39: 456–78.

Guthman, J. (2008), "'If They Only Knew': Color Blindness and Universalism in California Alternative Food Institutions", *The Professional Geographer*, 60: 387–97.

Guthman, J., and DuPuis, M. (2006), "Embodying Neoliberalism: Economy, Culture, and the Politics of Fat," *Environment and Planning D: Society and Space*, 24: 427–48.

Guthrie, J., Fox J., Cleveland L., and Welsh, S. (1995), "Who Uses Nutrition Labelling, and What Effects Does Labelling Have on Diet Quality?," *Journal of Nutrition Education*, 27: 163–72.

Guy, K. M. (1999), "Oiling the Wheels of Social Life: Myths and Marketing in Champagne during the Belle Epoque," *French Historical Studies*, 22: 211–39.

Guy, K. M. (2007), *When Champagne became French: Wine and the Making of a National Identity*, Baltimore, MD: Johns Hopkins University Press.

Haber, B. (1997), "Follow the Food," in A. V. Avakian (ed.), *Through the Kitchen Window: Women Explore the Intimate Meanings of Food and Cooking*, Boston: Beacon Press, 65–74.

Hacking, I. (1990), *The Taming of Chance*, Cambridge: Cambridge University Press.

Haig, M. (2006), *Brand Success: How the World's Top 100 Brands Thrive and Survive*, London, Philadelphia, New Delhi: Kogan Page.

Halbwachs, M. (1992), *On Collective Memory*, Chicago: University of Chicago Press.

Halkier, B. (2004), "Handling Food-related Risks: Political Agency and Governmentality," in M. E. Lien and B. Nerlich (eds.), *The Politics of Food*, Oxford: Berg, 21–38.

Halkier, B. (2009), "A Practice Theoretical Perspective on Everyday Dealings with Environmental Challenges of Food Consumption," *Anthropology of Food*, S5.

Halkier, B. (2010), *Consumption Challenged: Food in Medialised Everyday Lives*, Farnham: Ashgate.

Hall, S. (1980), "Encoding/decoding," in S. Hall, *Culture, Media, Language*, London: Hutchinson, 107–16.

Halweil, B., and Gardiner, G. (2000), *Underfed and Overfed: The Global Epidemic of Malnutrition*, Washington, D.C.: Worldwatch Institute.

Hamilton, S. (2008), *Trucking Country: The Road to America's Wal-Mart Economy*, Princeton, NJ: Princeton University Press.

Hannerz, U. (1992), *Cultural Complexity: Studies in the Social Organisation of Meaning*, New York: Columbia University Press.

Hansen, J., Holm, L., Frewer, L., Robinson, P., and Sandøe, P. (2003), "Beyond the Knowledge Deficit: Recent Research into Lay and Expert Attitudes to Food Risks," *Appetite*, 41: 111–21.

Hansen, S. (2008), "Society of the Appetite: Celebrity Chefs Deliver Consumers," *Food, Culture and Society*, 11: 49–67.

Hardin, R. (2006), *Trust*, Cambridge: Polity Press.

Hardt, M., and Negri, A. (2004), *Multitude*, New York: Penguin.

Hareven, T. K. (1982), *Family Time and Industrial Time: The Relationship between the Family and Work in a New England Industrial Community*, Cambridge: Cambridge University Press.

Harnack, L., Steffen, L., Arnett, D., Gao, S., and Luepker, R. (2004), "Accuracy of Estimation of Large Food Portions," *Journal of the American Dietetic Association*, 104: 804–6.

Harris, E. M. (2010), "Eat Local? Constructions of Place in Alternative Food Politics," *Geography Compass*, 4: 355–69.

Harris, M. (1985), *Good to Eat: Riddles of Food and Culture*, New York: Simon and Schuster.

Harrison, S., Pile, S., and Thrift, N. J. (eds.) (2004), *Patterned Ground: Entanglements of Nature and Culture*, London: Reaktion Books.

Hartley, J. (2005), *Communication Cultural and Media Studies: The Key Concepts*, 3rd ed., London, New York: Routledge.

Harvey, D. (1990), "Between Space and Time: Reflections on the Geographical Imagination," *Annals of the Association of American Geographers*, 80: 418–34.

Harvey, M., McMeekin, A., and Warde, A. (2004), *Qualities of Food*, Manchester: Manchester University Press.

Haskins, C. (2008), "The Return of Malthus," *Prospect*, 20 January.

Hastings, G., Stead, M., McDermott, L., Alasdair, F., MacKintosh, A. M., and Rayner, M. (2003), *Review of the Research on the Effects of Food Promotion to Children*, London: Food Standards Agency.

Havinga, T. (2008), "Actors in Private Regulation: Taking Responsibility or Passing the Buck?," Paper presented at the Symposium on Private Governance in the Global Agro-Food System, Munster, Germany.

Hawkes, C. (2007), *Marketing Food to Children: Changes in the Global Regulatory Environment 2004–2006*, Geneva: World Health Organization.

Hawkins, G. (2006), *The Ethics of Waste: How we Relate to Rubbish*, Lanham, MD: Rowman & Littlefield.

Hawkins, G. (2009), "The Politics of Bottled Water," *Journal of Cultural Economy*, 2: 183–95.

Hawkins, G., and Muecke, S. (2003), *Culture and Waste: The Creation and Destruction of Value*, Lanham, MD: Rowman & Littlefield.

Hayden, D. (1978), "Two Utopian Feminists and their Campaigns for Kitchenless Households," *Signs*, 4(2): 274–90.

Hayes-Conroy, A., and Hayes-Conroy, J. (2008), "Taking Back Taste: Feminism, Food and Visceral Politics," *Gender, Place and Culture*, 15: 461–73.

Hayes-Conroy, A., and Hayes-Conroy, J. (2010), "Visceral Difference: Variations in Feeling (Slow) Food," *Environment and Planning A*, 42: 2956–71.

Hayes-Conroy, A., and Martin, D. G. (2010), "Mobilising Bodies: Visceral Identification in the Slow Food Movement," *Transactions Institute of British Geographers*, 35: 269–81.

Hayes-Conroy, J., and Hayes-Conroy, A. (2012), "Veggies and Visceralities: A Political Ecology of Food and Feeling," *Emotion, Space and Society*. Available at http://www.sciencedirect.com/science/article/pii/S1755458611100879.

Hebdige, D. (1979), *Subculture: The Meaning of Style*, London: Routledge

Heidegger, M. (1978), *Being and Time*, Oxford: Blackwell.

Heldke, L. (1992), "Foodmaking as a Thoughtful Practice," in D. W. Curtin and L. Heldke (eds.), *Cooking, Eating, Thinking: Transformative Philosophies of Food*, Bloomington, Indianapolis: Indiana University Press, 203–29.

Heldke, L. (2003), *Exotic Appetites: Ruminations of a Food Adventurer*, London: Routledge.

Heldke, L. (2005), "But Is It Authentic?: Culinary Travel and the Search for the 'Genuine Article,'" in C. Korsmeyer (ed.) *The Taste Culture Reader: Experiencing Food and Drink*, Oxford: Berg, 385–94.

Heller, C. (2007), "Techne versus Technoscience: Divergent (and Ambiguous) Notions of Food 'Quality' in the French Debate over GM Crops," *American Anthropologist*, 109(4): 603–15.

Hennion, A. (2007a), "Those Things That Hold Us Together: Taste and Sociology," *Cultural Sociology*, 1: 97–114.

Hennion, A. (2007b), "Pragmatics of Taste," in M. D. Jacobs and N. W. Hanrahan (eds.), *The Blackwell Companion to the Sociology of Culture*, Oxford: Blackwell Publishing, 131–44.

Hervieu-Léger, D. (1996), "Tourisme, Tradition et Ethnologie," *Source*, 27: 55–86.

Heuzenroeder, A. (2006), "European Food Meets Aboriginal Food: To What Extent Did Aboriginal Food Cultures Influence Early German-Speaking Settlers in South Australia?," *Limina*, 12: 30–39.

Hewison, R. (1987), *The Heritage Industry: Britain in a Climate of Decline*, London: Methuen.

Hier, S. (2003), "Risk and Panic in Late Modernity: Implications of Converging Sites of Social Anxiety," *British Journal of Sociology*, 54: 3–20.

Higgins, V., Dibden, J., and Cocklin, C. (2008), "Building Alternative Agri-food Networks: Certification, Embeddedness and Agri-Environmental Governance," *Journal of Rural Studies*, 24: 15–27.

Hill, A. (2005), *Reality TV, Audiences and Popular Factual Television*, New York: Routledge.

Hilliard, D. (ed.) (2008), *The Black Panther Party: Service to the People Programs*, Albuquerque: University of New Mexico Press.

Hinchliffe, S., and Bingham, N. (2008), "Securing Life: The Emerging Practices of Biosecurity," *Environment and Planning A*, 40: 1534–51.

Hine, T. (1995), *The Total Package: The Evolution and Secret Meanings of Boxes, Bottles, Cans, and other Persuasive Containers*, London: Little, Brown and Company.

Hinrichs, C. (2000), "Embeddedness and Local Food Systems: Notes on Two Types of Direct Agricultural Market," *Journal of Rural Studies*, 16: 295–303.

Hinrichs, C. (2003), "The Practice and Politics of Food System Localization," *Journal of Rural Studies*, 19(1): 33–45.

Hirschman, A. O. (1970), *Exit, Voice and Loyalty: Responses to Decline in Firms, Organizations and States*, Cambridge, MA: Harvard University Press.

Hitlin, S., and Piliavin, J. A. (2004), "Values: Reviving a Dormant Concept," *Annual Review of Sociology*, 30: 359–93.

Hobsbawm, E. (1987), *The Age of Empire 1875–1914*, London: Abacus.

Hobsbawm, E., and Ranger, T. (1983), *The Invention of Tradition*, Cambridge: Cambridge University Press.

Hochschild, A. R. (1983), *The Managed Heart: The Commercialization of Human Feeling*, Berkeley, Los Angeles: University of California Press.

Hochschild, A. R. (1997), *The Time Bind: When Work Becomes Home and Home Becomes Work*, New York: Henry Holt & Co.

Hockey, J., Meah, A., and Robinson, V. (2007), *Mundane Heterosexualities: From Theory to Practices*, Basingstoke: Palgrave.

Hodkinson, P. (2011), *Media, Culture and Society: An Introduction*, London: Sage.

Holden, T. J. M. (2005), "The Overcooked and the Underdone: Masculinities in Japanese Food Programming," *Food and Foodways*, 13: 39–65.

Holdway, R., Walker, D., and Hilton, M. (2002), "Eco-Design and Successful Packaging," *Design Management Journal*, 13: 45–53.

Hollander, G. M. (2003), "Re-Naturalizing Sugar: Narratives of Place, Production and Consumption," *Social and Cultural Geography*, 4: 59–74.

Holloway, L. (2002), "Virtual Vegetables and Adopted Sheep: Ethical Relation, Authenticity and Internet-Mediated Food Production Technologies," *Area*, 34: 70–81.

Holloway, L., Kneafsey, M., Venn, L., Cox, R., Dowler, E., and Tuomainen, H. (2007), "Possible Food Economies: A Methodological Framework for Exploring Food Production-Consumption Relationships," *Sociologia Ruralis*, 47: 1–19.

Holloway, S., Valentine, G., and Jayne, M. (2009), "Masculinities, Femininities and the Geographies of Public and Private Drinking Landscapes," *Geoforum*, 40: 821–31.

Hollows, J. (2003a), "Oliver's Twist: Leisure, Labour and Domestic Masculinity in The Naked Chef," *International Journal of Cultural Studies*, 6: 229–48.

Hollows, J. (2003b), "Feeling like a Domestic Goddess: Postfeminism and Cooking," *European Journal of Cultural Studies*, 6: 179–202.

Hollows, J., and Jones, S. (2010), "At Least He's Doing Something: Moral Entrepreneurship and Individual Responsibility in Jamie's Ministry of Food," *European Journal of Cultural Studies*, 13: 307–22.

Holt, D. B. (2006a), "Towards a Sociology of Branding," *Journal of Consumer Culture*, 6: 299–302.

Holt, D. B. (2006b), "'Jack Daniels' America," *Journal of Consumer Culture*, 6: 355–77.

Holtzman, J. (2002), "Politics and Gastropolitics: Gender and the Power of Food in Two African Pastoralist Societies," *Journal of the Royal Anthropological Institute*, 8: 259–78.

Holtzman, J. (2006), "Food and Memory," *Annual Review of Anthropology*, 35: 361–78.

Holtzman, J. (2009), *Uncertain Tastes: Memory, Ambivalence, and the Politics of Eating in Samburu, Northern Kenya*, Berkeley: University of California Press.

hooks, b. (1990), *Yearning: Race, Gender, and Cultural Politics*, Toronto: Between the Lines.

hooks, b. (1992), "Eating the Other: Desire and Resistance," in *Black Looks: Race and Representation*, London: Turnaround, 21–39.

Horowitz, D. (2004), *The Anxieties of Affluence: Critiques of American Consumer Culture, 1939–1979*, Amherst: University of Massachusetts Press.

Howes, D. (2003), *Sensing Culture: Engaging the Senses in Culture and Social Theory*, Ann Arbor: The University of Michigan Press.

Howes, D. (2005), *Empire of the Senses: The Sensual Culture Reader*, Oxford: Berg.

Huggan, G. (1994), "The Postcolonial Exotic: Salman Rushdie and the Booker of Bookers," *Transition*, 62: 22–29.

Hughes, M. (1997), "Soul, Black Women and Soul Food," in C. Counihan and P. Van Esterik (eds.), *Food and Culture: A Reader*, New York: Routledge, 277–80.

Hume, D. (1757/2005), "Of the Standard of Taste," in C. Korsmeyer (ed.), *The Taste Culture Reader*, Oxford: Berg, 197–208.

Hutnyk, J. (2000), *Critique of Exotica: Music, Politics and the Culture Industry*, London: Pluto Press.

Hyder, A., Maman, S., Nyoni, J., Khasiani, S., Teoh, N., et al. (2005), "The Pervasive Triad of Food Security, Gender Inequity and Women's Health: Exploratory Research from Sub-Saharan Africa," *African Health Sciences*, 5: 328–34.

Ilbery, B., and Kneafsey, M. (2000a), "Registering Regional Speciality Food and Drink Products in the United Kingdom: The Case of PDOs and PGIs," *Area*, 32: 317–25.

Ilbery, B., and Kneafsey, M. (2000b), "Producer Constructions of Quality in Regional Speciality Food Production: A Case Study from South West England," *Journal of Rural Studies*, 16: 217–30.

Ilbery, B., Morris, C., Buller, H., Maye, D., and Kneafsey, M. (2005), "Product, Process and Place: An Examination of Food Marketing and Labelling Schemes in Europe and North America," *European Urban and Regional Studies*, 12: 116–32.

Ingold, T. (2000), *The Perception of the Environment: Essays in Livelihood, Dwelling and Skill*, London: Routledge.

Inness, S. A. (2001), *Dinner Roles: American Women and Culinary Culture*, Iowa City: University of Iowa Press.

Irwin, A. (2001), "Constructing the Scientific Citizen: Science and Democracy in the Biosciences," *Public Understanding of Science*, 10: 1–18

ISO 9000:2000 (2004), "Quality Management Systems: Fundamentals and Vocabulary." Available at http://www.iso.org/iso/catalogue_detail?csnumber=29280 (accessed May 21, 2012).

Jackson, P. (1991), "The Cultural Politics of Masculinity: Toward a Social Geography," *Transactions of the Institute of British Geographers*, 16: 199–213.

Jackson, P. (1992), "The Racialization of Labour in Post-war Bradford," *Journal of Historical Geography*, 18: 190–209.

Jackson, P. (2000), "Rematerializing Social and Cultural Geography," *Social and Cultural Geography*, 1: 9–14.

Jackson, P. (2002), "Commercial Cultures: Transcending the Cultural and the Economic," *Progress in Human Geography*, 26: 3–18.

Jackson, P. (ed.) (2009), *Changing Families, Changing Food*, Basingstoke: Palgrave Macmillan.

Jackson, P. (2010), "Food Stories: Consumption in an Age of Anxiety," *Cultural Geographies*, 17: 147–65.

Jackson, P., and Everts, J. (2010), "Anxiety as Social Practice," *Environment and Planning A*, 42: 2791–806.

Jackson, P., and Holbrook, B. (1995), "Multiple Meanings: Shopping and the Cultural Politics of Identity," *Environment and Planning A*, 27: 1913–30

Jackson, P., Lowe, M., Miller, D., and Mort, F. (2000), *Commercial Cultures: Economies, Practices, Spaces*, Oxford: Berg.

Jackson, P., Olive, S., and Smith, G. (2009), "Myths of the Family Meal: Re-Reading Edwardian Life Histories," in P. Jackson (ed.), *Changing Families, Changing Food*, Basingstoke: Palgrave Macmillan, 131–45.

Jackson, P., and Penrose, J. (eds.) (1993), *Constructions of Race, Place and Nation*, London: UCL Press.

Jackson, P., Perez del Aguila, R., Clarke, I., Hallsworth, A., De Kervenoael, R., and Kirkup, M. (2006), "Retail Restructuring and Consumer Choice 2: Understanding Consumer Choice at the Household Level," *Environment and Planning A*, 38: 47–67.

Jackson, P., Russell, P., and Ward, N. (2006), "Mobilising the Commodity Chain Concept in the Politics of Food and Farming," *Journal of Rural Studies*, 22: 129–41.

Jackson, P., Russell, P., and Ward, N. (2007), "The Appropriation of 'Alternative' Discourses by 'Mainstream' Food Producers," in D. Maye, L. Holloway, and M. Kneafsey (eds.), *Alternative Food Geographies: Representation and Practice*, Amsterdam: Elsevier, 309–30.

Jackson, P., Russell, P., and Ward, N. (2011), "Brands in the Making: A Life History Approach," in A. Pike (ed.), *Brands and Branding Geographies*, Cheltenham: Edward Elgar, 59–74.

Jackson, P., Ward, N., and Russell, P. (2009), "Moral Economies of Food and Geographies of Responsibility," *Transactions of the Institute of British Geographers*, 34: 908–24.

Jackson, P., Ward, N., and Russell, P. (2010), "Manufacturing Meaning along the Chicken Supply Chain: Consumer Anxiety and the Spaces of Production," in D. Goodman, M. Goodman, and M. Redclift (eds.), *Consuming Space: Placing Consumption in Perspective*, Aldershot: Ashgate, 163–88.

Jackson, P., Watson, M., and Piper, N. (in press), "Locating Anxiety in the Social: The Cultural Mediation of Food Fears," *European Journal of Cultural Studies*.

Jackson, S. (1999), *Heterosexuality in Question*, London: Sage.

Jacobsen, E. (2004), "The Rhetoric of Food," in M. Lien and B. Nerlich (eds.), *The Politics of Food*, Oxford: Berg, 59–78.

Jaivin, L. (1998), *Eat Me*, New York: Broadway Books.

James, A. (2005), "Identity and the Global Stew," in C. Korsmeyer (ed.), *The Taste Culture Reader: Experiencing Food and Drink*, Oxford: Berg, 372–84.

James, C. (2007), *Global Status of Commercialized Biotech/GM Crops*, Ithaca, NY: ISAAA.

Jamie Go Home (2008), "About." Available at http://jamiegohome.wordpress.com/about/ (accessed January 7, 2012).

Jasanoff, S. (1995), "Product, Process, or Programme: Three Cultures and the Regulation of Biotechnology," in M. Bauer ed. *Resistance to New Technology: Nuclear Power, Information Technology and Biotechnology*, Cambridge: Cambridge University Press, 311–31.

Jasanoff, S. (2005), *Designs on Nature: Science and Democracy in Europe and the United States*, Oxford: Princeton University Press.

Jefkins, F. (2000), *Advertising*, 4th ed., Harlow: Pearson Education.

Jenkins, R. (2004), *Social Identity*, London: Routledge.

Jessop, B. (1995), "The Regulation Approach, Governance and Post-Fordism: Alternative Perspectives on Economic and Political Change?," *Economy and Society*, 24: 307–33.

Joffe, H. (1999), *Risk and "The Other"*, Cambridge: Cambridge University Press.

Johnson, L. (2006), "Browsing the Modern Kitchen: A Feast of Gender, Place and Culture Part 1," *Gender, Place and Culture*, 13: 123–32.

Johnson, R. (2009), "Potential Farm Sector Effects of 2009 H1N1 'Swine Flu': Questions and Answers," in Congressional Research Service, Report for Congress, September 4. Available at http://assets.opencrs.com/rpts/R40575_20090904.pdf (accessed February 9, 2011).

Johnston, J., and Baumann, S. (2007), "Democracy versus Distinction: A Study of Omnivorousness in Gourmet Food Writing," *American Journal of Sociology*, 113: 165–204.

Johnston, J., and Baumann, S. (2010), *Foodies: Democracy and Distinction in the Gourmet Foodscape*, London: Routledge.

Jones, P., Comfort, D., and Hillier, D. (2006), "Healthy Eating and the UK's Major Food Retailers: A Case Study in Corporate Social Responsibility," *British Food Journal*, 108: 838–48.

Julier, A. P. (2004), "Entangled in our Meals: Guilt and Pleasure in Contemporary Food Discourses," *Food, Culture and Society*, 7: 13–21.

Julier, A. P., and Lindenfeld, L. (2005), "Mapping Men onto the Menu: Masculinities and Food," *Food and Foodways*, 13: 1–16.

Kant, I. (1790/2008), *The Critique of Judgement*, Oxford: Oxford University Press.

Karantininis, K., Sauer, J., and Furtan, W. H. (2010), "Innovation and Integration in the Agri-Food Industry," *Food Policy*, 35: 112–20.

Katrak, K. (1997), "Food and Belonging: At 'Home' in 'Alien-kitchens,'" in A. V. Avakian (ed.), *Through the Kitchen Window: Women Explore the Intimate Meanings of Food and Cooking*, Boston: Beacon Press, 263–73.

Kaufman, L. (1980), "Prime Time Nutrition," *Journal of Communication*, 30: 37–46.

Kaufmann, J.-C. (2010), *The Meaning of Cooking*, Cambridge: Polity Press.

Kelly, I. (2005), *Cooking for Kings: The Life of Antoine Carême, the First Celebrity Chef*, New York: Walker & Co.

Kemmer, D. (2000), "Tradition and Change in Domestic Roles and Food Preparation," *Sociology*, 34: 323–33.

Kennedy, E., and Peters, P. (1992), "Household Food Security and Child Nutrition: The Interaction of Income and Gender of Household Head," *World Development*, 20: 1077–85.

Kerr, M., and Charles, N. (1986), "Servers and Providers: The Distribution of Food within the Family," *Sociological Review*, 46: 48–72.

Ketchum, C. (2005), "The Essence of Cooking Shows: How the Food Network Constructs Consumer Fantasies," *Journal of Communication Inquiry*, 29: 217–34.

Kierkegaard, S. (1844/1980), *The Concept of Anxiety*, Princeton, NJ: Princeton University Press.

Kirschenblatt-Gimblett, B., and Bruner, E. (1992), "Tourism," in R. Baunman (ed.), *Folklore, Cultural Performances, and Popular Entertainments*, Oxford: Oxford University Press, 300–7.

Kirwan, J. (2004), "Alternative Strategies in the UK Agro-Food System: Interrogating the Alterity of Farmers' Markets," *Sociologia Ruralis*, 44: 395–415.

Kjaernes, U. (2006), "Trust and Distrust: Cognitive Decisions or Social Relations?," *Journal of Risk Research*, 9: 911–32.

Kjaernes, U., and Dulsrud, A. (1998), "Consumption and Mechanisms of Trust,"

Paper presented to the European Sociology Association conference on the Sociology of Consumption, Milan.

Kjaernes, U., Harvey, M., and Warde, A. (2007), *Trust in Food: A Comparative and Institutional Approach*, Basingstoke: Palgrave-Macmillan.

Klein, N. (2000), *No Logo*, London: Harper-Collins.

Kline, S. J. (1985), "What is Technology?," *Bulletin of Science Technology Society*, 1: 215–18.

Klintman, M. (2002), "The Genetically Modified (GM) Food Labelling Controversy: Ideological and Epistemic Crossovers," *Social Studies of Science*, 32: 71–91.

Kloppenburg, J. R.(2004), *First the Seed: The Political Economy of Plant Biotechnology*, 2nd ed., Madison: University of Wisconsin Press.

Kneale, J. (1999), "A Problem of Supervision: Moral Geographies of the Nineteenth-Century British Public House," *Journal of Historical Geography*, 25: 333–48.

Kneale, J., and French, S. (2008), "Mapping Alcohol: Health, Policy and the Geographies of Problem Drinking in Britain," *Drugs: Education, Prevention, and Policy*, 15: 233–49.

Knowles, T., Moody, R., and McEachern, M. G. (2007), "European Food Scares and Their Impact on EU Food Policy," *British Food Journal*, 109: 43–67.

Kopytoff, I. (1986), "The Cultural Biography of Things: Commoditization as Process," in A. Appadurai (ed.), *The Social Life of Things*, Cambridge: Cambridge University Press.

Korsmeyer, C. (1999), *Making Sense of Taste: Food and Philosophy*, Ithaca, NY: Cornell University Press.

Korsmeyer, C. (2002), "Delightful, Delicious, Disgusting," *The Journal of Aesthetic Art and Criticism*, 60: 217–25.

Korsmeyer, C. (ed.) (2005), *The Taste Culture Reader: Experiencing Food and Drink*, Oxford: Berg.

Krider, R., Raghubir, P., and Krishna, A. (2001), "Pizzas: π or square?: Psychophysical Biases in Area Comparisons," *Marketing Science*, 20: 405–25.

Kusenbach, M. (2003), "Street Phenomenology: The Go-Along as Ethnographic Research Tool," *Ethnography*, 4: 445–85.

Lagrange, L., and Valceschini, E. (2007), "Enjeux Internationaux et Institutionnels des Signes de Qualité et d'Origine," *Économie Rurale*, 3: 4–6.

Landecker, H. (2011), "Food as Exposure: Nutritional Epigenetics and the New Metabolism," *Biosocieties*, 6: 167–94.

Lang, T., Barling, D., and Caraher, M. (2009), *Food Policy: Integrating Health, Environment and Society*, Oxford: Oxford University Press.

Lang, T., and Heasman, M. (2004), *Food Wars: the Global Battle for Mouths, Minds and Markets*, London: Earthscan.

Lappé, F. M., Collins, J., Rosset, P., and Esparza, L. (1998), *World Hunger: Twelve Myths*, 2nd ed., New York: Grove Press.

Lash, S., and Urry, J. (1987), *The End of Organized Capitalism*, Cambridge: Polity Press.

Lash, S., and Urry, J. (1994), *Economies of Signs and Space*, London: Sage.

Laslett, P. (1965), *The World We Have Lost*, New York: Charles Scribner's Sons.

Latour, B. (1988), *The Pasteurization of France*, Cambridge, MA: Harvard University Press.

Latour, B. (2000), "When Things Strike Back: A Possible Contribution of 'Science Studies' to the Social Sciences," *British Journal of Sociology*, 51: 107–23.

Latour, B. (2004a), "How to Talk About the Body? The Normative Dimension of Science Studies," *Body and Society*, 10: 205–29.

Latour, B. (2004b), *The Politics of Nature*, Boston: Harvard University Press.

Latour, B. (2005), *Reassembling the Social: An Introduction to Actor-Network-Theory*, Oxford: Oxford University Press.

Law, L. (2001), "Home Cooking: Filipino Women and Geographies of the Senses in Hong Kong," *Cultural Geographies*, 8(3): 264–83.

Law, O. W., and Wong, S. K. (2000), "Contamination in Food from Packaging Material," *Journal of Chromatography A*, 882: 255–70.

Lawrence, C., and Shapin, S. (eds.) (1998), *Science Incarnate: Historical Embodiments of Natural Knowledge*, Chicago: University of Chicago Press.

Lawrence, F. (2008), "Britain on a Plate" (October 1). Available at http://www.guardian.co.uk/ lifeandstyle/2008/oct/01/foodanddrink.oliver (accessed January 14, 2013).

Lawson, N. (1999), "Gastroporn," *Talk*, October: 153–4.

Lazzarato, M. (1997), *Lavoro Immateriale*, Verona: Ombre Corte.

Leach, E. R. (1961), *Rethinking Anthropology*, London: Athlone Press.

Lears, J. (2009), *Rebirth of a Nation: The Making of Modern America, 1877–1920*, New York: Harper.

Lee, R. (2000), "Shelter from The Storm? Geographies of Regard in the Worlds of Horticultural Consumption and Production," *Geoforum*, 31: 137–57.

Lee, R. P. (2009), "Agri-Food Governance and Expertise: The Production of International Food Standards," *Sociologia Ruralis*, 49: 415–31.

Lee, R. P. (2012), "Knowledge Claims and the Governance of Agri-Food Innovation," *Agriculture and Human Values*, 29: 79–91.

Le Heron, K., and Hayward, D. (2002), "The Moral Commodity: Production, Consumption, and Governance in the Australasian Breakfast Cereal Industry," *Environment and Planning A*, 34: 2231–51.

Le Heron, R. (2003), "Creating Food Futures: Reflections on Food Governance Issues in New Zealand's Agri-Food Sector," *Journal of Rural Studies*, 19: 111–25.

Le Heron, R. (2011), "Performing Provenance in Contemporary Food Geographies," Paper presented at the Association of American Geographers annual meeting, Seattle, Washington.

Lehrer, A. (1969), "Semantic Cuisine," *Journal of Linguistics*, 5: 39–55.

Lester, R. J. (1995), "Emboded Voices: Women's Food Asceticism and the Negotiation of Identity," *Ethos*, 23: 187–222.

Leutchford, P. (2005), "Economic Anthropology and Ethics," in J. G. Carrier (ed.), *A Handbook of Economic Anthropology*, Cheltenham: Edward Elgar, 390–404.

Levenstein, H. A. (1993), *Paradox of Plenty: A Social History of Eating in Modern America*, New York: Oxford University Press.

Levenstein, H. A. (2003), *Revolution at the Table: The Transformation of the American Diet*, Berkeley, Los Angeles: University of California Press.

Lévi-Strauss, C. (1963), *Structural Anthropology*, New York: Basic Books.

Lévi-Strauss, C. (1969), *The Raw and the Cooked: Introduction to a Science of Mythology*, vol. 1, Chicago: University of Chicago Press.

Lewis, M. K., and Hill, A. J. (1998), "'Food Advertising on British Children's Television: A Content Analysis and Experimental Study with Nine-Year-Olds," *Journal of the International Association for the Study of Obesity*, 22: 206–214.

Lien, M. E. (1997), *Marketing and Modernity*, Oxford: Berg.

Lindgreen, A., and Hingley, M. (2003), "The Impact of Food Safety and Animal Welfare Policies on Supply Chain Management: The Case of the Tesco Meat Supply Chain," *British Food Journal*, 105: 328–49.

Lintott, S. (2003), "Sublime Hunger: A Consideration of Eating Disorders Beyond Beauty," *Hypatia*, 18: 65–86.

Llewellyn, M. (2004), "Designed by Women and Designing Women: Gender, Planning and the Geographies of the Kitchen in Britain 1917–1946," *Cultural Geographies*, 10: 42–62.

Lloyd, C., and James, S. (2008), "Too Much Pressure?: Retailer Power and Occupational Health and Safety in the Food Processing Industry," *Work, Employment and Society*, 22: 713–30.

Lloyd, J., and Johnson, L. (2004), "Dream Stuff: The Postwar Home and the Australian Housewife, 1940–1960," *Environmental and Planning D: Society and Space*, 22: 251–72.

Locander, W. B., and Hermann, P. W. (1979), "The Effect of Self-Confidence and Anxiety on Information Seeking in Consumer Risk Reduction," *Journal of Marketing Research*, 16: 268–74.

Lockie, S. (2009), "Responsibility and Agency within Alternative Food Networks: Assembling the Citizen Consumer," *Agriculture and Human Values*, 26: 193–201.

Loeber, A., Hajer, M., and Levidow, L. (2011), "Agro-Food Crises: Institutional and Discursive Changes in the Food Scares Era," *Science as Culture*, 20: 147–55.

Longhurst, R., Johnston, L., and Ho, E. (2009), "A Visceral Approach: Cooking 'At Home' with Migrant Women in Hamilton, New Zealand," *Transactions, Institute of British Geographers*, 34(3): 333–45.

Losey, J., Rayor, L., and Carter, M. (1999), "Transgenic Pollen Harms Monarch Larvae," *Nature*, 399: 214.

Lowe, P., Phillipson, J., and Lee, R. P. (2008), "Socio-Technical Innovation for Sustainable Food Chains: Roles for Social Science," *Trends in Food Science and Technology*, 19: 226–33.

Lowe, P., and Ward, N. (1998), "Regional Policy, CAP Reform and Rural Development in Britain," *Regional Studies*, 32: 469–74.

Lowenthal, D. (1985), *The Past is Another Country*, Cambridge: Cambridge University Press.

Lu, S., and Fine, G. A. (1995), "The Presentation of Ethnic Authenticity: Chinese Food as a

Social Accomplishment," *Sociological Quarterly*, 36: 535–53.

Luhmann, N. (1979), *Trust and Power*, Chichester: Wiley.

Luhmann, N. (1988), "Familiarity, Confidence, Trust: Problems and Alternatives," in D. Gambetta (ed.), *Trust: Making and Breaking Cooperative Relations*, Oxford: Oxford University Press, 94–107.

Lukanuski, M. (1993), "A Place at the Counter: The Onus of Oneness," in R. Scapp and B. Seitz (eds.), *Eating Culture*, New York: State University of New York Press, 112–20.

Lupton, D. (1994), "Food, Memory and Meaning: The Symbolic and Social Nature of Food Events," *Sociological Review*, 42: 664–85.

Lupton, D. (1996), *Food, the Body and the Self*, London: Sage.

Lury, C. (1996), *Consumer Culture*, Cambridge: Polity Press.

Lury, C. (2004), *Brands: The Logos of the Global Economy*, London: Routledge.

Lusk, J. L., Brown, J., Mark, T., Proseku, I., Thompson, R., and Welsh, J. (2006), "Consumer Behavior, Public Policy, and Country-of-Origin Labeling," *Applied Economic Perspectives and Policy*, 28: 284–92.

Lynch, K. (1960), *The Image of the City*, Cambridge, MA: MIT Press.

Lyotard, J.-F. (1979), *The Postmodern Condition: A Report on Knowledge*, Manchester: Manchester University Press.

MacCannell, D. (1973), "Staged Authenticity: Arrangements of Social Space in Tourist Settings," *American Journal of Sociology*, 79: 589–603.

Macht, M. (2008), "How Emotions Affect Eating: A Five-Way Model," *Appetite*, 50: 1–11.

Macintyre, S., Reilly, J., Miller, D., and Eldridge, J. (1998), "Food Choice, Food Scares and Health: Role of the Media," in A. Murcott (ed.), *The Nation's Diet: The Social Science of Food Choice*, London: Longman, 228–49.

Macleans (2007), "The Truth about 'Organic' Food." Available at http://www.macleans. ca/science/environment/article.jsp?cont ent=20070910_109141_109141 (accessed January 14, 2013).

Malam, S., Clegg, S., Kirwan, S., and McGinigal, S. (2009), "Comprehension and Use of UK Nutrition Signpost Labelling Schemes," BMRB Social Research for UK Food Standards Agency, April. Available at http://www.food. gov.uk/multimedia/pdfs/pmptechannexe.pdf (accessed March 21, 2012).

Malinowski, B. (1922), *Argonauts of the Western Pacific*, London: Routledge & Kegan Paul.

Malpas, J. (1999), *Place and Experience*, Cambridge: Cambridge University Press.

Mansfield, B. (2003), "Spatializing Globalization: A 'Geography of Quality' in the Seafood Industry," *Economic Geography*, 79: 1–16.

Marris, C., Wynne, B., Simmons, P., and Weldon, S. (2001), *Public Perceptions of Agricultural Biotechnologies in Europe*, Lancaster: University of Lancaster.

Mars, G. (1982), *Cheats at Work: An Anthropology of Workplace Crime*, London: George Allen & Unwin.

Marsden, T. (2000), "Food Matters and the Matter of Food: Towards a New Food Governance?," *Sociologia Ruralis*, 40: 20–29.

Marx, K. (1867/1976), *Capital: A Critique of Political Economy*, vol. 1, Harmondsworth: Penguin.

Massey, D. (1991), "A Global Sense of Place," *Marxism Today* (June): 24–29.

Massey, D. (1993), "Power-Geometry and a Progressive Sense of Place," in J. Bird, B. Curtis, T. Putnam, G. Robertson, and L. Tickner (eds.), *Mapping the Futures: Local Culture, Global Change*, London: Routledge, 60–70.

Massey, D. (1995), "Places and their Pasts," *History Workshop Journal*, 39: 182–92.

Massey, D. (2004), "Geographies of Responsibility," *Geografiska Annaler*, 86B: 5–18.

Massey, D. (2005), *For Space*, London: Sage.

Massumi, B. (2009), "National Enterprise Emergency," *Theory, Culture and Society*, 26: 153–85.

Mather, C., and Marshall, A. (2010), "Biosecurity's Unruly Spaces," *Geographical Journal*, 177: 300–10.

Matthews, J., Gunter, B., and Dickinson, R. (2009), *The Nature of Infant Formula and Follow-On Formula Advertising and Presentation*. Available at http://www2.le.ac.uk/departments/media/ documents/375-1-653-Research-project-1- report-for-publication-September-09.pdf (accessed July 15, 2011).

Mauss, M. (1923/1990), *The Gift: The Form and Reason for Exchange in Archaic Societies*, New York: W.W. Norton.

Mauss, M. (1925/1970), "Essai sur le don", *Année Sociologique*, reprinted as *The Gift: The Forms and Functions of Exchange in Archaic Societies*, London: Routledge.

Mauss, M. (1934/1973), "Techniques of the Body," *Economy and Society*, 2: 70–88.

May, J. (1996), "A Little Taste of Something More Exotic: The Imaginative Geographies of Everyday Life," *Geography*, 81: 57–64.

May, R. (1950), *The Meaning of Anxiety*, New York: Ronald Press.

Maye, D., Holloway, L., and Kneafsey, M. (2007), *Alternative Food Geographies: Representation and Practice*, Oxford: Elsevier.

McArdle, M. (2011), "The Joy of Not Cooking," *The Atlantic Magazine*. Available at http://www.theatlantic.com/magazine/archive/2011/05/the-joy-of-not-cooking/8442/ (accessed March 14, 2012).

McCluskey, J., and Swinnen, J. (2011), "The Media and Food-risk Perceptions," *European Molecular Biology Organisation Reports*, 12: 624–9.

McGee, T. G. (1973), *Hawkers in Hong Kong: A Study of Planning and Policy in a Third World City*, University of Hong Kong: Centre of Asian Studies.

McGuigan, J. (2009), *Cool Capitalism*, London: Pluto Press.

McLean, A. (2004), "Tasting Language: The Aesthetic of Pleasures of Elizabeth David," *Food, Culture and Society*, 7: 37–45.

McMahon, A. (1999), *Taking Care of Men: Sexual Politics in the Public Mind*, Cambridge: Cambridge University Press.

McMichael, P. (2005), "Global Development and The Corporate Food Regime," *Research in Rural Sociology and Development*, 11: 265–99.

McRobbie, A. (2009), *The Aftermath of Feminism: Gender, Culture and Social Change*, Los Angeles: Sage.

McWilliams, J. (2012), "Meat: What Big Agriculture and the Ethical Butcher Have in Common" (February 8). Available at http://www.theatlantic.com/health/archive/2012/02/meat-what-big-agriculture-and-the-ethical-butcher-have-in-common/252679/ (accessed January 14, 2013).

Meadows, D. H., Meadows, D. L., Randers, J., and Behrens III, J. (1972), *The Limits to Growth*, New York: Universe Books.

Meah, A. (2001), "Reflecting upon a Feminist Research Process: A Study of Gatekeeping in HIV/AIDS Organisations in Durban," PhD thesis, University of Manchester.

Meah, A., and Jackson, P. (2013), "Crowded Kitchens: the 'Democratisation' of Domesticity," *Gender, Place and Culture*, 20: 578–596.

Meah, A., and Watson, M. (2011), "Saints and Slackers: Challenging Discourses about the Decline of Domestic Cooking," *Sociological Research Online*, 16(2). Available at http://www.socresonline.org.uk/16/2/6.html.

Meah, A., and Watson, M. (2013), "Cooking up Consumer Anxieties about 'Provenance' and 'Ethics': Why it Sometimes Matters where Foods Come from in Domestic Provisioning," *Food, Culture and Society*, 16: 495–512.

Mennell, S. (1985), *All Manners of Food: Eating and Taste in England and France from the Middle Ages to the Present*, Oxford: Blackwell.

Mennell, S., Murcott, A., and van Otterloo, A. (1992), *The Sociology of Food, Eating, Diet and Culture*, London: Sage.

Merleau-Ponty, M. (1945/1962), *Phenomenology of Perception*, London: Routledge and Kegan Paul.

Metcalfe, A., Dryden, C., Johnson, M., Owen, J., and Shipton, G. (2009), "Fathers, Food and Family Life," in P. Jackson (ed.), *Changing Families, Changing Food*, Basingstoke: Palgrave Macmillan, 93–117.

Miele, M., and Evans, A. (2010), "When Food Becomes Animals: Rumination on Ethics and Responsibility in Care-Full Practices of Consumption," *Ethics, Place and Environment*, 13: 171–90.

Miele, M., and Murdoch, J. (2002), "The Practical Aesthetics of Traditional Cuisines: Slow Food in Tuscany," *Sociologia Ruralis*, 42: 312–28.

Miles, R. (1989), *Racism*, London: Routledge.

Miller, D. (1987), *Material Culture and Mass Consumption*, Oxford: Blackwell.

Miller, D. (1988), "Appropriating the State on the Council Estate," *Man*, 23: 353–72.

Miller, D. (1998a), *Material Cultures: Why Some Things Matter*, Chicago: University of Chicago.

Miller, D. (1998b), *A Theory of Shopping*, Ithaca, NY: Cornell University Press.

Miller, D. (1998c), "Coca-Cola: A Black Sweet Drink from Trinidad," in D. Miller (ed.), *Material Cultures*, London: UCL Press, 169–87.

Miller, D. (1999), "Risk, Science and Policy: Definitional Struggles, Information Management, the Media and BSE," *Social Science and Medicine*, 49: 1239–55.

Miller, D. (2000), "The Birth of Value," in P. Jackson, M. Lowe, D. Miller, and F. Mort (eds.), *Commercial Cultures*, Oxford: Berg, 77–83.

Miller, D. (2001), *The Dialectics of Shopping*, Chicago: University of Chicago Press.

Miller, D. (2008), *The Comfort of Things*, Cambridge: Polity.

Miller, D., Jackson, P., Holbrook, B., Thrift, N., and Rowlands, M. (1998), *Shopping, Place and Identity*, London: Routledge.

Miller, P., and O'Leary, T. (1994), "The Factory as Laboratory," *Science in Context*, 7: 469–96.

Miller, P., and Rose, N. (1995), "Production, Identity, and Democracy," *Theory and Society*, 24: 427–67.

Miller, R. (1991), "'Selling Mrs Consumer': Advertising and the Creation of Suburban Socio-Spatial Relations, 1910–1930," *Antipode*, 23: 263–301.

Miller, W. (1997), *The Anatomy of Disgust*, Cambridge, MA: Harvard University Press.

Mills, C. M., and Keil, F. C. (2005), "The Development of Cynicism," *Psychological Science*, 16: 385–90.

Mills, M. B. (2005), "From Nimble Fingers to Raised Fists: Women and Labour Activism in Globalising Thailand," *Signs*, 3: 117–44.

Millstone, E., Thompson, J., and Brooks, S. (2009), *Reforming the Global Food and Agriculture System: Towards a Questioning Agenda for the New Manifesto*, STEPS Working Paper 26, Brighton: STEPS Centre.

Milne, R. (2011), "A Focus Group Study of Food Safety Practices in Relation to Listeriosis among the Over-60s," *Critical Public Health*, 21: 485–95.

Milne, R. (in press), "Arbiters of Waste: Date Labels and the Contingent Definition of Good, Safe Food," *Sociological Review Monographs*.

Milne, R., Wenzer, J., Brembeck, H., and Brodin, M. (2011), "Fraught Cuisine: Food Scares and the Modulation of Anxieties," *Distinktion: Scandinavian Journal of Social Theory*, 12: 177–92.

Milton, A., and Mullan, B. (2010), "Consumer Food Safety Education for the Domestic Environment: A Systematic Review," *British Food Journal*, 112: 1003–22.

Mincyte, D. (2011), "Homogenizing Europe: Raw Milk, Risk Politics, and Moral Economies in Post-Socialist Lithuania," Paper presented at Ethical Foods and Food

Movements in Postsocialist Settings, London: SOAS.

Ming, X., Weber, G. H., Ayres, J. W., and Sandinde, W. E. (1997), "Bacteriocins Applied to Food Packaging Materials to Inhibit *Listeria monocytogenes* on Meats," *Journal of Food Science*, 62: 413–15.

Mintz, S. (1985), *Sweetness and Power: The Place of Sugar in Modern History*, New York: Viking Penguin.

Mintz, S. (1996), *Tasting Food, Tasting Freedom: Excursions into Eating, Culture, and the Past*, Boston: Beacon Press.

Mintz, S. (2006), "Food at Moderate Speeds," in R. Wilk (ed.), *Fast Food/Slow Food: The Cultural Economy of the Global Food System*, Walnut Creek, CA: Altamira Press, 3–12.

Mitchell, D. (1996), *The Lie of the Land: Migrant Workers and the California Landscape*, Minneapolis: University of Minnesota Press.

Mitchell, K. (1997), "Different Diasporas and the Hype of Hybridity," *Environment and Planning D: Society and Space*, 15: 533–53.

Mohun, S. (1991), "Machinery and Machinofacture," in T. Bottomore, L. Harris, V. G. Kiernan, and R. Miliband (eds.), *A Dictionary of Marxist Thought*, 2nd ed., Oxford: Blackwell, 331–32.

Mol, A. (2008), "I Eat an Apple: On Theorizing Subjectivities," *Subjectivity*, 22: 28–37.

Mol, A. (2009), "Good Taste: The Embodied Normativity of the Consumer-Citizen," *Journal of Cultural Economy*, 2: 269–83.

Mollering, G. (2001), "The Nature of Trust: From Georg Simmel to a Theory of Expectation," *Interpretation and Suspension Sociology*, 35: 403–20.

Molz, J. G. (2003), "Tasting an Imagined Thailand: Authenticity and Culinary Tourism in Thai Restaurants," in L. M. Long (ed.), *Culinary Tourism*, Lexington: University Press of Kentucky, 53–75.

Moon, Y. S. (2010), "How Food Ads Communicate 'Health' with Children: A Content Analysis of Korean Television Commercials," *Asian Journal of Communication*, 20: 456–76.

Moore, E. S. (2006), *It's Child's Play: Advergaming and the Online Marketing of Food to Children*, Menlo Park, CA: Kaiser Family Foundation.

Morgan, K. (2010), "Local and Green, Global and Fair: The Ethical Foodscape and the Politics of Care," *Environment and Planning A*, 42: 1852–67.

Morgan, K., Marsden, T., and Murdoch, J. (2006), *Worlds of Food: Place, Power, and Provenance in the Food Chain*, Oxford: Oxford University Press.

Morgan, K., and Murdoch, J. (2000), "Organic vs. Conventional Agriculture: Knowledge, Power and Innovation in the Food Chain," *Geoforum*, 31: 159–73.

Morley, D. (1980), *The Nationwide Audience*, London: British Film Institution.

Morley, D. (1992), *Television, Audiences and Cultural Studies*, London: Routledge.

Morley, D. (1993), "Active Audience Theory: Pendulums and Pitfalls," *Journal of Communication*, 43: 13–19.

Morris, J. (2007), *The Cappuccion Conquests: The Transnational History of Italian Coffee*, University of Hertfordshire, Exhibition Catalogue.

Mudry, J. (2009), *Measured Meals: Nutrition in America*, Albany: State University of New York Press.

Munro, M., and Madigan, R. (1999), "Negotiating Space in the Family Home," in I. Cieraad (ed.), *At Home: An Anthropology of Domestic Space*, Syracuse, NY: Syracuse University Press, 107–17.

Murcott, A. (1983a), "Cooking and the Cooked: A Note on the Domestic Preparation of Meals," in A. Murcott (ed.), *The Sociology of Food and Eating*, Aldershot: Gower, 178–93.

Murcott, A. (1983b), "It's a Pleasure to Cook for Him: Food, Mealtimes and Gender in some South Wales Households," in E. Gamarnikow, D. Morgan, J. Purvis, and D. Taylorson (eds.), *The Public and the Private*, London: Heinemann, 78–90.

Murcott, A. (1997), "Family Meals: A Thing of the Past?," in P. Caplan (ed.), *Food, Health and Identity*, London: Routledge, 32–49.

Murcott, A. (1999), "'Not Science but PR': GM Food and the Makings of a Considered Sociology," *Sociological Research Online*, 4(3): n.p.

Murcott, A. (2000), "Is it Still a Pleasure to Cook for Him? Social Changes in the Household and the Family," *Journal of Consumer Culture*, 24: 78–84.

Murcott, A. (2011), "The BSA and the Emergence of a 'Sociology of Food': A Personal View," *Sociological Research Online*, 16(3): 14. Available at http://www.socresonline.org.uk/16/3/14.html (accessed January 10, 2012).

Murdoch, J. (2005), *Post-Structuralist Geography: A Guide to Relational Space*, London: Sage.

Murdoch, J., Marsden, T., and Banks, J. (2000), "Quality, Nature, and Embeddedness: Some Theoretical Considerations in the Context of Food Systems," *Economic Geography*, 76: 107–25.

Murdoch, J., and Miele, M. (1999), "'Back to Nature': Changing 'Worlds of Production' in the Food Sector," *Sociologia Ruralis*, 39: 465–83.

Muxel, A. (1996), *Individu et Memoire Familiale*, Paris: Nathan.

Narayan, U. (1995), "Eating Cultures: Incorporation, Identity and Indian Food," *Social Identities*, 1: 63–86.

Natalier, K. (2003), "'I'm Not His Wife': Doing Gender and Doing Housework in the Absence of Women," *Journal of Sociology*, 39: 253–69.

National Restaurant Association (2011), *2011 Restaurant Industry Pocket Factbook*, Washington, D.C.: National Restaurant Association.

Nestle, M. (2002), *Food Politics: How the Food Industry Influences Nutrition and Health*, Berkeley, Los Angeles: University of California Press.

Nestle, M. (2010), *Safe Food: The Politics of Food Safety*, Berkeley, Los Angeles: University of California Press.

Newby, H. (1977), *The Deferential Worker: A Study of Farm Workers in East Anglia*, Harmondsworth: Penguin.

New York Times (1994), "Giuliani Broadens Crackdown to Banish All Illegal Vendors" (May 9). Available at http://www.nytimes.com/1994/05/09/nyregion/giuliani-broadens-crackdown-to-banish-all-illegal-vendors.html?src=pm (accessed January 14, 2013).

Nora, P. (1989), "Between Memory and History: Les Lieux de Memoire," *Representations*, 26: 7–25.

Novero, C. (2000), "Stories of Food: Recipes of Modernity, Recipes of Tradition in Weimar Germany," *Journal of Popular Culture*, 34: 163–82.

Nowotny, H. (1992), "Time and Social Theory," *Time and Society*, 1: 421–54.

Nygård, B., and Storstad, O. (1998), "De-Globalization of Food Markets? Consumer Perceptions of Safe Food: The Case of Norway," *Sociologia Ruralis*, 38: 35–53.

Oakes, T. (1999), "Eating the Food of the Ancestors: Place, Tradition, and Tourism in a Chinese Frontier River Town," *Ecumene*, 6: 123–45.

Oakley, A. (1974), *The Sociology of Housework*, London: Martin Robertson.

Obama, B. (2009), "Memorandum on Transparency and Open Government". Available at http://www.fda.gov/AboutFDA/Transparency/TransparencytoRegulatedIndustry/PhaseIIITransparencyReport/FDATransparencyInitiative/default.htm.

The Observer (2005), "Britain's Organic Food Scam Exposed" (August 21). Available at http://www.guardian.co.uk/uk/2005/aug/21/foodanddrink.organics1 (accessed January 14, 2013).

O'Brien, M. (2007), *A Crisis of Waste? Understanding the Rubbish Society*, London: Routledge.

Offer, A. (2006), *The Challenge of Affluence: Self-Control and Well-Being in the United States and Britain since 1950*, Oxford: Oxford University Press.

Ohnuki-Tierney, E. (1997), "McDonald's in Japan: Changing Manners and Etiquette," in J. Watson (ed.), *Golden Arches East: McDonald's in East Asia*, Palo Alto, CA: Stanford University Press, 161–82.

Oliver, J. (1999), *The Naked Chef*, London: Michael Joseph.

O'Neill, J., Holland, A., and Light, A. (2008), *Environmental Values*, New York: Routledge.

O'Neill, O. (2002), *A Question of Trust: The BBC Reith Lectures*, Cambridge: Newnham College.

Opie, F. D. (2008), *Hog and Hominy: Soul Food from Africa to America*, New York: Columbia University Press.

Organic Consumers Association (2006), "Business Week: Wal-Mart's Organic offensive", Available at: http:// www.organicconsumers.org/articles/article_204.cfm, accessed January 14, 2013.

Orwell, G. (1937), *The Road to Wigan Pier*, London: Victor Gollancz.

Orwell, G. (1970), "Politics and the English Language," in S. Orwell and I. Angus (eds.), *The Collected Essays, Journalism and Letters of George Orwell, Vol. 4: In Front of your Nose, 1945–1950*, Harmondsworth: Penguin, 156–70.

Ouma, S. (2010), "Global Standards, Local Realities: Private Agrifood Governance and the Restructuring of the Kenya Horticulture Industry," *Economic Geography*, 86: 197–222.

Ozdemir, M., and Floros, J. D. (2010), "Active Food Packaging Technologies," *Critical Reviews in Food Science and Nutrition*, 44: 185–93.

Packard, V. (1957), *The Hidden Persuaders*, New York: Simon & Schuster.

Pain, R., and Smith, S. (eds.) (2008), *Fear: Critical Geopolitics and Everyday Life*, Aldershot: Ashgate.

Parasecoli, F. (2008), *Bite Me: Food in Popular Culture*, Oxford: Berg.

Parfitt, J., and Barthel, M. (2011), *Global Food Waste Reduction: Priorities for a World in Transition*, Science Review SR56, Foresight Project on Global Food and Farming Futures, London: Stationery Office.

Parkin, K. J. (2006), *Food is Love: Food Advertising and Gender Roles in Modern America*, Philadelphia: University of Pennsylvania Press.

Parkins, W., and Craig, G. (2006), *Slow Living*, Sydney: University of New South Wales Press.

Parrott, N., Wilson, N., and Murdoch, J. (2002), "Spatializing Quality: Regional Protection and the Alternative Geography of Food," *European Urban and Regional Studies*, 9: 241–61.

Pascali, L. (2006), "Two Stoves, Two Refrigerators, *due cucine*: The Italian Kitchen Immigrant Kitchens," *Gender Place and Culture*, 13: 685–95.

Patel, R. (2007), *Stuffed and Starved: Markets, Power and the Hidden Battle for the World's Food System*, London: Portobello Books.

Paterson, M. (2006), *Consumption and Everyday Life*, London, New York: Routledge.

Paxson, H. (2005), "Slow Food in a Fat Society: Satisfying Ethical Appetites," *Gastronomica*, 5: 14–18.

Paxson, H. (2011), "The 'Art' and 'Science' of Hand Crafting Cheese in the United States," *Endeavour*, 35(2–3): 116–24.

Peel, C. S. (1933), *Life's Enchanted Cup: An Autobiography*, London: John Lane.

Peet, R., and Watts, M. (eds.) (1996), *Liberation Ecologies: Environment, Development, Social Movements*, London: Routledge.

Peine, E., and McMichael, P. (2005), "Globalization and Global Governance," in V. Higgins and G. Lawrence (eds.), *Agricultural Governance: Globalization and the New Politics of Regulation*, London: Routledge, 19–34.

Peñaloza, L. (1994), "Atravesando Fronteras/Border Crossings: A Critical Ethnographic Exploration of the Consumer Acculturation of Mexican Immigrants," *Journal of Consumer Research*, 21: 32–54.

Perks, R. (2010), "'Corporations are People Too!' Business and Corporate Oral History in Britain," *Oral History*, 38: 36–54.

Perks, R., and Thomson, A. (eds.) (2006), *The Oral History Reader*, London: Routledge.

Perrow, C. (1999), *Normal Accidents: Living with High-Risk Technologies*, Princeton, NJ: Princeton University Press.

Peterson, R., and Kern, R. (1996), "Changing Highbrow Taste: From Snob to Omnivore," *American Sociological Review*, 61: 900–7.

Peterson, R. A. (1997), *Creating Country Music: Fabricating Authenticity*, Chicago: University of Chicago Press.

Petridou, E. (2001), "The Taste of Home," in D. Miller (ed.), *Home Possessions: Material Culture Behind Closed Doors*, Oxford: Berg, 87–104.

Petrini, C. (2004), *Slow Food: The Case for Taste*, New York: Columbia University Press.

Phillips, A., and Taylor, B. (1980), "Sex and Skill: Notes Towards a Feminist Economics," *Signs*, 6: 79–88.

Phillips, J., and French, M. (1998), "Adulteration and Food Law, 1899–1939," *Twentieth Century British History*, 9(3): 350–69.

Phillips, Lord N., Bridgeman, J., and Ferguson-Smith, M.A. (2001), *The BSE Inquiry*, London: Stationery Office.

Pickering, A. (1995), *The Mangle of Practice: Time, Agency and Science*, Chicago: University of Chicago Press.

Pike, A. (ed.) (2011), *Brands and Branding Geography*, Cheltenham: Edward Elgar.

Pile, S., and Thrift, N. (eds.) (2000), *City A–Z: Urban Fragments*, London: Routledge.

Pinch, T. J., and Bijker, W. E. (1984), "The Social Construction of Facts and Artifacts: Or How the Sociology of Science and the Sociology of Technology might Benefit Each Other," *Social Studies of Science*, 14: 399–441.

Piore, M. J. (1979), *Birds of Passage: Migrant Labour and Industrial Societies*, Cambridge: Cambridge University Press.

Piper, N. (2011), "Engaging with Jamie Oliver in Rotherham and Tunbridge Wells," Paper presented to the Association of American Geographers annual meeting, Seattle, Washington.

Piper, N. (in press), "Audiencing Jamie Oliver: Embarrassment, Voyeurism and Reflexive Positioning," *Geoforum*.

Pitts, M., Pattie, C., and Dorling, D. (2007), "Christmas Feasting and Social Class: Christmas Feasting and Everyday Consumption," *Food, Culture and Society*, 10: 407–24.

Polanyi, K. (1944/1957), *The Great Transformation: The Political and Economic Origins of Our Time*, New York: Holt, Rinehart & Winston.

Pollan, M. (2002), *The Botany of Desire: A Plant's-Eye View of the World*, New York: Random House.

Pollan, M. (2006), *The Omnivore's Dilemma: Natural History of Four Meals*, New York: Penguin.

Pollan, M. (2009), *Food Rules: An Eater's Manual*, London: Penguin.

Pollay, R. W., and Gallagher, K. (1990), "Advertising and Cultural Values: Reflections in the Distorted Mirror," *International Journal of Advertising*, 9: 361–74.

Poole, S. (2012), "Let's Start the Foodie Backlash", *The Guardian* (September 28). Available at: http://www.guardias.co.

Popay, J., Hearn, J., and Edwards, J. (1998), *Men, Gender Divisions and Welfare*, London: Routledge.

Popkin, B. M. (2004), "The Nutrition Transition: An Overview of World Patterns of Change," *Nutrition Reviews*, 62: S140–S143.

Popkin, B. M. (2007), "The World is Fat," *Scientific American*, 297: 88–95.

Potter, C., and Tilzey, M. (2005), "Agricultural Policy Discourses in the European Post-Fordist Transition: Neo-Liberalism, Neo-Mercantilism and Multifunctionality," *Progress in Human Geography*, 29: 581–600.

Pratten, J. D. (2003), "What Makes a Good Chef?," *British Food Journal*, 105: 454–9.

Pretty, J., Sutherland, W. J., Ashby, J., Auburn, J., Baulcombe, D., et al. (2010), "The Top 100 Questions of Importance to the Future of Global Agriculture," *International Journal of Agricultural Sustainability*, 8: 219–36.

Probyn, E. (2000), *Carnal Appetites: Food Sex Identities*, London, New York: Routledge.

Probyn, E. (2012), "In the Interests of Taste and Place: Economies of Attachment," in G. Pratt and V. Rosner (eds.), *The Global and the Intimate: Feminism in Our Time*, New York: Columbia University Press, 57–84.

Proust, M. (1913/1922), *Remembrance of Things Past. Volume 1: Swann's Way, within a Budding Grove*, New York: Vintage.

Pryer, D., and Hewitt, P. (2010), "CJD: Risk Communication in a Healthcare Setting," in P. G. Bennett, K. Calman, S. Curtis, and D. Fischbacher-Smith (eds.), *Risk Communication* and *Public Health*, 2nd ed., Oxford: Oxford University Press, 163–80.

Pullman, M. E., and Dillard, J. (2010), "Values-Based Supply Chain Management and Emergent Organizational Structures," *International Journal of Operations and Production Management*, 30: 744–71.

Quested, T., and Parry, A. (2011), *New Estimates for Household Food and Drink Waste in the UK*, Banbury: WRAP.

Ram, U. (2007), "Liquid Identities: Mecca Cola versus Coca-Cola," *European Journal of Cultural Studies*, 10(4): 465–84.

Rampton, S., and Stauber, J. (2002), *Trust Us, We're Experts!: How Industry Manipulates Science and Gambles with Your Future*, New York: Penguin Putnam Inc.

Rancière, J. (2004), *The Politics of Aesthetics: The Distribution of the Sensible*, London: Continuum.

Rathje, W., and Murphy, C. (1992), *Rubbish! The Archaeology of Garbage*, New York: Harper Collins.

Rausing, S. (1998), "Signs of the New Nation: Gift Exchange, Consumption and Aid on a Former Collective Farm in North-West Estonia," in D. Miller (ed.), *Material Cultures: Why Some Things Matter*, London: UCL Press, 189–213.

Ray, K. (2004), *The Migrant's Table: Meals and Memories in Bengali-American Households*, Philadelphia: Temple University Press.

Reardon, J. (1994), *M.F.K. Fisher, Julia Child and Alice Waters: Celebrating the Pleasures of the Table*, New York: Harmony Books.

Reckwitz, A. (2002), "Toward a Theory of Social Practices: A Development in Culturalist Theorizing," *European Journal of Social Theory*, 5: 243–63.

Reid, S. E. (2002), "Cold War in the Kitchen: Gender and the De-Stalinization of Consumer Taste in the Soviet Union under Khrushchev," *Slavic Review*, 61: 211–52.

Reilly, J. (1999), "Just another Food Scare?: Public Understanding and the BSE Crisis," in G. Philo (ed.), Message *Received Glasgow Media Group Research 1993–1998*, Essex, New York: Longman, 128–45.

Reilly, J., and Miller, D. (1997), "Scaremonger or Scapegoat: The Role of the Media in the Emergence of Food as a Social Issue," in P. Caplan (ed.), *Food, Health and Identity*, London: Routledge, 234–51.

Reimer, S., and Leslie, D. (2004), "Identity, Consumption, and the Home," *Home Cultures*, 1: 187–208.

Reissig, C. J., Strain, E. C., and Griffiths, R. R. (2009), "Caffeinated Energy Drinks: A Growing Problem," *Drug and Alcohol Dependence*, 99: 1–10.

Relph, E. C. (1976), *Place and Placelessness*, London: Pion.

Renard, M. (2005), "Quality Certification, Regulation and Power in Fair Trade," *Journal of Rural Studies*, 21: 419–31.

Rhodes, R. (1997), *Deadly Feasts: Tracking the Secrets of a Terrifying New Plague*, New York: Simon & Schuster.

Ribeiro, R., and Collins, H. (2007), "The Bread-Making Machine: Tacit Knowledge and Two Types of Action," *Organization Studies*, 28: 1417–33.

Rich, E. (2011), "'I See Her Being Obesed!': Public Pedagogy, Reality Media and the Obesity Crisis," *Health*, 15: 3–21.

Richards, C., Lawrence, G., and Burch, D. (2011), "Supermarkets and Agro-industrial Foods: The Strategic Manufacturing of Consumer Trust," *Food, Culture and Society*, 14: 29–47.

Richards, P. (1985), *Indigenous Agricultural Revolution: Ecology and Food Production in West Africa*, London: Hutchinson.

Richmond, M. (1990), *The Microbiological Safety of Food: Report of the Committee on the Microbiological Safety of Food*. London: HMSO.

Ritzer, G. (1993), *The McDonaldization of Society*, Thousand Oaks, CA: Pine Forge Press.

Ritzer, G. (1998), *The McDonaldization Thesis: Extensions and Explorations*, London: Sage.

Robson, E. (2006), "The 'Kitchen' as Women's Space in Rural Hausaland, Northern Nigeria," *Gender, Place and Culture*, 13: 669–76.

Roche, E. (2004), "If You Can't Stand the Heat, Get Some Balls," *The Guardian*. Available at http://www.guardian.co.uk/theguardian/2004/jan/28/features11.g21 (accessed March 14, 2012).

Roden, C. (1974), *A Book of Middle Eastern Food*, New York: Vintage.

Roe, E. J. (2006), "Things Becoming Food and the Embodied, Material Practices of an Organic Food Consumer," *Sociologia Ruralis*, 46: 104–21.

Rojek, C. (2001), *Celebrity*, London: Reaktion.

Rollin, F., Kennedy, J., and Wills, J. (2011), "Consumers and New Food Technologies," *Trends in Food Science and Technology*, 22: 99–111.

Roos, G., Prättälä, R., and Koski, K. (2001), "Men, Masculinity and Food: Interviews with Finnish Carpenters and Engineers," *Appetite*, 37: 47–56.

Røpke, I. (2009), "Theories of Practice: New Inspiration for Ecological Economic Studies on Consumption," *Ecological Economics*, 68: 2490–7.

Rousseau, G., and Porter, R. (eds.) (1990), *Exoticism in the Enlightenment*, Manchester: Manchester University Press.

Rowe, G., and Frewer, L. J. (2000), "Public Participation Methods: A Framework for Evaluation," *Science, Technology and Human Values*, 25: 3–29.

Rozin, P. (1976), "The Selection of Foods by Rats, Humans and other Animals," in J. S. Rosenblatt, R. A. Hinde, E. Shaw, and C. Beer (eds.), *Advances in the Study of Behavior*, vol. 6, London, New York: Academic Press, 21–76.

Rozin, P. (1999), "Food is Fundamental, Fun, Frightening and Far-Reaching," *Social Research*, 66: 9–30.

Rozin, P., Fischler, C., Imada, S., Sarubin, A., and Wrzesniewski, A. (1999), "Attitudes toward Food and the Role of Food in Life in the USA, Japan, Flemish Belgium and France: Possible Implications for the Diet-Health Debate," *Appetite*, 33: 163–80.

Rozin, P., Haidt, J., and McCauley, C. R. (2008), "Disgust: The Body and Soul Emotion in the 21st Century," in D. McKay and O. Olatunji (eds.), *Disgust and its Disorders*, Washington, D.C.: American Psychological Association, 9–29.

Ruark, J. K. (1999), "A Place at the Table," *The Chronicle of Higher Education* (9 July), A17–A19.

Russell, P. (2003), "Narrative Constructions of British Culinary Culture," PhD diss., University of Sheffield.

Russell, P. (2008), "Manufacturing Memories: Commercial, Team and Individual Narratives in Poultry Production," *Oral History*, 36: 81–94.

Rutherford, J. (1990), "A Place Called Home," in J. Rutherford (ed.), *Identity: Community, Culture, Difference*, London: Lawrence and Wishart, 9–27.

Saarikangas, K. (2006), "Displays of the Everyday Relations between Gender and the Visibility of Domestic Work in the Modern Finnish Kitchen from the 1930s to the 1950s," *Gender, Place and Culture*, 13: 161–72.

Sack, R. (1992), *Place, Modernity and the Consumer's World*, Baltimore, MD: Johns Hopkins University Press.

Sack, R. (1997), *Homogeographicus: a Framework for Action, Awareness and Moral Concern*, Baltimore, MD: Johns Hopkins University Press.

Sack, R. (2003), *A Geographical Guide to the Real and the Good*, London: Routledge.

Safran Foer, J. (2009), *Eating Animals*, London: Penguin.

Sahlins, M. D. (1972), *Stone Age Economics*, Berlin: Aldine de Gruyter.

Said, E. W. (1978), *Orientalism*, New York: Pantheon Books.

Saito, Y. (2001), "Everyday Aesthetics," *Philosophy and Literature*, 25: 87–95.

Saldanha, A. (2006), "Reontologising Race: The Machinic Geography of Phenotype," *Environment and Planning D: Society and Space*, 24: 9–24.

Salecl, R. (2004), *On Anxiety*, London: Routledge.

Salvatore, A., and Sassatelli, R. (2004), "Trust and Food: A Theoretical Discussion," Working Paper, Consumer Trust in Food: A European Study of the Social and Institutional Conditions for the Production of Trust. Available at http://www.trustinfood.org (accessed March 21, 2012).

Samuel, R., and Thompson, P. (eds.) (1990), *The Myths We Live By*, London: Routledge.

Sanders, L. (2009), "Consuming Nigella," in S. Gillis, and J. Hollows (eds.), *Feminism Domesticity and Popular Culture*, New York: Routledge, 151–64.

Sassatelli, R., and Davolio, R. (2010), "Consumption, Pleasure and Politics: Slow Food and the Politico-Aesthetic Problematization of Food," *Journal of Consumer Culture*, 10: 202–32.

Sassatelli, R., and Scott, A. (2001), "Novel Food, New Markets and Trust Regimes: Responses to the Erosion of Consumers' Confidence in Austria, Italy and the UK," *European Societies*, 3: 213–44.

Sayer, A. (2000), "Moral Economy and Political Economy," *Studies in Political Economy*, Spring: 79–103.

Scanlan, J. (2005), *On Garbage*, London: Reaktion Books.

Schatzki, T. (1996), *Social Practices: A Wittgensteinian Approach to Human Activity and the Social*, Cambridge: Cambridge University Press.

Schatzki, T. (2002), *The Site of the Social: A Philosophical Account of the Constitution of Social Life and Change*, University Park: Pennsylvania State University Press.

Schiefenh vel, W., and Blum, P. (2007), "Insects Forgotten and Rediscovered as Food: Entomophagy among the Eipo, Highlands of West-New Guinea, and in Other Traditional Societies," in J. MacClancy, J. Henry, and H. Macbeth (eds.), *Consuming the Inedible: Neglected Dimensions of Food Choice*, Oxford: Berghahn, 163–76.

Schmiechen, J., and Carls, K. (1999), *The British Market Hall: A Social and Architectural History*, London: Yale University Press.

School of Artisan Food (2011), "About us". Available at http://www.schoolofartisanfood.org (accessed July 22, 2011).

Schroeder, K. (2006), "A Feminist Examination of Community Kitchens in Peru and Bolivia," *Gender, Place and Culture*, 13: 663—8.

Schudson, M. (1981), "Criticizing the Critics of Advertising: Towards a Sociological View of Marketing," *Media, Culture and Society*, 3: 3–12.

Schumpeter, J. A. (1943), *Capitalism, Socialism and Democracy*, London: George Allen and Unwin.

Schwarzweller, H. K. (1971), "Tractorization of Agriculture: The Social History of a German Village," *Sociologia Ruralis*, 11: 127–39.

The Scotmsan (2006), "M&S Lochmuir Salmon ... Only Lochmuir Doesn't Exist" (August 10). Available at http://www.scotsman.com/news/uk/m-amp-s-lochmuir-salmon-only-lochmuir-doesn-t-exist-1-1131606 (accessed January 14, 2013).

Scott, J. C. (1976), *The Moral Economy of the Peasant: Rebellion and Subsistence in Southeast Asia*, New Haven, CT: Yale University Press.

Scott, M. L., Nowlis, S. M., Mandel, N., and Morales, A. C. (2008), "The Effects of Reduced Food Size and Package Size on the Consumption Behavior of Restrained and Unrestrained Eaters," *Journal of Consumer Research*, 35: 391–405.

Scott, S., and Brindley, P. (2012), "New Geographies of Migrant Settlement in the UK," *Geography*, 97: 29–38.

Scottish Government (2008), "Healthy Eating, Active Living: An Action Plan to Improve Diet, Increase Physical Activity and Tackle Obesity, 2008–2011." Available at www.scotland.gov.uk/Publications/2008/06/20155902/0 (accessed February 15, 2011).

Scrinis, G. (2008), "On the Ideology of Nutritionism," *Gastronomica*, 8: 39–48.

Seaman, W. R. (1992), "Active Audience Theory: Pointless Populism," *Media, Culture and Society*, 14: 301–11.

Segal, L. (2007), *Slow Motion: Changing Masculinities, Changing Men*, London: Virago.

Self, W. (2011), "Why Captain Birdseye is my Slightly Fishy Culinary Hero," *New Statesman* (July 4). Available at http://www.newstatesman.com/food/2011/07/birds-eye-traditional-chicken (accessed December 3, 2011).

Sell, S. (2009), "Corporations, Seeds, and Intellectual Property Rights Governance," in J. Clapp and D. Fuchs (eds.), *Corporate Power in Global Agrifood Governance*, Cambridge, MA: MIT Press, 187–224.

Sellerberg, A. M. (1991), "In Food we Trust? Vitally Necessary Confidence and Unfamiliar Ways of Attaining it," in E. Furst, R. Prättälä, M. Ekström, L. Holm, and U. Kjaernes (eds.), *Palatable Worlds: Sociocultural Food Studies*, Oslo: Solum, 193–201.

Sen, A. (1981), *Poverty and Famines: An Essay on Entitlement and Deprivation*, Oxford: Clarendon Press.

Sennett, R. (2008), *The Craftsman*, New Haven, CT: Yale University Press.

Sennett, R., and Cobb, J. (1972), *The Hidden Injuries of Class*, New York: Vintage Books.

Seremetakis, C. N. (1994), *The Senses Still: Perception and Memory as Material Culture in Modernity*, Boulder, CO: Westview Press.

Seremetakis, C. N. (2005), "The Breast of Aphrodite," in C. Korsmeyer (ed.) *The Taste Culture Reader: Experiencing Food and Drink*, Oxford: Berg, 297–303.

Seyfang, G. (2006), "Ecological Citizenship and Sustainable Consumption: Examining Local Organic Food Networks," *Journal of Rural Studies*, 22: 383–95.

Shapin, S. (2012), "The Sciences of Subjectivity," *Social Studies of Science*, 42: 170–84.

Shapiro, L. (1986), *Perfection Salad: Women and Cooking at the Turn of the Century*, New York: Farrar, Straus and Giroux.

Shapiro, L. (2004), *Something from the Oven: Reinventing Dinner in 1950s America*, New York: Penguin.

Shaw, A. (1999), "What are 'They' Doing to our Food?: Public Concerns About Food in the UK," *Sociological Research Online*, 4.

Shaw, A. (2004), "Discourses of Risk in Lay Accounts of Microbiological Safety and BSE: A Qualitative Interview Study," *Health, Risk and Society*, 6: 151–71.

Sheldon, R., Cleghorn, N., Penfold, C., Brown, A., and Newmark, T. (2009), *Exploring Attitudes to GM Food: Final Report National Centre for Social Research*, Prepared for the Social Science Research Unit, London: Food Standards Agency.

Shephard, S. (2000), *Pickled, Potted, and Canned: The Story of Food Preserving*, London: Headline.

Shiva, V. (1991), *The Violence of the Green Revolution: Third World Agriculture, Ecology and Politics: Ecological Degradation and Political Conflict*, London: Zed Books.

Short, F. (2006), *Kitchen Secrets: The Meaning of Cooking in Everyday Life*, Oxford: Berg.

Shove, E. (2003), *Comfort, Cleanliness and Comfort: The Social Organization of Normality*, Oxford: Berg.

Shove, E. (2009), "Everyday Practice and the Production and Consumption of Time," in E. Shove, F. Trentmann, and R. Wilk (ed.), *Time, Consumption, and Everyday Life*, Oxford: Berg, 17–33.

Shove, E., Pantzar, M., and Watson, M. (2012), *The Dynamics of Social Practice*, London: Sage.

Shove, E., and Southerton, D. (2000), "Defrosting the Freezer: From Novelty to Convenience: A Narrative of Normalization," *Journal of Material Culture*, 5: 301–19.

Shove, E., Watson, M., Hand, M., and Ingram, J. (2007), *The Design of Everyday Life*, Oxford: Berg.

Siegrist, M., Cousin, M. E., Kastenholz, H., and Wiek, A. (2007), "Public Acceptance of Nanotechnology Foods and Food Packaging: The Influence of Affect and Trust," *Appetite*, 49: 459–66.

Silva, E. (2000), "The Cook, the Cooker and the Gendering of the Kitchen," *Sociological Review*, 48: 612–28.

Silverstone, R., and Hirsch, E. (eds.) (1992), *Consuming Technologies: Media and Information in Domestic Spaces*, London: Routledge.

Simmel, G. (1903), "The Metropolis and Mental Life," reprinted in D. N. Levine (ed.) (1971), *Georg Simmel: On Individuality and Social Forms*, Chicago: University of Chicago Press, 324–39.

Simmel, G. (1906), "The Sociology of Secrecy and of Secret Societies," *American Journal of Sociology*, 11: 441–98.

Simmel, G. (1971), *On Individuality and Social Forms*, Chicago: University of Chicago Press.

Simmons, D. (2008), "Starvation Science: From Colonies to Metropole," in A. Nützenadel and F. Trentmann (eds.), *Food and Globalization*, Oxford: Berg, 173–91.

Simon, B. (2009), *Everything but the Coffee: Learning about America from Starbucks*, Berkeley: University of California Press.

Simonsen, K. (2010), "Encountering O/other Bodies: Practice, Emotion and Ethics," in B. Anderson and P. Harrison (eds.), *Taking-Place: Non-Representational Theories and Geography*, Farnham: Ashgate, 221–41.

Sinclair, U. (1906/1965), *The Jungle*, Harmondsworth: Penguin Modern Classics.

SIRC (2006), *The Tio Pepe Eating In Study*, Oxford: Social Issues Research Centre.

Skeggs, B. (1997), *Formations of Class and Gender: Becoming Respectable*, London: Sage.

Slocum, R. (2007), "Whiteness, Space and Alternative Food Practice," *Geoforum*, 38: 520–33.

Slow Food (2011), "Our Philosophy." Available at http://www.slowfood.com/international/2/our-philosophy (accessed December 1, 2011).

Slow Food (2012), "How We Operate." Available at http://www.slowfood.com/international/3/how-we-operate (accessed April 7, 2012).

Smart, C., and Neale, B. (1999), *Family Fragments?*, Cambridge: Polity Press.

Smith, A. (1759), *The Theory of Moral Sentiments*, London: A. Millar.

Smith, A. (1776), *An Inquiry into the Nature and Causes of the Wealth of Nations*, London: Methuen & Co.

Smith, E., Marsden, T., Flynn, A., and Percival, A. (2004), "Regulating Food Risks: Rebuilding Confidence in Europe's Food?," *Environment and Planning C: Government and Policy*, 22: 543–67.

Smith, G., and Winchester, H. (1998), "Negotiating Space: Alternative Masculinities at the Work / Home Boundary," *Australian Geographer*, 29: 327–39.

Smith, M. (2008), *Sensing the Past: Hearing, Smelling, Tasting, and Touching in History*, Berkeley: University of California Press.

Sobal, J., and Maurer, D. (eds.) (1999a), *Interpreting Weight: The Social Management of Fatness and Thinness*, New York: Aldine de Gruyter.

Sobal, J., and Maurer, D. (eds.) (1999b), *Weighty Issues: Fatness and Thinness as Social Problems*, New York: Aldine de Gruyter.

Sobal, J., and Wansink, B. (2007), "Kitchenscapes, Tablescapes, Platescapes and Foodscapes: Influences of Microscale Built Environments on Food Intake," *Environment and Behavior*, 39: 124–42.

Sonnino, R., and Marsden, T. (2006), "Beyond the Divide: Rethinking Relationships between Alternative and Conventional Food Networks in Europe," *Journal of Economic Geography*, 6: 181–99.

Southerton, D. (2009), "Re-Ordering Temporal Rhythms: Coordinating Daily Practices in the UK in 1937 and 2000," in E. Shove, F. Trentmann, and R. Wilk (eds.), *Time, Consumption, and Everyday Life*, Oxford: Berg, 49–66.

Speedy, A. W. (2003), "Global Production and Consumption of Animal Source Foods," *The Journal of Nutrition*, 133: 4048S.

Stanziani, A. (2004), "Wine Reputation and Quality Controls the Origins of the AOCs in 19th Century France," *European Journal of Law and Economics*, 18: 149–67.

Stanziani, A. (2005), *Histoire de la qualité alimentaire (XIX–XX siècle)*, Paris: Seuil.

Stanziani, A. (2007), "Negotiating Innovation in a Market Economy: Foodstuffs and Beverages Adulteration in Nineteenth-Century France," *Enterprise and Society*, 8: 375–412.

Steinbeck, J. (1937), *Of Mice and Men*, London: Heinemann.

Steinberg, S. (1998), "Bubbie's Challah," in R. Scapp and B. Seitz (eds.), *Eating Culture*, New York: State University of New York Press, 295–7.

Steingarten, J. (1997), *The Man Who Ate Everything*, London: Headline.

Stephens, N. (2010), "In Vitro Meat: Zombies on the Menu?," *SCRIPTed*, 7(2): 394. Available at http://www.law.ed.ac.uk/ahrc/script-ed/vol7-2/stephens.asp (accessed March 21, 2012).

Stice, E., and Shaw, H. (1994), "Adverse Effects of the Media Portrayed Thin-Ideal on Women and Linkages to Bulimic Symptomatology," *Journal of Social and Clinical Psychology*, 13: 288–308.

Stilgoe, J., Irwin, A., and Jones, K. (2006), *The Received Wisdom: Opening up Expert Advice*, London: Demos.

Stirling, A. (2007), "Risk, Precaution and Science: Towards a More Constructive Policy Debate, Talking Point on the Precautionary Principle," *EMBO Reports*, 8: 309–15.

Stoker, G. (1998), "Governance as Theory: Five Propositions," *International Social Science Journal*, 155: 17–28.

Stoller, P., and Olkes, C. (1989), "The Taste of Ethnographic Things," in P. Stoller (ed.), *The Taste of Ethnographic Things: The Senses in Anthropology*, Philadelphia: University of Pennsylvania Press, 465–79.

Strand, C. (1999), *Hello, Fruit Face!: The Paintings of Guiseppe Archimboldo*, New York: Prestel Publishing.

Strasburger, V., and Wilson, B. (2002), *Children, Adolescents and the Media*, London: Sage.

Strasser, S. (1982), *Never Done: A History of American Housework*, New York: Pantheon Books.

Strasser, S. (2000), *Waste and Want: A Social History of Trash*, New York: Owl Books.

Stuart, T. (2009), *Waste: Uncovering the Global Food Scandal*, London: Penguin.

Sullivan, O. (2000), "The Division of Domestic Labour: Twenty Years of Change?," *Sociology*, 34: 437–56.

Supski, S. (2006), "'It Was Another Skin': The Kitchen as a Home Australian Post-War Immigrant Women," *Gender, Place and Culture*, 13: 133–41.

Sutton, D. (2001), *Remembrances of Repasts: An Anthropology of Food and Memory*, Oxford: Berg.

Sutton, D. (2006), "Cooking Skill, the Senses and Memory: The Fate of Practical Knowledge," in C. Gosden, R. Phillips, and E. Edwards (eds.), *Sensible Objects: Colonialism, Museums and Material Culture*, Oxford: Berg, 87–128.

Swenson, R. (2009), "Domestic Divo: Televised Treatments of Masculinity, Femininity and Food," *Critical Studies in Media Communication*, 26: 36–53.

Swinbank, V. (2002), "The Sexual Politics of Cooking: A Feminist Analysis of Culinary Hierarchy in Western Culture," *Journal of Historical Sociology*, 15: 464–94.

Sztompka, P. (1999), *Trust: A Sociological Theory*, Cambridge: Cambridge University Press.

Tacitus, C. (2003), *The Annals of Imperial Rome*, London: Penguin.

Takeda, H. (2008), "Delicious Food in a Beautiful Country: Nationhood and Nationalism in Discourses on Food in Contemporary Japan," *Studies in Ethnicity and Nationalism*, 8: 5–29.

Tansey, G., and Rojette, T. (eds.) (2008), *The Future of Control of Food: A Guide to International Negotiations and Rules on Intellectual Property, Biodiversity and Food Security*, London: Earthscan.

Tansley, A. F. (1935), "The Use and Abuse of Vegetational Terms and Concepts," *Ecology*, 16: 284–307.

Taussig, M. (1980), *The Devil and Commodity Fetishism in Latin America*, Chapel Hill: University of North Carolina Press.

Taylor, C. (1971), "Interpretation and the Sciences of Man," *The Review of Metaphysics*, 25: 3–51.

Taylor, C. (1992), *The Ethics of Authenticity*, Cambridge, MA: Harvard University Press.

Taylor, M. (2011), "Implementation of the U.S. Food Safety Modernization Act: Building a Partnership for Prevention," Remarks at the China International Food Safety and Quality Conference and Expo Beijing, China, November 2. Available at http://www.fda.gov/ Food/FoodSafety/FSMA/ucm278215.htm (accessed April 12, 2012).

Tchoukaleyska, R. (2009), "The Markets of Montpellier: Food Culture, Identity and Belonging in France," MA thesis, University of British Columbia.

Teil, G., and Hennion, A. (2004), "Discovering Quality or Performing Taste?" in M. Harvey, A. McMeekin, and A. Warde (eds.), *Qualities of Food*, Manchester, New York: Manchester University Press, 19–37.

Thaler, R. H., and Sunstein, C. R. (2008), *Nudge: Improving Decisions about Health, Wealth and Happiness*, New Haven, CT: Yale University Press.

Thien, D. (2005), "After or Beyond Feeling? A Consideration of Affect and Emotion in Geography," *Area*, 37: 450–4.

Thøgersen, J. (1999), "The Ethical Consumer: Moral Norms and Packaging Choice," *Journal of Consumer Policy*, 22: 439–60.

Thomas, N. (1991), *Entangled Objects: Exchange, Material Culture, and Colonialism in the Pacific*, London: Harvard University Press.

Thompson, C., Locander, W. and Pollio, H. (1990), "The Lived Meaning of Free Choice: An Existential-Phenomenological Description of Everyday Consumer Experiences of Contemporary Married Women". *Journal of Consumer Research*, 17: 346–61.

Thompson, E. P. (1967), "Time, Work-Discipline, and Industrial Capitalism," *Past and Present*, 38: 56–97.

Thompson, E. P. (1971), "The Moral Economy of the English Crowd in the Eighteenth Century," *Past and Present*, 50: 76–136.

Thompson, M. (1979), *Rubbish Theory: The Creation and Destruction of Value*, Oxford: Oxford University Press.

Thompson, P. (1996), "Markets, Moral Economy and the Ethics of Sustainable Agriculture," in W. Heijman, H. Hetsen, and J. Frouws (eds.), *Rural Reconstruction in a Market Economy*, Wageningen: Wageningen Agricultural University, 39–54.

Thoreau, H. D. (1854), *Walden or, Life in the Woods*, Harmondsworth: Penguin Classics.

Thrift, N. (2007), *Non-Representational Theory: Space, Politics, Affect*, London: Routledge.

Tomlinson, M., and Warde, A. (1993), "Social Class and Change in Eating Habits," *British Food Journal*, 95: 3–10.

Trentmann, F. (ed.) (2006), *The Making of the Consumer*, Oxford: Berg.

Trentmann, F. (2007), "Before 'Fair Trade': Empire, Free Trade, and the Moral Economies of Food in the Modern World," *Environment and Planning D: Society and Space*, 25: 1079–1102.

Trilling, L. (1972), *Sincerity and Authenticity*, Cambridge, MA: Harvard University Press.

Trubek, A. (2000), *Haute Cuisine: How the French Invented the Culinary Profession*, Philadelphia: University of Pennsylvania Press.

Trubek, A. (2008), *The Taste of Place: a Cultural Journey into Terroir*, Berkeley: University of California Press.

Truninger, M. (2011), "Cooking with Bimby in a Moment of Recruitment: Exploring Conventions and Practice Perspectives," *Journal of Consumer Culture*, 11: 37–59.

Tuan, Yi-Fu (1974), *Topophilia: a Study of Environmental Perception, Attitudes and Values*, New York: Columbia University Press.

Tuan, Yi-Fu (1977), *Place and Space: the Perspective of Experience*, Minneapolis: University of Minnesota Press.

Tuan, Yi-Fu (1993), "Pleasures of the Proximate Senses: Eating, Taste and Culture," reprinted in C. Korsmeyer (ed.) (2005), *The Taste Culture Reader: Experiencing Food and Drink*, Oxford: Berg, 35–62.

Tuhiwai Smith, L. (1999), *Decolonising Methodologies: Research and Indigenous Peoples*, New York: Zed Books.

Turner, B. S. (1984), *The Body and Society: Explorations in Social Theory*, Oxford: Blackwell.

Turner, J. (2005), *Spice: The History of a Temptation*, New York: Vintage.

Turner, K. L. (2006), "Buying, Not Cooking: Ready-to-Eat Food in American Working-Class Neighbourhoods 1880–1930," *Food, Culture and Society*, 9: 13–39.

Twenge, J. M. (2000), "The Age of Anxiety? Birth Cohort Change in Anxiety and Neuroticism, 1952–1993," *Journal of Personality and Social Psychiatry*, 79: 1007–21.

Tyrer, P. (1999), *Anxiety: A Multidisciplinary Review*, London: Imperial College Press.

Ungar, S. (2001), "Moral Panic versus the Risk Society: The Implications of the Changing Sites of Social Anxiety," *British Journal of Sociology*, 52: 271–91.

Urry, J. (1990), *The Tourist Gaze*, London: Sage.

Valentine, G. (1999), "Eating In: Home, Consumption and Identity," *Sociological Review*, 47: 491–524.

Vanclay, F., Howden, P., Mesiti, L., and Glyde, S. (2006), "The Social and Intellectual Construction of Farming Styles: Testing Dutch Ideas in Australian Agriculture," *Sociologia Ruralis*, 46: 61–82.

Van Der Ploeg, J. D. (1985), "Patterns of Farming Logic, Structuration of Labour and Impact of Externalisation: Changing Dairy Farming in Northern Italy," *Sociologia Ruralis*, 25: 5–25.

Van Leeuwen, T. (2003), "What is Authenticity?," *Discourse Studies*, 3: 392–7.

Vannini, P., and Williams, J. P. (eds.) (2009), *Authenticity in Culture, Self, and Society*, Aldershot: Ashgate.

Van Zwanenberg, P., and Millstone, E. (2005), *BSE: Risk, Science, and Governance*, Oxford: Oxford University Press.

Verbeke, W. (2005), "Agriculture and the Food Industry in the Information Age," *European Review of Agricultural Economics*, 32: 347–68.

Verrill, L., Lando, A., and O'Connell, K. (2012), "Consumer Vegetable and Fruit Washing Practices in the United States, 2006 and 2010," *Food Protection Trends*, 32: 164–72.

Versteegen, H. (2010), "Armchair Epicures: The Proliferation of Food Programmes on British TV," in M. Gymnich (ed.), *The Pleasures and Horrors of Eating: The Cultural History of Eating in Anglophone Literature*, Bonn: Bonn University Press, 447–64.

Von Schomberg, R. (2006), "The Precautionary Principle and its Normative Challenges," in J. Jones and R. von Schomberg (eds.), *Implementing the Precautionary Principle: Perspectives and Prospects*, Cheltenham: Edward Elgar Publishing, 19–42.

Wade-Gayles, G. (1997), "'Laying on Hands' through Cooking: Black Women's Majesty and Mystery in Their Own Kitchens," in A. V. Avakian (ed.), *Through the Kitchen Window: Women Explore the Intimate Meanings of Food and Cooking*, Boston: Beacon Press, 95–103.

Wales, C., Harvey, M., and Warde, A. (2006), "Recuperating BSE: Trust in Food and Institutional Change in Britain," *Appetite*, 47: 187–95.

Wallace Center (2011), "Sysco's Journey from Supply Chain to Value Chain." Available at http://www.wallacecenter.org (accessed December 1, 2011).

Warde, A. (1997), *Consumption, Food and Taste: Culinary Antinomies and Commodity Culture*, London: Sage.

Warde, A. (1999), "Convenience Food: Space and Timing," *British Food Journal*, 101: 518–27.

Warde, A. (2005), "Consumption and Theories of Practice," *Journal of Consumer Culture*, 5: 131–53.

Warde, A., Cheng, S. L., Olsen, W., and Southerton, D. (2007), "Changes in the Practice of Eating," *Acta Sociologica*, 50: 363–88.

Warde, A., and Martens, L. (2000), *Eating Out: Social Differentiation, Consumption and Pleasure*, Cambridge: Cambridge University Press.

Wardrop, J. (2006), "Private Cooking, Public Eating: Women Street Vendors in South Durban," *Gender, Place and Culture*, 13: 677–83.

Watson, J. L. (ed.) (1997), *Golden Arches East: McDonalds in East Asia*, Palo Alto, CA: Stanford University Press.

Watson, M., and Meah, A. (2013), "Food Waste and Safety: Negotiating Conflicting Social Anxieties into the Practices of Provisioning," in D. Evans, A. Murcott, and H. Campbell (eds.),

Waste Matters: New Perspectives on Food and Society, Oxford: Wiley-Blackwell, 102–120.

Watts, M. J. (1983), *Silent Violence: Food, Famine, and Peasantry in Northern Nigeria*, Berkeley, Los Angeles: University of California Press.

Weatherell, C., Tregear, A., and Allinson, J. (2003), "In Search of the Concerned Consumer: UK Public Perceptions of Food, Farming and Buying local," *Journal of Rural Studies*, 19: 233–44.

Weiss, C. R., and Wittkopp, A. (2005), "Retailer Concentration and Product Innovation in Food Manufacturing," *European Review of Agricultural Economics*, 32: 219–44.

Welsh Assembly Government (2006), "Food and Fitness: Promoting Healthy Eating and Physical Activity for Children and Young People in Wales: 5 Year Implementation Plan." Available at www.wales.gov.uk/topics/health/improvement/food/food-fitness/plan/?lang=en (accessed February 15, 2011).

Wenzer, J. (2010), "Eating Out Practices among Swedish Youth: Gothenburg Area Foodscapes," *CFK rapport 2010:03*, Göteborg: Centrum för konsumtionsvetenskap.

Whatmore, S. J. (1991), *Farming Women: Gender, Work and Family Enterprise*, London: Macmillan.

Whatmore, S. J. (2002a), "From Farming to Agribusiness: Global Agri-food Networks," in R. J. Johnston, P. J. Taylor, and M. J. Watts (eds.), *Geographies of Global Change*, 2nd ed., Oxford: Blackwell, 57–67.

Whatmore, S. J. (2002b), *Hybrid Geographies: Natures Cultures Spaces*, London: Sage Publications.

Whatmore, S. J.,Munton, R., Little, J., and Marsden, T. J. (1987), "Towards a Typology of Farm Businesses in Contemporary British Agriculture," *Sociologia Ruralis*, 27: 21–37.

Whatmore, S., Stassart, P., and Renting, H. (2003), "What's Alternative about Alternative Food Networks?," *Environment and Planning A*, 35: 389–91.

Whatmore, S., and Thorne, L. (1997), "Nourishing Networks: Alternative Geographies of Food," in D. Goodman and M. J. Watts (eds.), *Globalizing Food: Agrarian Questions and Global Restructuring*, London: Routledge, 287–304.

WHO (2003), "Diet, Nutrition and the Prevention of Chronic Disease," *Report of a Joint WHO/FAO Expert Consultation*, Geneva: World Health Organization.

WHO (2007), "Food Safety and Foodborne Illness," Factsheet No. 237. Available at http://www.who.int/mediacentre/factsheets/fs237/en/ (accessed December 14, 2012).

WHO (2012), "Food Safety." Available at http://www.who.int/foodsafety/en/ (accessed April 12, 2012).

WHO/FAO (2003), "Diet, Nutrition and the Prevention of Chronic Diseases," in World Health Organization (ed.), *WHO Technical Report Series*, Geneva: World Health Organization, 1–148.

Wilcock, A., Pun, M., Khanona, J. and Aung, M. (2004), "Consumer Attitudes, Knowledge and Behaviour: a Review of Food Safety Issues", *Trends in Food Science and Technology*, 15: 56–66.

Wilcox, H. C., Conner, K. R., and Caine, E. D. (2004), "Association of Alcohol and Drug Use Disorders and Completed Suicide: An Empirical Review of Cohort Studies," *Drug and Alcohol Dependence*, 76 (Supplement): S11–S19.

Wilk, R. (2002), "Food and Nationalism: the Origins of 'Belizean Food,'" in W. Belasco and P. Scranton (eds.), *Food Nations: Selling Taste in Consumer Societies*, New York: Routledge, 67–89.

Wilk, R. (2004), "Morals and Metaphors: The Meaning of Consumption," in K. M. Ekström and H. Brembeck (eds.), *Elusive Consumption*, Oxford: Berg, 11–26.

Wilk, R. (2006a), "Bottled Water: The Pure Commodity in the Age of Branding," *Journal of Consumer Culture*, 6: 303–25.

Wilk, R. (2006b), *Home Cooking in the Global Village: Caribbean Food from Buccaneers to Ecotourists*, London: Berg.

Wilkinson, I. (1999), "Where is the Novelty in our Current 'Age of Anxiety'?" *European Journal of Social Theory*, 2: 445–67.

Wilkinson, I. (2001), *Anxiety in a Risk Society*, London: Routledge.

Wilkinson, R., and Pickett, K. (2009), *The Spirit Level: Why Equality is Better for Everyone*, London: Penguin.

Williams, J. (2011), "'The Ethic of Regard': Artisan Practice and the Stuff of Food," PhD diss., University of Sheffield.

Williams, L., and Parker, H. (2001), "Alcohol, Cannabis, Ecstasy and Cocaine: Drugs of Reasoned Choice Amongst Young Adult Recreational Drug Users in England,"

International Journal of Drug Policy, 12: 397–413.

Williams, R. (1958), *Culture and Society, 1780–1950*, Harmondsworth: Penguin.

Williams, R. (1976), *Keywords: A Vocabulary of Culture and Society*, New York: Oxford University Press.

Wilson, B. (2008), *Swindled: The Dark History of Food Fraud, from Poisoned Candy to Counterfeit Coffee*, Princeton, NJ: Princeton University Press.

Wilson, M. (2012), "Moral Economies of Food in Cuba," *Food, Culture and Society*, 15: 277–91.

Wilson, W. J. (1987), *The Truly Disadvantaged: the Inner City, the Underclass, and Public Policy*, Chicago: University of Chicago Press.

Winickoff, D. E., and Bushey, D. M. (2010), "Science and Power in Global Food Regulation: The Rise of the Codex Alimentarius," *Science, Technology and Human Values*, 35: 356–81.

Winickoff, D., Jasanoff, S., Busch, L., Grove-White, R., and Wynne, B. (2005), "Adjudicating the GM Food Wars: Science, Risk, and Democracy in World Trade Law," *Yale Journal of International Law*, 30: 81–123.

Winson, A. (2004), "Bringing Political Economy into the Debate on the Obesity Epidemic," *Agriculture and Human Values*, 21: 299–312.

Winter, M. (2003), "Embeddedness, the New Food Economy and Defensive Localism," *Journal of Rural Studies*, 19: 25–32.

Witt, D. (2004), *Black Hunger: Soul Food and America*, Minneapolis: University of Minnesota Press.

Witz, A., Warhurst, C., and Nickson, D. (2003), "The Labour of Aesthetics and the Aesthetics of Organization," *Organization*, 10: 33–54.

Wolf, O. H. N. (2002), *Reversed Food Chain- From the Plate to the Farm: Priorities in Food Safety and Food Technology in European Research*, Brussels: European Commission, EUR 20416 EN.

Wolfenstein, M. (1951), "The Emergence of Fun Morality," *Journal of Social Issues*, 7: 15–25.

Woodham Smith, C. (1962), *The Great Hunger: Ireland 1845–9*, New York: Harper and Row.

Woodruffe-Burton, H., Eccles, S., and Elliott, R. (2002), "Towards a Theory of Shopping: An Holistic Framework," *Journal of Consumer Behaviour*, 1: 256–66.

WRAP (2011), "Consumer Insight: Date Labels and Storage Guidance," *Report by Brook Lyndhurst for the Waste and Resources Action Programme May 2011*. Available at http://www.wrap.org.uk/sites/files/wrap/Technical_report_dates.pdf (accessed March 17, 2012).

Wright, P. (2009), *On Living in an Old Country*, Oxford: Oxford University Press.

Wrigley, N., Coe, N. M., and Currah, A. (2005), "Globalising Retail: Conceptualising the Distribution-Based Transnational Corporation (TNC)," *Progress in Human Geography*, 29: 437–57.

Wrigley, N., Warm, D., and Margetts, B. (2003), "Deprivation, Diet, and Food-Retail Access: Findings from the Leeds 'Food Deserts' Study, *Environment and Planning A*, 35: 151–188.

Wynne, B. (1992), "Misunderstood Misunderstanding: Social identities and Public Uptake of Science," *Public Understanding of Science*, 1: 281–304.

Wynne, B. (2001), "Creating Public Alienation: Discourses of Risk and Ethics on GMO's," *Science as Culture*, 10: 445–81.

Yan, Y. (1997), "McDonald's in Beijing: The Localization of Americana," in J. Watson (ed.), *Golden Arches East McDonald's in East Asia*, Palo Alto, CA: Stanford University Press, 39–76.

Young, B. (2003), "Does Food Advertising Influence Children's Food Choices? A Critical Review of Some of the Recent Literature," *International Journal of Advertising*, 22: 441–59.

Young, E. M. (2010), "Deadly Diets: Geographical Reflections on the Global Food System," *Geography*, 95: 60–69.

Yudkin, J. (1972), *Pure, White and Deadly: The Problems of Sugar*, London: Davis-Poynter.

Yudkin, J., and McKenzie, J. (1964), *Changing Food Habits*, London: McGibbon and Kee.

Zachman, K., and Østby, P. (2011), "Food, Technology, and Trust: An Introduction," *History and Technology*, 27: 1–10.

Zerubavel, E. (1981), *Hidden Rhythms: Schedules and Calendars in Social Life*, Chicago: University of Chicago Press.

Zukin, S. (1995), *The Cultures of Cities*, Oxford: Blackwell Publishers.

Zukin, S. (2004), *Point of Purchase: How Shopping Changed American Culture*, New York: Routledge.

Zukin, S. (2008), "Consuming Authenticity: From Outposts of Difference to Means of Exclusion," *Cultural Studies*, 22: 724–48.

Index

the United States, Alice Waters promotes the use of organic food and advocates the use of locally grown produce in her restaurant Chez Panisse as well as in her educational program "Edible Schoolyard" at a local Berkeley school. Celebrity chefs do not just teach us how to cook, they can also potentially teach us what to cook. So, for example, Joanne Hollows and Steve Jones (2010) note how Nigella Lawson could be viewed as a postfeminist exemplar where cooking and the business of being a "domestic goddess" embody a form of feminine enjoyment through indulgence and self-directed pleasure, rather than what Marjorie DeVault (1991) refers to as the confines of "feeding work." Celebrity chefs, then, can also show us how we might feel about cooking, reworking (however spuriously) the cultural interpretation of cookery. If Lawson and her ilk promote a preoccupation with pleasure, then it is likely that even minimally studious audiences are critical enough to discern that visually hedonistic food programs skim over domestic realities like washing up. The pleasures of viewing celebrity chefs may not be transformed seamlessly into culinary experimentation in the kitchen and may well stop as some form of "vicarious consumption." But there is nothing vicarious about such practices since people are directly experiencing themselves as viewers. Nonetheless, the point remains that celebrity chefs might be seen more as entertainers than as cookery teachers (Caraher et al. 2000).

The concern that celebrity chefs are functioning merely to provide vicarious consumption "experiences" for viewers (Adema 2000) is paralleled by concerns about the implications of watching, rather than doing, cooking. So it is for Signe Hansen (2008) who sees that the "real" role of the celebrity chef is to generate and fashion people into consumers of media whose desires are to be fashioned, kept alive, and never sated by food media and the advertising it supports. Perhaps this highlights a more general concern and resistance toward a perceived step in the mediatization of everyday life, where traditionalists see a shift from the real to the virtual as genuinely detrimental to human experience (Baudrillard 1970).

Celebrity chefs are remarkable in their ability to arouse the normative concerns of both media critics and viewers. The centrality of food to many people's existence and social life is now fused to the centrality of media in our lives. The implied normative position is that the seductive power of media spectacle is supplanting genuine social and culinary experiences. A corollary argument runs that audiences of celebrity chefs are effectively the subjects of advertising campaigns and of the submerged logic of consumer capitalism.

Authors such as Annette Hill (2005) conclude that audiences are far from duped even if processes of economic manipulation do occur, whereas David Morley (1993) has cautioned against the pitfalls of accepting audience activity as significant in and of itself (see also Seaman 1992). Research by Nick Piper (in press) has shown how the audiences of Oliver are aware of their own multiple, often contradictory, relationships with this celebrity chef. Audience research shows that he can be read as a philanthropist and a cynical capitalist, a "normal bloke" and a celebrity, for example. Many people seem unwilling to form a finite judgment about the character and role of celebrity chefs and instead report their ambivalence toward them. Audience ambivalence should come as no surprise given the complexity of issues and practices in which celebrity chefs and their audiences are involved. The common experience of ambivalence—when attempting to balance the need for financial gain with the desire to act morally, for example— is one reason people cite for identifying with and forming an affectionate attachment to celebrity chefs.

The celebrity chefs of today are a product of the culinary and social fields in which they operate as well as significant semiautonomous agents of cultural change. Along with their audiences, they help to determine the nature of future engagements with food and media but at the same time are conditioned by the mediated culinary history that has passed before them. One should not forget that the celebrity chefs of today are also the audiences of the chefs before them, as are their agents, their publicists, and the numerous other "cultural intermediaries" who assist them (Rojek 2001). What a celebrity